Crime Mapping and Spatial Aspects of Crime

Crime Mapping and Spatial Aspects of Crime

Second Edition

DEREK J. PAULSEN

Eastern Kentucky University

MATTHEW B. ROBINSON

Appalachian State University

Prentice Hall
Upper Saddle River, New Jersey 07458
Columbus, Ohio

Library of Congress Cataloging-in-Publication Data

Paulsen, Derek J.
Crime mapping and spatial aspects of crime / Derek J. Paulsen,
  Matthew B. Robinson.— 2nd ed.
     p. cm.
Includes bibliographical references and index.
Rev. ed. of: Spatial aspects of crime. ©2004.
ISBN-13: 978-0-205-60945-1 (alk. paper)
ISBN-10: 0-205-60945-7 (alk. paper)
   1. Criminology.   2. Crime.   3. Space and time—Sociological aspects.
I. Robinson, Matthew B.   II. Paulsen, Derek J. Spatial aspects of crime.   III. Title.
HV6018.P377 2009
364.01—dc22

                                                                  2008019539

Editor in Chief: Vernon Anthony
Senior Acquisitions Editor: Tim Peyton
Editorial Assistant: Alicia Kelly
Media Project Manager: Karen Bretz
Director of Marketing: David Gesell
Marketing Manager: Adam Kloza
Marketing Coordinator: Alicia Dysert
Production Manager: Kathy Sleys
Creative Director: Jayne Conte
Cover Design: Kristine Carney
Cover Illustration/ Photo: © Image Source/Images.com
Full-Service Project Management/ Composition: Sadagoban Balaji/Integra Software Services, Inc.

Credits and acknowledgments borrowed from other sources and reproduced, with permission, in this textbook appear on appropriate page within text.

Pearson Education Ltd., London
Pearson Education Singapore, Pte. Ltd
Pearson Education Canada, Inc.
Pearson Education–Japan
Pearson Education Australia PTY, Limited

Pearson Education North Asia, Ltd., Hong Kong
Pearson Educación de Mexico, S.A. de C.V.
Pearson Education Malaysia, Pte. Ltd.
Pearson Education Upper Saddle River, New Jersey

Prentice Hall
is an imprint of

www.pearsonhighered.com

ISBN-13: 978-0-20-560945-1
ISBN-10:   0-20-560945-7

Contents

CHAPTER 3

Social Disorganization   46

CHAPTER 4

Ecological Theories of Crime   68

CHAPTER 5

Behavioral Geography and Criminal Behavior   104

WORKBOOK SECTION **IV** Aggregate Data Analysis 289

WORKBOOK

Preface

As indicated by the title, **Crime Mapping and Spatial Aspects of Crime** deals with the theoretical and practical aspects of crime mapping and spatial analysis of crime. This topic has become increasingly important in the last ten years because of the increase in law enforcement agencies that are using GIS and crime mapping. In response to this increased use of crime mapping, the federal government has enlarged support to law enforcement agencies conducting crime mapping. Most visibly, this support has been through the National Institute of Justice (NIJ) Maps Office and Community Oriented Policing MORE grants, which seek to improve the effective implementation of GIS and crime mapping within the criminal justice system.

In response to the increased use of crime mapping, there has been an increased demand for crime mapping education and training. In order to fill this need, universities and community colleges have begun to provide education and training in crime mapping and spatial analysis. However, a void exists in terms of textbooks on this subject. Currently, there are no books specifically designed to provide education concerning either the theoretical or practical aspects of mapping for criminal justice purposes. This book is designed to fill this void. First, the text is designed to provide a solid understanding of the theoretical and empirical realities of the spatial aspects of crime. Second, the text is designed to provide students with the practical tools necessary to conduct effective crime mapping and spatial analyses of crime. This text will include the most recent research regarding the current state-of-the art uses for GIS in the criminal justice system, theoretical aspects of the geography of crime, and practical instruction and exercises on how to use GIS to conduct crime mapping and spatial analysis of crime.

ORGANIZATION OF THE TEXT

In order to meet the goal of providing a comprehensive understanding of both theoretical and practical issues surrounding spatial aspects of crime, the text is divided into three different parts. Part I is designed to introduce students to the empirical realities of the geography of crime as well as major criminological theories that discuss spatial variation in crime. Empirical realities of the geography of crime are discussed first (Chapter 2, Crime and Place), and subsequent chapters discuss theoretical areas such as Social Disorganization (Chapter 3), Routine Activities and Crime Pattern Theory (Chapter 4), Behavioral Geography (Chapter 5), and Epidemics, Diffusion, and Displacement of Crime (Chapter 6).

Part II of the book provides a two-chapter picture of the practical application of crime mapping and the geography of crime. Chapter details the historical, contemporary, and future uses of crime mapping in the three areas of the Criminal Justice System: Policing, Courts, and Corrections. Chapter then follows up with a discussion of the major issues facing the use of crime mapping, including barriers to effective use, data issues, and critical issues in crime mapping, and finishes with a discussion of legal and ethical issues.

Part III of the textbook completes the book by providing hands-on instruction in how to use GIS software for analyzing and understanding spatial patterns of crime.

Divided into four sections, the workbook is designed to allow students to take theoretical and practical concepts they learned in the first two sections of the textbook and apply them to spatial data using GIS software. Specifically, students learn how to view, analyze, and better understand patterns of crime by analyzing crime spatially through the use of computerized mapping. Although not designed to substitute for an in-depth class on the use of a GIS or a class on spatial statistics, the workbook will provide students with a thorough understanding of both areas. Students wishing to learn more about GIS or spatial statistics concepts discussed in the different chapters are encouraged to pursue the "Further Readings" suggested at the end of each chapter.

The first section of the workbook is designed to provide a basic introduction to GIS software (Chapter 1), spatial data used for crime mapping (Chapter 2), entering (Chapter 3) and manipulating data (Chapter 4), and basic fundamentals of map making (Chapter 5). The second section of the workbook introduces students to basic spatial analysis techniques, including proximity analysis (Chapter 6), spatial distribution analysis (Chapter 7), and distance analysis (Chapter 8). The third section of the workbook takes the student one step further, providing instruction on advanced spatial analysis techniques. These advanced techniques include hot spot analysis (Chapter 9), density mapping (Chapter 10), and spatial dispersion mapping (Chapter 11). The final section of the workbook introduces students to analyzing aggregate data, including finding and working with aggregate data (Chapter 12), exploratory spatial data analysis (Chapter 13), and spatial autocorrelation analysis (Chapter 14). Overall, the workbook is designed to walk the student from beginner to advanced level in both point and aggregate spatial data analyses.

SPECIAL FEATURES OF THE TEXT

To facilitate students' understanding, the book is filled with numerous eye-catching, instructive, and unique features. These features include:

- **Focus Boxes:** These in-chapter sections cover important issues and individuals related to the chapter in a more in-depth manner. Topics discussed include Testing Social Disorganization Theory, NIJ MAPS Office, and Next Event Forecasting.
- **Case Studies:** Similar in function to the Focus On boxes, case studies allow students to review more in-depth research related to subjects discussed within the chapter. Cases studies covered include Hate Crimes, the Chicago Area Project, and the Geography of Social Control.
- **List of Major Research Findings:** Each chapter ends with a listing of the major research findings and important points from the chapter. This is designed to act as both a chapter review and quick fact area for students.
- **Implications of Research Findings for Crime Mapping:** Included in each chapter is a discussion of the implications of the research findings of that chapter for practical crime mapping applications. This is designed to facilitate the understanding of how research findings can impact real-world analysis of crime data.

WORKBOOK FEATURES

- **Dedicated Webpage:** The textbook, and the workbook in particular, is designed to work in concert with a dedicated webpage (www.mappingcrime.org). This webpage contains various Internet resources including on-line figures to assist with understanding, instructions on how to acquire GIS and spatial analysis software used in the workbook, enhanced workbooks labs that use screen shots to help explain the workbook, and links to online resources. This site can also be accessed through the publisher's website at www.ablongman.com/paulsen1e.

- **Step-by-Step Instructions:** The workbook is designed to walk students step-by-step through the use of GIS software. With instructions that run the gamut from basic (opening GIS software) to advanced (dual kernel density interpolation), the workbook provides easy-to-follow instruction for users of all levels of GIS and computer knowledge.
- **Enhanced Workbook Labs**: In addition to the step-by-step instructions in the workbook, pdf files can be downloaded from the dedicated website that provides screen capture images and instructions for each lab. These enhanced labs are designed to facilitate instruction of the GIS lab work by making the instructions even easier to understand.
- **Leading GIS Software:** The workbook instructs students in how to use the leading GIS software (Arcview 9.2), making skills learned easily transferable to the marketplace. In addition, the bundled software makes learning and retaining GIS skills easier than ever.
- **Sample Data:** Data designed specifically for completing the exercises in the workbook are available for students to download from the webpage.
- **Interpretation of Output:** The output of each spatial analysis technique is discussed thoroughly and in easy-to-understand terms.
- **Review Questions and Further Readings:** Each chapter of the workbook ends with review questions and suggested "Further Readings" to advance the learning experience of students.

Instructor Resource Center

Register today at www.prenhall.com to access instructor resources digitally.

To access supplementary materials online, instructors need to request an instructor access code. Go to www.pearsonhighered.com/irc, where you can register for an instructor access code. Within 48 hours after registering, you will receive a confirming e-mail, including an instructor access code. Once you have received your code, go to the site and log on for full instructions on downloading the materials you wish to use.

ACKNOWLEDGMENTS

The authors would like to thank numerous people who have helped with the production of this book. Many thanks to Jennifer Jacobson, Dave Repetto, and the staff at Allyn and Bacon. Thanks also to the reviewers whose comments and insights helped to make this a better book: Bruce Bayley, California State University, Sacramento; Gisela Bichler-Robertson, California State University, San Bernardino; George Rengert, Temple University; Issac T. Van Patten, Radford University; Thomas Mueller,

California University of Pennsylvania; George Higgins, University of Louisville; and Susan C. Smith (Wernike), Shawnee Police Department. The authors would also like to thank those who helped influence them: Rolando del Carmen, Kelly Damphousse, Jim Marquardt, Victoria B. Titterington, Vic Kappeler, Pete Kraska, Garry Potter, as well as those who provided both direct and indirect help in the book, George Rengert, Paul and Patricia Brantingham, Keith Harries, and Richard and Becky Block. A special thanks needs to go to Ned Levine for answering numerous questions about all things spatial. Thanks also need to go to the faculty and administration at both Eastern Kentucky University and Appalachian State University for their support of this project. There is also no way that this book would have been possible without the love and support of the authors' friends and families, including all the Paulsens, Creekmores, and Robinsons, and the numerous students who sat through various iterations of this book. An extra thank you goes to Gaige B. Paulsen for his years of assistance and support of all things technical and computer. Finally, a very large and heartfelt thank you goes to our wives and children who had to put up with late hours and stress in the writing of this book.

Crime Mapping and Spatial Aspects of Crime

CHAPTER 1

Introduction to Spatial Aspects of Crime
Theory and Practice

The main purposes of this chapter are to introduce criminological theory and identify and discuss its main problems as related to spatial analysis and crime mapping. We also briefly introduce each main section and chapter of the book.

Chapter Outline

INTRODUCTION TO CRIMINOLOGICAL THEORY

Although you have likely heard of the word *theory* and probably even use it occasionally, few people have a good understanding of what the word really means. Theories are basically statements or sentences (commonly called *propositions* or *hypotheses*) that relate two or more real-world things (often called *concepts* or *variables*) in order to explain and/or predict some phenomenon. Theories of crime tend to *explain* why criminal behaviors occur and/or *predict* where and when they are more likely to occur.

An example of a criminological theory is Robert Merton's *strain theory* (Merton, 1938). This theory is based on the assumption that all Americans are taught, through socialization in our capitalistic culture, to want to achieve the "American Dream." Achieving the American Dream means acquiring financial independence and/or wealth. Unfortunately, even though we all share the same *goals*, the *means* to achieve these goals are not available to all, and are in fact structured by social class. That is, opportunities for success are not equally available to all. When people are unable to achieve their financial goals through legitimate means (such as school and work), they will be likely to *innovate* in order to achieve their goals. One way of doing this is by creating illegitimate means (such as stealing, robbing, or selling drugs) in order to obtain wealth. According to this theory, crime is caused by a *disjunction between one's goals and means*, which is another way of saying that crime occurs when people cannot achieve their goals legally. In America's culture of consumption, inevitably some people will be unable to succeed through legitimate means and thus will commit crime because of their experiences of strain (Robinson, 2004).

Shifting the Focus to the Criminal Event

Most criminological theories, like Merton's strain theory, are aimed at explaining what motivates people to commit criminal acts. These theories offer biological, psychological, sociological, cultural, economic, and other reasons why people want to offend, engage in deviance, or break the law. Far less common are theories that try to explain the criminal event in its entirety. According to *environmental criminologists* (e.g., Brantingham and Brantingham, 1991a), a crime consists of four elements:

1. A law;
2. An offender;
3. A target; and
4. A place.

In order for a crime to occur, all of these elements must be present. There must be a law in order to make an act or behavior illegal and thus criminal. An offender must be present—he or she is the one who acts or behaves in a way that violates the law. And for the criminal event to actually occur, there must also be a target (e.g., a piece of property that can be stolen or a person that can be harmed), as well as a place for the criminal event to occur. A place is "a very small area, usually a street corner, address, building, or street segment" or a "specific location within larger social environments" (Eck and Weisburd, 1995:1, 3). Places provide the context or backdrop on which criminal events occur. While targets have been integrated into some explanations of crime, such as *routine activity theory* and *lifestyle/exposure theory* (discussed in Chapter 4), the importance of place in criminal events has received far less examination by criminologists. More importantly, spatial analysis techniques such as crime mapping have exploded onto the scene in criminology and related disciplines. Criminological theory, we believe, has yet to catch up.

For example, few of our theories make predictions about where and when crime is most likely to happen. The where and when of criminal events are highly relevant for crime mapping and spatial analysis of crime, as you will see throughout this book. Consider this example: There is a man who is, for whatever reason, highly motivated to commit a criminal act. He seeks a house to burglarize in order to steal household property to fence for money. The man walks about a neighborhood and finds no suitable targets to victimize. People are home at virtually every house in the neighborhood, small children are playing in the area, and many people are nearby to supervise the homes and property in the vicinity. Some homes are left unoccupied but their doors and windows—his entry points—are visible to neighbors and passersby, and they are not accessible to him because they are protected by heavy-duty locks and some have alarms. Rather than taking a chance, the man walks on from this neighborhood to some other place in pursuit of a suitable criminal opportunity. No crime has been committed in this neighborhood despite the presence of a motivated offender. Why?

Almost no criminological theories can account for why this would-be criminal did *not* commit a crime in the neighborhood, for most theories of crime are aimed only at explaining what motivated the man to want to commit a crime. Most criminological theories focus on the offender and ignore what makes targets suitable for victimization and places suitable to host crimes. Most criminological theories thus ignore the *situational context* of crime. The situational context of crime refers to the conditions in which something exists or occurs. For example, an assault that occurs at a bar is typically preceded by heavy drinking and some insult, each of which can be considered part of the situational context of assaults.

To the degree that criminological theory is only focused on the factors that cause a person to commit criminal behavior, it cannot explain crime. Another example provides further clarification: The factors that produce a would-be murderer are not sufficient to explain a murder. In order for a murder to occur, there must also be a crime scene (a place and time of the event), a murder victim, and a situational context that precipitated the murder. Every criminal event rests on a suitable opportunity, as well. So, the situational context of any crime includes not only an offender, but also a place and time where the crime occurs, a victim of crime, and an opportunity for crime that is worth taking.

It is almost certain that you heard all about the sniper attacks that gripped much of the nation when more than a dozen people were shot at from a parked car in Washington, D.C., Maryland, and Virginia, over a one-month period. Criminological theories typically aim to explain why people become motivated to commit such horrific acts. They rarely, however, aim to explain why this motivation manifests itself through the particular behaviors it does. For example, why did the offender choose the victims he did? Were the attacks random or did they follow some pattern? Why did he shoot at people at particular gas stations, stores, and some isolated areas? Did he have some purpose in mind? Did the placement of the shooting attacks that were plotted on maps by virtually every media institution have some meaning? Similar questions are being asked about the recent mass murder at the Virginia Polytechnic Institute and State University, where 32 students were murdered by another student (before he took his own life). Most criminological theories do not consider such questions because they are not concerned with the situational context of crime. The factors that motivate people to commit murder are indeed important; they just are not sufficient to explain actual murders.

An Example: Broken Windows Theory.   Some criminological theories do focus on the situational context of crime. One such theory is commonly referred to as the "broken windows theory." According to its authors, Wilson and Kelling (1982), disorder and crime are thought to be inextricably linked in a developmental sequence. They provide the following example that explains where the name of the theory emerged:

> Social psychologists and police officers tend to agree that if a window in a building is broken and is left unrepaired, all the rest of the windows will soon be broken. This is as true in nice neighborhoods as in run-down ones. Window-breaking does not necessarily occur on a large scale because some areas are inhabited by determined window-breakers whereas others are populated by window-lovers; rather, one unrepaired broken window is a signal that no one cares, and so breaking more windows costs nothing. (It has always been fun.)

The most important word in the above paragraph is *signal*. According to the broken windows theory, any sign of disorder sends a signal to would-be offenders that residents in this neighborhood do not care about their property, that police are not aware of this property, and thus, it is unlikely that anyone will defend this property. This theory has been tested under the concept of *incivilities* (discussed in Chapter 3), which are any signs of an uncivil area, including but not limited to, abandoned buildings with boarded or broken windows, abandoned lots with an accumulation of trash, litter in streets, walkways, and parking areas, graffiti on buildings and walls, groups of people loitering/arguing/fighting on streets, derelicts and "winos" reclining in doorways and alleyways, poorly lighted streets and dark entries to buildings and alleys, and the presence of illegal drug activity.

The main difference between the theory of strain introduced earlier and the broken windows theory is that the former is aimed at explaining what motivates people to commit criminal acts (in this case, the disjunction between one's goals and means), whereas the latter assumes offenders are already motivated and really aims to explain why some places are more prone to criminal victimization than others. Strain theory assumes people are motivated to commit crimes when they cannot achieve what they want legally. It says nothing about what they are likely to target and at what places they are most likely to offend. Broken windows theory does not really explain what motivates offenders to commit crimes; it merely assumes that there are would-be offenders in the neighborhood and that certain environmental cues (such as broken windows or any signs of incivilities) trigger criminal events. It seeks to explain why some types of residences (targets) are victimized by crime more than others and why some neighborhoods (places) have higher crime rates than others.

How Theories are Created and Evaluated

Typically, a theory is created to explain a set of observations that have already been witnessed. Alternatively, a theory may be posited in advance and then later tested by collecting real-world data. As criminologists, we spend much of our time reading about "facts of crime" that are consistently found regardless of the type of crime being studied. We have found, for example, that men typically commit more crime than women. We have learned that younger people are typically more aggressive than older people (except for acts of white-collar and corporate crimes). We have witnessed that poor people are at a greater risk for most forms of criminal victimization. Such facts need to be explained so that they can be understood, and thus numerous theories have been offered to explain these facts, to make sense of them.

Anyone can create a theory of crime. For example, create a list of things that you think:

- Make a person more likely to break the law (e.g., assault another person);
- Make a person more likely to be victimized by crime (e.g., become a victim of an assault);
- Make a person's home more attractive to a criminal (e.g., a house that is noticed by a would-be burglar);
- Make a person's personal property more attractive to a criminal (e.g., a car that is noticed by a would-be thief); and
- Make crime more likely to happen at a given place (e.g., a place you hang out or frequently visit).

If you were to list some things that you thought answered these questions, and state them in sentence form, you would in essence be involved in the first stages of building a theory of crime. The key criterion that makes such sentences or propositions theories is that they are *testable*. Theories are tested by collecting data through some form of observations (e.g., phone surveys, questionnaires, experiments) in order to see if empirical evidence is consistent with the proposed hypotheses. When evidence is consistent with the theory, we can say that the theory is supported or has been verified. When evidence is inconsistent with the theory, we can say that the theory is not supported. When evidence is repeatedly contradictory to what was expected, we can say that the theory has been refuted or even falsified (which means disproven).

The most important criterion we use to evaluate any theory is *empirical validity*— the degree to which it is supported by real-world observations and data. Robinson (2004) reviewed most theories of crime, including strain theories and the broken windows theory introduced earlier. In terms of empirical validity of strain theory, Robinson concluded that perceptions of strain by individuals appear to be related to increased antisocial behavior and criminality, so that the greater one experiences strain, the more likely he or she is to commit an official act of criminality. Of all sources of strain, however, the most important seem to be nonfinancial in nature. Instead, sources of *general strain* seem to best account for antisocial behavior (Mazerolle and Maahs, 2000). General strain occurs not only when one is prevented from achieving his or her goals by other people, but also when one loses something of financial or sentimental value, or when one experiences some undesirable stimulus. Delinquency is viewed as a normal reaction to strain; it in fact is a means to cope with it (Brezina, 1996). Delinquency is viewed as a rational, problem-solving behavior committed by an individual dealing with emotional strain. In essence, the research shows that much antisocial behavior and criminality is motivated by negative affective states such as anger, frustration, depression, and so on.

In terms of broken windows theory, several studies find support for its key premise that disorder and crime are related. The main problem with this theory is that the relationship between *incivilities* and crime appears to be *spurious* (or false), because both disorder and crime are produced by other factors. In Chapter 3, we report recent data that illustrate that poverty, high levels of immigrant populations, and mixed land uses can result in both disorder and crime, suggesting a causal relationship between disorder and crime that actually does not exist (Robinson, 2004). Even so, police departments in major cities such as New York have used the logic of broken windows theory to clean up "problem areas" in their cities. Police officials claim that, as a result of sending out the signal to would-be offenders that the city does not tolerate even minor offenses such as graffiti, reductions in serious crimes were achieved. Serious crime rates did decline in New York following these efforts and police officials were quick to take credit, but evidence suggests the declines began before the crackdown on disorder was launched and that similar declines occurred in most other major cities across the country, including many that did not implement policies of eliminating disorder (Robinson, 2005).

There are literally more than one hundred other theories of criminal behavior (Vold, Bernard, and Snipes, 2001). Most of these theories are aimed at *explanation*—explaining why people break the law and/or commit some form of antisocial/deviant or harmful behaviors. Far fewer of these theories are aimed at *prediction*—stating in advance where and when such behaviors will be more likely to occur. We suggest that, because of this, criminological theory is not as useful as it could be and should be in the real world, especially when it comes to crime mapping and spatial analysis of crime.

The Usefulness of Criminological Theory

Although the word "theory" likely brings forth the conception of something that is "just theoretical" and "not practical," the truth is that theory is very useful in the real world. As we said earlier, theory is aimed at explaining things we have observed. Theory thus allows us to make sense out of what we experience and of the world in general. As for criminological theories, they attempt to explain why criminality occurs, based on the many observations about criminal behavior that have been witnessed over the years. For example, why do men commit more crime than women? Why are younger people more aggressive than older people? Why are poor people at a greater risk for most forms of criminal victimization? All of these are questions that pertain to observations about crime in the real world.

Theories allow us to answer these questions and ultimately learn the answers. This makes theory tremendously useful in the real world. Theory allows us to understand why criminal behavior happens, and where and when it is most likely to happen. Ultimately, we can use the findings from tests of theories to then prevent criminal behavior or lessen the likelihood that it will occur.

Spatial analysis techniques, such as crime mapping software, can aid tremendously in these efforts. The main advantage that these techniques offer over non-spatial techniques is that they allow us to visually depict observations by place and time. This has tremendous significance because being able to "see" facts is crucial to understanding them. It is also advantageous because social facts can be mapped along with individual criminal events or crime rates in order to assess relationships between these facts and crime. Figure 1.1, created using crime mapping software, provides an example of how such relationships may be mapped in order to study relationships between spatial and temporal features and criminal events.

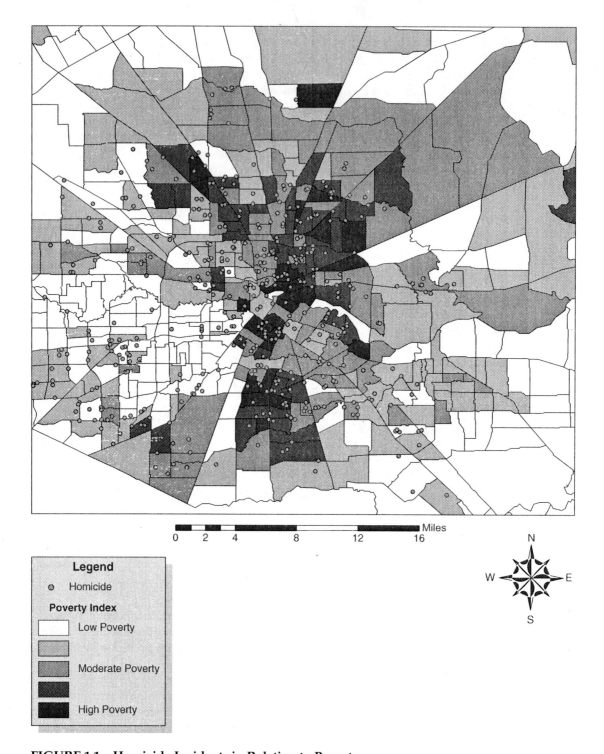

FIGURE 1.1   Homicide Incidents in Relation to Poverty

This figure illustrates average poverty rates by census tracts, according to government data, over a five-year period in an American city. Also plotted on the map are addresses of homicides during the same period. What is the relationship between poverty and murder, according to this figure? Even a quick glance at the image suggests that homicides are more likely to occur in areas with higher rates of poverty. Additionally, you may notice that homicide tends to cluster into groups, including more than a dozen in some places. Finally, you can probably tell that there are more murders toward the center of the city illustrated in the map. Why is murder more common in poor areas? Why does murder cluster? Why do more murders occur closer to the center of the city?

The theories discussed in this book are aimed at answering such questions by explaining why such facts occur. These "spatial theories" are intended to make sense out of these real-world observations. Additionally, the "spatial analysis" techniques discussed in this book are utilized for the purpose of analyzing relationships between factors such as poverty (as well as many others) and criminal events and crime rates.

As we noted in the Preface, this book is unique in that we show how spatial theories and spatial analysis can be used to study and more fully understand crime. Our goal is to link crime mapping techniques and the theories that underlie them, in order to illustrate their enormous utility for understanding and ultimately being able to predict crime.

AN INTRODUCTION TO THE BOOK

The book is organized into three main parts with a total of 19 chapters. Part I, titled, "Theory" includes chapters on "Crime and Place" (Chapter 2), "Social Disorganization" (Chapter 3), "Ecological Theories of Crime" (Chapter 4), "Behavioral Geography and Criminal Behavior" (Chapter 5), and "Epidemics, Diffusion, and Displacement of Crimes" (Chapter 6). Its purpose is to present theoretical considerations related to spatial analysis of crime.

In Chapter 2, we introduce the issue of crime and place and examine empirical realities of crime rate differences internationally, regionally within the United States, between urban and rural areas within the United States, and within American cities. We also examine spatial aspects of fear of crime and public perception of crime and various issues related to media coverage of crime. The goal of Chapter 2 is to provide a comprehensive overview of the geographic distribution of crime in order to demonstrate what needs to be explained by criminological theories.

In Chapter 3, we examine the well-known social disorganization theory. We briefly examine the early development of social disorganization theory and provide a detailed account of the development of the "Chicago School of Criminology." We conclude with a discussion of empirical findings from more modern social disorganization research. In Chapter 3, we hope to show how critical social disorganization theory was to the development of crime mapping.

In Chapter 4, we examine in great depth other ecological theories of crime, including defensible space, Crime Prevention Through Environmental Design (CPTED), situational crime prevention, routine activity theory, and crime pattern theory. We lay out the main hypotheses of each, discuss research findings, and conclude with the major limitations of each. In Chapter 4, we show the modern examples of criminological theories that are aimed at accounting for why some places and times are plagued by more crime than others. This chapter is particularly useful for understanding the links between theory and practice in spatial analysis.

In Chapter 5, we examine issues related to behavioral geography and criminal behavior. Key concepts related to crime mapping are introduced and discussed, including mental maps and awareness space. In this chapter we also focus on journey to crime research and the growing use of geographic profiling. Chapter 5 is particularly helpful in illustrating how spatial analysis techniques can illuminate offender decision-making processes in terms of where offenders commit crimes and how potential victims are selected.

In Chapter 6, we focus on crime epidemics, diffusion of crime, and displacement of crime. Research in this chapter illustrates how and why crime and crime prevention can grow and spread across time and place. This chapter also provides very important research related to spatial analysis of crimes and numerous examples are provided in order to show how social scientists currently use crime mapping techniques to explain why some places and times are more prone to crime than others and to predict where and when crime is most likely to occur.

Part II, titled "Practice," includes chapters on "Mapping in the Criminal Justice System" (Chapter 7), and "Major Issues in the Practice of Crime Mapping" (Chapter 8). Its purpose is to illustrate more practical issues related to spatial analysis of crime.

In Chapter 7, we provide a brief history of mapping in criminal justice, paying particular attention to the development of mapping in American policing and focusing on its many uses by law enforcement agencies. We also provide some discussion of mapping uses in courts and corrections, including its potential benefits to probation and parole officers and researchers of correctional issues. We also discuss future uses of GIS and crime mapping.

In Chapter 8, we discuss barriers to computerized mapping, including costs associated with crime mapping and department needs, as well as database integration and planning for implementation. We examine several issues related to crime mapping data and then discuss various critical, ethical, and legal issues in crime mapping. This chapter will be of particular interest for any person or agency considering the adoption and implementation of crime mapping techniques.

In each of the above-mentioned chapters, we conclude with a list of major research findings relating to the topics covered, as well as a discussion of implications of theoretical research findings for the practice of crime mapping and spatial analysis in general. Each chapter also contains relevant and contemporary case studies and "Focus On" boxes that briefly introduce key concepts and notable individuals who have advanced the theory and practice of spatial analysis of crime through their work.

Part III of the book, titled "Crime Mapping Workbook," provides the most practical aspects of crime mapping. It is a hands-on tutorial aimed at teaching the reader how to use crime mapping software. The workbook introduces crime mapping software, teaches basic crime mapping techniques, and then illustrates some more advanced uses of crime mapping. Chapters include "Getting Started with ArcGIS" (Chapter 1), "Understanding Data Sources" (Chapter 2), "Entering Data" (Chapter 3), "Querying and Joining Data" (Chapter 4), "Understanding Layouts and Map Design" (Chapter 5), "Proximity Analysis" (Chapter 6), "Spatial Distribution Analysis" (Chapter 7), "Distance Analysis" (Chapter 8), "Hot Spot Analysis" (Chapter 9), "Density Mapping" (Chapter 10), "Spatial Dispersion Mapping" (Chapter 11), "Working with Aggregate Data" (Chapter 12), Exploratory Spatial Data Analysis (Chapter 13), and Spatial Autocorrelation (Chapter 14).

Each of the chapters in the workbook contains useful exercises to assist with learning both basic and more advanced crime mapping techniques. Each chapter also concludes with review questions and assignments for further readings, as well as links to the on-line web pages associated with the book.

THEORY

CHAPTER 2

Crime and Place

The purpose of this chapter is to provide a comprehensive overview of the geographic distribution of crime. In this chapter, we will specifically discuss differences in crime distributions on various levels including international differences, regional differences within the United States, urban versus rural differences within the United States, and intra-city differences within the United States. We also assess spatial aspects of fear of crime and public perception of crime. Our goal in this chapter is to provide an understanding of the major geographic realities of crime and their implications for crime mapping and crime prevention.

Chapter Outline

INTRODUCTION TO CRIME AND PLACE

As we noted in the previous chapter, every crime involves the elements of an offender, a law, a place, and a victim, which provide the context for criminal events. Without these elements, a crime cannot occur. Many criminologists focus on these elements of the crime event. For example, Cornish (1993:355) developed what he called a "human action theory," which views actions (i.e., behaviors) as "the outcome of person-situation interactions" taking place over time, where situations include "settings and their physical objects as well as other people" that have "enabling or constraining effects on action." Felson's (2008) *Crime and Everyday Life* illustrates how the patterns of daily routines affect the location of crime. Sacco and Kennedy's (2002) *The Criminal Event* attempts to describe the how, when, and where of criminal events.

In this chapter, we concern ourselves with the issue of the *place* of crime. As first introduced in Chapter 1, a place is "a very small area, usually a street corner, address, building, or street segment" or a "specific location within larger social environments" (Eck and Weisburd, 1995:1, 3). In this chapter, we illustrate differences in crime distributions on various levels of places, including international differences, regional differences within the United States, urban versus rural differences within the United States, and intra-city differences within the United States. We also show how fear of crime and public perception of crime are affected by spatial elements. This chapter presents what can essentially be considered the key facts of crime at places, that place-oriented theories are aimed at explaining, and that crime mapping software is aimed at depicting and analyzing. Interestingly, you will see that *most* explanations of crime rate variation across places identified in the literature pay little or no attention to the factors unique to places. We attempt to rectify this by injecting our own thoughts about relevant spatial factors that may account for crime rate variations across places.

INTERNATIONAL DIFFERENCES IN CRIME DISTRIBUTION

According to the United Nations' *Global Report on Crime and Justice* (Newman, 1999), crime is everywhere, in every country. This report suggests that the risks of being victimized are highest in Latin America and sub-Saharan Africa. Yet, the United States has more crime than any other nation in the world (Barclay and Tavares, 2002). According to the Bureau of Justice Statistics (2006), U.S. residents aged 12 or older experienced approximately 23 million crimes in 2005. Of these crimes, 78 percent (18.2 million) were property crimes, and 22 percent (5.2 million) were crimes of violence. These crime data come from the National Crime Victimization Survey (NCVS), a survey of crime victims in a nationally representative sample of American households.

Although *crime frequencies* (actual number of crimes in a given place) are the highest in the United States, America does not have the highest *crime rates* (number of crimes divided by the population). Some American crime rates are among the highest in the world. For example, the United States has one of the highest rates of gun murders in the world, especially when comparing only Western, industrialized nations (Kleck, 2005). It is difficult to make comparisons between countries because crime data from many countries are simply not available. Additionally, countries collect data differently from their criminal justice organizations, and there are clearly differences in the amount of crimes citizens report to police in different countries. Countries also obviously define crimes differently. In some places, acts may not be illegal whereas in others they are, and when different countries each have similar crimes, the specific behaviors that fall within each type of crime are not the same. For these reasons, comparisons between recorded crime levels in different countries can be misleading (Barclay and Tavares, 2002). Homicide rate comparisons are thought be more valid, although there are some differences in how they are counted across cultures. With these caveats in mind, we examine the empirical realities of crime rate variation across the globe.

Empirical Realities

The United States has a very high homicide rate relative to most countries, although it does not have the highest rate. The United States also historically has had very high violent crime rates. For example, Reiss and Roth (1993:3) write:

> Homicide rates in the United States far exceed those in any other industrialized nation. For other violent crime, rates in the United States are among the world's highest. . . . Among 16 industrialized countries surveyed in 1988, the United States had the highest prevalence rates for serious sexual assaults and for other assaults including threats of physical harm.

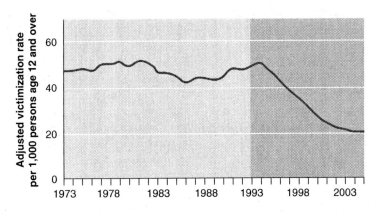

FIGURE 2.1   Trends in Violent Crime in the United States

Source: Bureau of Justice Statistics (www.ojp.usdoj.gov/bjs)

More recent data suggest other countries have overtaken the United States as leaders in homicide rates. According to Barclay and Tavares (2002), the average rate of homicides in European Union countries from 1998 to 2000 was 1.7 homicides per 100,000 citizens, with the highest rates in Northern Ireland (3.1), Spain (2.8), Finland (2.6), Scotland (2.2), and Sweden (2.1). The highest rates for non-European nations include South Africa (54.3), Russia (20.5), Estonia (11.4), Lithuania (8.9), Latvia (6.5), and the United States (5.9).

Barclay and Tavares (2002) report that although official crime rates fell in the United States from 1996 to 2000 by 14 percent and in Canada by 11 percent, they rose in many European countries. Crime rates did fall in other European nations, however. Some European nations saw large increases in violent crime during this time period, including Spain (38 percent increase), France (36 percent increase), the Netherlands (35 percent increase), Portugal (28 percent increase), Italy (20 percent increase), Denmark (17 percent increase), and England and Wales (15 percent increase). The only decreased rate was for Ireland (49 percent decrease). Other countries that saw large increases in violent crime from 1996 to 2000 included Japan (72 percent), Poland (49 percent), Slovenia (26 percent), Lithuania (23 percent), and Slovakia (19 percent). Violent street crime in the United States decreased 16 percent from 1996 to 2000. This continued four earlier years of consecutive declines in violent crime in the United States as measured by police statistics in the Uniform Crime Reports (UCR). Figure 2.1 illustrates trends in violent crime in the United States according to the NCVS; NCVS data are generally thought to be more valid for examining *crime trends*—crime over time, meaning that the top line is the most accurate measure of violence trends in the United States. Note that the NCVS was redesigned in 1992 to better capture victimization experiences; the darker shaded region beginning in 1993 depicts victimization data after the redesign.

Figure 2.2 depicts trends in property crime in the United States. This figure is also based on NCVS data. From these data, we can clearly see that street crime has declined in the United States.

According to the International Crime Victims' Survey (ICVS), which assesses crime across numerous countries, crime rose in most countries between 1988 and 1991, stabilized in 1995, and then declined until 1999. The trends were different in North America and Europe, however. The ICVS is the most comprehensive crime survey conducted. Key findings from the 2000 ICVS, conducted in 17 industrialized countries (van Kesteren, Mayhew, and Nieuwbeerta, 2001), show the following:

■ Countries where more than 24 percent of citizens were victims of any crime included Australia, England and Wales, the Netherlands, and Sweden;

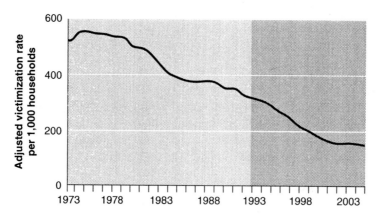

FIGURE 2.2 Trends in Property Crime in the United States

Source: Bureau of Justice Statistics (www.ojp.usdoj.gov/bjs)

- Countries where between 20 and 24 percent of citizens were victims of any crime included Canada, Scotland, Denmark, Poland, Belgium, France, and the United States; and
- Countries where less than 20 percent of citizens were victims of any crime included Finland, Spain, Switzerland, Portugal, Japan, and Northern Ireland.

The most common crime in any country is a crime against property, and is typically theft of someone's property by another.

In terms of an individual's risk of criminal victimization from specific crimes, the 2000 ICVS finds the following:

- The highest risks of contact crime (robbery, assaults with force, and sexual assaults) were in Australia, England and Wales, Canada, Scotland, and Finland (all over 3 percent);
- The highest risks of theft were in Australia, Sweden, and Poland (between 5 and 6 percent);
- The highest risks of burglary were in Australia (7 percent), England and Wales (5 percent), and Canada, Denmark, and Belgium (all at 4 percent); and
- The highest risks of car theft were in England and Wales (2.6 percent), Australia (2.1 percent), and France (1.9 percent).

Based on the above data, the United States does not rank at the top of all nations for any crime rate. Yet, our homicide rates far exceed those of most industrialized nations and our gun homicide rate is among the highest in the world, as noted earlier.

Explanations

There are several reasons why crime rates vary so greatly across the globe. Goldstein (1994:75–76) blames higher crime rates in the United States on high levels of economic inequality, cultural legitimization of violence, and low levels of community stability coupled with high levels of relative deprivation. The explanations of international crime rate variation can be grouped into at least two categories, including so-called *grand theories* and *structural theories*. As defined by Howard, Newman, and Pridemore (2000:148), grand theories "entail a high level of abstraction and usually assume that one major theoretical construct, such as a nation's level of modernization or its placement in the world's political economy, has the greatest impact on its level of crime." Structural theories, according to Howard, Newman, and Pridemore, "attempt to explain the spatial variation in rates of offending via subcultures (i.e., social learning), status-induced strain, or social control." In other words, explanations of differential crime rates tend to be offered in line with one of four major theories of crime— anomie, strain, social learning, and social control theories. According to Robinson (2004), anomie theory posits that criminality is caused by sudden changes in society, such as rapid development of a country through population growth and industrialization brought on by globalization. Strain theories are related to anomie and attribute increased crime to economic and emotional frustration brought about by conditions in society.

Cultural deviance or subcultural theories assert that criminality is caused by conflicts between social groups and the emergence of criminal groups who develop values, norms, and attitudes that are inconsistent with mainstream society. Social learning theories say that criminality is learned in a process of communication between individuals; people learn not only how to commit crime but also how to justify their illegal acts. Finally, social control theories suggest that criminality is normal and expected in the absence of social control. To the degree that people do not have a stake in conformity (i.e., they do not have something of value to lose) and are not controlled by institutions of society (e.g., family, school, the law), they are free to deviate. Conformity can also be threatened in times of economic success or turmoil.

Grand Theories.   According to Howard, Newman, and Pridemore (2000:148), grand theories include so-called

- Modernization theory;
- Civilization theory;
- Opportunity theories; and
- World system theories.

Each of these is discussed below.

Modernization theory is just another name for anomie theory, put forth by Emile Durkheim (1893, 1897). His research suggested that "as nations develop, they are characterized by an increasingly intricate web of social and economic relations. These complex divisions are suspected of undermining mechanical solidarity and its control over the collective conscience. Thus, rapid social change engenders the breakdown of traditional values, resulting in . . . a higher crime rate" (Howard, Newman, and Pridemore, 2000:148). As a society becomes modernized and technologically advanced, it is likely to experience increased industrialization and urbanization. The result is often increased conflict between groups (called *culture conflict* by criminologist Thorsten Sellin, 1938) and increased *social inequality* between classes. These are the main contributors to increased crime rates according to modernization theory (Heiland and Shelley, 1992). In essence, this theoretical perspective is based on the assumption that as nations develop, increased crime is inevitable. This "developing countries" argument is the one most cited as relevant to rising crime rates by the United Nations.

It should be pointed out that modernization also creates good outcomes. For example, Fernandez and Kuenzi (2006:1) write that "modernization leads to increasing wealth, leading to an increase in citizen support for democracy." Yet, even these authors note that "industrialization and urbanization produce a rapid increase in the complexity of social and economic relations. Technical and industrial development reshapes economic, market and labor relations. These transformations in turn change social relationship by increasing social differentiation and, potentially, increasing inequality. Industrialization and urbanization may well cause a breakdown in traditional structures and values, and an increase in social interaction, tension and conflict. These social changes then contribute to the emergence of criminal activity" (p. 2).

This argument has found some support in studies of property crime in Colombia (Bouley and Vaughn, 1995), gangs in the Caribbean (Mahibir, 1988), and larger works across numerous countries (Huang, 1995; Ortega et al., 1992). Crime increases in the Czech Republic following the transition to democracy are also consistent with the argument that modernization produces crime (Fernandez and Kuenzi, 2006).

Similarly, an examination of crime rate changes in Russia after the fall of communism suggests that global anomie may contribute to higher crime rates there (Passas, 2000). The process of globalization (the spread of capital, labor, management, news, and data across country borders that is pursued by transnational corporations, transnational media organizations, intergovernmental organizations, and non-governmental organizations) is criminogenic.

According to Passas, the spread of capitalism to the former Soviet Union led to anomie and crime in Russia in the 1990s. The key mechanisms he identifies as relevant for understanding increased crime rates in Russia include increased inequalities, greater amounts of poverty, and the promotion of unsustainable growth. Results include increased street crime, increased corporate crime, increased corruption, increased ecosystem deterioration, as well as lower worker productivity, higher unemployment, and a disappearance of traditional safety nets. Passas asserts not only that globalization provides more motivation and opportunities to commit deviance, but also that it leads to a less efficacious institutional control system.

Civilization theory "expects decreasing crime rates as governments and their citizens become more human and civilized" (Howard, Newman, and Pridemore, 2000:150). As a country becomes modernized or civilized, "individuals learn to inhibit their urges and societies become less violent as a result." This perspective, at first glance, seems to suggest the opposite of the modernization theory, yet it not only is aimed at explaining lower levels of violent crime in nations but also is meant to explain increased acts of suicide and drug abuse in countries. Howard, Newman, and Pridemore (2000:150) explain that as industrialization increases:

> It creates a complex division of labor that demands a high degree of interdependency. As this organic solidarity grows stronger, people exercise a higher degree of internal control over their behavior because others increasingly depend on them (Heiland and Shelley, 1992). This internalization of control is expected to lead to a decrease in crime rates, especially in violence. As individuals increasingly repress their urges, however, they are likely to experience an increase in psychological pathologies (Freud, 1962) and self-inflicted victimization (e.g., suicide and drug abuse).

There is very little empirical evidence in support of this theoretical perspective.

Opportunity theories link higher crime rates in nations to increased opportunities for crime created by changes in society's structures, institutions, culture, and social processes. Every society has a unique *social structure*, which symbolizes the main, permanent, interrelated features of the society that determine how the society as a whole functions. A society's social structure contains various *institutions* and includes the regular, persistent social relations shared by individual members and between groups and communities. Institutions are the significant practices and organizations in a society or culture, including economic institutions, political institutions, educational institutions, moral institutions, and so forth. Society also includes the general *culture* of the society as a whole and the various *subcultures* that exist within the society. A culture can be understood as "the integrated pattern of human knowledge, belief, and behavior that depends upon man's capacity for learning and transmitting knowledge to succeeding generations; the customary beliefs, social forms, and material traits of a racial, religious, or social group" (*Merriam-Webster's Collegiate Dictionary*, 2001). The various events that occur within society's structures, institutions, and its general culture make up the *social processes* of the society, or the way in which the society itself generally operates.

Opportunity theories include *routine activity theory* (Cohen and Felson, 1979), *lifestyle exposure theory* (Hindelang, Gottfredson, and Garofalo, 1978), and related approaches. Each of these is addressed in Chapter 4 in the discussion of *ecological theories* of crime. For the purposes of international crime rate differences, these opportunity theories attribute higher crime rates to changes in society's routines and opportunities, as indicated by economic productivity, and amount of time spent away from home at work and in recreation. For example, societies that produce more goods, particularly low weight and highly portable goods, will have higher rates of theft. Theft would also increase as societies became more egalitarian with women working away from the home as much as men (Felson, 2008). The result of such changes is an increased likelihood that suitable targets to steal would be left at home unguarded and thus more likely to be stolen. Increases in residential mobility and cultural heterogeneity are also thought to make it more difficult for residents to get to know each other, develop close interpersonal relationships, and control crime naturally. This makes opportunity theories related to the theory of *social disorganization*, which is addressed in Chapter 3.

The theory of social disorganization and the opportunity theories of routine activity and lifestyle exposure have been used to explain crime rate differences within cities, which we discuss later in this chapter. These theories have not been widely applied to national crime rate differences, mostly because of the difficulty associated with collecting measures of the key concepts in so many countries with different value systems and cultures related to work, recreation, and so forth.

The final grand theory is *world system theory*. According to Howard, Newman, and Pridemore (2000:152), this perspective "borrows from the Marxist perspective to explain the impact of an ever-expanding capitalism on nations that vary in their level of development." An uneven expansion of capitalism across the globe means "(1) nations are no longer autonomous political and economic entities but are instead actors in an international political-economic system, and (2) weaker countries are politically and economically exploited by stronger ones." As capitalism expands, the result is a disruption of indigenous cultures and their normal way of life. New forms of exploitation and inequalities are created. "Political and legal formations are disrupted, and social dislocations become widespread. The rural population begins to migrate to cities in search of employment, creating class conflict and competition for scarce resources (Castells, 1977; Gilbert and Gugler, 1982). Social relationships are replaced by market relations, and consumerism replaces traditional use patterns (see Fromm, 1976)." Ultimately, poverty, inequality, and increased feelings of unfairness lead to increased crime rates.

Unfortunately for the world system theory, most of the tests are case studies of one or two nations and are only descriptive in nature. The theories are so grand that they are difficult to test in the real world.

We conclude that, of the grand theories, the ones that hold the most promise for explaining why crime rates vary across countries are modernization theory and opportunity theories. Envision a map of the world whereby one could determine the presence of income inequality and valuable possessions. These are factors identified as criminogenic by modernization theory and opportunity theories, respectively. Areas high in income inequality (e.g., poor people living near wealthy people) and high in suitable targets (e.g., cellular phones) would be expected to have higher crime rates.

Structural Theories.   As mentioned above, structural theories explain differences in international crime rates in terms of subcultures (i.e., social learning), strain, and social control factors. Structural theories include:

- Cultural theories;
- Strain theories; and
- Social disorganization.

Each of these is discussed below.

Cultural theories attribute crime rate differences to differences in belief systems, attitudes, values, norms, and ways of life of unique groups. According to this line of thought, some groups are more violent and/or deviant given the environmental conditions in which they live; over time, violence and/or deviance becomes normal and expected when confronted with noxious stimuli. Eventually, unacceptable behaviors become acceptable—values that justify such behavior are passed down or transmitted over generations. As explained by Howard, Newman, and Pridemore (2000:155), "cultural norms may promote or condone violence in certain situations, meaning that the attitudes and values of individuals within cultures that have higher rates of crime or violence should be distinguishable from those with lower rates." Unfortunately, such evidence is hard to come by and thus the validity of this theoretical approach is questionable. It is difficult to independently identify "criminal" or "deviant" values of any group, particularly across many cultures.

Strain theories posit that frustration—usually caused by economic conditions—leads to higher rates of crime. Typically, strain is measured through indicators of *absolute deprivation* (e.g., poverty levels in a nation) or *relative deprivation* (e.g., the gap between the wealthy and the poor in a nation). Although many more studies have been conducted within the United States and other individual countries, studies across nations tend to be consistent with the strain perspective. For example, as economic conditions increase in a country, homicide rates tend to decrease (Neapolitan, 1994, 1996).

Social disorganization theory attributes higher crime rates in any area, including a nation, to a breakdown in the bonds that normally hold citizens to society and its laws. The conditions that are thought to erode social bonds are factors such as high levels of poverty, ethnic or racial heterogeneity (diversity of the population), high levels of residential mobility (or population turnover), family disruption, and even high levels of population density. When this theory is used to explain cross-national crime rates, it suggests that nations with higher crime rates are socially disorganized. Given the weight of evidence related to modernization theory, it is likely that this approach can help us explain higher crime rates in some countries. Social disorganization seems to be a mechanism through which globalization and economic development affect crime rates. Social disorganization theory is discussed in more depth as it applies to crime rate differences within cities and across regions later in this chapter, and is discussed in more depth in Chapter 3.

We can conclude that, of the structural theories, strain and social disorganization theories are the most useful for explaining crime rate variations between countries. Crime mapping software ought to allow us to visually depict and analyze factors unique to these theoretical perspectives as they change over time within countries, in order to see if such change affects crime rates over time. Such efforts have been lacking in the literature pertaining to spatial analysis of crime.

REGIONAL DIFFERENCES IN CRIME DISTRIBUTION WITHIN THE UNITED STATES

Although if you watch the news, you might think that your risk of being victimized by serious crime is relatively constant wherever you are within the United States, crime rates vary widely within the borders of the nation. Place of residence in the country can have a large impact on one's likelihood of being victimized by street crime. Historically, crime rates have been highest in the southern United States, particularly the Southeast.

Empirical Realities

Perhaps the first to demonstrate that crimes were highest in the southern United States was Redfield (1880), who showed that homicide rates were concentrated mostly in this region of the country. According to Ousey (2000), several facts can be stated with regard to street crimes, as measured in the UCR. Figure 2.3 illustrates homicide trends in the United States over nearly 20 years, by region of the country. The solid area represents the trend for the United States as a whole while the individual lines are the trends for

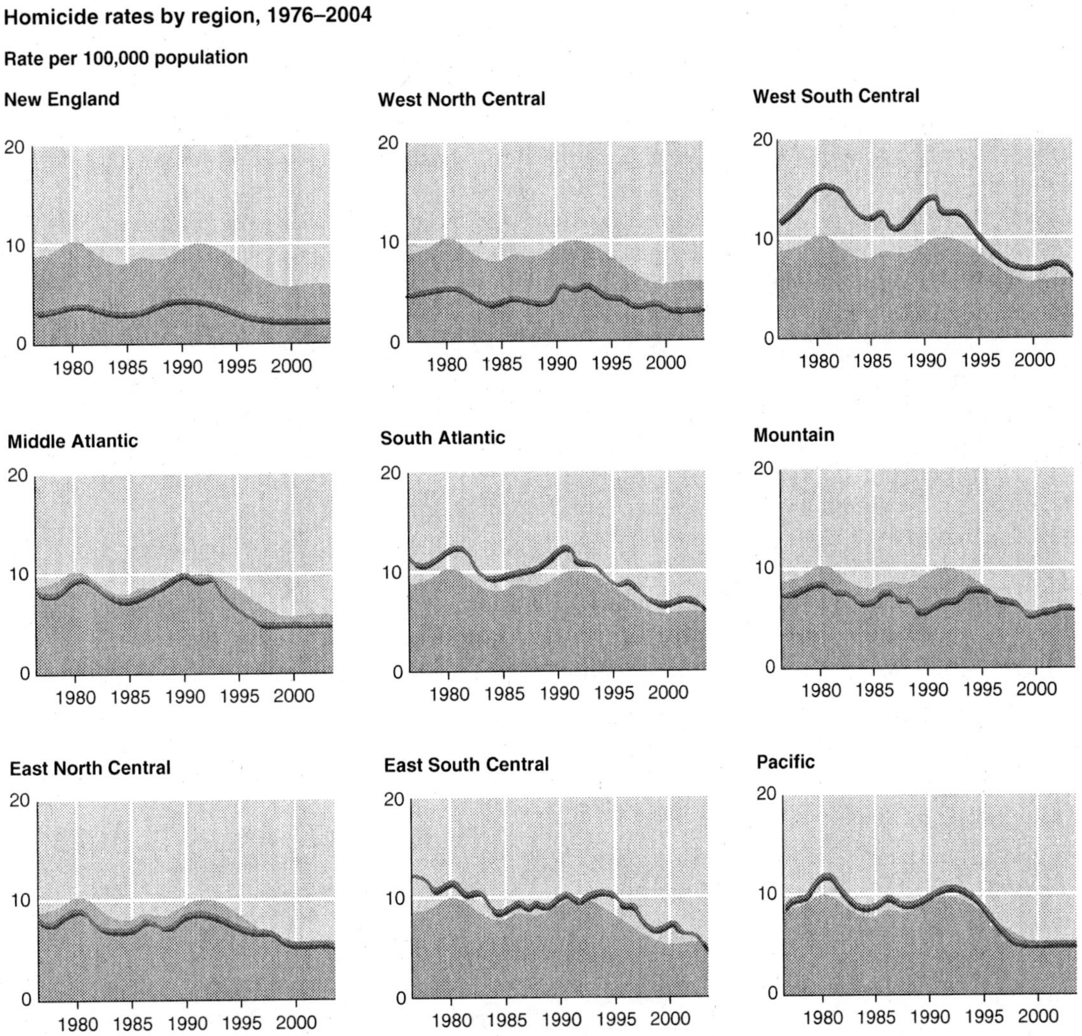

Homicide rates by region, 1976–2004

Rate per 100,000 population

FIGURE 2.3   Homicide Trends in the United States, by Region

Source: Ousey, G. (2000). "Explaining regional and urban variation in crime: A review of the research." Washington, DC: US Department of Justice.

each specific region. As you can see, homicide rate trends are almost identical for all regions of the country, meaning that although the rates varied widely by region, generally homicide rates fell and rose at similar times across the whole country. As explained by Ousey (2000:264), "there is tremendous continuity in the South's position as the most homicidal region of the United States. Consistent with the findings reported by many previous scholars, the South has the highest homicide rate every year between 1960 and the present day." At the same time, the gap between the South and the other regions of the country has narrowed over the past 40 years.

Figure 2.4 illustrates robbery trends in the United States over a slightly different time period, by region of the country. Interestingly, the South has relatively low rates of this violent crime. Even though trends over time for robbery are very similar in every region of the country, the South had the lowest rates of robbery through the 1980s and the second lowest through the 1990s. Again, over time, the gap between the highest regions, the Northeast and the West, and the lowest regions narrowed over the past several decades.

Figure 2.5 illustrates burglary trends in the United States, by region of the country. Burglary is perhaps the most serious of all street crimes against property. Burglary trends by region of the country are very similar over time except for a brief rise in the

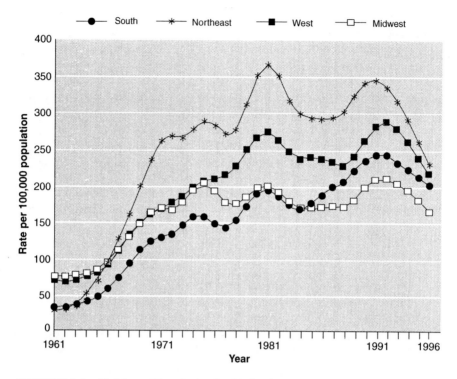

FIGURE 2.4 **Robbery Trends in the United States, by Region**

Source: Ousey, G. (2000). "Explaining regional and urban variation in crime: A review of the research." Washington, DC: US Department of Justice.

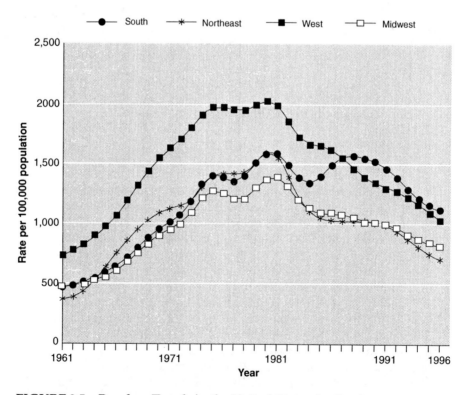

FIGURE 2.5 **Burglary Trends in the United States, by Region**

Source: Ousey, G. (2000). "Explaining regional and urban variation in crime: A review of the research." Washington, DC: US Department of Justice.

South in the 1980s. Rates of burglary were highest in the West until the 1980s, when the South took over as the nation's highest burglary region.

The most notable finding of UCR data shows that homicide rates in the South are much higher than in the non-South. Thus, it is not surprising that an entire theoretical perspective is developed to explain this difference. We look at the southern subculture of violence thesis later in this chapter.

It should be pointed out that there is much evidence in regional crime rate data of what can be called "divergence." Part of this can be attributed to increases in crime in the West, what some scholars have called "Westward movement" (see Goldstein, 1994:70). Figure 2.6 shows crime rate differences by state, according to the 2005 UCR.

Regional Crime Rates 2005
Violent and Property Crimes per 100,000 Inhabitants

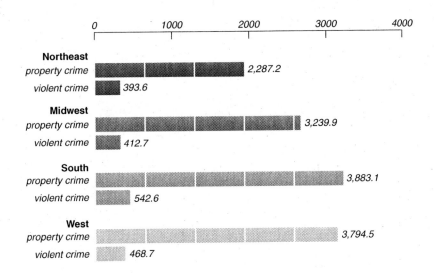

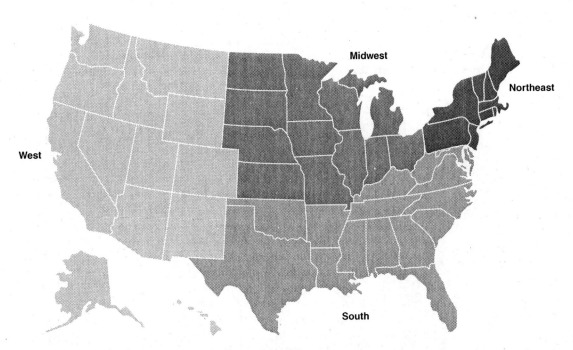

FIGURE 2.6   2001 National Index Crime Rate and Rank (in parentheses) per 100,000 Population
Source: Oklahoma DOC Data Analysis & Statistics Unit.

As you can see, the largest volume of serious street crime occurs in states in the South, which is the most populous region of the country. The next highest crime rate, according to the UCR, is in the West, followed by the Midwest and the Northeast. Just over 36 percent of U.S. residents lived in the South in 2005, yet more than 40 percent of all serious crimes occur in the South. Crime is thus over-represented in states in the South. Meanwhile, serious street crime is under-represented in states in the Northeast. Just over 18 percent of U.S. residents lived in the Northeast in 2005, yet less than 15 percent of all serious crimes occur in the Northeast.

The rate of serious property crimes in 2005 was also highest in the South, followed by the West, the Midwest, and the Northeast. The rate of serious violent crime followed a different pattern, with the West leading, followed by the South, the Northeast, and the Midwest. Table 2.1 illustrates crime rates by region of the country, according to the UCR.

In terms of individual violent crimes, the pattern varies. For aggravated assault, the most common violent crime, the rate per 100,000 inhabitants was highest in the South (354.5), followed by the West (292.3), the Northeast (219.4), and the Midwest (246.2). The South also had the highest rate per 100,000 inhabitants of murder victims (6.6), followed by the West (5.8), the Midwest (4.9), and the Northeast (4.4). The Midwest had the highest rates per 100,000 females of rapes (36.2), closely followed by the South (33.1), the West (32.7), and the Northeast (22.1). Finally, the Northeast led the nation in robberies per 100,000 inhabitants (147.7), closely followed by the South (148.4), the West (137.9), and the Midwest (125.3).

Also in terms of individual property crimes, the pattern varies. For theft, the most common property crime, rates per 100,000 inhabitants were highest in the South (3,883.1), followed by the Midwest (3,259.9), the West (3,794.5), and the Northeast (2,287.2). Burglary rates per 100,000 inhabitants were highest in the South (898.1), followed by the West (757.3), the Midwest (666.2), and the Northeast (424.5). As for motor vehicle theft, the highest rate per 100,000 inhabitants was for the West (685.1), followed by the South (383.3), the Midwest (341.8), and the Northeast (237.6). Interestingly, theft of trucks and buses is far more common in the West and South than in the Midwest and Northeast, whereas cars are stolen more frequently in the Northeast and Midwest. This is likely a function of the types of automobiles available for theft and desired by thieves across regions of the country. Finally, with regard to arson, the West

TABLE 2.1   Crime Rates by Region of the Country
Source: http://www.fbi.gov/ucr/05cius/data/table_04.html

	VIOLENT CRIME	MURDER	RAPE	ROBBERY	AGGRAVATED ASSAULT
US	**469.2**	**5.6**	**31.7**	**140.7**	**291.1**
Northeast	393.6	4.4	22.1	147.7	219.4
Midwest	412.7	4.9	36.2	125.3	246.2
South	542.6	6.6	33.1	148.4	354.5
West	468.7	5.8	32.7	137.9	292.3

	PROPERTY CRIME	THEFT	BURGLARY	MOTOR VEHICLE THEFT
US	**3,429.8**	**2,286.3**	**726.7**	**416.7**
Northeast	2,287.2	1,625.0	424.5	237.6
Midwest	3,259.9	2,251.9	666.2	341.8
South	3,883.1	2,601.7	898.1	383.3
West	3,794.5	2,352.1	757.3	685.1

saw the highest rate per 100,000 inhabitants (39.5), closely followed by the Midwest (39.1), the South (35.5), and the Northeast (31.6).

Based on the above data, the southern United States has the highest rates of homicide and other serious street crimes. The northeast generally has the lowest rates of serious street crimes, except for the crime of robbery.

Explanations

Ousey (2000) suggests there are two competing explanations for regional differences in crime rates in the United States. These include the southern subculture of violence and the economic deprivation explanations. Each of these is discussed below.

Southern Subculture of Violence.   The *southern subculture of violence* theory blames higher crime rates in the South on "cultural values that evolved from that region's unique history" (Ousey, 2000:268). As a result of the many violent historical facts of the South, including slavery, lynchings, Reconstruction and the Jim Crow era, resistance to the Civil Rights movement, and so forth, a unique culture emerged that is associated with higher rates of murder in the South. "Two prominent aspects of this culture are an exaggerated sensitivity to derision and the expectation that indignities will be handled personally, promptly, and violently" (Ousey, 2000:268). Goldstein (1994:67) says this perspective is based on the notion "that more than a century's series of experiences had shaped southern attitudes and behaviors in ways decidedly facilitative of the enhanced likelihood of aggression" including a "much greater incidence of gun ownership and use, dueling as an accepted means of dispute resolution, vigilante groups, local militia, military training, military titles, and the several ways in which the South, much more fully than the North, could still be described as a frontier society."

As indicated by the title of the approach, the southern subculture of violence is a subcultural explanation. A *subculture* is a culture within a culture, or more specifically, "an ethnic, regional, economic, or social group exhibiting characteristic patterns of behavior sufficient to distinguish it from others within an embracing culture or society" (*Merriam-Webster's Collegiate Dictionary*, 2001). All cultural explanations are based on the social learning approach, which holds that criminality is learned through intimate interactions with others. Whereas social learning theorists focus on how individuals learn to commit deviance and to justify it in the context of intimate social groups (e.g., peers, families), subcultural theorists aim to explain how entire groups of people maintain established traditions of violence; they presume these traditions are learned over time or culturally transmitted.

An example of this thesis comes from the work of Nisbett and Cohen (1996), who "observed that high homicide rates in the South are almost entirely the result of very high rates among rural white males. For females and for minority males, there are only minor differences between homicide rates in the South and in other regions of the country" (Weisheit and Donnermeyer, 2000:345). The high homicide rates among rural whites are supposedly due to a "culture of honor," which encourages or even mandates a violent response when one is confronted by another person, depending on the circumstances of the confrontation. Another example is that capital punishment is highest in the South. Studies show that the number of executions in a state is correlated with the number of lynchings in the same states (Robinson, 2008).

Economic Deprivation.   The *economic deprivation* explanation to differences of crime rates within regions of the country is synonymous with strain theories, introduced earlier in this chapter. In terms of regional crime rate differences, strain is thought to encompass *absolute deprivation* (e.g., poverty levels in a region) or *relative deprivation* (e.g., the gap between the wealthy and the poor in a region). In other words, higher crime rates in the South are thought to reflect reactions to financial or economic difficulties more than they are to cultural differences in the people who live there.

According to Ousey (2000:269), "studies testing the merits of these two competing perspectives have produced inconsistent results." Some studies show that homicide rate differences still exist after controlling for economic factors (Fowles and Merva, 1996; Ousey, 1999; Parker and McCall, 1997; Peterson and Krivo, 1993) while others do not (Chamlin and Cochran, 2006; Corzine and Huff-Corzine, 1992; Harer and Steffesnmeier, 1992; Messner and Golden, 1992; Phillips, 1997; Smith, 1992). More advanced studies that correct for methodological problems find support for both the Southern subculture of violence model and the economic deprivation model (Land, McCall, and Cohen, 1990; Williams and Flewelling, 1988).

Finally, with regard to explanations of crime centered around economic deprivation, research on *income inequality* and crime is relevant. Generally, the research shows a positive relationship between the amount of income inequality in an area and that area's crime rates, although findings for different types of crime are inconsistent (Witt, Clarke, and Fielding, 1999). According to Hsieh and Pugh (1993), who reviewed more than 30 studies assessing relationships between poverty, income inequality, and violent crimes, almost all of the studies find positive relationships between income inequality and homicide, assault, robbery, and rape. Other research into income inequality has produced similar findings (Fowles and Merva, 1996; Hagan and Peterson, 1994). A review of 45 studies by Vieraitis (2000) describes relationships between income inequality, poverty, and violent crimes: (1) inequality and homicide is typically positive; (2) poverty and homicide is typically positive; and (3) inequality and assault is typically positive. This means that as income inequality and poverty increase, so too do these types of crimes.

Ousey (2000:271–272) thus concludes,

> Although not entirely consistent, there is evidence of a Southern region effect on some violent crimes. In particular, research suggests that compared with other regions, southern areas of the United States have higher primary and conflict homicide rates and higher assault rates. On the other hand, rates of instrumental violence (e.g., robbery and felony homicides) are lower in the South than in other regions.

In summary, both the Southern subculture of violence and the economic deprivation models seem to account for part of why some crime rates are higher in the South. It would be theoretically possible to use crime mapping software to visually depict and analyze subcultural factors and economic deprivation variables in order to show their effects on crime rates across regions of the country. Such large-scale crime mapping rarely occurs, but it would be possible to map poverty rates from the U.S. Census or another measure of poverty against crime rates, as we did for one city in Chapter 1. The poorest areas would be expected to have the highest rates of criminal victimization for most street crimes.

DIFFERENCES IN URBAN AND RURAL DISTRIBUTIONS OF CRIME WITHIN THE UNITED STATES

Just as crime rates are higher in some regions of the country than in others, so too are crime rates higher in some types of areas than in others. For example, for virtually every type of street crime, levels have always been higher in urban areas than in rural areas. Although roughly 75 percent of the U.S. population lives in urban areas, nearly 95 percent of street crime occurs in urban areas (Ousey, 2000), meaning that the disproportionate amount of street crime in urban areas cannot be accounted for solely on the basis of higher populations.

According to Weisheit and Donnermeyer (2000:310), there are roughly 65 million rural citizens, who make up roughly one-quarter of the population of the United States. And rural areas make up about 70 percent of the land mass in United States. Thus, most places in the United States are rural.

Empirical Realities

Both the UCR and the NCVS show that crime rates are highest in urban areas. For example, Ousey (2000) analyzes rates of homicide, robbery, and burglary from 1961 to 1996 and finds that size of city is related to rates of these street crimes. He labels "large" cities as those with 1 million population or more, "medium-large" cities as those with 500,000–999,999 people, "medium" as those cities with 250,000–499,999 people, "medium-small" as those cities with 10,000–249,999 people, and finally, "small" as those cities with less than 10,000 people.

Overall, Ousey shows that homicides are highest in large cities, except in the 1960s when medium-large cities had higher rates of homicide. The largest homicide declines in the 1990s were for large cities, so that by 1996, rates of homicide for large and medium cities were nearly identical. Figure 2.7 shows trends in homicide by city size.

Ousey also shows that robbery rates are positively associated with city size. They are highest in cities with more than one million people and lowest in cities with less than 100,000 people. Figure 2.8 shows trends in robbery by city size.

Finally, rates of burglary over the time period of study are highest in medium cities. Interestingly, in the 1990s, rates of burglary were lower in large cities than in medium-small, medium, and medium-large cities. Figure 2.9 shows trends in burglary by city size.

A special focus on rural crime shows some interesting facts. First, Weisheit and Donnermeyer (2000:312) discuss the stereotypes of rural crimes: "One image is of a bucolic countryside where crime is rare. . . . Another image is of serious violent crime perpetrated by 'rednecks' or 'white trash'" who are "amoral, revengeful, and violent." According to the literature of rural crime in America, most crimes are less common in rural areas than in urban areas, the greatest difference is for the crime of robbery, and

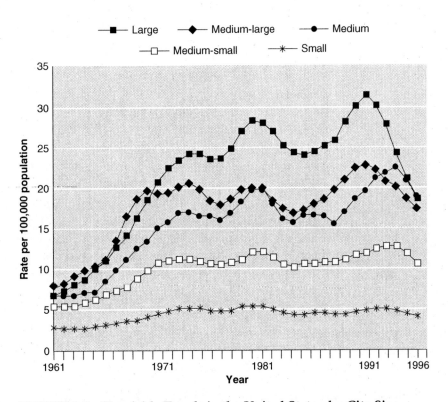

FIGURE 2.7   Homicide Trends in the United States, by City Size

Source: Ousey, G. (2000). "Explaining regional and urban variation in crime: A review of the research." Washington, DC: US Department of Justice.

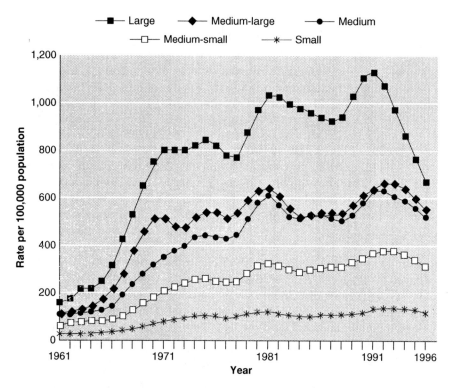

FIGURE 2.8   Robbery Trends in the United States, by City Size

Source: Ousey, G. (2000). "Explaining regional and urban variation in crime: A review of the research." Washington, DC: US Department of Justice.

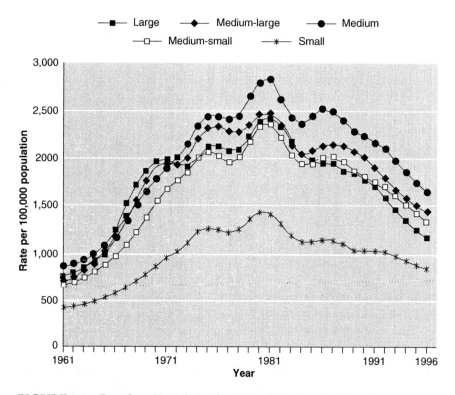

FIGURE 2.9   Burglary Trends in the United States, by City Size

Source: Ousey, G. (2000). "Explaining regional and urban variation in crime: A review of the research." Washington, DC: US Department of Justice.

for some crimes, the differences are small (Donnermeyer, 1994; Weisheit, Falcone, and Wells, 1994). Additionally, some crimes are actually unique to rural areas. The gap between urban and rural violent crime is greater than the gap between urban and rural property crimes (Weisheit, Falcone, and Wells, 1994).

In the remainder of this section, we discuss the specifics of rural crime in order to provide a comparison with urban crime in the United States. Rates of violent and property crimes in urban areas have always been higher than those in rural areas, although there has been some modest convergence between the rates recently. Violent crimes are still roughly five times as frequent in urban areas than in rural areas. As noted by Weisheit and Donnermeyer (2000:316), "Where convergence has occurred, it is between suburban and rural areas. This has more to do with drops in suburban victimization than with increased rural victimization."

Recent UCR data (2000) show that cities outside metropolitan areas had higher rates of serious street crimes (4,485 per 100,000 inhabitants) than metropolitan areas (4,428 per 100,000 inhabitants) and rural counties (1,864 per 100,000 inhabitants). Rates of violent crime were higher in metropolitan areas (561.4 per 100,000 inhabitants) than in cities outside metropolitan areas (401.5 per 100,000 inhabitants) and rural counties (209.7 per 100,000 inhabitants). Property crime rates showed a similar pattern, as rates were higher in the cities (4,419.6 per 100,000 inhabitants) than in suburban counties (2,628.8 per 100,000 inhabitants) and rural counties (1,714.9 per 100,000 inhabitants). Rates per 100,000 inhabitants are much lower in rural counties (17.7) than in suburban counties (33.9) or large cities of 250,000 people or more (67.2).

With regard to individual property crimes, rates per 100,000 inhabitants for the most common crime of theft were higher in cities outside metropolitan areas (3,125.1) than in metropolitan areas (2,631.9) and rural counties (999.7). For burglaries, the rate per 100,000 inhabitants was highest in cities outside metropolitan areas (759.2), followed by metropolitan areas (754.9) and rural counties (532.3). Rates per 100,000 inhabitants of motor vehicle theft in metropolitan areas were high overall (479.9) and were highest in cities with over 250,000 people (929.1), but much lower in cities with fewer than 10,000 people (217.3) and cities outside metropolitan areas (199.2). Rural counties had the lowest rates per 100,000 inhabitants (122.3). Although crime trends in cities, suburbs, and rural areas are similar in terms of recent declines, crimes in cities have always been notably higher.

For the most common violent crime of aggravated assault, rates per 100,000 inhabitants were higher in metropolitan areas (349.2) than in cities outside metropolitan areas (302.5) and rural counties (167.8). The highest rates per 100,000 inhabitants of murder were in metropolitan areas (5.9) while both cities outside metropolitan areas and rural counties had lower rates per 100,000 inhabitants (3.8). The highest rates per 100,000 females of rape were for cities outside metropolitan areas (69.0), closely followed by metropolitan areas (65.0) and then rural counties (43.4). The fastest rise in murders, however, from 1999 to 2000, was in cities with populations less than 10,000 people (11.7 percent increase). For robbery, the highest rates per 100,000 inhabitants were for metropolitan areas generally (173.0), followed by cities outside metropolitan areas (59.9) and rural areas (15.9). The highest rates per 100,000 inhabitants of robbery were for cities with more than 1 million people (440.2), followed by cities with 250,000 or more (413.4), suburban counties (67.6), and rural counties (15.5). Similar to murder, the highest increase in robbery from 1999 was for cities with less than 10,000 people (3.1 percent increase).

According to studies on rural crime, gun ownership is higher in rural areas, but gun crimes are lower in rural areas than in urban areas. Additionally, gang membership is lower in rural areas, although rural gangs are more likely to be found in areas that are adjacent to major cities. Crimes with small differences between urban and rural areas include alcohol use, illicit drug use, and domestic violence. Domestic violence data are not necessarily valid anywhere given the low rate at which domestic violence is reported, but research suggests that rates of abuse are similar in rural and urban areas. Websdale's (1998) *Rural Women Battering* illustrates how isolation in rural areas contributes to the initiation and the continuation of abuse victimization in rural Kentucky.

Crimes that are more common in rural areas than in urban areas include driving under the influence of alcohol (DUI), tobacco use by youth, and some forms of drug manufacturing (Bai, 1997; Clayton, 1995; Howlett, 1997; Kirn, 1998; McCormick and O'Donnell, 1993; Stewart and Sitaramiah, 1997; Tyson, 1996; Weisheit and Donnermeyer, 2000). Crimes that are nearly unique to rural areas include some forms of crimes against the environment, crimes in the name of the environment, and wildlife crimes.

In terms of DUI, it is not necessarily that more people in rural areas actually drink more or are more inclined because of their culture to drive while impaired, it is the fact that they are in rural areas that increases the likelihood that they will find themselves behind the wheel of the car while impaired. Consider young people, for example. Peters, Oetting, and Edwards (1992:25) speculate,

> Similar rates of alcohol use . . . may be more of a problem for rural than for urban youth because rural youth must spend more time on the roads. The distances that must be traveled from homes to school and other entertainment events, or even to visit friends, are generally much greater for rural youth than for urban youth. The lack of availability of public transportation means that these youth spend a significant amount of time in cars. . . . With many rural roads in poor conditions, poorly marked for hazards, and poorly lit, these youth are already at higher risk of accidents leading to injury or death.

The nature of some crimes is also different in rural and urban areas. Increasingly, homicides in the nation's cities are being committed by strangers (Robinson, 2005). Yet, violent crimes such as homicide, rape, and assault are more likely between acquaintances than in urban areas (Weisheit, Falcone, and Wells, 1994:1). Place of victimization also differs, as rural crime victims are more likely to be victimized away from their own communities than urban victims.

Based on the above data, we can conclude that street crime is generally higher in larger cities within the United States, with the exception of burglary. Additionally, crime rates are generally higher within cities and metropolitan areas outside cities than in rural areas. One exception is the crime of robbery. High rates per 100,000 inhabitants of robberies on streets or highways are less likely as the population decreases, but high rates per 100,000 inhabitants of robberies of convenience stores are more likely as population goes down. This likely reflects the more common presence of highways in larger cities and the isolated nature of convenience stores in the nation's small cities and rural areas. Crime mapping software can be effectively used to identify isolated, rural highways, and to plot convenience stores on these roads in order to predict likely robbery sites. Our Figure 2.10 shows an example from a study that found that more isolated roadways suffer from higher rates of convenience store robbery than roads that have greater levels of traffic.

Explanations

It may seem logical to you that urban and rural crime rates would be vastly different, given your own experiences with urban and rural areas. Weisheit and Donnermeyer (2000) suggest that it is the uniqueness of rural areas that explains their lower crime rates. Rural areas can be differentiated from urban areas in terms of their physical distance and isolation (whereas urban areas are more congested and have higher population densities), meaning it is usually more difficult for neighbors to keep an eye on each other's property. Routine activity theory (discussed in Chapter 4) suggests this could actually increase the likelihood of crime. Burglars, for example, prefer to enter unoccupied residences that are not easily seen by neighbors or passersby (Robinson, 2000).

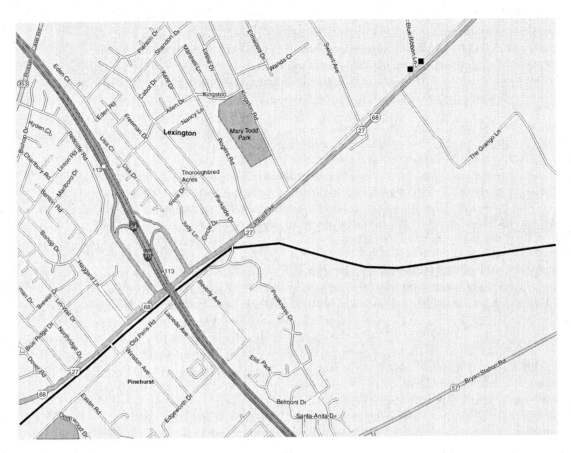

FIGURE 2.10   Traffic on Roadways and Convenience Store Robbery

Rural areas also tend to have a different culture than urban areas. It can be described as higher in "informal social control, a mistrust in government, and a reluctance to seek outside assistance" (Weisheit and Donnermeyer, 2000:328). High levels of informal social control—characterized by closer friendship networks, for example—inhibit criminal victimization. Other facts of rural life are non-criminogenic, including higher levels of population stability of the local population and greater homogeneity of the population. The mistrust of government and the reluctance to seek outside assistance could account for lower levels of reported crime to the police in rural areas.

As rural areas grow, they are thought to be more susceptible to criminality, in line with the anomie theory, discussed earlier. As explained by Donnermeyer (1994:1), "economic, social, and cultural forces associated with rising levels of crime, violence, delinquency, and gangs appear first in urban areas then spread to the hinterlands." Weisheit, Falcone, and Wells. (1994:2) report that in 21 of 23 studies reviewed, crime grew faster than the population in rural communities that were characterized by rapid population growth. Population growth in the United States historically was from rural areas to urban areas, but since the 1970s this has reversed. With more people moving from the nation's cities to the rural areas, bringing with them not only higher populations but also increased development and diversity, it is possible that rural crime rates will likely rise in the future. It is suggested that rural communities that witness rapid growth may see crime increase as much as four times faster than in urban areas (Freudenburg and Jones, 1991), particularly as crime spills over from urban areas (Wells and Weisheit, 1998). However, the U.S. population is aging, including in rural areas. Therefore, large increases in street crime in rural areas are not likely.

The main explanations for urban versus rural crime rate differences include:

- Social stratification; and
- Social control.

According to Ousey (2000:281), the social stratification model "asserts that crime is related to economic conditions." As mentioned earlier in the chapter, social control theories suggest that criminality occurs when normal lines of social control are eroded or weakened.

Social Stratification.   *Social stratification* as an explanation for higher urban crime rates relative to rural crime rates is very similar to previous explanations examined in this chapter. Recall the grand theory of modernization and the structural theories of strain and social disorganization aimed at explaining international crime rate variations. Each of these explanations suggested crime rates are higher in some nations because of economic conditions. Also recall the economic deprivation model aimed at explaining regional crime rate variations in the United States. This perspective attributes higher crime rates in some regions of the country (e.g., the South) to economic conditions.

The economic conditions identified by each of these perspectives, including culture conflict, inequality, anomie, frustration, and relative and absolute deprivation, are relevant for the social stratification model, as well. For example, there is the *absolute deprivation model*, which "emphasizes the crime-producing effects of earning an income that falls below a level necessary to maintain basic subsistence." Like strain theory, this theory sees crime as a normal method of adapting to economic frustration, that "stressful and dehumanizing effects of a life of severe economic disadvantage produce frustration and anger that become expressed through physical aggression." And the *relative deprivation model* "emphasizes the criminogenic aspects of socioeconomic inequality" so that as people become aware of the gap between their status and those who are better off around them, "a sense of deprivation, resentment, and anger develops" (Ousey, 2000:281).

Some research produces findings opposite to those predicted by the absolute deprivation model, so that rates of poverty are either unrelated to violent crime or are associated with lower rates of it (Blau and Blau, 1982; Messner, 1982). Although methodological flaws in these studies suggest the findings could be in error, Ousey suggests that the relationship between poverty and violent crime is inconclusive. Studies of relative deprivation also produce inconsistent results. Yet, as noted by Ousey (2000:282) himself, most of the studies of income inequality and crime do find a positive relationship, so that as inequality is greater, crime rates are greater as well. Additional research finds support for a measure of ethnic-specific inequality and homicide rates (Balkwell, 1990). Thus, if income inequality is higher in urban areas than in rural areas, and if ethnic inequality is prevalent, this could be one explanation as to why crime rates are so much higher in urban areas.

Although Ousey (2000:284) did not list social disorganization as an explanation of urban versus rural crime rates, he did mention it as "new avenues in social stratification-crime research." For example, research by Shihadeh and Ousey (1996, 1998) shows that high rates of serious street crime are associated with what they call suburbanization and industrial restructuring. As cities expand outward into the suburbs and ultimately into rural areas, the mass exodus of people and their jobs from the inner cities lead to a class of remaining people called the "truly disadvantaged" (Wilson, 1987). So, "as rates of poverty, joblessness, welfare dependence, and family breakdown have increased, there has also been a corresponding increase in rates of serious crime" (Ousey, 2000:284). This finding is consistent with social disorganization theory, discussed earlier in this chapter and in more depth in Chapter 3.

Social Control.   The *social control* perspective has been discussed previously in this chapter as relevant for crime rate differences across nations and regions of a particular country. It is also relevant for urban versus rural crime rate differences. Research using social disorganization variables, such as residential mobility and population density, finds that areas characterized by low levels of residential stability and large populations tend to have higher rates of violent and property crimes. In essence, any factor that weakens the social cohesion of an area is thought to increase crime rates. Larger populations characterized by racial and ethnic heterogeneity interfere with the ability of a population to regulate its own members. Other factors such as family disruption also achieve this result, and are associated with higher rates of homicide rates and other serious crimes (Miethe and Meier, 1994; Phillips, 1997).

This makes social control and social disorganization theories relevant for urban versus rural crime rate differences, as rural areas are thought to be characterized by higher levels of informal social control and lower levels of social disorganization. This issue is returned to below. Ousey (2000:289) concludes that

> Social stratification and social control models are more appropriately conceptualized as complementary, rather than competing, explanations of crime. Several studies indicate that social stratification affects crime by reducing informal social control. That is, greater economic disadvantage (e.g., joblessness, inequality) decreases informal social control (e.g., two-parent households), which in turn, increases crime.

We can conclude that the social stratification and social control theories have promise in helping to account for crime rate variations between urban and rural areas within the United States. Earlier, we suggested that social stratification variables can be plotted on crime maps. Movement of people seeking work is another example of a factor that can be mapped and compared with crime rate fluctuations over time. Areas characterized by higher levels of mobility would be expected to have higher overall crime rates.

INTRA-CITY DIFFERENCES IN DISTRIBUTIONS OF CRIME WITHIN THE UNITED STATES

The amount of crime at any place within a given city depends on characteristics of neighborhoods, residences, activities and traffic patterns of surrounding streets and sidewalks, and other similar factors. Every city seems to have its seedy parts, as it also has its desirable areas. Chances are you could easily identify the area in your community or city where you would not wish to find yourself alone because of your perception that there is more crime there.

Empirical Realities

Research on crime in cities shows at least two clear facts: (1) some areas incur a great amount of crime while far more experience no crime; and (2) some people incur a great amount of criminal victimization while far more experience no criminal victimization. Areas that are high in crime are called *hot spots of crime*, and when people are victimized more than once by criminals, it is called *revictimization*. Both of these phenomena can be considered subsets of *clustering of crime*. In this section, we present some facts about hot spots and revictimization in order to illustrate how crime clusters among certain places and people.

Sherman, Gartin, and Buerger (1989:37) analyzed spatial data on 323,979 calls to the police over an estimated 115,000 addresses and intersections in Minneapolis, Minnesota, in one year. These researchers reported that "a majority (60 percent) of all addresses generated at least one call over the course of the year, but almost half of those addresses produced one call and no more." Thus, many addresses produced more than one call to police. For example, all 15,901 calls to police for burglary in a year in Minneapolis came from only 11 percent of all street addresses ("hot spots"). More strikingly, 50 percent of all calls to police came from 3 percent of places, while all calls for rape came from 1.2 percent of places, all calls for auto thefts came from 2.7 percent of places, and all calls for robberies came from 2.2 percent of places. The number of places calculated by Sherman, Gartin, and Buerger included street addresses and intersections. The high concentration of crime by place is thus partly due to the fact that these researchers calculated crimes by places, not merely by residences. This was necessary because many crimes occur away from residences.

In this study, "relatively few 'hot spots' produce(d) most calls to police . . . because crime is both rare . . . and concentrated" (Sherman, Gartin, and Buerger, 1989:27). Thus, even though many (9,032) residences suffered from one burglary, even more (97,449) were not victims of burglary at all. The authors write, "To be sure, most of the absence of crime by place is due to crime's overall rarity, rather than its concentration" (p. 43).

Carolyn and Richard Block have demonstrated, in numerous studies, the presence of hot spots of crime, including homicides in Chicago (Block and Christakos, 1995; Block and Block, 1998), street gang violence (Block and Block, 1995b), and liquor-related crime (Block and Block, 1995a). Hot sports of crime and fear of crime are common for virtually every type of crime (Brantingham and Brantingham, 1999), including drug crimes (Green, 1995; Eck and Weisburd, 1995), gun violence (Sherman and Rogan, 1995), and burglary (Robinson, 1998). Common hot spots of crime include street blocks near bars (Roncek and Maier, 1991), entertainment districts (Cochran, Bromley, and Branch, 2000), and even bus stops (Loukaitou-Sideris, 1999). In fact, it has been shown that hot spots of crime exist around the world, caused by unique problems in certain areas, such as gang problems in Los Angeles, California, drug cartels in Mexico City, Mexico, street muggings in London, England, and murder in Johannesburg, South Africa, among many others. Figure 2.11 illustrates several hot spots of burglary in an American city, generated using crime mapping software.

Numerous recent studies verify the reality that a small portion of all places generate a large portion of all crimes in any given location. For example, a study by Zhu, Gorman, and Horel (2004) explores whether alcohol outlets were associated with greater occurrences of drug-related and violent crimes. They found that places that host a lot of drug crime also are plagued by high violent crime rates. Another study of a popular public park found it to be a hot spot for alcohol- and drug- related crimes as well as vandalism (Thomas and Wolfer, 2003). Interestingly, studies of hot spots also help explain why crime declined across the United States in the 1990s. One major study found that declines in small portions of some cities in many states (previous hot spots of crime) were responsible for most of the decline in the nation's crime rate, and in most places, crime was remarkably stable (Weisburd et al., 2004).

Part of the reason that some places become hot spots of crime is because some people are victimized more than once by crime. Revictimization "occurs when the same person or place suffers from more than one criminal incident over a specified period of time" (Ross, 1994:1). For more on the phenomenon of repeat victimization, see the Focus On box.

Explanations

Why people and places suffer from revictimization—why crime clusters in any given area—is still being debated. Sparks (1981:772–778) was one of the first modern theorists to hypothesize about the causes of revictimization. He discusses many concepts that he believed were relevant, including victim facilitation, vulnerability, opportunity, target attractiveness, impunity, and lifestyle. He writes that a multiple victim may "facilitate its commission . . . by deliberately, recklessly, or negligently placing himself at special risk. . . . Anyone who fails to take reasonable precautions against crime may be said to have facilitated a crime against him."

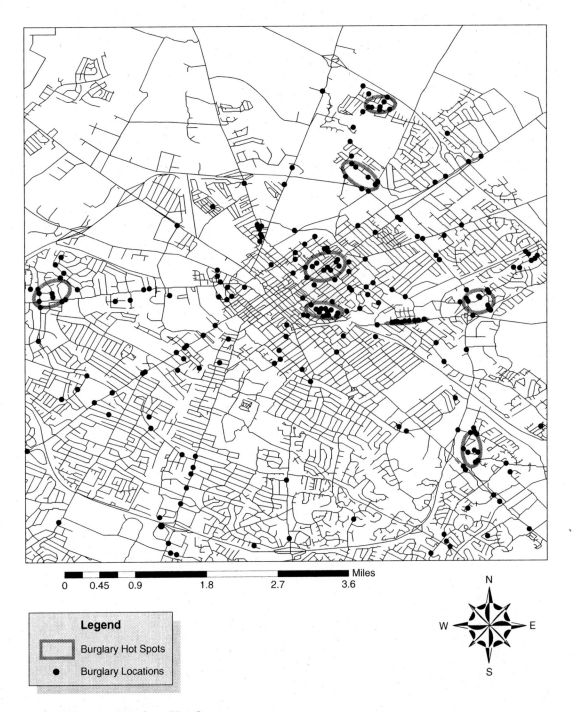

FIGURE 2.11   Burglary Hot Spots

FOCUS ON
CRIMINAL REVICTIMIZATION

Research shows that very small segments of the population suffer from disproportionate amounts of criminal victimization and that this phenomenon is not due to simple chance alone (Farrell, 1994; Polvi et al., 1990, 1991). A tremendous volume of literature now verifies the existence of this problem (see Robinson, 1998).

(continued)

Many studies have focused on both violent and property offenses. Sampson and Phillips (1992) demonstrate that two-thirds of families in a study were revictimized by racial attacks. It has been estimated that 90 percent of domestic violence involves systematic beatings (Hammer and Stanko, 1985). Forrester, Chatterton, and Pease (1988) show in a study that a previously burglarized house was four times more likely than one that had not been burglarized to be burglarized again. Of all crimes reported by 33 schools in England, 98 percent were repeat crimes (Burquest, Farrell, and Pease, 1992). Less than 10 percent of motor vehicle theft victims accounted for nearly one-fourth of all incidents of motor vehicle thefts in three surveys (Mayhew, Maung, and Mirrlees-Black, 1993). In a period of a year, 39 percent of businesses in an area were re-burglarized at least once more (Tilley, 1993). Hope (1982) demonstrates that from 1977 to 1978, 19 percent of schools studied had ten or more burglaries, while another 17 percent were victims of between five and nine burglaries. Another 45 percent of schools suffered from between one and four burglaries. At the same time, 19 percent had no burglaries at all.

Repeatedly victimized people and places may account for a large portion of all crime (National Board for Crime Prevention, 1994:2). For example, one-half of all victimized respondents of the 1992 British Crime Survey were repeat victims. They suffered from 81 percent of all reported crimes. Furthermore, 4 percent of those who suffered from criminal victimizations more than once were victimized four or more times in a year, and accounted for 44 percent of all reported crimes (Farrell and Pease, 1993).

Polvi et al. (1990) show that revictimization made up a significant portion of all the victimization of burglary in the area they studied (Saskatoon, Canada). Of the 70,343 dwellings in the area, only 2,966 (4.2 percent) were burglarized. Of those burglarized units, 1,848 (62.3 percent) were burglarized only once, versus 118 (4.0 percent) residences that were burglarized more than once. Polvi et al. also demonstrate that there was an increased chance for revictimization immediately after an initial burglary. According to Polvi et al., dwellings in Saskatoon in 1987 were almost four times more likely to be burglarized again following a first burglary. This chance for revictimization decreased with time. Specifically, the risk of being burglarized a second time was highest within the same month as the initial burglary. In fact, 28 percent of repeat burglaries occurred in the same day or adjacent days, while a full 50 percent occurred within seven days, and 74 percent occurred within 16 days. A follow-up study by Polvi et al. (1991:413) on burglaries between 1984 and 1987 in the same area shows that the elevated risk of being revictimized by burglary extended only over a short period, and that after six months, the risk of repeat victimization ceased to exist. Robinson (1997) demonstrates that one percent of residences accounted for 26 percent of all burglaries in one high-crime police zone in Tallahassee, Florida, between 1992 and 1994. When residences were revictimized, most of the revictimization occurred within one month of the initial offenses. More recent research indicates that not only are recently burglarized residences at an increased risk of revictimization, but so too are other residences within 400 meters of the original residence (Bowers, Johnson, and Pease, 2004).

Although many studies of revictimization have been conducted on property crimes, there is also a growing literature on revictimization from sex crimes and abuse (Arata, 1999; Classen et al., 2001; Mayall and Gold, 1995; Messman-Moore and Long, 2000; Shapiro, 1998). This research shows that revictimization

- Is concentrated in very few people;
- Is more likely to occur to people who have been victimized as children; and
- Is predicted by certain victim lifestyles.

As noted by Robinson (1998:79), "The results of the growing body of research leaves one with the sense that revictimization is a reality across all crime types, all locations, and all periods of study (Farrell, Phillips, and Pease, 1995:501)."

Also, some people, "because of their attributes, usual behavior, or their place in a social system, may be very vulnerable" to revictimization. Vulnerability factors may be related to status (sex, class) or may be ecological (living in a bad neighborhood). It is now common knowledge that some groups suffer from higher rates of criminal victimization than others. The likelihood of criminal revictimization is said to be higher for these groups who are most vulnerable in society (Pease, 1992). But the meaning of a bad neighborhood is ambiguous, and an "open empirical question . . . i.e., whether the risk of crime is randomly or evenly distributed throughout the neighborhood, or so concentrated in some parts of the neighborhood that other parts are relatively safe" (Sherman, Gartin, and Buerger, 1989:29). Whichever the case, the rate of criminal revictimization is reportedly three times higher in high-crime areas than in low-crime areas (Trickett et al., 1992). Thus, where crime tends to cluster (hot spots of crime), rates of revictimization will be higher.

According to Sherman (1998), the following community-level factors may explain why some neighborhoods have higher crime rates than others. These factors may also account for hot spots of crime.

- *Community composition*—with higher rates of some types of people living in a community, crime rates are found to be higher. This includes "unmarried or divorced adult males, teenage males, non-working adults, poor people, persons with criminal histories and single parents";
- *Community social structure*—crime rates are also affected by the way in which inhabitants of an area interact. For example, communities with a high percentage of single-parent households reduce the ability of parents to supervise their children, thereby increasing the likelihood of children associating with other children without parental supervision;
- *Oppositional culture*—high-crime neighborhoods are thought to be characterized by an "oppositional culture" or subcultural values that stem from frustration arising out of financial strains. People in high-crime areas develop "values that oppose the protective factors of marriage and family, education, work and obedience to the law";
- *Criminogenic commodities*—rates of youth violence tend to be associated with the presence of places where alcohol use, drug use, and gun ownership are prevalent; and
- *Social and physical disorder*—high crime rate areas tend to be characterized by incivilities, which are signs that a neighborhood is in disarray.

Each of these factors is related to social disorganization theory and is discussed in more depth in Chapter 3.

Similar to Sherman (1998), Goldstein (1994:77) suggests that three theoretical perspectives can help us understand inter-city crime rate variations. These include:

- Deterministic theories;
- Compositional theories; and
- Subcultural theories.

Deterministic theories posit that characteristics of the community directly act on those who live there and cause them to become aggressive and deviant. *Compositional theories* posit that the ethnic and racial make-up of communities determines the crime rates. *Subcultural theories* were introduced earlier, but Goldstein suggests they are a combination of the previous two approaches. Goldstein (1994:78) also lists the following factors as possibly explanatory of crime rate differences across cities: level of direct, face-to-face contacts between residents; size of city; population density; population heterogeneity; income levels; income inequality; residential instability; stress; and unemployment. Many of these were discussed earlier.

In terms of social disorganization, communities or cities that have higher levels of friendship networks, organizational participation, and supervision of peer groups have lower rates of serious street crime (Sampson and Groves, 1989). Urbanized areas with higher levels of residential instability tend to be characterized by lower levels of local friendship networks, and areas that are more well off tend to have higher levels of organizational participation and supervision of peer groups (in part because they are inhabited by more two-parent families). The impacts of socioeconomic status (e.g., poverty), heterogeneity (ethnic and racial diversity), and residential instability (population turnover) on crime rates are mediated by weak social interactions (Bellair, 1997), although this model may only apply to white, middle-class communities (Warner and Rountree, 1997).

The main question yet to be definitively answered about hot spots of crime and criminal revictimization is whether they occur because of enduring characteristics about targets which make them attractive or suitable to multiple offenders (the *risk heterogeneity argument*), or if they occur because of factors related to the initial victimization (the *state-dependent argument*). Is it because some people and places are different in some way that attracts offenders or is it because initial victimizations result in the reinforcement of offenders' criminal behaviors? It is likely that the answer to each of these questions is yes.

In summary, we believe variations in crime rates within cities are a function of community composition and community social structure factors, as well as the presence of criminogenic commodities. Each of these offers opportunities for study by crime mapping users. For example, community composition and community structure (e.g., presence of single parents), the presence of criminogenic commodities (e.g., bars, gun shops), and the presence of disorder (e.g., abandoned buildings) can be identified with crime mapping software and compared with area crime rates (Levine, 2006). Figure 2.12 illustrates the proportion of homicides that occurred near bars in an American city.

SPATIAL ASPECTS OF FEAR OF CRIME AND PUBLIC PERCEPTION OF CRIME

The geography of crime can be divided into two different, but related fields of study: the geography of objective crime patterns and the geography of perceptual crime patterns (Brantingham, Brantingham, and Butcher, 1986). The geography of objective crime patterns involves the mapping and analysis of official crime data, such as police records of calls for service, arrests, and crime incident locations. It is the mapping and analysis of official data that the majority of this chapter has focused on and which the majority of all spatial analysis of crime patterns focuses on. By contrast, the geography of perceptual crime patterns focuses on the mapping and analysis of perceptual beliefs about crime and fear of crime (Brantingham, Brantingham, and Butcher, 1986). Specifically, the geography of perceptual crime patterns focuses on people's perceptions of where crime occurs, where they fear crime the most, and those areas that people label as dangerous or high-crime areas. Because of its focus on perception of crime patterns, the geography of crime perception relies on survey research and other unofficial sources of data to try and gain an understanding of where people perceive crime as occurring and why. While the amount of research into perceptual crime patterns is significantly smaller than that dealing with objective crime patterns, it is only through research into perceptual crime patterns that a true picture of crime distribution in an area can be created.

In looking at public perceptions of crime patterns, the overall findings have concluded that there are distinct differences in how people perceive crime and that these perceptions are not consistent with crime patterns of official data. In his study of spatial patterns of crime in Akron, Ohio, Pyle (1980) found that perceptions of high-crime areas

FIGURE 2.12   Homicides within 1,500 Feet of Bars

varied by numerous social characteristics including race, gender, age, income, education, and where in a city an individual lived. Importantly, Pyle (1980) found that large portions of the city center were mistakenly perceived as high crime while areas in the suburbs with high crime rates were mistakenly perceived as safe. Consistent with this, research has found that most people perceive their neighborhood to be relatively crime free and safe as compared with other neighborhoods in a city, regardless of the actual crime levels in their neighborhood.

Studies tend to show that people perceive risks to their personal safety in conditions of physical disorder (Doran and Lees, 2005; Robinson et al., 2003; Roh and Oliver,

2005; Simon and Shepherd, 2007). A series of studies on a university campus found that students, faculty, and staff perceived the greatest threats to their personal safety in areas where criminal victimization rarely occurred, such as in dark parking lots, alleys behind dorms, and even in a pedestrian tunnel that runs under a main campus street (Robinson and Mullen, 2001; Robinson and Roh, 2007).

In addition to citizens' perceptions of crime patterns, other researchers have studied the spatial perceptions of police officers as they relate to crime patterns within a city and found that they, too, are incorrect. Specifically, Ratcliffe and McCullagh (2001a) found that the accuracy of officers' perceptions varied by crime types, with officers being more accurate in their perceptions of where burglaries were concentrated and less accurate in their perceptions of other crimes such as auto theft and non-residential burglary. Rengert and Pelfrey (1997) found similar results when they analyzed the spatial perceptions of police recruits as they related to downtown Philadelphia, Pennsylvania. Importantly, Rengert and Pelfrey (1997) found that the degree of familiarity and knowledge of the downtown area had no impact on accuracy of spatial perceptions of crime.

Although reasons for these incorrect perceptions are not necessarily known, speculation centers around several different potential causes, including preconceived notions, presence of nuisance crimes, and the impact of media coverage. In their research, Rengert and Pelfrey (1997) found that perceived safety of an area was highly related to the perception that an area was predominately white in population. Conversely, areas that were perceived as being "unsafe" were highly associated with perceptions that an area was predominately minority in population. These results bring to light serious issues of race and class and how they interact to impact our perceptions as to whether an area is safe or unsafe. By contrast, Brantingham, Brantingham, and Butcher (1986) found that reasons for labeling an area a "criminal area" were highly associated with the perception that it was a center of nuisance behaviors (solicitation of prostitution or panhandling) as opposed to a center of serious criminal activity. This seems to indicate, as with the findings by Rengert and Pelfrey, that perceptions of crime are not driven by actual crime statistics. Finally, research by Paulsen (2002) found that media coverage of homicides was more likely to focus on homicide incidents that occurred in the city-center area than in outer areas of a city. Importantly, homicides that occurred in the city-center area were more likely to receive celebrated news coverage than those that occurred elsewhere, despite homicides in the city center being less likely. This finding about media coverage of crime raises the possibility that mainstream media are a major factor in the creation of spatial perceptions of crime.

The impact of these inaccurate spatial perceptions cannot be understated as these "ecological labels" can have serious impacts on personal behavior. *Ecological labeling* is a term that refers to the labels that people place on areas (dangerous, safe, high crime) and the impact that these labels in turn have on the actions of people. Research has shown that negative ecological labels, often driven by inaccurate perceptions of crime patterns, can contribute to the decline of shopping areas and city centers (Pyle, 1980). Other research has shown that "high crime" labels create a destructive feedback loop in which property values decline, causing areas to become less viable socially (Miller, 1991). Still other research has shown that increasing crime rates follow the wide-scale application of "criminal area" labels to specific neighborhoods, almost encouraging crime (Baldwin and Bottoms, 1976; Miller, 1991). Overall ecological labeling of areas as "high-crime" or "dangerous" can have serious ramifications for the long-term health of a community. Moreover, as stated above, the rationale for why these areas are labeled as "dangerous" often is based on factors far removed from the actual amount of crime that occurs in these areas.

Crime mapping technology is particularly useful for illustrating factors such as fear of crime and perceptions of crime risk, as well as for comparing and contrasting areas that promote fear and risk perception relative to actual crime and victimization rates. For example, Robinson and Roh (2007) used GIS software to plot calls for police service at a comprehensive regional university in the South. They then compared the places on campus that host the most crime with the places users of the space (i.e., students, faculty, and staff) identified as being the most dangerous. Generally, findings showed that the places where perceptions of crime risk were greatest were the same places where actual criminal victimization was highest. Additionally, students, faculty, and staff feared going some places that hosted virtually no crime, likely due to the nature of the environmental conditions at these places (e.g., dark, isolated parking lots). Finally, the researchers found that the places characterized by the highest levels of calls for crimes such as assault, vandalism, theft, and harassment were the same areas that had the most calls for alcohol violations and illicit drug use, suggesting a correlation between these factors.

SUMMARY

List of Major Research Findings

In this chapter, you learned the following important facts pertaining to geographic differences in crime:

1. Crime occurs everywhere, in every country;
2. The United States has more crime (higher crime frequencies) than any other nation in the world;
3. Most crimes in the United States are committed against property and are non-violent in nature;
4. America's crime rate (the number of crimes per capita) is *not* the highest in the world;
5. It is difficult to make comparisons of crime rates across countries because data are often not available, countries collect their crime data differently, and the behaviors that constitute crime vary across countries;
6. Homicide rates can be compared across countries more safely than other crimes;
7. The highest rates of homicide in the world are found in South Africa and Russia;
8. The U.S. murder rate is about one-tenth that of South Africa;
9. The highest murder rate in Europe is found in Northern Ireland and Spain;
10. According to the National Crime Victimization Survey (NCVS), violent crime rates declined in the United States beginning in the 1990s;
11. According to the NCVS, property crime rates declined in the United States beginning in the 1970s;
12. According to the International Crime Victims' Survey (ICVS), crime rates rose in most countries between 1988 and 1991, then stabilized through 1995, and began declining again through 1999;
13. According to the ICVS, countries whose citizens are most likely to be victimized by crime of some type include Australia, England and Wales, the Netherlands, and Sweden;
14. According to the ICVS, between 20 and 24 percent of Americans can expect to be victimized by some type of crime;
15. The most common crime in any country is property crime, typically theft of property;
16. According to the ICVS, the highest risks of contact crimes such as robbery, assaults, and sexual assaults are found in Australia, England and Wales, Canada, Scotland, and Finland;
17. According to the ICVS, the highest risks of theft are found in Australia, Sweden, and Poland;
18. According to the ICVS, the highest risks of burglary are found in Australia, England and Wales, Canada, Denmark, and Belgium;

19. According to the ICVS, the highest risks of car theft are found in England and Wales, Australia, and France;

20. Explanations of international crime rate variations can be grouped into two categories—grand theories and structural theories;

21. Grand theories include modernization theory, civilization theory, opportunity theories, and world system theory;

22. Structural theories include cultural theories, strain theories, and social disorganization;

23. Modernization theory, also known as the developing countries argument, explains higher crime rates as a result of anomie—a breakdown of the controlling influence of morality due to economic changes, social inequality, and culture conflict;

24. Civilization theory explains low crime rates as a result of increased modernization and civilization;

25. Opportunity theories, such as routine activity theory and lifestyle exposure theory, explain crime rates as a function of opportunities created by a society's structures, institutions, culture, and social processes;

26. World system theory explains crime rates as a function of disruption of normal life by economic expansion and reactions to exploitation of weaker countries by stronger countries;

27. Cultural theories explain crime rates as a function of belief systems, attitudes, values, norms, and ways of life of particular groups;

28. Strain theories explain crime as a result of frustration caused by economic conditions, manifested through absolute deprivation and relative deprivation;

29. Social disorganization theory explains crime as a function of a breakdown in bonds that normally hold society together, caused by factors such as poverty, ethnic or racial heterogeneity, residential mobility, family disruption, and population density;

30. Of the grand theories, modernization theory and opportunity theories hold the most promise for explaining crime rate variations across countries;

31. Of the structural theories, strain and social disorganization theories hold the most promise for explaining crime rate variations across countries;

32. Crime rates vary widely within the borders of any nation;

33. Rates of homicide and serious property crimes have historically been higher in the southern United States, but the differential between the rate of homicide in the South and other regions of the country has narrowed over the past 40 years;

34. The rate of crime in the South is disproportionately high, while it is disproportionately low in the Northeast;

35. Robbery rates are highest in the Northeast and West, but the gap between the highest and lowest regions has narrowed over the past 40 years;

36. Rates of burglary were highest in the West until the 1980s and since have been highest in the South;

37. The West leads the nation in overall rates of serious violent crime, although the South has the highest rates of homicides and aggravated assaults;

38. The rate of rape in the United States is highest in the Midwest;

39. The rate of robbery in the United States is highest in the Northeast;

40. The rate of theft in the United States is highest in the South;

41. The rate of burglary in the United States is highest in the South;

42. The rate of motor vehicle theft in the United States is highest in the West;

43. The rate of arson in the United States is highest in the West;

44. Explanations of regional crime rate variation in the United States include the Southern subculture of violence thesis and the economic deprivation hypothesis;

45. The Southern subculture of violence thesis suggests that crime is highest in the South because of its unique cultural values that both tolerate and celebrate violence;

46. The economic deprivation hypothesis, identical to strain theory, suggests that crime rates are highest when people live in conditions of absolute deprivation, relative deprivation, and income inequality;

47. Both the Southern subculture of violence thesis and the economic deprivation hypothesis explain why overall crime rates are highest in the South;

48. Virtually every type of street crime rate in the United States is higher in urban areas than in rural areas;

49. Large cities with more than one million inhabitants generally have higher street crime rates than medium-large cities with 500,000 to one million people, medium cities with 250,000 to 500,000 people, medium-small cities with 10,000 to 250,000 people, and small cities with less than 10,000 people;

50. Homicide trends have fluctuated over time and declined in the 1990s;

51. Homicide rates in the United States have been highest in large cities, but large cities saw the largest declines in homicide rates in the 1990s and, thus, the rate of homicide in medium-large cities is virtually identical to that of large cities;

52. Robbery rates in the United States are highest in the large cities;

53. Burglary rates in the United States are highest in the medium cities;

54. Violent crimes are roughly five times as likely to occur in urban areas as in rural areas;

55. Overall violent crime rates are highest in metropolitan areas, followed by cities outside of metropolitan areas and rural counties;

56. Overall property crime rates are highest in metropolitan areas, followed by cities outside of metropolitan areas and rural counties;

57. Rates of theft in the United States are highest in cities outside of metropolitan areas;

58. Rates of burglary in the United States are highest in cities outside of metropolitan areas;

59. Rates of aggravated assault in the United States are highest in metropolitan areas;

60. Rates of murder in the United States are highest in metropolitan areas;

61. Rates of rape in the United States are highest in cities outside of metropolitan areas;

62. Rates of robbery in the United States are highest in cities outside of metropolitan areas;

63. Rates of gun ownership are higher in rural areas, yet rates of gun crimes are higher in urban areas;

64. Crimes with small differences between urban and rural areas include alcohol use, illicit drug use, and domestic violence;

65. Crimes that are more common in rural areas include driving under the influence of alcohol (DUI), tobacco use by youth, and some forms of drug manufacturing;

66. Homicides by strangers are more common in urban areas, whereas homicides by acquaintances are more common in rural areas;

67. Rural areas can be differentiated from urban areas in terms of their physical distance and isolation, as well as in their culture;

68. Growth in rural areas usually is followed by increased crime rates;

69. The main explanations of urban versus rural crime rate differentials in the United States include social stratification and social control theories;

70. The social stratification perspective asserts that crime rates are higher in urban areas because of economic hardship, similar to strain theory;

71. The social control perspective asserts that crime rates are higher in urban areas because of breakdowns in the ability of residents to control their own neighborhood because of conditions of social disorganization;

72. Both the social stratification and social control perspectives help explain why crime rates are higher in urban areas than in rural areas;

73. Crime statistics within cities show that some areas are more prone to crime than others and that some people are more prone to victimization than others;

74. Hot spots are areas or places that host a great deal of crime;
75. Repeat victimization occurs when the same person or place is victimized by more than one crime;
76. Neighborhood street crime rate variation is explained by community composition factors such as the percentage of single-parent families, by community social structure factors such as less supervision of children in neighborhoods, and by criminogenic commodities such as places that sell alcohol, drugs, and guns;
77. The geography of crime is divided into two different aspects, the geography of objective crime patterns and the geography of perceptual crime patterns;
78. The geography of objective crime patterns involves the mapping and analysis of official crime data, such as police records of calls for service, arrests, and crime incident locations;
79. The geography of perceptual crime patterns focuses on the mapping and analysis of peoples' perceptions of where crime occurs, where they fear crime the most, and those areas that people label as dangerous or high-crime areas;
80. Public perception of crime varies by race, gender, age, income, education, and where in a city an individual lives, and in general is not consistent with actual crime patterns;
81. Perceptions of crime are influenced by various factors including the racial make-up of an area, the level of perceived nuisance crimes in an area, and media coverage of crime;
82. Ecological labeling is a term that refers to the labels that people place on areas (dangerous, safe, high-crime) and the impact that these labels in turn have on the actions of people;
83. Research has shown that negative ecological labels, often driven by inaccurate perceptions of crime patterns, can contribute to the decline of shopping areas and city centers;

Implications of Findings for Crime Mapping and Spatial Analysis

The above findings have tremendous implications for crime mapping and spatial analysis generally. Most importantly, we believe that if practitioners can learn to predict crime even fairly accurately—whether across countries, regions of the country, urban versus rural areas, or within cities and particular neighborhoods, they will ultimately be able to prevent many crimes from happening. This can be accomplished by launching well-planned interventions in the places where they are most needed based on scientific evidence like that reviewed here. Advice can also be given to people living in particular places about how they should go about their lives given their relative crime risks.

For example, we showed that modernization theory, opportunity theories, and strain and social disorganization theories hold the most promise for explaining crime rate variations across countries. Thus, predictions can be aimed at the cross-national level asserting that crime will be higher in countries characterized by conditions of anomie due to being developed rapidly, that provide suitable opportunities for crimes, that are characterized by blocked opportunities for success, and that are experiencing conditions that make it difficult for communities to utilize the effective informal social controls of their own people.

We saw in this chapter that rates of homicide, aggravated assault, and serious property crimes have historically been higher in the southern United States, and that the West leads the nation in overall rates of serious violent crime. Because these facts are explained by both the Southern subculture of violence thesis and the economic deprivation hypothesis, we can predict that areas that tolerate and promote violence and that do not provide legitimate opportunities for success will have higher crime rates.

We also learned in this chapter that rates of virtually every type of street crime in the United States are higher in urban areas than in rural areas. Exceptions to this rule include DUI, tobacco use by youth, and some forms of drug manufacturing, which are more prevalent in rural areas. These crime rate differences are explained by the social stratification and social control perspectives; thus, efforts can be directed at eliminating economic hardships and increasing the ability of families to spend time with and supervise their children.

The research on crime statistics within cities described in this chapter illustrates that some areas are more prone to crime than others (hot spots of crime) and that some people are more prone to repeat criminal victimization than others. These crime facts seem to be explained by community composition factors such as the percentage of single-parent families, by community social structure factors such as less supervision of children in neighborhoods, and by criminogenic commodities such as places that sell alcohol, drugs, and guns. In addition, hot spots and revictimization are greatly affected by opportunities for crime.

Crime mapping software, as we attempted to demonstrate in this chapter, can allow these crime facts to be visually depicted in a clear format that is easy to understand. Predictions can also be mapped using the same software, and data analysis techniques allow researchers and practitioners to gain understanding as to why some people and places are more prone to crime than others. Crime mapping provides a type of understanding of crime that no other methodology allows. Hot spots and regional variations in crime rates are most easily graphically represented and analyzed using mapping software, and are probably of most interest to criminal justice practitioners and citizens alike. Crime mapping allows fairly accurate predictions to be made about where street crime is most likely to occur at the region and city level of analysis, as well as even at the street and block level of analysis.

CASE STUDY
HATE CRIMES AND SPACE

The Southern Poverty Law Center (SPLC) began to monitor "hate activity" in 1981 after a noted resurgence of the Ku Klux Klan (KKK). Using its Intelligence Project, the SPLC follows the activities of at least 888 racist and neo-Nazi groups in the United States (as of 2007). In 1994, after the SPLC discovered links between white supremacist organizations and elements of the antigovernment "Patriot" movement, the Intelligence Project began monitoring the activities of militias and other extremist antigovernment groups. The purpose of the Intelligence Project is to monitor and investigate suspected hate groups in order to provide comprehensive updates to law enforcement agencies, the media, and the general public.

According to the organization's website, it warned the U.S. Attorney General of an impending disaster six months before the Oklahoma City bombing, based on "the new mixture of armed militia groups and those who hate." At what it calls the peak of the Patriot movement in the mid-1990s, the SPLC followed more than 800 militia-like Patriot groups, but the number thought to exist today is less than 200. For example, in 2001, the Intelligence Project identified 158 "Patriot" groups, including 73 militias, two "common-law courts," and scores of publishers, ministries, and citizens' groups with a racist and/or antigovernment orientation. According to the Project's website, "Patriot groups define themselves as opposed to the 'New World Order' or advocate or adhere to extreme antigovernment doctrines." Groups included in the Project's lists do not necessarily advocate or engage in violence or other criminal activities.

The Project tracked hate incidents in 2007 committed by 888 hate groups, including Klan groups, neo-Nazi groups, racist skinhead groups, Christian identity groups, neo-Confederate groups, Black separatist groups, and other groups.

Even though official statistics suggest that there are about 10,000 hate crimes in the United States every year, the Project estimated that 50,000 hate crimes occur each year and that the vast majority is committed by people not affiliated with extremist organizations.

(continued)

CASE STUDY   CONTINUED

According to the organization's website,

Two recent studies—a 2001 investigation by the Southern Poverty Law Center's *Intelligence Report* and a 2000 academic study funded by the U.S. Department of Justice— found that the U.S. hate crime reporting system is riddled with errors, omissions and even outright falsification of data.

The Hate Crime Statistics Act defines a hate crime as "a criminal act in which a victim is selected because of the perpetrator's prejudice against the victim's race, ethnicity, national origin, religion, sexual orientation and/or disability." Hate crimes include crimes against property (e.g., burning someone's home or property) and crimes against persons (e.g., assaulting or killing someone).

Figure 2.13 identifies hate groups by state and by category of group type. As you can see from the map, there is a geographic element to hate group location in the United States. As one might expect, the vast majority of neo-Confederate groups (*n* = 102 groups) and White Nationalist groups (*n* = 110 groups) are located in the Southeast United States, whereas neo-Nazi groups (*n* = 191 groups) are located throughout the United States, but especially the East Coast. Most Klan groups (*n* = 165 groups) are also located in the Southeast, although they exist in the Midwest and Northeast, as well. Racist skinhead groups (*n* = 78 groups) and Christian identity groups (*n* = 37 groups) are fewer in number and are spread across the United States. Most Black separatist groups (*n* = 88) and "general" hate groups (*n* = 73) are located in the Southeast United States, which is not surprising given that Black populations are high in the Southeast and that the "other" category includes some anti-Black groups.

What this map shows is that the presence of hate groups is specific to areas of the country. Geographic studies of hate crimes show that they tend to be clustered in areas based on levels of certain socio-demographic factors (such as racial and ethnic heterogeneity and poverty). Hate groups are more prevalent in rural areas and suburban areas, and in areas where there is ethnic diversity and high levels of poverty. An example is a study of the presence of the KKK in Pennsylvania by Flint (2001).

His research, which mapped KKK cells in Pennsylvania in the 1920s and the 1980s and 1990s, showed that in the 1920s rural regions of Pennsylvania, such as counties in the northern tier, had higher numbers of KKK cells. "I wasn't surprised about the rural areas," says Flint. "What struck me is that it is so low in the suburban areas. Other research has

FIGURE 2.13   The Geography of Hate Groups

Source: Southern Poverty Law Center
(http://www.splcenter.org/images/dynamic/intel/hatemaps/5/ hate_map_ir125_adjusted.pdf)

shown the Klan to be strong in areas where there have been labor tensions based on ethnic divides, such as Pittsburgh and the anthracite coal mining regions," says Flint. "Those areas don't pop up here."

Flint's research suggests that KKK clusters are in rural areas because of major social changes that were taking place during the 1920s, such as the fear of modernization and change. Flint suggests that people joined hate groups or committed hate crimes because they were perceiving changes in society which they thought threatened them, and they reasoned that the changes were being brought about by non-white people.

For the 1984–1999 period, Flint mapped "tension incidents" that were reported to the Pennsylvania Human Relations Committee and found high concentrations of activity in the suburban areas of Philadelphia, Harrisburg, and York. The pattern was different from the 1920s: Hate activity moved from rural areas to suburban areas.

Flint reports that he had seen this in other exploratory research, including mapping of hate activity in the Atlanta area which showed "a donut of activity around the city, in the suburban areas." According to such research, modern hate activity seems to occur in suburban areas. Crime mapping allows this to be witnessed and ultimately explained.

Sources: "Patterns of hate." [On-line]. Available: www.rps.psu.edu/0105/patterns.html; Southern Poverty Law Center. "Fight hate and promote tolerance." [On-line]. Available: www.tolerance.org/maps/hate/index.htm.

CHAPTER 3

Social Disorganization

The purpose of this chapter is to provide a comprehensive discussion of one of the foundations of American criminological theory—social disorganization theory. In this chapter, we trace the history of social disorganization theory in order to accurately assess the research findings related to this theory. Finally, we discuss the implications for crime mapping and spatial analysis of crime.

Chapter Outline

INTRODUCTION TO SOCIAL DISORGANIZATION

Scholars at the University of Chicago created what has been variously called the "Chicago School of Human Ecology" and the "Chicago School of Criminology" in the early twentieth century. The University of Chicago's Department of Sociology was founded in 1892 when Albion Small was made Head Professor of Sociology. Small's colleagues and successors included W. I. Thomas, Robert Park, and Ernest Burgess, all of whom are considered founders of social disorganization theory.[1]

This theory, and the school of thought out of which it emerged, came about largely as a result of environmental and social conditions that materialized at the turn of the twentieth century in Chicago, including extensive foreign immigration, high rates of juvenile delinquency, and other social problems in the city. As you will see,

---

[1]This account is derived from the websites of The University of Chicago's Department of Sociology, located at http://sociology.uchicago.edu/overview/history.html.

these conditions were first described by sociologists at the University of Chicago and then explanations centered around the concept of *social disorganization* were used to explain why these conditions materialized and survived.

The concept of social disorganization was defined by Thomas and Znaniecki (1958:128) as a "decrease of the influence of existing social rules of behavior upon individual members of the group." Vold, Bernard, and Snipes (1998:147) summarize social disorganization theory: "The formal social organizations that existed in the neighborhood tend to disintegrate as the original population retreats. Because the neighborhood is in transition, the residents no longer identify with it, and thus they do not care as much about its appearance or reputation. There is a marked decrease in 'neighborliness' and in the ability of the people of the neighborhood to control their youth."

This trend is worsened by high mobility of residents, high population turnover, culture conflict, high levels of immigration, and similar features of urban life. Social disorganization is essentially *anomie* at the community or neighborhood level (Walsh, 2002:171–172). Anomie can be understood as "social instability resulting from a breakdown of standards and values; also personal unrest, alienation, and uncertainty that comes from a lack of purpose or ideals" (*Merriam-Webster's Collegiate Dictionary*, 2002).

There is also a *theory of anomie* put forth by French sociologist Emile Durkheim in two books, *The Division of Labor in Society* (1893) and *Suicide* (1897). Anomie occurs when societal institutions can no longer regulate members of society, and when individual members of society no longer feel integrated into the whole; thus, anomie can also be understood as a lack of regulation and integration.

Walsh (2002) explains that social disorganization affects neighborhood crime rates in two ways: first, it erodes informal social control networks between neighbors; and second, it provides positive incentives to commit antisocial behaviors. Similarly, Wikstrøm (1998) claims that crime rate variations are affected by changes in community *rules*, *resources*, and *routines*. This means when conditions of social disorganization arise, families find it harder to assert authority over children, children find it more difficult to resist deviant temptations, and children will engage in behaviors that take them into dangerous and risky places where delinquency is likely to occur (which may very well be their own neighborhoods).

PREHISTORY OF SOCIAL DISORGANIZATION THEORY: CARTOGRAPHIC SCHOOL OF CRIMINOLOGY

Prior to the emergence of social disorganization theory, others explored the effects of ecological factors on crime. There have been three distinct waves of research pertaining to crime and place,[2] including (1) that conducted by nineteenth-century French and Belgian statisticians, who essentially described spatial patterns of crime in an atheoretical manner; (2) that conducted by early twentieth-century American sociologists, who started by describing ecological conditions in Chicago, and then turned to sociological variables to explain the occurrence of high-crime areas; and (3) that conducted beginning in the 1970s by people such as Jeffery (1971) and Newman (1972a), and continued into the 1990s by others such as Crowe (1991), who focused on urban design and architecture and how they influenced crime and feelings of safety. The first and second waves of research are discussed in this chapter, for each directly relates to social disorganization. The final wave of research is discussed under the titles of "Crime Prevention Through Environmental Design" and "Defensible Space" in Chapter 4 (ecological theories of crime).

---

[2]The research conducted into crime and place is often referred to as *environmental criminology*. As noted in Chapter 1, a crime consists of a law, an offender, a target, and a place. Environmental criminology is the study of the last element—the place.

Phillips (1972) suggests that "hundreds of spatially oriented studies of crime and delinquency have been written by sociologists and criminologists since about 1830 . . ." and he recognizes the so-called *cartographic* or *geographic school of criminology* (1830–1880). The first systematic studies of ecology in the field of criminology were realized by A. M. Guerry and Adolphe Quetelet. Levin and Lindesmith (1971:63) claim these works were the first ecological studies of crime. These scholars were also among the first in the world to ever use mapping in studies of crime. Both Guerry and Quetelet analyzed and mapped French criminal statistics. Each found specific distributions of crime occurrences across the country, including high crime rates in some areas and low crime rates in other areas, differences in violent and property crime rates, and stability of such rates over time. The works of these two men helped construct the foundation for contentions made about criminal etiology, in general, and environmental criminology, in particular.

Vold (1958) writes that it was Guerry who published what many scholars consider to be the first work in scientific criminology, in which he held that the opportunity to steal was critical in determining criminal activity (Morris, 1957). Guerry forecasted the inevitable development of future emphasis on opportunities for crime that now underlie ecological theories (discussed in Chapter 4).

According to Morris (1957), A. M. Guerry was appointed to collect judicial statistics for the City of Paris. With his collaborator, Adriano Balbi, Guerry created a statistical map that compared educational levels with crime in France. Guerry used the cartographic method to present statistics related to crime and social phenomena, which would later be done by others in England and Wales and the United States. For example, Guerry divided up France into five regions, North, South, East, West, and Centre, and used shaded maps to show the following:

- Crimes in France from 1825 to 1830, by type;
- Gender (i.e., sex) and crime;
- Age and crime;
- Seasonal variations and crime;
- Education and crime;
- Illegitimacy and crime;
- Charitable donations and crime; and
- Distributions of suicides.

Guerry showed, among other things, that crime rates against both people and property varied across different regions of France. Crimes against property in the North were about twice as high as crimes against persons, while in the South crimes against people were twice as high as crimes against property. Guerry also found that most crimes against a person were more common in the summer whereas crimes against property were more common in the winter. Guerry speculated causes of crime as poverty, lack of education, and population density. Each of these is relevant to the Chicago School and to social disorganization theory, discussed later in the chapter. Finally, Guerry found that suicides were highest in urbanized areas. Morris (1957) reasons that the influence of Guerry was greatest in two areas: (1) using valid statistics to test theoretical hypotheses about behavior; and (2) showing that social factors affect behavior and can be objectively verified.

Adolphe Quetelet has been referred to as the "father of modern statistics," as he attempted to measure social phenomenon statistically (Voss and Peterson, 1971:3). Quetelet was one of the most influential social statisticians of the nineteenth century, although many still refer to his work in the area of "moral statistics," which was the original term for social statistics. Quetelet was born in Belgium in 1796 and conducted numerous studies that would have a large impact on social scientists such as sociologists in the nineteenth and twentieth centuries in England and Wales and the United States. Quetelet believed it was possible to gather statistics and ultimately compare the behavior of populations against the "average man" and attempted to map physical and moral statistics of populations.

As explained by Morris (1957:74), Quetelet "was impressed by the regularity of social data, and noticed their degree of concomitance with such variables as age, sex, and climate. Quetelet wrote about man, his physical qualities, what causes behavior, birth, death, morality, politics, and human development. He also wrote about the propensity for criminality at different ages."

The significance of these early studies of crime for spatial analysis is that they generated curiosity about spatial elements of crime and demonstrated the potential of crime maps. Early social disorganization theorists would focus on features of community-level spatial factors and would also use primitive maps to study crime.

EARLY SOCIAL DISORGANIZATION THEORIES

The city of Chicago was growing by leaps and bounds in the early 1900s. Vold, Bernard, and Snipes (1998:141) describe the immigration that accounted for the growth: "Chicago at that time had a population of over 2 million; between 1860 and 1910 its population had doubled every ten years, with wave after wave of immigrants." According to Figlio, Hakim, and Rengert (1986:xi), early sociological theorists such as Thomas and Znaniecki argued that urban areas were more crime-prone than rural areas: "Perhaps the most influential of these theorists was Louis Wirth, who observed that life in cities creates anomie at the societal level and alienation at the individual level. Similarly, Tonnies, Simmel, and Maine viewed urban living as essentially amoral and normless." Other significant studies during this early period of the twentieth century include Thomas and Znaniecki's *The Polish Peasant in Europe and America* (1920), Frederick Thrasher's *The Gang* (1927), and Shaw's books, *The Jackroller* (1930), *The Natural History of a Delinquent Career* (1931), and *Brothers in Crime* (1938), among many others.

These works showed the following:

- Delinquents could not be differentiated from members of conventional society on the basis of biological or psychological factors;
- Delinquency often resulted from a disintegration of conventional traditions and clear approval by parents of delinquent behavior;
- Close-knit immigrant families unraveled in the conditions of the new world, and their attitudes changed in line with those in inner-city America;
- Areas where delinquency was higher were characterized by numerous opportunities for illegitimate activities but few opportunities for legitimate success;
- Delinquency began early in the lives of many children as part of play;
- Adolescents served as role models in crime for younger children; and
- Informal social controls could not prevent delinquency in these areas.

Delinquency was thus seen as a legitimate response to abnormal living conditions. Delinquent behavior became normal over time as, slowly, conventional traditions and customs of immigrants were eroded and ultimately replaced with ones that supported delinquency.

Park and Burgess: *The City* (1925)

Human Ecology.   In the early 1900s, Robert Park investigated various social conditions of the city of Chicago. In 1914, he was appointed to the Sociology Department at the University of Chicago. Park eventually became interested in the similarities between the natural distribution of plant life and the societal organization of human life. From the field of plant ecology, he borrowed two concepts that helped him form what he called the *theory of human ecology*. Felson (1983:665) notes that this field of human ecology encompasses the field of the ecology of crime, but in turn it is encompassed by the more general field of ecology.

The first concept borrowed by Robert Park (1915:577–612) was from Eugenius Warming. Warming posited that plant communities were made up of individual organisms, each having its own characteristics. These characteristics in combination resembled the original organism. Thus, each plant community was analogous to a distinct organism. Park (1952:118) saw the city in a similar way—as a super-organism. He noted that many areas existed where different types of people lived. Like the natural areas of plants, each area of the city had an organic unity of its own. Divisions in the city existed, including racial and ethnic divisions, income and occupational divisions, industrial and business divisions, and physical divisions separated by architectural and natural structures.

The second concept Park borrowed from plant ecology revolved around how the balance of nature in an area changed. The primary mechanisms identified by Park were *invasion*, *domination*, and *succession*. As noted by Figlio, Hakim, and Rengert (1986:xi), "Park viewed communities as functionally specialized areas within an industrial economy. The patterning of communities was determined by competition, and changes were determined by invasion and social succession." These mechanisms can be seen in nature (e.g., the natural evolution of a pasture into a deciduous forest, where plant species invade, dominate, and eventually take over original species). They can also be seen in human societies (e.g., the shift from small, closely knit communities to large, unfamiliar cities through the process of immigration).

Later ecological studies focused on ecological spatial patterns of cities, such as Burgess' (1925) *concentric circles*, Hoyt's (1943) *sectors*, and Shaw and McKay's (1929a, 1942) work on *delinquency areas*. For example, Ernest Burgess, Park's associate, explored the processes of invasion, dominance, and succession. He used them to explain the growth of cities. According to Burgess, cities expand outward from the center of the city in patterns of concentric circles.

Concentric Zones.   Burgess portrayed the city of Chicago in five zones. Figure 3.1 shows these zones. They include the loop, the zone in transition, the zone of workingmen's homes, the residential zone, and the commuters' zone. The loop was the central business district. The zone in transition was the oldest section of the city and was being invaded by business and industry. Residential housing there was deteriorated, and residents were generally poor immigrants. The zone of workingmen's homes was occupied by those who had managed to escape the zone in transition. The residential zone consisted of single-family houses and expensive apartments. Finally, the commuters' zone was a growing zone that was in the process of expanding outward through a process of invasion, dominance, and succession (Robinson, 1997).

Of course, the portrayal created by Burgess does not represent a perfect account of any given city. After all, any city contains natural areas, such as lakes and rivers, and architectural features, such as railroad tracks and highways. Nevertheless, within this

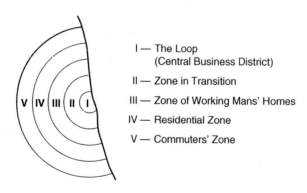

I — The Loop
(Central Business District)

II — Zone in Transition

III — Zone of Working Mans' Homes

IV — Residential Zone

V — Commuters' Zone

FIGURE 3.1   Chicago's Concentric Zones

framework, Burgess and Park studied Chicago and its social problems. The most crime reportedly occurred in the least desirable residential section of the city, which was the zone in transition.

THE CHICAGO SCHOOL OF CRIMINOLOGY

Shaw and McKay: *Juvenile Delinquency in Urban Areas* (1942)

Clifford Shaw utilized Park's theories as a foundation for studying juvenile delinquency in Chicago. Shaw believed that juvenile delinquency resulted from the juvenile's *detachment from conventional groups*. This would lead to *social control theories*, popularized by scholars such as Travis Hirschi (1969) and Michael Gottfredson (Gottfredson and Hirschi, 1990), which attribute delinquency, criminality, and other forms of antisocial behavior to a weak bond to society and a low degree of self-control. Such factors are usually measured by one's *attachment* to parents, *commitment* to school and work, *involvement* in legitimate conventional activities such as recreation, and one's *belief* in the morality of the law. These theories place the blame for juvenile delinquency and adult criminality at the feet of everyday, normal citizens (mostly parents).

Shaw wanted to determine how detachment from conventional groups occurred. Shaw felt that delinquent activities somehow came out of individuals' environments. Therefore, he analyzed characteristics of the neighborhoods out of which delinquents arose, and compiled case histories for individual delinquents, in order to find out how they had related to their environments. This meant his analyses were limited to delinquents known to the criminal justice system through court records (Robinson, 1997). For more on Clifford Shaw, see the Focus On box.

Later, Henry McKay co-authored studies with Shaw. Shaw and McKay pinpointed the residence of juveniles identified by the police or courts as delinquent over several decades. They produced maps that pinpointed these residences of juveniles involved in the justice system. Other maps showed percentages of the juvenile population who were involved in the criminal justice system. Through zone maps, a general tendency for concentration of delinquency emerged toward the city's center. Specific findings related to delinquency showed that it had roots in the physical and economic status of the neighborhood, and in the population composition of the neighborhood. Specifically, the scholars found that areas with the highest official rates of juvenile delinquency were characterized by high industry and commerce, high levels of foreign-born families, and a low level of economic status (Robinson, 1997).

Their study also found high-crime neighborhoods had the highest levels of welfare, infant mortality, tuberculosis, and insanity. Thus, disadvantages of all kinds tended to cluster in the same areas. *Comorbidity* is a term that means that events tend to cluster together in the same people and places, and criminological research has long shown that bad things tend to occur to the same people and in the same places (Robinson, 2004). Perhaps the most important finding of Shaw and McKay was, regardless of the decade or the nature of the population, the same areas of the city always had the highest rates of delinquency within the zone in transition. Shaw and Mckay did produce zone maps showing that rates of delinquency were highest in the same areas over many decades.

Had crime mapping software been available, it would have been possible to carefully depict and assess the effects of numerous physical, economic, and social factors on crime rates. Today, studies of crime in large cities, including Chicago, use crime mapping to explain and predict high crime rate areas (e.g., Bowers, Johnson, and Pease, 2004; Gorman, Zhu, and Horel, 2005; Levine, 2006; Tita and Griffiths, 2005).

Clifford R. Shaw was born in 1896 in Luray, Indiana, and was the fifth of ten children. His father was a farmer and owned a small general store. Shaw became a sociologist who devoted his life to finding the causes of crime in large cities.

Shaw often related his own brush with delinquency as a young boy. Caught stealing bolts from a blacksmith, Shaw was initially scolded by the blacksmith and then asked why he took the bolts. Later, the blacksmith helped Shaw repair his toy wagon with the bolts. This experience was used by Shaw to illustrate small town reaction to delinquency, and the importance of reincorporating the offender into conventional society became a key component in his methods to dissuade a youngster from committing future crimes.

While in graduate school at the University of Chicago, Shaw worked part-time from 1921 to 1923 as a parole officer for the Illinois State Training School for Boys in St. Charles, Illinois. From 1924 to 1926, he was a parole officer at the Cook County Juvenile Court. Many of his ideas grew out of these "real life" experiences, as well as his association with colleagues at the University of Chicago Institute for Juvenile Research.

In 1927, Shaw was appointed director for the newly created Department of Research Sociology. Working with Henry McKay, whom Shaw had known in graduate school, he plotted the residences of official delinquents on maps of Chicago and found them to be overwhelmingly concentrated in areas adjacent to commerce and industry. This concentration of crime in specific areas over long periods of time was offered as striking evidence against the then-popular theory that psychological factors were the cause of crime.

Shaw also developed the use of the personal life-history of individual delinquents and criminals, which he gathered through contacts at reform schools and prisons. Several were published containing the official juvenile and criminal records of the individual along with the delinquent's biography told in his own words. In 1930, the first of these autobiographies, *The Jack Roller*, was published and it became a classic in criminology. The life-history approach was used by Shaw to explain how the social factors that dominated areas of high crime were responsible for encouraging delinquent acts, not any particular personality flaws on the part of the delinquent.

In 1932, the Chicago Area Project (CAP) was begun in three of the city's highest crime areas to text juvenile delinquency prevention techniques. As director of the research department and later as CAP's first director, Shaw developed both private and public sources of funding to expand the program to other areas of Chicago throughout the 1940s. His failing health during the last ten years of his life lessened his activist role and he died in 1957 before the full impact of CAP on public policy was realized. For more on CAP, see the Case Study at the end of this chapter.

The CAP became the prototype for delinquency prevention and welfare programs. Its principles of community organization, self-determination, and using natural leaders indigenous to a neighborhood were quite radical when first proposed by Shaw in the early 1930s, but are used by many groups today to successfully solve local problems.

Source: http://chicagoareaproject.org/FAQ.htm

Social Disorganization

These types of findings, along with summary case studies of individual delinquents, led to the theory of *social disorganization*. According to Veysey and Messner (1999:159), social disorganization operates "through the processes of value and norm conflicts, cultural change and cultural vacuums, and the weakening of primary relationships. This, in turn, is believed to reduce internal and external social control, which then frees individuals to engage in deviant behavior." Characteristics of the community, including *urbanization, residential mobility, racial or ethnic heterogeneity, socioeconomic status* (SES), *family disruption or single parent households,* and others, inhibit a community's ability to impose social controls over people in the community. For more details about these terms, see the Focus On box.

The criminogenic influence of social disorganization operates through processes such as reduced friendship networks, less involvement in community organizations, and less supervision of young people (Sampson and Groves, 1989). Social disorganization is also thought to increase associations between an individual and deviant peers (Cattarello, 2000), meaning social learning theory underlies the process of social disorganization. *Social learning theories* suggest that criminal behavior originates in the context of associations with criminals who hold definitions favorable to violating the law, when observers imitate the behavior of these people. Criminal behaviors are continued when reinforced either directly by reward or pleasure, or when an individual observes others being rewarded for criminal behavior. Structural conditions such as income inequality, poverty, and so forth increase the likelihood that one will associate with criminal or delinquent peers.

The opposite of social disorganization is referred to as *collective efficacy*. Taylor (2001:128) explains the differences between a socially disorganized neighborhood and one that is high in collective efficacy:

> A locale is socially disorganized if several things are true: residents do not get along with one another; residents do not belong to local organizations geared to bettering the communities and thus cannot work together effectively to address common problems; residents hold different values about what is and what is not acceptable behavior on the street; and residents are unlikely to interfere when they see other youths or adults engaged in wrongdoing.

An area has collective efficacy if

> residents will work together on common, neighborhood-wide issues, will get along somewhat with one another, and will take steps to supervise activities of youth or teens taking place in the immediate locale. It consists of several features of community social life including organizational participation . . . informal social control . . . and local social ties based on physical proximity.

A neighborhood is high in collective efficacy if it is organized to fight crime. Taylor took the works of Shaw and McKay and turned them on their head; he has studied opposite conditions and labeled them collective efficacy.

Through the writings of Shaw and McKay, the ecological approach was committed to "the stability of the ecological substructure of the city" (Figlio, Hakim, and Rengert, 1986). For example, Shaw and McKay saw the city's stable delinquency areas as "specialized habitation niches for low income migrants into the city" which "would be used by a succession of immigrant groups from different ethnic backgrounds at different time periods." Thus, even when the ethnic composition of the inner city changed from German and Irish to Italian and Polish, high crime rates were consistently found closest to the center of the city, because "as the social and economic situation of groups improved, they would move into the mainstream of American life, leaving space for the new immigrant groups" in the "breeding ground for the city's criminal population." Those who were left behind can be thought of as socially isolated from the middle class. The recognition of *hot spots* of crime (discussed in Chapter 2) undoubtedly started here.

FOCUS ON
TESTING SOCIAL DISORGANIZATION

The main concepts of studies testing relationships between social disorganization and crime rates rely on the following definitions. *Nominal definitions* are like dictionary definitions, telling us what the concepts mean. *Operational definitions* are more specific and define the concepts in a way that can be measured or counted in a study.

- *Social disorganization* (Nominal)—an inability of inhabitants to control the behavior of residents and users of neighborhood space because of deleterious social conditions; (Operational)—any evidence of deleterious social conditions, including the presence of

(continued)

poverty, residential mobility, immigration, heterogeneity, population density, incivilities, and family disruption, typically measured using official sources of data such as government census data, and/or surveys of residents of a neighborhood and on-site observations of neighborhood conditions

■ *Poverty or SES* (Nominal)—the presence of lower class people in a community; (Operational)—the proportion of lower class people in a neighborhood, city, or other area, as measured by official government statistics such as census data

■ *Residential mobility, instability, or transiency* (Nominal)—the degree of population turnover in a neighborhood; (Operational)—the degree of turnover among residents in a neighborhood, as measured by official government data or surveys of residents that assess the relative stability of residential status

■ *Immigration* (Nominal)—the amount of people moving into a neighborhood; (Operational)—evidence of large-scale moving by people from outside a neighborhood, as measured by government statistics such as census data

■ *Racial or ethnic heterogeneity* (Nominal)—diversity of a neighborhood among race and ethnic groups; (Operational)—the degree of diversity in a neighborhood, as measured by government statistics such as census data

■ *Population density* (Nominal)—a heavy concentration of people residing in an area; (Operational)—the number of people living in a neighborhood, as measured by government statistics such as census data

■ *Physical disorder or incivilities* (Nominal)—the presence of untended property and untended people and behavior in an area; (Operational)—the degree of presence of conditions such as abandoned buildings with boarded or broken windows, abandoned lots with an accumulation of trash, litter in streets, walkways, and parking areas, graffiti on buildings and walls, groups of people loitering/arguing/fighting on streets, derelicts and winos reclining in doorways and alleyways, poorly lighted streets and dark entries to buildings and alleys, and the presence of illegal drug activity, usually measured through surveys of residents and/or on-site observations

■ *Family disruption or single-parent families* (Nominal)—the presence of single-parent families in a neighborhood; (Operational)—the degree of family break-up, single parents, or divorce, as measured by government statistics such as census data

■ *Collective efficacy* (Nominal)—the degree of cohesion in a neighborhood; (Operational)—evidence that a neighborhood is well suited to protect itself from deviant influences, as measured by friendship networks, involvement in community organizations and activities, and supervision of children, usually measured in surveys of neighborhood residents

■ *Crime rates* (Nominal)—an aggregate measure of crime in an area; (Operational)—an official measure of total crime divided by the population (crimes per capita), typically crimes known to the police

Source: Robinson, M. (2004). *Why Crime? An Integrated Systems Theory of Antisocial Behavior.* Upper Saddle River, NJ: Prentice-Hall.

Park and Burgess of the Chicago School originated their search into the etiology of deviance by *describing* environmental factors. Shaw and McKay essentially began attempts to *explain* why these environmental factors were important. In other words, "the work of Park and Burgess was used by Shaw and McKay to study the ecology of crime" (Jeffery, 1990:260). For example, certain areas of Chicago characterized by high rates of delinquency were differentiated from areas with lower rates of delinquency, in terms of "physical, economic, and population characteristics" (Voss and Petersen, 1971:87). Shaw and McKay then turned to "more subtle differences in values, standards, attitudes, traditions, and institutions," in order to explain such differences.

Examples of explanations of crime provided by "the Chicago sociologists" included *urbanization, culture conflict, immigration, poverty, ecology,* and *socialization* (Jeffery, 1990:256). From this, American criminology turned largely to sociological variables in attempts to explain criminal and deviant behavior, leaving the physical environment behind (Jeffery and Zahm, 1993:326). Thus, it was out of the early works of the ecological theorists that the sociological theories which have been greatly emphasized in American criminology arose. We could conclude, then, that social disorganization theory led criminology away from spatial analysis of crime, which is ironic given its early focus on spatial factors.

Specifically, the theories of *strain* (Merton, 1938), *differential opportunity* (Cloward and Ohlin, 1960), *social control* (Hirschi, 1969), and *social learning* (Akers, 1977) can all be traced back to social disorganization research. Strain and differential opportunity theories were discussed in Chapter 2, and social control and social learning theories were discussed earlier in this chapter. Vold, Bernard, and Snipes (1998:156) write that the "Chicago School of Human Ecology can be described as a gold mine that continues to enrich criminology today . . . the social disorganization theory forms the basis for several other theories in contemporary criminology."

Despite the important position that social disorganization theory has played in American criminology, the theory and its key concept have been severely criticized. Later in the chapter, we outline the main problems with the theory, but for now, it is important to differentiate social disorganization from *differential social organization*. Differential social organization is a term coined by Sutherland (1947), which simply suggests that no neighborhood is truly disorganized. Instead, neighborhoods may be organized differently, according to different rules of conduct, and thus differentially socially organized. The term social disorganization implies a form of chaos in a neighborhood, which is inaccurate. Differential social organization implies a different set of values, attitudes, and way of life than traditional middle-class neighborhoods.

MODERN SOCIAL DISORGANIZATION RESEARCH

There have literally been hundreds of studies testing relationships between various aspects of social disorganization and crime (e.g., see Bursik, 1988; Bursik and Grasmick, 1993; Sampson, 1985; Sampson and Groves, 1989; Sampson and Wilson, 1995; Sampson and Wooldredge, 1987; Sampson, Raudenbush, and Earls, 1997; Smith and Jarjoura, 1988; Stark, 1987; Taylor, 1997; Warner and Pierce, 1993; Warner and Rountree, 1997). Most of these studies focus on community-level factors and their relationships to neighborhood crime rates (Sampson, 2000). Stark (1987), for example, suggests that structural characteristics such as high population density, high levels of transiency, high poverty, mixed land uses, and dilapidation of buildings all lead to higher crime rates.

Figure 3.2 is a map showing that neighborhood burglary rates vary based on opportunities created in conditions of social disorganization. The map shows that renter-occupied units, presence of substandard housing conditions, and visual signs of disorder are related to higher rates of burglary.

Stark's *theory of dangerous places* is based on the assertion that such factors in the physical environment lead to moral cynicism among residents, to increased opportunities and motivation for crime, and interfere with the ability of residents to control the behavior of those who occupy the space. His theory is related not only to *social disorganization* theory but also to *social learning, anomie,* and *social control* theories, all introduced earlier in this chapter, as well as to opportunity theories such as *routine activity theory* and *crime pattern theory* (discussed in Chapter 4). This theory of dangerous places can be used to explain why certain groups of people engage in criminality more

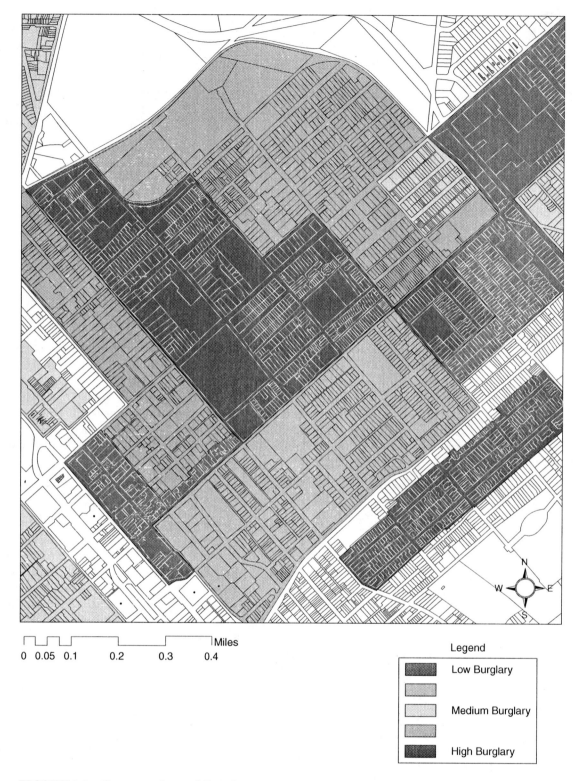

Miles
0 0.05 0.1   0.2   0.3   0.4

Legend

Low Burglary	
Medium Burglary	
High Burglary	

FIGURE 3.2 Opportunity and Burglary

than others, without relying on individual level factors as explanations. It holds that the reason some people commit more crime than others is because of where they live, who they interact with, and the conditions they experience in their neighborhoods.

Sampson and Groves (1989) test their model of social disorganization using data from 238 British neighborhoods. They find that urbanization, family disruption, SES, residential stability, and ethnic heterogeneity are all related to unsupervised peer groups, that SES is related to participation in community organizations, and that residential stability and urbanization are related to local friendship networks. They also find that family disruption and urbanization have direct effects on victimization, as do reduced friendship networks, less involvement in community organizations, and less supervision of young people. Specifically, friendship ties decrease robbery and burglary but not assault, rape, auto theft, or vandalism. Veysey and Messner (1999:169) summarize and speculate that

> SES affects both organizational participation and supervision of peer groups. Poor communities lack money and resources, and therefore, have fewer organizational opportunities for youth and adults. In addition, poverty is believed to undermine formal and informal social controls, thus affecting the community's ability to monitor youth. Urbanization is negatively related to friendship networks and reduced organizational participation. Ethnic heterogeneity reduces community consensus and increases distrust among community members. Communities then become fragmented along ethnic lines, which impedes communication and, therefore, effective supervision of youths. Family disruption directly affects community members' ability to supervise teenage peer groups. Finally, residential mobility is predicted to disrupt friendship networks.

A review by Sampson (1995) of numerous studies testing the effects of poverty on official crime rates finds that poverty combined with residential mobility is associated with higher levels of violent street crime. Other factors at the community level associated with higher crime rates include high numbers of apartments and various forms of family disruption (e.g., divorce, single-parent households).

A study of juvenile violence in rural areas (Osgood and Chambers, 2000) finds that residential instability, ethnic heterogeneity, and family disruption are associated with higher arrest rates for rape, assault, and weapons offenses. Yet, the study finds no relationships between these crimes and poverty or unemployment, which is not surprising given that the research suggests such factors are most related to property crimes (Robinson, 2004).

According to many studies, different elements of social disorganization are interrelated because they affect one another. For example, Rountree and Warner (1999) find that community stability increases the proportion of women in the community with close ties, and that ethnic heterogeneity lessens ties between women in the community. Furthermore, not all aspects of social disorganization have equal effects on crime; some elements of social disorganization are mediated by others while some act directly on crime (Taylor, 2001). For example, Veysey and Messner (1999) measure the effects of SES, residential mobility, ethnic heterogeneity, family disruption, urbanization, friendship networks, unsupervised teenage peer groups, and organizational participation on total victimization rates from street crimes. They find that their measure of unsupervised peer groups is the strongest predictor of victimization, followed by urbanization and family disruption. They also find that SES and urbanization are related to organizational participation, and that urbanization and residential stability are related to friendship networks. SES is largely mediated by organization participation and peer groups, meaning that poverty interferes with a community's ability to participate in organizations and to supervise children.

The effects of social disorganization depend in part on neighborhood characteristics not usually measured by social disorganization theorists. For example, Rountree and Warner (1999), in a study of crime in Seattle, find that female social ties are more closely related to lower violent crime rates and that these ties are most effective when communities are characterized by fewer female-headed households. The suspected reason that female-headed households have a greater difficulty controlling crime is that men provide monetary support for families, which allows a greater assurance of supervision of children, and the potential for a strong authority figure in the household. This finding is consistent with McLoyd's (1998:189) assertion that "mediating pathways can vary with age, race, gender, and ethnicity." Ties to the community imply that neighbors know each other and share things, watch out for each other, and so on. Additionally, the effects of social ties on assault are dependent in part on race (Warner and Rountree, 1997).

From these studies, it can be argued that areas characterized by what scholars call social disorganization lack *social capital* and *human capital*, both of which are needed to prevent social problems in the community. Scholars contend that low levels of social capital, also referred to as *collective efficacy* (Taylor, 2001:128), combine with larger level factors in society such as *income inequality* to increase crime rates. One study illustrates this link, showing that burglary and violent crimes are associated with higher levels of income inequality when social capital is low (Kawachi, Kennedy, and Wilkinson, 1999). High-crime areas also tend to be characterized by other negative social conditions, including overall mortality rates.

When discussing the role of mass incarceration in the United States in the development of social disorganization, Rose and Clear (1998:456) differentiate between the effects of an incarceration in a socially organized and a socially disorganized neighborhood: "Socially organized areas have sufficient assets and resources to overcome the loss of an offender's asset in order to remove the offender's liability from the neighborhood. In socially disorganized areas, however, assets are already sufficiently depleted that the neighborhood feels the loss of the asset just as it rejoices in the loss of the liability." This is related to the notions of social capital and human capital. Social capital is

> the social skills and resources needed to effect positive change in neighborhood life. It is the aspect of structured groups that increases the capacity for action oriented toward the achievement of group goals (Hagan, 1994). . . . Social capital is the essence of social control for it is the very force collectives draw upon to enforce order. It is what enables groups to enforce norms, and, as a result, to increase their level of informal control.

Human capital is

> the human skill and resources individuals need to function effectively, such as reading, writing, and reasoning ability. It is the capital individuals acquire through education and training for productive purposes (Hagan, 1994) . . . neighborhoods rich in social capital exert more control over individual residents, thus helping to produce more highly educated, employable, and productive members of the community.

Factors of social disorganization make it more difficult for community members to regulate the behavior of their residents: "Poverty, family disruption, and residential instability . . . result in anonymity and the lack of relationships among neighborhood residents and low participation in community organizations and in local activities" (Vold, Bernard, and Snipes, 1998:152). Studies tend to consistently find relationships between high levels of poverty, residential mobility, racial heterogeneity, population density, single-parent households, and rates of both property and violent crimes (Petee and Kowalski, 1993; Petee, Kowalski, and Duffield, 1994; Warner and Pierce, 1993). Regardless of who lives in a community, these conditions will breed street crime and other social problems.

Consider adolescent delinquency, for example. Sampson (2000) uses data from 80 Chicago neighborhoods to explore how changes in residential stability and neighborhood advantages are related to measures of informal social control. He reports that concentrated poverty and low levels of residential stability are associated with higher rates of juvenile delinquency. The main causal factor in the relationship is the level of informal social control; high levels of informal social control inhibit delinquency. Similarly, Taylor (1996) finds that high levels of neighborhood stability are related to higher levels of local attachment and social involvement.

This suggests the importance of the family in informal community social controls. Social disorganization rests on the assumption that families are less able to monitor and correct the behavior of their children when conditions of social disorganization prevail. Yet, the effects of social disorganization variables on crime depend on other factors—other factors also appear to be important for helping understand some of the relationships between crime and community factors in urban areas. For example, people living in conditions of social disorganization may over time begin to see deviance as normal or not so bad and/or as a legitimate response to economic deprivation. Social disorganization also affects quality of parenting. According to Simons et al. (2001) living in poor neighborhoods produces present-orientation in parents, as well as poor organizational and planning skills. It also increases the chance of experiencing *strain* and reduces social support.

Recent research on social disorganization theory and crime supports its key propositions. For example, studies show that neighborhood conditions (e.g., social disadvantage, housing density, land use) are associated with rates of assault, robbery, and other crimes (Lockwood, 2007). Other studies find significant relationships between unemployment and crime (Andresen, 2006; Oh, 2005). Further, studies show that increased concentrations of the poor in urban low-income neighborhoods experience worse economic, employment, and educational opportunities; physical and mental health conditions; as well as many forms of violent crime (Chun-Chung, Johnson, and Austin, 2005; Stretesky, Schuck, and Hogan, 2004), as well as some forms of property crime (Larsson, 2006). Changes in income inequality also help explain why criminal victimization is becoming more concentrated among the poor (Thacher, 2004). Factors such as resource disadvantage (i.e., poverty, income inequality, unemployment) are associated with crime rate growth in those areas of non-metropolitan areas that are losing population, presumably due to an increased interference with the tightly knit community that is well equipped to fight crime in a neighborhood (Mencken and Barnett, 1999).

Modern social disorganization research suggests that social control (or social support) can be understood across different levels of analysis. For more on these levels, see the Focus On box.

It is clearly possible to plot social disorganization variables at the neighborhood level and assess their effects on crime rates using crime mapping software. For example, degree of poverty/SES, residential mobility, immigration, population heterogeneity, population density, disorder, and family disruption/single-parent families can be gleaned from government data sources and mapped by census tract. Additionally, the social disorganization variables of friendship levels, participation in community organizations, and levels of supervision of young people in a neighborhood can be identified from surveys, interviews, and on-site observations in neighborhoods. Each of these could be compared with census tract and neighborhood-level crime rates.

The block level of informal social control seems to hold the most promise for crime mapping research. For example, it is possible to map the presence of two-parent families in a city in order to assess relationships between family structure and crime rates.

Incivilities and Crime

The study of *incivilities* informs the findings from tests of social disorganization theory. Incivilities have been generally described as "untended property" and "untended people and behavior" (Wilson and Kelling, 1982). More specifically, these include abandoned buildings with boarded or broken windows, abandoned lots with an accumulation of trash, litter in streets, walkways, and parking areas, graffiti on buildings and walls, groups of people loitering/arguing/fighting on streets, derelicts and

---

FOCUS ON
LEVELS OF SOCIAL CONTROL

Social control is exercised on individuals by groups in society. It reinforces morality and stops individuals from acting on their deviant and criminal impulses. Bursik and Gasmick (1993) discuss the following levels of social control:

- *Private*—social control exercised by important people such as family members and close friends;
- *Parochial*—social control exercised by relatively less important people (e.g., acquaintances and neighbors);
- *Public*—social control exercised in conjunction with outside assistance (e.g., with government agencies).

Taylor (1997:114) clarifies,

> The control processes operating at each level are qualitatively different. The primary level of control "is grounded in the intimate informal primary groups that exist in the area. . . . Social control is usually achieved through the allocation or threatened withdrawal of sentiment, social support, and mutual esteem" (Bursik and Grasmick, 1993:16). At the parochial level, control is achieved through "the effects of the broader local interpersonal networks and the interlocking of local institutions such as stores, schools, churches, and voluntary organizations" (p. 17). Parochial control relies on "weak" ties and secondary groups, both perhaps emerging partly from participation in local institutions. Public control is achieved by local organizations as they "secure public goods and services that are allocated by agencies located outside the neighborhoods." (p. 17)

Social control networks can also be conceptualized within physical spaces. For example, Taylor (1997) asserts that the street block, commonly referred to as a *face block* in research, is in essence a closely knit neighborhood or community. Residents on a block share a common "pyschogeography" according to Taylor, or a common sense of community based on their proximity to one another. Strongly bonded blocks would deter criminality, according to social disorganization theorists, for the following reasons: people get to know each other through their interactions; as people get to know each other, they are more likely to be neighborly and look out for each other; over time, the neighborhood will develop norms for acceptable behavior; and community activities will not only specify opportunities for criminality but also inhibit them. Such a neighborhood would be characterized by a greater ability to recognize outsiders and to cooperate in protecting common space. If such street blocks are characterized by higher levels of nonresidential land uses (e.g., less homes but more vacant lots or businesses), they will likely be characterized by more physical deterioration (Taylor, Shumaker, and Gottfredson, 1985), including conditions of incivilities.

Source: Robinson, M. (2004). *Why Crime? An Integrated Systems Theory of Antisocial Behavior.* Upper Saddle River, NJ: Prentice-Hall.

---

winos reclining in doorways and alleyways, poorly lighted streets and dark entries to buildings and alleys, and the presence of illegal drug activity (Covington and Taylor, 1991; Hunter, 1978; Lewis and Salem, 1981; Rohe and Burby, 1988).

These conditions have been variously referred to as *signs of crime* (Skogan and Maxfield, 1981), *early signs of danger* (Stinchcombe et al., 1980), *urban unease* (Wilson, 1968), *perceived neighborhood problems* (Gates and Rohe, 1987), *non-normal appearances* (Goffman, 1971), *disorder* (Skogan, 1990), *soft crimes* (Reiss, 1985), *prelude to trouble* (Skolnick, 1966), and *cues to danger* (Warr, 1990). It is not surprising that environmental conditions are also associated with high rates of actual victimization, especially for offenses such as robbery (Camp, 1968; Tiffany and Ketchell, 1979), rape (Stoks, 1983), and burglary (Robinson, 1997, 1999; Taylor and Nee, 1988).

According to Robinson (1998b), the presence of incivilities can be understood as an indication that an area is low in aesthetics. Aesthetics refers to beauty, qualities that are pleasing to the senses. Insofar as environmental characteristics of urban areas are concerned, the term may be generally taken to include well-maintained buildings, neat vacant properties, as well as grounds immediately surrounding buildings, clean streets/parking areas/walkways, attractive natural foliage and plantings, bright lighting of all public use areas, and orderly, unobtrusive behavior of people. In essence, a high level of aesthetics is equivalent to a low level of incivilities.

A number of research studies have reported a significant relationship between conditions of incivility (or aesthetics) and fear of crime and/or perception of risk of victimization (Appleton, 1975; Biderman et al., 1967; Box, Hale, and Andrews, 1988; Covington and Taylor, 1991; Gates and Rohe, 1987; Green and Taylor, 1988; Hunter, 1978; Lewis and Maxfield, 1980; Lewis and Salem, 1986; Maxfield, 1984, 1987; Pate et al., 1986; Skogan, 1986; Taylor, Shumaker, and Gottfredson, 1985; Wilson, 1968). Areas with incivilities are found to have high levels of fear of crime and perceptions of crime risk, as well as dissatisfaction with one's neighborhood (Doran and Lees, 2005; Robinson et al., 2003; Roh and Oliver, 2005; Simon and Shepherd, 2007).

Sampson and Raudenbush (2001) summarize key relationships between disorder in urban neighborhoods and crime. Their results from 196 Chicago neighborhoods suggest that crime stems from the same conditions as disorder—neighborhood conditions such as concentrated poverty. They explain the process,

> disorder may operate in a cascading fashion by motivating residents to move out of their neighborhoods, thereby increasing residential instability. And because people move only if they have the financial means to do so, out-migration would increase the concentration of poverty among those left behind. Because residential instability and concentrated poverty are associated with lower collective efficacy and higher crime and disorder, over the course of time this process would lead to more crime and disorder.

This study finds a link between disorder and robbery but suggests that the relationship is spurious (false), or caused by other factors such as poverty, high levels of immigrant populations, and mixed land uses. These factors decrease collective efficacy, or the ability of residents to reduce crime in their own neighborhoods.

A longitudinal study of crime data from British Crime Survey (1984–1992) finds that low SES, ethnic heterogeneity, family disruption, and residential instability increase neighborhood disorder (incivilities) and that community cohesion reduces disorder (Markowitz et al., 2001). Incivilities appear to be a result of social disorganization and thus be considered as indicators of it.

PROBLEMS AND CRITICISMS OF THEORY

One of the most significant criticisms levied against social disorganization theory is that its *scope* is small. This means it cannot explain much crime or many types of crime (Robinson, 2004). Yet, tests of social disorganization have been used to explain homicide (Bachman, 1994; Frye and Wilt, 2001), gang membership and related criminality (Toy, 1992), assault and theft (Rollin, 1997), convenience store robbery (D'Alessio and Stolzenberg, 1990), drug use (Bell, Carlson, and Richard, 1998), school disorder (Welsh, Stokes, and Greene, 2000), violence among discharged mentally ill patients (Silver, 1999), suicide (Nomiya, Miller, and Hoffman, 2000), and even cyberspace deviance (Evans, 2001). Furthermore, it is related to higher levels of fear of crime and perceptions of crime risk (Taylor, 1997).

Social disorganization seems relevant only to street crimes committed within urban areas. At least one study finds that conditions of residential instability, family disruption, and ethnic heterogeneity explain rural violence committed by juveniles in 264 counties (Osgood and Chambers, 2000), but this study utilizes *arrests* for homicide, rape, assault, robbery, and weapons offenses as a measure of *crime*. The authors point out that other studies also relate social disorganization to measures of citizens' calls for police assistance (Warner and Pierce, 1993), self-reports of victims (Sampson, 1985; Sampson and Groves, 1989), and self-reports of offenders (Elliott et al., 1996; Gottfredson, McNeil, and Gottfredson, 1991; Simcha-Fagan and Schwartz, 1986). Social disorganization theory is rarely applied to areas outside of the inner-city environment.

Social disorganization does not explain individual behavior. Instead, it is aimed at explaining variations in *crime rates*, or the number of crimes per capita. For example, studies of neighborhoods show that crime rates are highest in neighborhoods with higher levels of social disorganization. These neighborhoods tend to have higher levels of minority residents (indeed, minority residents or racial or ethnic heterogeneity is one commonly used measure of social disorganization). To conclude, however, that higher crime rates in socially disorganized areas are attributable to the fact that they house more Blacks and Hispanics is incorrect. Given that police enforcement behaviors are aimed more at neighborhoods containing higher levels of Blacks, it is highly possible that higher crime rates are actually a better indication of police behavior than of residents' behavior (Robinson, 2002). For example, many studies show that the mere presence of racial minorities in a community is associated with higher arrest rates for offenses such as drug crimes, not necessarily because there is actually more drug use in the area (e.g., see Mosher, 2001).

Another weakness of social disorganization theory is that it is difficult to measure because it is not clearly defined. Most problematic, some measures of social disorganization itself often include measures of crime, making the theory *tautological*. A theory is tautological if it is true by definition. A theory is tautological when its key concepts cannot be measured separately from the behaviors they are supposed to explain. As explained by Veysey and Messner (1999:159), "Variation in official crime rates across communities is likely to reflect not only variation in crime but also variation in social control, which might itself systematically be related to the hypothesized determinants of social disorganization."

Part of the tautology problem arises because social disorganization is not actually measured in studies. Veysey and Messner (1999:159) explain, "Perhaps the most important limitation of virtually all of the research on social disorganization theory . . . is the lack of any direct measure of social disorganization itself. Indicators for many of the structural elements thought to cause social disorganization, such as poverty and residential mobility, are routinely collected, but direct indicators of social disorganization are lacking in standard data sources. To compensate, researchers have been forced to infer social disorganization processes that they cannot, in fact, observe in their data to interpret observed associations." The research by Sampson and Raudenbush (1999) that measures the degree of collective efficacy in a neighborhood is promising because it is the closest we can come to measuring social disorganization.

The concept of incivilities is also tautological. Sampson and Raudenbush (1999) point out that many forms of disorder, such as graffiti, public drug use, and loitering, are actually crimes. Thus, a relationship between incivilities and crime should be expected. Markowitz et al. (2001:295) add, "Moreover, even if disorder and other crimes are considered conceptually distinct, it may be that any association between them is due to common causes, such as collective efficacy and neighborhood demographic structure." This means the relationship may be spurious or false.

The use of official crime rate data raises the troublesome issue of class bias. If police are in socially disorganized communities, shouldn't we expect there to be more crime known to the police in those areas? This is a major weakness of theories such as social disorganization.

Another problem with tests of social disorganization theories is that they cannot resolve the debate about causal order: Which comes first, crime or social disorganization?

Much research shows that crime often precedes social disorganization and is a source of it. It appears that the relationship is reciprocal (Bellair, 1996; Skogan, 1991; Stark, 1996). Markowitz et al. (2001:297) state,

> Clearly, there is some evidence, although mixed, that crime is not only an important personal event, having consequences for both offenders and victims, but also that crime rates and the presence of disorder are important social facts, having consequences for social areas. It seems reasonable to expect that people avoid living, working, and playing in high crime areas. If they can afford to live elsewhere, they do; if they live there, they move out; and if they live there and cannot afford to move, they withdraw from social life or sharply alter their social interaction to avoid being victimized.

Finally, social disorganization theory does not explain from where social disorganization arises. Factors such as poverty unemployment, income inequality, and so forth do not just occur randomly and for no reason. Instead, each is created by decisions made by policy-makers in the form of economic (e.g., tax cuts) and social (e.g., mass imprisonment) policies. As such, social disorganization results from the decision-making of elites.

SUMMARY

List of Major Research Findings

In this chapter, you learned the following important facts pertaining to social disorganization:

1. Social disorganization has been defined as a "decrease of the influence of existing social rules of behavior upon individual members of the group," caused by social changes at the neighborhood or community level of analysis;
2. The first systematic studies of ecology and crime were conducted by A. M. Guerry and Adolphe Quetelet, who found high crime rates in some areas of the countries they studied and low crime rates in others, differences in violent and property crime rates by area, and stability of crime rates over time;
3. Social disorganization theory grew out of Durkheim's theory of anomie and the early social conditions in the city of Chicago at the beginning of the twentieth century;
4. Early social disorganization research demonstrated that delinquency often resulted from a disintegration of conventional traditions and parental approval of deviance: families of newly arriving immigrants sometimes unraveled in the conditions of the new world; areas where delinquency flourished were characterized both by high levels of opportunities for crime and low levels of opportunities for legitimate success; delinquency began early in life as a form of play for many delinquents; adolescents often served as role models in crime for children; and informal social controls could not prevent crime in delinquent areas;
5. Robert Park identified the processes of invasion, domination, and succession to describe how a small, closely knit community evolved into a larger, heterogenous community that was ill-equipped to ward off crime;
6. Ernest Burgess illustrated the city of Chicago using five zones, including the loop, the zone in transition, the zone of workingmen's homes, the residential zone, and the commuters' zone. Delinquency rates were consistently found to be higher in the zone of transition;
7. Clifford Shaw and Henry McKay identified how detachment for conventional groups encouraged delinquency among Chicago youth;
8. Shaw and McKay used pin maps and zone maps to document how juvenile delinquency tended to be found in higher levels in the center of the city and to decrease as one moved away in concentric circles;

9. Findings suggested that delinquency had its roots in the physical and economic status of the neighborhood, including high rates of delinquency in areas characterized by high industry and commerce, high levels of foreign-born families, high levels of welfare, high levels of infant mortality, high levels of illness, and low levels of economic status;

10. Significant characteristics used to predict rates of crime and delinquency by social disorganization theorists include urbanization, residential mobility, racial and ethnic heterogeneity, socioeconomic status (SES), and family disruption or single-parent households;

11. The elements of social disorganization—urbanization, residential mobility, racial and ethnic heterogeneity, SES, and family disruption or single-parent households—tend to reduce friendship networks in neighborhoods, involvement in community organizations, and supervision of young people by their parents;

12. The term that means the opposite of social disorganization is collective efficacy, which is present when neighborhoods are well equipped to work together to prevent crime before it occurs because of strong friendship networks in neighborhoods, involvement in community organizations, and supervision of young people by their parents;

13. In communities characterized by social disorganization, or lacking in collective efficacy, crime rates tend to be higher regardless of the makeup of the community;

14. Modern studies of social disorganization find that high crime rates tend to be found in areas with high population density, high levels of population turnover or transience, high rates of poverty, mixed land uses, and dilapidation of buildings;

15. Social disorganization theorists turn to social bonding or social control theory to explain why crime rates are higher in certain neighborhoods than others;

16. Levels of informal social control are thought to operate on at least three levels, private, parochial, and public;

17. Private social control is imposed by family members and friends;

18. Parochial social control is imposed by acquaintances and neighbors;

19. Public social control is imposed with assistance from outside influences;

20. Areas with low levels of private, parochial, and public social control are found to be characterized by higher crime rates;

21. Socially disorganized areas have low levels of social capital and human capital;

22. Social capital is the social skills and resources needed to bring about positive change in a community, such as community groups;

23. Human capital is the human skills and resources needed to function properly in society, such as reading and writing skills;

24. High crime areas tend to be characterized by incivilities;

25. Incivilities are signs of disorder, such as abandoned buildings, broken windows, the presence of litter or trash, graffiti, and so forth;

26. Aesthetics are the opposite of incivilities, and signify a well-maintained environment that is pleasing to the senses;

27. Many studies find relationships between high levels of incivilities/low levels of aesthetics and crime, fear of crime, and perceptions of crime risk;

28. Crime often precedes social disorganization, so that the relationship is likely reciprocal in nature;

29. Relationships between incivilities and crime are likely spurious or explained by other factors.

Implications of Findings for Crime Mapping and Spatial Analysis

As one of the classic ecological theories—one of the first that focused on the influence of spatial characteristics and processes on crime—social disorganization has significance for crime mapping and spatial analysis generally.

Social disorganization exists when existing social rules are too weak to moderate the behavior of people in a community or neighborhood because of a disintegration of conventional traditions caused by social change. The process of social disorganization rests on the presence of high levels of opportunities for crime and low levels of opportunities for legitimate success, factors that theoretically can be identified with crime mapping techniques. For example, poverty is often treated as a measure of criminal opportunities and can be mapped and compared to crime rates.

Additionally, the processes of invasion, domination, and succession that lead to social disorganization can be visualized with a careful longitudinal study in order to illustrate how a small, closely knit community evolves into a larger, heterogenous community that is less well equipped to ward off crime.

Maps created by the original social disorganization theorists illustrated the city of Chicago in five zones, including the loop, the zone in transition, the zone of working-men's homes, the residential zone, and the commuters' zone. Delinquency rates were consistently found to be higher in the zone in transition. Scores of studies have used this modern crime mapping technology to illustrate relationships between crime rates and location in the city, showing, for example, that most murders cluster around the center of the city.

More primitive pin maps and zone maps still are used to visually identify where crime and delinquency are most likely to occur. Such maps originated with the early social disorganization theorists. Findings from hundreds of studies have continued to suggest that delinquency and crime have their roots in the physical and economic status of the neighborhood. Modern social disorganization theorists continue to use factors such as urbanization, population density and population turnover, residential mobility, racial and ethnic heterogeneity, SES, family disruption or single-parent households, mixed land uses, and dilapidation of buildings to predict and explain crime rate variations across place. The effects of these factors on crime and on friendship networks, involvement in community organizations, and supervision of young people by their parents can be mapped to illustrate why crime is more likely to occur in some places than others. The ultimate goal of the social disorganization studies is to better understand how these factors produce crime in order to ultimately prevent it.

CASE STUDY
CHICAGO AREA PROJECT

The Chicago Area Project (CAP) was created in 1932 by the sociologist Clifford R. Shaw to address the problems of juvenile delinquency in some of the poorest communities in Chicago, and it operated for 25 consecutive years. It has since been reopened and is in existence today. Twenty-two neighborhood centers in six areas of the city were created, and control of the community centers was entrusted to the local residents. As noted by Kobrin (1994:439), without the participation of local residents, "the prevention of delinquency was a lost cause."

The community centers had "two primary functions. First, they were to coordinate community resources such as churches, schools, labor unions, industries, clubs, and other groups in addressing and resolving community problems. Second, they were to sponsor a variety of activity programs including recreation, summer camping and scouting activities, handicraft workshops, discussion groups, and community projects" (Vold, Bernard, and Snipes, 1998:148).

According to Kobrin's (1959) assessment of the CAP, it "rested on a conception of human nature which was optimistic concerning the prevention of delinquency and the rehabilitation of the delinquent. Delinquency was regarded as, for the most part, a reversible accident of the person's social experience" (Kobrin, 1994:438).

The CAP was aimed at reducing juvenile delinquency in the city, based on the theory of social disorganization. As noted by Kobrin (1994:443), one overriding goal of CAP was to

(continued)

"develop plans for the supervision of delinquent youngsters; visiting boys committed to training schools and reformatories; working with boys' gangs in the informal settings of the neighborhood; and assisting adult parolees in their problems of returning to the community." The accomplishments of the CAP included the following: (1) it created youth welfare organizations in high-delinquency areas; (2) it was the first such project aimed at reaching out to wayward youth in inner-city America; and (3) it passed judgment on more formal methods of dealing with juvenile delinquents (Kobrin, 1994:444). Yet, as noted by Kobrin and later by Vold, Bernard, and Snipes (1998), never has it been verified empirically that the CAP actually reduced juvenile delinquency.

The values and philosophy of CAP today are centered around improving the quality of neighborhood life with special focus on solving problems faced by young people and their families. Through its many affiliate programs, CAP provides direct services to diverse communities throughout Cook County. Through its community-based affiliate organizations and special projects, the CAP staff collectively provides human and financial resources to its affiliates to promote leadership in youth, parents, and their entire community.

In 1932, the CAP was begun in three of the city's highest crime areas to test juvenile delinquency prevention techniques. As director of the research department and later as CAP's first director, Shaw developed both private and public sources of funding to expand the program to other areas of Chicago throughout the 1940s.

The CAP became the prototype for delinquency prevention and welfare programs. Its principles of community organization, self-determination, and using natural leaders indigenous to a neighborhood were quite radical when first proposed by Shaw in the early 1930s, but are used by many groups today to successfully solve local problems.

Today, CAP is a private, not-for-profit organization with a distinguished history and demonstrable track record of over 60 years of work in delinquency prevention and service in disadvantaged urban neighborhoods. The original mission of CAP has not changed since its inception: to work toward the prevention and eradication of juvenile delinquency through the development and support of affiliated local community self-help efforts, in communities where the need is greatest.

The CAP's philosophy is to improve the quality of neighborhood life with a special focus on solving problems faced by young people and their families. The agency believes that residents must be empowered through the development of community organizations so that they can act together to improve neighborhood conditions, hold institutions serving the community accountable, reduce anti-social behavior by young people, protect them from inappropriate institutionalization, and provide them with positive role models for personal development.

The goals of the CAP are to develop special projects and establish locally controlled organizations that implement the directives put forth in CAP's mission and philosophy. Projects and affiliates are mandated to positively impact areas in the Chicago vicinity with high rates of juvenile delinquency or other symptoms of social disorganization.

The objectives for CAP projects and affiliated organizations include the following:

- To develop local leadership broadly representative of the communities that are being served;
- To conduct an annual community survey to assess needs and develop an action plan with a clear set of goals and objectives;
- To improve the climate for the positive development of young people by achieving such improvements as increases in educational achievement levels and vocational skills;
- To develop young people's leadership skills by involving them in youth-initiated community improvement activities or in cooperative projects with adults;
- To set measurable goals and show progress in improving undesirable conditions;
- To demonstrate an ability to raise funds, manage staff, and be accountable financially and programmatically;
- To promote and inform the community about all programs;
- To develop a referral/resource network with other agencies and institutions;
- To develop and maintain all contractual record-keeping documents as required.

The CAP model uses a three-pronged approach to address issues affecting youth, families, and communities:

- *Advocacy:* The CAP is dedicated to advocacy on behalf of youth and other resident concerns;
- *Direct Service:* CAP provides direct service for youth and adults; and
- *Community Organizing:* CAP facilitates community organizing directed toward improving the quality of neighborhood life.

CAP believes in strengthening Chicago's neighborhoods through action. Nothing offers a greater chance for raising a child who shares society's values than a neighborhood where everyone works together in a positive, cooperative way to care for the children growing up in their community. But how do you mobilize a neighborhood? How do you get people to work together? Can a child survive the complicated urban problems inner-city neighborhoods face? The answer lies in tapping the natural leadership and concern for community found within each neighborhood. While some delinquency prevention programs try to impose outside policies upon local residents, CAP's philosophy is to encourage people who live in the neighborhood to seek their own solutions. This is done by forming a community committee as the primary force for change. The committee consists of local citizens who encourage participation and effective representation in decisions affecting their neighborhood.

The CAP has over 40 affiliates and special projects throughout the city. Over the years, the programs and issues have changed, just as the neighborhood changed. But the democratic ideals of self-determination and self-improvement remain the same, and these key principles of CAP continue to serve its neighborhood.

CAP programs are organized activities designed to provide constructive outlets for addressing social, economic, and other needs that have a direct or indirect influence on the quality of life of participants. Under the CAP model, programs are a means toward the end of getting those affected to take steps that will remedy their problems by getting to their root causes. Within the context of "community," members' involvement in the process is key. A further aspect is the utilization of community resources as a definite strategy, as well as the development of community organizations to orchestrate this process. CAP programs include the Community Service Program (CSP), Community Organizing (CO), Juvenile Justice Diversion, and Title XX (a social services grant program).

Special projects are assigned to departments within CAP and designed to address specific problems within a specified time frame. CAP special projects include African-American Male Rites of Passage (ROP), Mentoring, Training & Employment (MTE), the Open Book Program, the Statewide Youth Advisory Board, Teen Reach, Women in Transition (WIT), Youth as Resources (YAR), YouthNet (Phillips High School), and YouthNet (Roseland).

While many of these services are not place-specific, others are. It is possible, with crime mapping software, to map high-delinquency areas and compare them to location of services for juvenile delinquency in order to assess the degree to which they match. Ideally, services will be offered in the areas in which they are most needed.

Source: "Chicago Area Project." [On-line]. Available: http://www.chicagoareaproject.org.

CHAPTER 4

Ecological Theories of Crime

The purpose of this chapter is to provide a comprehensive discussion of the myriad ecological theories of crime and the crime prevention policies that stem from them. In this chapter, we summarize major findings of this rich body of research and discuss the implications for crime mapping and spatial analysis.

Chapter Outline

INTRODUCTION TO THE MAJOR SCHOOLS OF THOUGHT IN ECOLOGICAL THEORY

In the 1970s, when Oscar Newman and C. Ray Jeffery published their respective books, *Defensible Space* and *Crime Prevention Through Environmental Design*, it marked a significant turning point with regard to thinking about the etiology of criminal behavior. These works are well known and have influenced academicians, governmental agencies, architectural design, and corporate and business initiatives related to crime prevention (Robinson, 1999).

Ecological theory goes back much farther than Oscar Newman and C. Ray Jeffery, as we illustrated in our discussion of the Chicago School of Human Ecology (discussed in Chapter 3). Moreover, as we showed, the Chicago theorists actually used primitive maps—pin maps and zone maps, for example—to illustrate where rates of street crime and delinquency were highest in the city. The development of modern crime mapping can be directly attributed to the work of more modern ecological theorists, including those who have worked in the areas of defensible space, crime prevention through environmental design (CPTED), situational crime prevention, routine activity theory, and crime pattern theory.

In this chapter, we discuss the main hypotheses and major findings with each of these schools of ecological theory, and then outline major problems and criticisms of these theories. Finally, we discuss the implications of the findings for crime mapping and spatial analysis of crime.

DEFENSIBLE SPACE

Major Hypotheses

The concept of *defensible space* was introduced by Oscar Newman in his book *Defensible Space: People and Design in the Violent City* (1972). This term is used to describe a residential environment designed to allow and even encourage residents themselves to supervise and be seen by outsiders as responsible for their neighborhoods (Mayhew, 1981:150).

Newman's notion of environmental design is based on

the development of coordinated design standards—for architecture, land use, street layout and street lighting—which improve security. Its goal is to create environments which reduce the opportunities for crime while encouraging people to use public space in ways that contribute to their safety and enhance their sense of community. (LEAA Newsletter, 1974, 4, 3:12–13)

Newman's notion of environmental design is more complex than simply redesigning space. It also includes redesigning residential environments so that residents use the areas and become willing to defend their territory.

According to the National Crime Prevention Institute (1986:121), defensible space design changes strengthen two basic kinds of social behavior, *territoriality* and *natural surveillance*. The goal of the defensible space approach is "to release the latent sense of territoriality and community among inhabitants so as to allow these traits to be translated into inhabitants' assumption of responsibility for preserving a safe and well-maintained living environment" (Newman, 1976:4), and to increase the potential for residents to see and report likely offenders, thereby enabling residents to control the physical environments in which they reside. Newman's work was an attempt to reduce both crime and fear of crime in a specific type of environment (public housing), by means of reducing opportunity for crime and fostering positive social interaction among legitimate users (Taylor and Harrell, 1996:3–4).

Areas low in defensible space (such as large cities) were thought to be more vulnerable to crime because in these areas feelings of ownership and community spirit were not generated by residents. In these areas, residents were thought to be less likely to be able to recognize outsiders as potential criminals. In smaller areas, the presence of defensible space was thought to increase the effectiveness of informal social control and make crime less likely (Murray, 1994:351). Newman's work was based on previous research by Elizabeth Wood, Jane Jacobs, and Schlomo Angel, among others.

According to Newman (1973:119), "one of the prime advocates of the importance of physical design considerations in achieving social objectives was Elizabeth Wood."

Wood's (1961:4) belief was that managers of residential areas could never do enough to stop the damaging actions of even a small group of hostile or indifferent tenants. While Wood worked for the Chicago Housing Authority, she strove to make surrounding residential environments of lower class citizens more rich and fulfilling (Newman, 1973:119). As she attempted to bring about design changes aimed at enhancing quality of life for residents and increasing the aesthetic qualities of the residential environment, she also developed a series of guidelines for improving security conditions of these environments (Newman, 1973:122).

One of her design goals was to improve *visibility* of apartment units by residents; another was to create spaces where residents could gather, thereby increasing the potential for resident *surveillability*. Surveillability is understood in the literature to mean "the extent to which a residence is overseen and observable by neighbors or passersby" (Cromwell, Olson, and Avary, 1991:35). As discussed by Newman (1973:122), "Miss Wood's concept of the social control of residential areas is predicated on the presence of and natural surveillance by residents. Areas that are out of view and unused are simply without control." As Jane Jacobs after her, Wood recognized that certain types of designs could translate into loss of opportunity for informal social control by residents (National Crime Prevention Institute, 1986:119). Newman (1973:126) wrote that "Elizabeth Wood was perhaps the foremost practitioner of social design in the field of housing." Yet, given the fact that Wood's ideas were never widely put into practice, the validity of her ideas was never actually subjected to rigid empirical testing.

Jacobs's work, *The Death and Life of Great American Cities* (1961), really began the search for how both physical and social urban factors affected people and their interactions. Hers was among the earliest discussions of urban decay and its relationship to crime. C. Ray Jeffery, who founded the term "crime prevention through environmental design" or "CPTED" (discussed below), has often stated that it was Jane Jacobs who sparked the widespread interest in how environmental conditions could be related to crime prevention (e.g., see Jeffery and Zahm, 1993:331–332). In fact, Jeffery reported that reading Jacobs's work caused him to "think about writing a book on crime prevention" (Jeffery, personal communication March 28, 1996), which, of course, he later did. Jacobs hypothesized that urban residential crime could be prevented by reducing conditions of anonymity and isolation in those areas (Murray, 1994:349).

Jacobs's work was "an indictment of post-war urban planning policies that gave precedence to the needs of the automobile at the expense of conditions fostering local community life" (Clarke, 1995a:2). Jacobs (1961:31) felt that cities were custom-made for crime: The way they were designed and built meant that citizens would not be able to build or maintain informal social control networks necessary for effective self-policing. It was Jacobs's contention that crime flourished when people did not know and meaningfully interact with their neighbors, for they would thus be less likely to notice an outsider who may be a criminal surveying the environment for potential targets or victims.

Jacobs (1961) discussed the effects of street surveillance by neighbors, and claimed that high levels of natural surveillance created a safe environment. Jacobs stated that city streets often do not have the three primary qualities needed in order to make them safer: (1) a clear demarcation between public and private space; (2) diversity of street use; and (3) fairly constant sidewalk use, which translated into "eyes on the street." Residential streets that promote multiple land uses promote natural and informal surveillance by pedestrians, and therefore, potentially increase residents' safety (National Crime Prevention Institute, 1986:118). To Jacobs, active streets served as a *deterrent* to crime. A deterrent is something that acts to create fear in a would-be offender so that he or she decides not to commit a criminal act.

Jacobs's ideas about how the physical environment is related to risks of crime are related to social control theory. This is not surprising given "another common sense understanding about crime: One of our best protections against crime is to live in a community where neighbors watch out for each other and stand ready to call the police

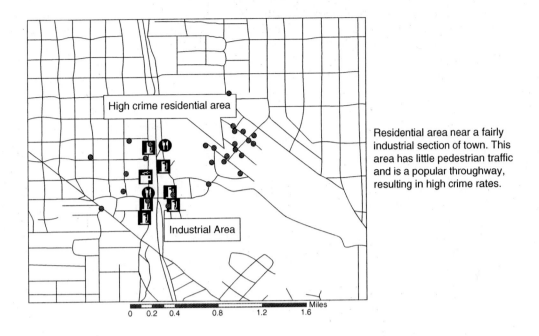

Residential area near a fairly industrial section of town. This area has little pedestrian traffic and is a popular throughway, resulting in high crime rates.

Residential area near a large and active residential park complex. Due to active pedestrian traffic in this neighborhood area, crime is relatively infrequent.

FIGURE 4.1   Pedestrian Traffic and Crime Incidents

or to intervene directly when they spot a malefactor" (Murray, 1994:349). We discussed social control theories in Chapters 2 and 3.

Schlomo Angel (1968), in *Discouraging Crime Through City Planning*, noted how citizens could take an active role in preventing crime, starting with a diagnosis of which environments afford the most opportunities for crime to occur. Angel thought that certain areas suffer from higher rates of crime than other areas because of the higher levels of opportunity on which rational offenders could capitalize. Angel reasoned that offenders chose their specific targets through a decision-making process in which they weighed the effort and risk against potential payoffs. With more opportunity and a higher potential payoff, it was thought that at least one successful target offering little risk would be found. Angel posited that deterrents to crime included high-intensity use of an area because this provides large numbers of effective witnesses and low-intensity land use because this reduces the number of potential victims (Newman, 1973:132). In between high- and low-intensity use, in periods of moderate use, criminal opportunities were thought to abound because there were enough victims to choose from but there weren't enough witnesses to deter crime (also see National Crime Prevention Institute, 1986:119). Angel's ideas regarding changing the physical design of environments revolved around channeling pedestrian traffic and zoning businesses into areas where mass transit and parking facilities are near.

It is possible to create maps of streets in neighborhoods to indicate the levels of typical traffic patterns. We would expect areas with higher pedestrian traffic to have lower rates of property crimes (such as burglary). Figure 4.1 provides one example. This map shows two areas of a city, the first with very little pedestrian traffic and near a major thoroughfare, producing high calls for police service. The second part of the city captures areas near neighborhoods and parks that have higher levels of pedestrian traffic and far fewer calls for police service.

Major Findings

Newman's research began in 1969 when the National Institute of Law Enforcement and Criminal Justice (NILECJ, now the National Institute of Justice) undertook a series of projects to appraise the relationship between the physical environment and risk of criminal victimization (Wallis, 1980:2). A result of these efforts was Oscar Newman's book. Within two years of the original publication, demonstration projects were initiated, and within one more year, the Law Enforcement Assistance Administration (LEAA) funded a multi-million dollar project to study crime in a commercial strip, a residential area, and a school. Eventually, public housing projects were designed based upon Newman's ideas. Newman's ideas may still be greatly influencing the design of public housing all over the world (Clarke, 1992:6; also see Coleman, 1985).

According to Jeffery and Zahm (1993:332–333), under a grant from LEAA, the Westinghouse Electric Corporation designed a school crime prevention project in Broward County, Florida, a commercial crime prevention project in Portland, Oregon, and a residential/mixed use crime prevention project in Hartford, Connecticut. These are among the most well-known defensible space efforts incorporating "physical, social, law enforcement, and management techniques to achieve its goal of reducing crime and the fear of crime" (National Crime Prevention Institute, 1986:124). Crime prevention strategies aimed at these goals included *controlling access* (or reducing *accessibility*), increasing *surveillance*, *activity support*, and *reinforcement*, or in other words, *defensible space* and *target hardening*. Target hardening can be understood as any mechanism aimed at making it more difficult for an offender to gain access to a target or crime victim (Robinson, 1998).

The Broward County school project "used Newman's concept of natural surveillance and an increased sense of responsibility on the part of students for crime prevention" (Jeffery, 1990:413). The Portland commercial area project made changes "in outdoor lighting, emergency phones, landscaping, special bus shelters, security surveys, neighborhood watch programs, traffic patterns and one-way streets, and the amount of cash carried or kept in stores." In Hartford, roads "were closed or narrowed, some streets were made one-way streets, community anti-crime groups were formed, and police-community relations were improved" (also see National Crime Prevention Institute, 1986:124–129).

Throughout the 1970s, until 1979 when LEAA was eliminated, Newman's book of crime prevention guidelines for public housing continued to be well received and projects based on it continued to be funded by governmental entities (LEAA Newsletter, 1976, 6, 2:8). For example, one of the defensible space designs Newman created was applied at two new housing developments—one in Indianapolis and another in Newark—with funding of more than $100,000 from NILECJ and $50,000 from the Department of Housing and Urban Development (HUD). This strategy was aimed at assigning different types of residents to the kinds of buildings they would best be able to control, subdividing buildings and corridors to promote a feeling of ownership by residents, and increasing surveillability through design.

Other defensible space projects included the South Loop New Town Security Project, a residential development of mixed-income populations in Chicago (Jeffery and Zahm, 1993:333) that "employed a broader orientation of Newman's philosophies developed by Richard Gardiner (1978)" under the concept of environmental security. Other programs spurred on by Newman included the Kansas City Lighting study, the Washington, D.C., burglary study conducted by Scarr, and the Boston residential crime study conducted by Reppetto (LEAA Newsletter, 1974, 4, 3:19). Newman's defensible space approach was actually first tested at two public housing projects in New York City—Clason Point and Markham Gardens. The design changes at these areas established play areas, improved the appearance of the projects, and also included installing better lighting, introducing fencing to divide areas into semi-private spaces, and erecting barriers to channel pedestrian traffic (Murray, 1994:352).

According to the National Crime Prevention Institute (1986:119–120), the first model developed by NILECJ that was aimed at modifying architectural design for entire neighborhoods was the Residential Neighborhood Crime Control project in Hartford, Connecticut (LEAA Newsletter, 1974, 4, 1:8). Under an Institute grant of almost $500,000, the Hartford Institute of Criminal and Social Justice developed and implemented a defensible space project in two Hartford neighborhoods, one a highly transient, apartment-dominated area and the other a family area containing mostly row houses—Asylum Hill and Clay Hill-Sand, respectively. In this project, streets were closed or narrowed in order to change traffic patterns, community groups were established or strengthened to increase a sense of "community," and police-community relations were strengthened (Murray, 1994:352; National Crime Prevention Institute, 1986:128). Such changes to streets can be illustrated using crime mapping software, and the effects of street closures and narrowing on crime rate trends can be determined.

Evidence of studies suggests that each of these projects had minimal impacts on actual occurrences of street crime (Robinson, 1999). As you will see in the section that follows, this ecological theory of crime is plagued by significant problems that threaten the validity of any conclusions of the above studies.

Problems and Criticisms of Theory

Despite Newman's (1973:1) own assertions that this concept of defensible space was applicable beyond public housing units "to the residential settings of most income groups" such as the neighborhoods discussed above, the validity of his concept has been seriously challenged (e.g., see Jeffery and Zahm, 1993). Murray (1994:352–353) called evidence of crime reduction through defensible space "ambiguous" and even wrote that "it did not reduce crime." In addition, in a test by Greenberg and Rohe (1984:45, 58) of two perspectives on the effects of the physical design of buildings and sites of neighborhoods on crime (*defensible space* versus *opportunity theory*), far more support was generated for the opportunity model of crime than for the defensible space model. This is similar to tests of Durkheim's anomie theory (Vold, Bernard, and Snipes, 2001). Opportunity theories simply assert that levels of crime in an area are a function of available and especially suitable targets or victims for crime (opportunity theories are discussed in more depth later in this chapter). The opportunity model was more supported because the physical characteristics differentiating high- and low-crime neighborhoods reflected differential levels of opportunity and access, not latent territorial control on the part of the residents (Jeffery and Zahm, 1993:333).

In an updated version of his book, Newman (1996) reported that changes to the external environment of a public housing complex, including reducing pedestrian travel routes, dividing up the complex into separate spaces, improving lighting conditions, and increasing the aesthetic qualities of the buildings, are associated with significant crime rate reductions, including serious crimes. This study was conducted in one place, without a control group, and is really not related directly to the key components of defensible space. The findings could be spurious (false, or explained away by some other factors) and also can be interpreted as support for a more general opportunity model.

A significant problem with Newman's concept of defensible space is that it is limited to modifications of the *external* physical environment in order to produce changes in the *external* social environment, while completely neglecting the *internal* physical environment of the offender. For example, Newman advocated "reducing the size and height of blocks" in public housing and "reducing the number of dwellings sharing a single entrance and making public areas visible from dwellings" (Clarke, 1995a:9, citing Coleman, 1985), as well as "enhanced lighting, the hiring of concierges and porters, and the installation of entry phones, fences and barriers" (Clarke, 1995a:9, citing Wekerle and Whitzman, 1995). Obviously, none of these actually addresses the root causes of criminality, particularly those that lie within the offender. This is a serious drawback to defensible space, for it may only move crime—called *displacement*—rather than actually prevent it (displacement is discussed in Chapter 6).

Nevertheless, Newman's work continues to influence governmental and architectural decision making with regard to physical design changes (Jeffery and Zahm, 1993:333–334). For example, many government-operated public housing projects, including the Outhwaite Homes Project in Cleveland, Ohio, and Renaissance Homes in Washington, D.C. (Cisneros, 1995), have adopted defensible space crime prevention strategies. Also, neighborhoods in Atlanta, Georgia, Richmond, Virginia, and St. Louis, Missouri, limit traffic and encourage resident associations, based on the principles of defensible space (Cisneros, 1995). Other neighborhoods, such as Five Oaks in Dayton, Ohio, Miami Shores in Florida, and an area of Bridgeport, Connecticut, have created neighborhood-wide defensible space strategies focusing primarily on limiting access to neighborhoods by outsiders so that residents will be more likely to recognize outsiders and to increase a sense of community among residents (Cisneros, 1995). Other examples of Newman's continuing influence on government thinking with regard to CPTED and architectural design abound (for discussion, see Eck, 1997).

CRIME PREVENTION THROUGH ENVIRONMENTAL DESIGN

Major Hypotheses

Crime prevention through environmental design (CPTED) is aimed at "identifying conditions of the physical and social environment that provide opportunities for or precipitate criminal acts . . . and the alteration of those conditions so that no crimes occur . . ." (Brantingham and Faust, 1976:289, 290, 292). Because it is aimed at preventing occurrences of criminality, CPTED is conceptually distinct and significantly different from the reactive (and largely failing) strategies employed by police, courts, and correctional facilities in the American criminal justice system (Robinson, 2002).

The notion of CPTED came to the forefront of criminological thought with Jeffery's *Crime Prevention Through Environmental Design* (1971), a work written simultaneously and therefore without influence from Oscar Newman's *Defensible Space* (1972). According to the National Crime Prevention Institute (1986:120), Jeffery's book encouraged crime prevention strategies aimed at changes to the physical environment and increased citizen involvement and proactive policing. Jeffery contended that the way to prevent crime is to design the "total environment" in order to reduce opportunities for crime. The total environment includes the internal environment of the offender.

Jeffery's work was based on the precepts of experimental psychology represented in modern learning theory (Jeffery and Zahm, 1993:329). Jeffery's CPTED concept arose out of his experiences with a rehabilitative project in Washington, D.C., that attempted to control the school environment of juveniles in the area. Rooted deeply in the psychological learning theory of B. F. Skinner, Jeffery's CPTED approach emphasized the role of the physical environment in the development of pleasurable and painful experiences for the offender that would have the capacity to alter behavioral outcomes. His original CPTED model was a stimulus–response (S-R) model positing that the organism learned from punishments and reinforcements in the environment. Jeffery "emphasized material rewards . . . and the use of the physical environment to control behavior" (Jeffery and Zahm, 1993:330). The major idea here was that by removing the reinforcements for crime, it would not occur. Jeffery's 1971 book was an early argument for crime prevention which rejected the more popular crime control goals of revenge, just deserts, or retribution and deterrence, as well as punitive crime control strategies employed by the criminal justice system. Jeffery's book was much more of an academic exercise rebelling against the current state of criminal justice practice than was Newman's practical guide to crime prevention.

Because Jeffery's (1971) approach was largely founded on Skinner's behavioral learning theory, it is not surprising that no attention was paid to the individual organism (in this case, the offender). Skinner was known for his criticisms of earlier "introspective" or "mentalistic" theories of behavior that are not empirically testable, are not falsifiable, and involve the logical error of circular reasoning. As introduced in Chapter 1, a theory is *testable* if it can be measured in the real world in order to see if it is supported or not. All theories are *falsifiable*, meaning if they are wrong, they can be proven wrong. Finally, *circular reasoning* occurs when a scholar labels a behavior (e.g., criminal behavior) and then uses that label to explain the same behavior. An example would be labeling a violent, repetitive criminal a psychopath because he has committed multiple violent crimes and then using the condition of psychopathy to explain the person's violent crimes (Robinson, 2004).

To make his theories testable, falsifiable, and to avoid circular reasoning, Skinner ignored the physical organism completely. He reasoned that there was no way to know what was going on in the organism's brain or mind; Skinner was thus content with merely observing and describing what he saw, rather than resorting to conjecture about what he could not see in the organism's brain or mind.

Jeffery's original work did not take into account either the mind or the brain of the organism. In the 1971 edition of his book, "Jeffery mentioned the biological basis of behavior and the role of the brain in behavior (pp. 171–172), but then dropped the concept from further discussion" (Jeffery and Zahm, 1993:330). Consequently, his first statement of the CPTED model in 1971 contained the flaw of the "empty organism." That is, the logical implication of Jeffery's original CPTED model was that the environment directly affected the behavior of the organism, without first entering the organism either physically or mentally. Figure 4.2 illustrates the logic of this model. You'll note that Jeffery originally proposed that environmental conditions affected behavior in a one-way relationship without first affecting the offender.

Jeffery's second edition of *Crime Prevention Through Environmental Design* (1977) involved a complete revision of the underlying theoretical approach for CPTED. While his 1971 edition was very limited in terms of its inclusion of material related to biology or the physical organism, the 1977 edition "included statements about human genetics and brain functioning from modern biology and psychobiology" (Jeffery and Zahm,

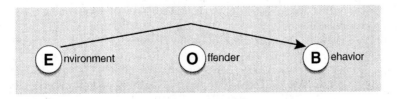

FIGURE 4.2   Jeffery's Original CPTED Model

1993:330). His empty organism approach was replaced by a new model commonly referred to as the "integrated systems model" of human behavior (e.g., see Jeffery, 1990). This model utilizes systems logic rather than sequential logic. It denies or at least questions the logic of time-ordered causal reasoning, and instead posits continuous interactive effects of organisms and environments which have reciprocal influences on one another, among all levels of analysis, from cell to society (including genetics, the brain, the individual, the group, the community, organizations, society, and so forth).

According to Fishbein (personal communication March 28, 1996), Jeffery was the first scholar in the field of criminology to fill the empty organism with knowledge he had learned from studying biology. Jeffery was preparing to develop a CPTED model aimed at modifying both the external environment and the internal environment of the offender. For more on C. Ray Jeffery, see the Focus On box.

Jeffery's 1977 work was based on a biological rather than a social ecology model, meaning that Jeffery's model of human behavior contained both a concrete physical environment *and* a concrete physical organism. This CPTED model does not focus on abstract sociological concepts such as *social disorganization* and *social learning* that tend to minimize the concrete physical environment in favor of the abstract social environment (Jeffery, 1996:4; Jeffery and Zahm, 1993: 326–329). Jeffery's shift from an S-R model of human behavior to an integrated systems approach was motivated by research into the role of the brain in human learning conducted by researchers outside the field of criminology in the early 1970s (Jeffery,

---

FOCUS ON
C. RAY JEFFERY

C. Ray Jeffery was Professor Emeritus of Criminology at Florida State University and past president of the American Society of Criminology, a recipient of the Sutherland Award from that association, a Fulbright-Hays research fellow to the Netherlands, and the founding editor of *Criminology: An Interdisciplinary Journal.* He held fellowships to the University of Chicago Law School and the University of Wisconsin Law School.

Dr. Jeffery's primary professional focus was on crime prevention and the biological foundations of criminal behavior. His major books include *Crime Prevention Through Environmental Design, Biology and Crime,* and *Criminology, an Interdisciplinary Approach.* His emphasis was on integrating crime prevention approaches including biology, psychology, sociology, and law.

Jeffery received his Ph.D. in Sociology/Political Philosophy from Indiana University in 1954. Given that Jeffery attended Indiana University, where B. F. Skinner was chair of the psychology department, and that Jeffery spent some time at Arizona State University, known as the "Fort Skinner of the West" (Crimnotes, 1995:1), it is to be expected that Jeffery's work was influenced by Skinner.

Jeffery's crime prevention ideas evolved from psychological in nature to biological as he learned about the role of biology in behavior. Jeffery has written and spoken a great deal about how his ideas evolved into a more integrated model. Unfortunately, criminological theory and crime prevention practice are still decades behind Jeffery.

However, recent efforts by criminologists have made significant headway in the past ten years. Scholars have put forth and begun to test integrated theories of crime based in part on Jeffery's research model (e.g., Robinson, 2004, 2005).

C. Ray Jeffery served as Director of the Crime Prevention Through Environmental Design Project (HUD Grant, Albany, Georgia, 1990–1991), the Director of the Biochemical Aspects of Antisocial Behavior Project (Thomasville and Albany, Georgia, 1990–1991), the Director of the Campus Crime Research Project (Florida State University, 1991–1992), and the Director of the Crime Prevention and Crime Project in Tallahassee (1991–1992).

C. Ray Jeffery died in December 2007. His influence on criminology was enormous and lives on through his students and others who have read his enormous body of work.

personal communication March 28, 1996). Jeffery's CPTED model evolved into a general crime prevention model. Thus, his later model includes both the external environment of the place *and* the internal environment of the offender.

This CPTED model was much more fully developed in Jeffery's *Criminology: An Interdisciplinary Approach* (1990). The basic assumption of the CPTED approach of Jeffery, as it stood in the 1990 book, and as it stands today, is that

> the response [i.e., behavioral adaptation] of the individual organism to the physical environment is a product of the brain; the brain in turn is a product of genetics and the environment. The environment never influences behavior directly, but *only through the brain*. Any model of crime prevention must include *both* the brain and the physical environment. (Jeffery and Zahm, 1993:330; also see Jeffery, 1996:4)

There are then two critical elements to CPTED in the Jeffery model: (1) the place where the crime occurs; and (2) the person who commits the crime. According to Jeffery's (1990:418) CPTED model, we can successfully prevent crime by altering the organism and/or the external environment. Because the approach contained in Jeffery's CPTED model is today based on many academic fields, a focus on only external environmental crime prevention is inadequate as it ignores another entire dimension of CPTED—the internal environment. This revised conception of CPTED is depicted in Figure 4.3. You'll note that Jeffery's revised model is reciprocal, so that environmental conditions affect behavior and behavior affects the environment, and that the offender is depicted in the model.

Crime mapping has not yet evolved to the point of being able to visually depict what is going on inside the brain of offenders. Yet, brain imaging techniques such as the functional magnetic resonance imaging (MRI) can visually depict images of brain activity during aggressive behaviors and emotional states (Robinson, 2004). These can, for all intents and purposes, be considered crime maps in the brain.

Over the years, a number of variations and refinements of the basic CPTED concept have been offered. Generally, CPTED, as practiced in the real world of crime prevention, "focuses on the settings in which crimes occur and on techniques for reducing vulnerability of the settings" (Taylor and Harrell, 1996:1), because its central premise is that crime can be facilitated or inhibited by features of the physical environment (Clarke, 1995a:2). According to Fleissner and Heinzelmann (1996), the basic principles of CPTED include designing and managing the physical environment of buildings, changing residential neighborhoods and businesses through target hardening, increasing surveillance, and encouraging territorial reinforcement. Crowe's (1991:3) *Crime Prevention Through Environmental Design: Applications of Architectural Design and Space Management Concepts* utilizes the "Three D" approach based on the three dimensions of human space (Designation, Definition, and Design) to describe useful CPTED strategies that can be used in various environments, including commercial, residential, and school environments. For more on the Three D's of CPTED, see the Focus On box.

These are the approaches promoted by organizations such as the International CPTED Association, International Security Management & Crime Prevention Institute, and international conferences on CPTED.

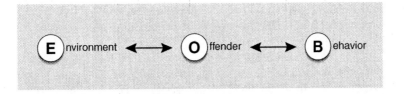

FIGURE 4.3   Jeffery's Revised CPTED Model

FOCUS ON
THREE D'S OF CPTED

Using the Three D's as a guide, one can evaluate any given space by asking the following types of questions:

DESIGNATION

- What is the designated purpose of this space?
- For what purpose was it originally intended?
- How well does the space support its current use or its intended use?
- Is there conflict?

DEFINITION

- How is space defined?
- Is it clear who owns it?
- Where are its borders?
- Are there social or cultural definitions that affect how space is used?
- Are the legal or administrative rules clearly set out and reinforced in policy?
- Are there signs?
- Is there conflict or confusion between purpose and definition?

DESIGN

- How well does the physical design support the intended function?
- How well does the physical design support the desired or accepted behaviors?
- Does the physical design conflict with or impede the productive use of the space or the proper functioning of the intended human activity?
- Is there confusion or conflict in the manner in which physical design is intended to control behavior?

Source: "Crime Prevention Through Environmental Design." [On-line]. Available: www.stpete.org/police/cpted.htm

CPTED is the "specific management, design, or manipulation of the immediate environment in which crimes occur in a systematic and permanent way" (Bennett and Wright, 1984). While CPTED generally involves changing the environment to reduce the opportunity for crime, it is aimed at other outcomes, including reducing fear of crime, increasing the aesthetic quality of an environment, and increasing the quality of life for law-abiding citizens, especially by reducing the propensity of the physical environment to support criminal behavior (Clarke, 1995a:8; Crowe, 1991:1, 28–29, 40).

We've used crime mapping software to illustrate areas on a college campus that were indicated in surveys of space users to be home to more crime, higher levels of fear of crime, and higher levels of perceived risk of crime. Figure 4.4 illustrates the findings relevant for calls to police service. The places with the largest stars in the figure—typically parking lots and dark, isolated areas—were the areas that had the most calls for police service. These were the same areas that generated the most fear of crime and perceived crime risk among the campus users. A follow-up study of the same campus more than five years later found that crimes clustered in the same places. In fact, places with the highest numbers of alcohol and drug violations were also most likely to experience greatest numbers of various crimes, including theft, vandalism, harassment, and assault (Robinson and Roh, 2007).

The underlying logic of designing a specific external environment in order to prevent crime makes sense for several reasons. For example, crime prevention efforts

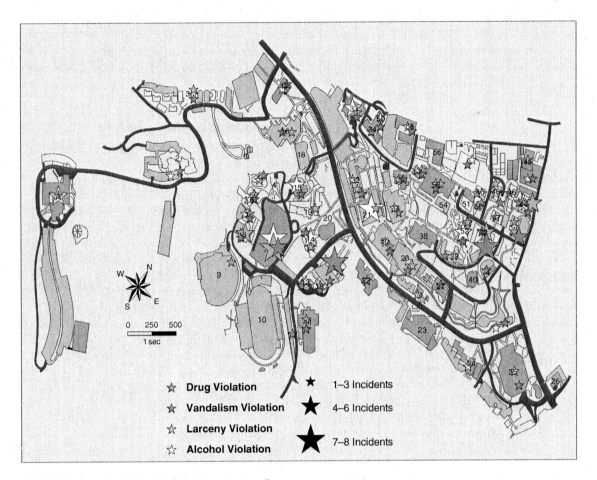

FIGURE 4.4   Calls for Police Service on Campus

aimed at people through methods such as "general deterrence" and "special deterrence" (Packer, 1968) are less sure to work, for the placement of people in the physical environment is temporary owing to their mobile nature—i.e., they are not permanent fixtures of most environments for an extended period of time. Things such as buildings and other physical features of the environment are "relatively permanent" (Nasar and Fisher, 1992:48–49). As a result, CPTED can produce effects on crime and perceptions of personal crime risks. Yet, the idea that CPTED only applies to the external physical environment is limited. To be more effective, CPTED should be applied to both external *and* internal environments, or to the environments of the place and the offender, respectively.

Major Findings

First, it should be stated unequivocally that Jeffery's most recent version of CPTED has not been subjected to widespread empirical testing. Thus, the validity of his theory remains unknown. Most tests of CPTED have been conducted with regard to the effects of modifications to the external physical environment on crime, fear of crime, perceptions of crime risk, and appreciation of environmental aesthetics (Robinson and Mullen, 2001).

Widespread CPTED projects began in the 1970s when the NILECJ, the research and development arm of the LEAA, sponsored and conducted research on crime prevention. Their basic program would target hardening measures—"such things as security locks, street lighting, residential security systems, and housing design" (LEAA Newsletter, 1971, 1, 6:7). Almost immediately thereafter, issues of the LEAA

Newsletter, a document distributed by NILECJ, contained detailed reports of crime prevention programs being implemented across the United States, including one in Washington, D.C., which included only the installation of high-intensity street lighting (LEAA Newsletter, 1971, 1, 7:3). According to Murray (1994:353), 41 recorded street-lighting projects were undertaken up to 1977, with results showing that "occasional short-term improvements were ephemeral." Results of street-lighting projects in Baltimore, Milwaukee, Tucson, Denver, and Minneapolis found that they did reduce perceptions of safety among residents (Murray, 1994:353), a stated goal of CPTED researchers. Although some of these street-lighting projects preceded Jeffery's original work, his 1971 book would announce that this type of strategy clearly would not be sufficient for crime prevention.

Nevertheless, when NILECJ allocated the majority of its $31-million budget for fiscal 1973 on large-scale research projects aimed at goals such as reducing opportunities for crime, the main thrust of its efforts was on target hardening approaches such as increased building security, burglar alarms, and more street lighting and architectural design changes. Other LEAA Newsletters were devoted to grants awarded for target hardening approaches, including one in Tyler, Texas, which focused on "making burglary harder" (LEAA Newsletter, 1973, 3, 3:6).

Later editions of the LEAA Newsletter (1973 3, 3:12) noted that LEAA earmarked $2 million for a defensible space project and would invite other federal agencies (Department of Housing and Urban Development, National Science Foundation, Education and Welfare, and the Department of Transportation) to participate in founding a "Program for Crime Prevention Through Environmental Design" that would eventually initiate studies to be conducted by the Westinghouse Electric Corporation of Baltimore, Maryland. This program would focus on residential, school, and commercial environments. Although obviously borrowing Jeffery's title, it was based on Newman's ideas of defensible space rather than Jeffery's CPTED model (e.g., see Jeffery, 1977:225). Thus, these projects were discussed in the section on defensible space earlier in the chapter.

In the most heralded crime prevention study ever done, John Eck (1997) summarized the findings related to crime and place and makes this same conclusion. For example, he asked this perplexing question: "How much can we conclude about specific types of intervention, at specific places, against specific crimes? The answer is, we usually cannot be confident about what works where" (p. 3). The reason this is so is because most evaluative studies of the effects of place-specific prevention efforts are conducted at only one site, many of the studies investigate the effects of not one but numerous interventions that were put into place at the same time, and the studies were not rigorous enough to allow for firm conclusions.

The study summarized findings from research in the following areas:

1. Residential places;
2. Money-spending places (retail stores, banks and money-handling businesses, and bars and drinking establishments);
3. Transportation places (e.g., public transportation facilities, parking lots, and airports);
4. Other public places (e.g., open urban spaces and public coin machines).

The study found that "as of yet, there are no place-focused crime prevention programs proved to be ineffective. However, relative to other areas of crime prevention, few place-focused crime prevention methods have been studied by criminologists in the United States" (Sherman et al., 1998:9). The findings of the study are summarized in Table 4.1.

TABLE 4.1   Summary of Place-Specific Findings

	WORKS	DOES NOT WORK	PROMISING	UNKNOWN
Residential	Nuisance abatement			Target hardening Restricting movement Guards CCTV Cocoon watch Property marking
C.ommercial Stores			Multiple clerks Store design	EAS CCTV Target hardening Frequent inventory counts Prohibiting offenders Electronic monitoring Ink tags Guards Cameras Restricting movement
Banking and money handling				Cameras Target hardening Guards
Bars and taverns			Server training	
Transport Public transportation				Removing targets Rapid cleanup Design Informal watching CCTV Guards Restricting movement
Parking lots				
Airports			Metal detectors Guards	
Public Settings Open spaces			Street closures	CCTV Prohibiting offenders Controlling drinking Lighting
Public facilities			Target hardening	Removing targets Signs

Problems and Criticisms of Theory

Not once during the entire 1970s did C. Ray Jeffery's name appear in any edition of the LEAA Newsletter when CPTED was discussed. As noted by Murray (1994:583), Jeffery (1971) antedated Newman and "originated the acronym CPTED... which has remained a common label in the technical literature but (for obvious reasons) never grabbed the public imagination in the way that 'defensible space' did." Murray did not explain what those "obvious reasons" were, but Jeffery (personal communication, September 20, 1996) stated that he re-read his 1971 edition of *Crime Prevention Through Environmental Design* in order to try to understand why "no one paid any attention to it," and he reasoned that it was because of his call for more research and the foundation of a crime-related research institute at a time when people were looking for practical applications for preventing crime. Jeffery's original work in 1971 contained no detailed recipes for crime prevention at a time when government leaders were looking for them and giving wide publicity to those they found (Jeffery personal communication, September 20, 1996; also see Jeffery and Zahm, 1993:330).

By contrast, other works related to CPTED, such as Newman's book in 1972, included specific suggestions for how to reduce crime—at least in public housing facilities—through such techniques as lowering building height, lowering the number of apartments sharing a common hallway, increasing lobby visibility, and altering entrance design and site layout to enhance surveillability (also see National Crime Prevention Institute, 1986:122–123 for other specific architectural guidelines based on Newman's defensible space approach to crime prevention). Such suggestions were promulgated by widely recognized publishing firms and in government documents. As a result, Jeffery (personal communication, March 28, 1996) has said that he could "only scream and holler for funding" while all the money went to defensible space research, to projects like those discussed above. Because Newman argued that physical environments could be designed in order to "encourage residents to assume the behavior necessary for deterring crime" (Wallis, 1980:2), his work fit with a popular sentiment about people helping themselves. As noted by Newman (1973:1), "the physical mechanisms we have isolated as contributing to the creation of defensible space have the purpose of *enabling inhabitants* to themselves assume primary authority for insuring safe, well-maintained residential areas" (emphasis added). Ideas related to crime prevention are more likely to be well received when they include or revolve around provisions that allow citizens to play meaningful roles. This may be the same reason that community-oriented policing is so widely practiced in law enforcement today: It focuses on developing a partnership between the police and the community, where citizens take an active role in problem solving (e.g., see Fleissner and Heinzelmann, 1996; Wrobleski and Hess, 1993).

As CPTED now exists in government, architecture, academia, and corporate business, little if any consideration is given to the internal, physical environment of the offender. Rather, attention is given only to the external physical environment of the place. In academia particularly, CPTED has been developed only with regard to the external environment, which usually is not even treated as physical, but instead as some set of abstract social factors. This is ironic given our discussion of criminological theory in Chapter 1. Most criminologists study only the offender; place-oriented or environmental criminologists tend to study only the place of crime.

When the internal environment of the offender or victim is taken into account, it is typically treated as non-physical or "mental" (see the discussion of crime mapping theory later in this chapter). This is a serious limitation of the current body of CPTED literature. Rather than arguing for a primary crime prevention model aimed at identifying conditions both in the external environment of the place *and* in the internal environment of the offender, CPTED research based on rational choice, opportunity, routine activity theory, or crime pattern theory (all discussed in the chapter) leads to crime prevention projects aimed at reducing *opportunities* for *rational* offenders through increasing surveillance, deterrence, target hardening and removal, access control, and so forth. Instead of leading to complete CPTED projects, they have led to projects related to CPTED that assume a rational offender who seeks to maximize utility, benefit, or pleasure and to minimize cost or loss of pain.

According to Clarke (1995a:3), interest in CPTED research did decline in the 1980s because Newman's ideas had been dismissed as "environmental determinism" and many thought he oversimplified the problem of crime by neglecting important social causes (e.g., poverty, unemployment, and racism). Moreover, CPTED studies were not proving to be very effective, and some scholars at the time began to question whether the causes of crime were beyond the control of CPTED (Clarke, 1995a:4). Thus, relative to other crime prevention measures, such as *situational crime prevention* (discussed below), CPTED support by governmental agencies declined:

> In Britain as well as in some other European countries, situational prevention has become an integral part of government policy. In the United States, comparatively less success has been enjoyed by CPTED because of the failure of some ambitious projects funded by the federal government and also . . . because CPTED, unlike situational prevention, has generally been confined to projects involving buildings and facilities. (Clarke, 1992:6)

Examples of the failed CPTED projects discussed by Clarke include the Westing-house projects discussed above, aimed at reducing crime in other types of physical environments. These were troublesome to implement and proved meager in terms of crime prevention (Murray, 1994:354) because they attempted to extend the defensible space concept to inappropriate areas such as school and commercial sites where "'territorial' behavior is much less natural than in the residential context" (Clarke, 1995b:97). According to Murray (1994:354): "In retrospect, it seems to have been a mistake to apply defensible space and territorial concepts in environments where a broader conception of CPTED would have been more appropriate." It seems very ironic now that it was Jeffery who has been arguing all along for a conception of CPTED that is *broader* than Newman's notion of defensible space. Changes to the external environment should be only a part of a larger crime control package in order to be effective (Murray, 1994:354). This was Jeffery's argument in his 1971, 1977, and 1990 books.

These failing CPTED measures led Murray (1994:354) to claim that no strategies exist for altering the built environment that will reduce crime, and the lesson is that it all depends on the specific *situation*. This lesson no doubt influenced the development of *situational crime prevention*, discussed below (Clarke, 1983).

SITUATIONAL CRIME PREVENTION

Major Hypotheses

Situational crime prevention is aimed at eliminating opportunities for crime. It includes opportunity-reducing measures that are "directed at highly specific forms of crime . . . that involve the management, design or manipulation of the immediate environment in as systematic and permanent way as possible . . . so as to increase the effort and risks of crime and reduce the rewards as perceived by a wide range of offenders" (Clarke, 1992:3–4).

Situational crime prevention (Clarke, 1983) is practiced by crime prevention units within central governments of Holland and Great Britain and semiautonomous governmental agencies in countries such as Sweden (Clarke, 1995b:92). The situational crime prevention model originated from lessons learned from research on correctional treatments by the British government's Home Office Research Unit that demonstrated the potential for designing out misbehavior by manipulating situational factors in the immediate environment of institutions (Clarke, 1992:4–5; also see Clarke, 1995b:94–96; Clarke and Cornish, 1985).

This research, combined with the "the action research model," in which researchers and practitioners work together to analyze and define problems, identify and implement possible solutions, and evaluate results (Clarke, 1992:5), led to the

TABLE 4.2   Situational Crime Prevention Techniques

INCREASE THE EFFORT	INCREASE THE RISKS	REDUCE THE REWARDS	REDUCE PROVOCATIONS	REMOVE THE EXCUSES
1. Harden Targets immobilizers in cars anti-robbery screens	*6. Extend guardianship* cocooning neighborhood watch	*11. Conceal targets* gender-neutral phone directories off-street parking	*16. Reduce frustration and stress* efficient queuing soothing lighting	*21. Set rules* rental agreements hotel registration
2. Control access to facilities alley-gating entry phones	*7. Assist natural surveillance* improved street lighting neighborhood watch hotlines	*12. Remove targets* removable car radios pre-paid public phone cards	*17. Avoid disputes* fixed cab fares reduce crowding in pubs	*22. Post instructions* "No parking" "Private property"
3. Screen exits tickets needed electronic tags for libraries	*8. Reduce anonymity* taxi driver ID's "how's my driving?" signs	*13. Identify property* property marking vehicle licensing	*18. Reduce emotional arousal* controls on violent porn prohibit pedophiles working with children	*23. Alert conscience* roadside speed display signs "shoplifting is stealing"
4. Deflect offenders street closures in red light district separate toilets for women	*9. Utilize place managers* train employees to prevent crime support whistle blowers	*14. Disrupt markets* checks on pawn brokers licensed street vendors	*19. Neutralize peer pressure* "idiots drink and drive" "it's ok to say no"	*24. Assist compliance* little bins public lavatories
5. Control tools/weapons toughened beer glasses photos on credit cards	*10. Strengthen formal surveillance* speed cameras CCTV in town centers	*15. Deny benefits* ink merchandise tags graffiti cleaning	*20. Discourage imitation* rapid vandalism repair V-chips in TV's	*25. Control drugs/alcohol* breathalyzers in pubs alcohol-free events

Source: www.popcenter.org

development of the theory underlying situational crime prevention, as well as the standard methodology it uses (Clarke, 1995b:91). According to Clarke, the concept of situational crime prevention was "soon influenced by two independent (Jeffery, 1977), but nonetheless related strands of policy research in the United States"—defensible space (Newman, 1972a) and CPTED (Jeffery, 1971)—"both of which had preceded situational prevention, but, because of the transatlantic delay in the dissemination of ideas, had not been the spur to its development." Later, situational crime prevention was influenced by the notion of "problem-oriented policing" (e.g., Goldstein, 1979), an approach aimed at identifying and solving the problems of particular communities rather than waiting for those problems to result in criminal behavior, which is viewed as a symptom of the underlying problems (e.g., see Wrobleski and Hess, 1993).

Clarke (1992:7) has written that situational crime prevention is broader than CPTED, because the former "encompasses the entire range of environments (and objects) involved in crime and because it encompasses legal and management as well as design solutions," while CPTED "tends to be focused on design of the built environment" (also see Fleissner and Heinzelmann, 1996:1). This may be true in terms of how CPTED has been applied to physical design in a comprehensive, planned way (National Crime Prevention Institute, 1986:123). Yet, Jeffery's CPTED model has evolved beyond these strategies to include both the external environment of the place *and* the internal environment of the offender. Clarke (1992:6) acknowledged that Jeffery's (1977) volume argued for a crime prevention approach that "took due account of both genetic predisposition and the physical environment." Therefore, Jeffery's theoretical concept of CPTED is actually broader than situational crime prevention, for Jeffery discusses crime prevention strategies that involve both the external environment of the place and the internal environment of the offender. Situational crime prevention only takes into account the nature of the external physical environment of the place (e.g., see Clarke, 1992, 1995b:109) and makes inferences to the offender based on what must be going on in the offender's mind. Offenders are treated as a homogenous group of *rational* beings. The internal environment of the offender is treated as mental instead of physical.

Table 4.2 illustrates the types of approaches available in situational crime prevention. As you can see, there are 25 different ways to reduce opportunities for crime through situational crime prevention. The five major categories of situational crime prevention include increasing the effort for offenders; increasing the risks of crime; reducing the rewards of crime; reducing provocations for crime; and removing excuses for crime. Examples of each type are provided in the table.

Major Findings

Scholars involved in founding and developing situational crime prevention in theory and evaluating it in the real world celebrate its many successes. For example, Weisburd (1997:7) mentions that "an array of applied studies point to the success of situational measures in reducing crime and crime-related problems." Ronald Clarke (2001:7), its founder, claimed "more than 100 documented successes" including the following:

- Street closing in London to prevent prostitution in cars;
- Identification requirements to prevent check frauds in Sweden in the 1980s;
- Improved street lighting in council housing estates in England;
- Responsible drinking practices to control public drunkenness in Australia;
- Cash reduction in U.S. convenience stores;
- Worldwide airport baggage screening;
- CCTV in British town centers;
- Automatic cameras at traffic lights in Scotland;
- Graffiti cleaning on the New York subway; and
- Anti-robbery screens in London post offices.

Clarke's book *Situational Crime Prevention: Successful Case Studies* (1997) contains 23 of these success stories. Most of the successful crime prevention initiatives concern relatively minor types of crimes and tend to be those committed against either private corporations or public facilities with private interests. However, Clarke (2001:17) claimed,

> When first developed [situational crime prevention] was mainly used in reducing opportunities for conventional 'street' crimes of robbery, burglary, vandalism and car theft. . . . It has since been applied in a wider variety of contexts. It has been used in commercial settings to reduce crimes such as shoplifting, fare evasion, and thefts by employees. It has helped to reduce drunkenness and disorder at sporting events, in nightlife districts and in city centers. And it has been deployed against crimes committed by ordinary people such as tax and welfare frauds, sexual harassment and driving offenses.

Weisburd (1997:8) did point out, in agreement with the earlier summary by John Eck, that "in most of these studies, the methods of evaluation used meet only minimal technical standards, follow up is often short, and reliable control groups are generally absent." He also suggested that in some areas of situational crime prevention, such as problem-oriented policing, "the rhetoric of success has clearly outstripped the empirical evidence available" (p. 11). Even so, virtually everyone is satisfied that situational crime prevention works to reduce crime, perhaps because it so strongly appeals to our common sense.

Problems and Criticisms of Theory

Like most theories that underlie the practice of crime prevention, situational crime prevention ignores the offender. In fact, it views the offender as irrelevant because it does not address offender motivation. As we noted above, situational crime prevention efforts assume that offenders are rational and can be deterred by altering the physical environment. To the degree that situational crime prevention is a theory, it leads to circular reasoning, which we defined earlier. Situational crime prevention assumes rationality of offenders without ever actually measuring it, and only infers offender rationality based on crime rate changes that may or may not be affiliated with changes to the physical environment.

One significant limitation of situational crime prevention is that it protects commercial interests, meaning it is "pro status quo." Large businesses and governments can protect their assets without having to actually do the dirty work of trying to change the conditions in the environment that cause (or more accurately, increase the risk of) criminality. If you believe that one of the basic obligations of government is to protect its citizens—not only from crime but also from harmful conditions that lead to crime—situational crime prevention is inconsistent with this goal. Instead of addressing the root causes of crime, it merely removes opportunities for it thus never affecting the level of motivation in offenders.

To this charge, Felson and Clarke (1998:1) respond,

> Criminological theory has long seemed irrelevant to those who have to deal with offenders in the real world. This irrelevance seems partly from attributing the causes of crime to distant factors, such as child-rearing practices, genetic makeup, and psychological or social processes. These are mostly beyond the reach of everyday practice, and their combination is extremely complicated for those who want to understand crime, much less do something about it.

As we showed in Chapter 1 of this text, crimes require more than just offenders, they also must include a place or setting. Felson and Clarke (1998:1) assert, "Most criminological theory pays attention only to the first, asking why certain people might be more criminally inclined or less so. This neglects the second, the important features of each setting that help to translate criminal inclinations into action."

Situational crime prevention aims not to change criminal inclinations, except by altering opportunities to commit crime. As Felson and Clarke (1998:1) explain, "To be sure, no single cause of crime is sufficient to guarantee its occurrence; yet opportunity above all others is necessary and therefore has as much or more claim to being a 'root cause.' "

Finally, it was originally believed that efforts to remove or change the situational inducements to crime would simply move crime rather than actually prevent it—called *displacement*. This would be a serious limitation to situational crime prevention. According to most of the evidence, displacement does not appear to be a reality. Those crimes that are displaced do not seem to equal those that are prevented. Additionally, there is evidence of a *diffusion of benefits*—when efforts are made to prevent a single type of crime, other types of crime also are prevented. The issues of displacement and diffusion are discussed in Chapter 6.

One of the benefits of studying the relationship between opportunity and crime is that opportunities for crime can be mapped and studied using crime mapping software. Figure 4.5 illustrates how opportunities are related to crime. In this case, you see that low levels of household occupancy are related to higher criminal

Level of Occupation

- very high
- high
- average
- low
- very low

FIGURE 4.5   Daytime Occupation of Homes and Burglary Incident Locations

victimization. The more time one spends at home, the less likely he or she is to be victimized by crime, which is a key finding of routine activity theory. Criminologists believe this to be true.

ROUTINE ACTIVITY THEORY

Major Hypotheses

According to the original statement of *routine activity theory*, crime results from the convergence of three elements in time and space: a presence of likely or motivated offenders; a presence of suitable targets; and an absence of capable guardians to prevent the criminal act (Cohen and Felson, 1979:588).

A *likely offender* includes anyone with an inclination to commit a crime (Felson, 1983:666). A *suitable target* includes any person or thing that may evoke criminal inclinations, which would include the actual value of the target and the monetary and symbolic desirability of it for offenders, the visibility to offenders or their informants, the access to it, the ease of escape from the site, as well as the portability or mobility of objects sought by offenders (Felson, 1983:666). A *guardian* is a person who can protect a target (Eck and Weisburd, 1995:5), including friends and formal authorities such as police and security personnel, *intimate handlers* such as parents, teachers, coaches, friends, employers, and *place managers* such as janitors and apartment managers (e.g., see Eck, 1994; Eck and Weisburd, 1995:5, 6, 55; Felson, 1986, 1995:21). Eck (1994) writes that potential targets are supervised by guardians, potential offenders by handlers, and potential places of crime by place managers. The guardian, handler, and manager must be absent or ineffective from the potential target, the potential handler, and the place, respectively, for crime to occur (Eck and Weisburd, 1995:21).

An *absence of capable guardians* can be produced by average citizens going about their daily life (Felson, 1983:666). In fact, the most important guardians are ordinary citizens going about their daily routines (Felson, 1994:31). The typical guardian is not a police officer or security guard in most cases, but is a neighbor, friend, relative, bystander, or owner of property (Clarke and Felson, 1993:3). This means that routine activities of potential victims can not only facilitate criminal victimization, but they may also prevent it.

The term *routine activities* means "any recurrent and prevalent activities which provide for basic population and individual needs, whatever their biological or cultural origins . . . including formalized work, leisure, social interaction, learning . . . which occur at home, in jobs away from home, and in other activities away from home" (Cohen and Felson, 1979:593). Routine activities are the means people use to satisfy their needs, which are specific to their lifestyles. When these routine activities are performed within or near the home, lower risks of property crime are expected because they enhance guardianship capabilities (Cohen and Felson, 1979:594; Felson, 1983:667; Felson, 1987:125–126). That is, because higher levels of guardianship increase the likelihood that offenders will be seen, the risk of criminal victimization is reduced.

Routine activity theory was used by Cohen and Felson (1979) to explain rising crime rates in the United States. Other theories, according to the authors, could not account for the rise. Cohen and Felson explained that crime rates could vary without actual changes in the number of potential offenders or offender motivations. For example, with more women in the workplace, a greater number of homes would be left unguarded, meaning that burglary would increase. Felson and Clarke (1998:5) put forth the acronym VIVA to clarify the four elements that influence a target's risk of being victimized by crime. They are *value, inertia, visibility,* and *access.* Value refers to what the target is worth to the offender—items high in value are more attractive. Inertia refers to the ability of a target to be taken—those that can be taken more easily are more attractive. Visibility refers to how easily targets are seen by offenders—more visible targets are more vulnerable. Access refers to how easily targets can be accessed by offenders—more accessible items are more vulnerable. Each of these elements is important to routine activity theory and can lead to increases in crime without any change in the offender population.

Routine activity theory also points to factors unique to lifestyles or potential offenders and victims as these are affected by larger social processes. The importance of victim lifestyles is also indicated by the *lifestyle/exposure theory*, which was developed by Hindelang, Gottfredson, and Garofalo (1978:243). This model of criminal events links victimization risks to the daily activities of specific individuals, especially potential victims (Goldstein, 1994:54; Kennedy and Forde, 1990a:208).

Lifestyles are patterned, regular, recurrent, prevalent, or "routine activities" (Robinson, 1997). Lifestyles consist of the activities that people engage in on a daily basis, including both *obligatory activities* and *discretionary activities.* LeBeau and Coulson (1996:3; also see LeBeau and Corcoran, 1990) assert that "The former are activities that *must* be undertaken while the latter because they are pursued by choice are called discretionary. An activity is discretionary if there is a greater chance of *choice* than constraint, and obligatory if there is a greater degree of constraint than choice" (Chapin, 1974:38).

The lifestyle/exposure model suggests that lifestyles, which encompass differences in various demographic factors (e.g., age, sex, marital status, family income, and race), affect daily routines of people and thus vulnerability to criminal victimization (Kennedy and Forde, 1990a:208). Because lifestyles vary, victimization is not evenly distributed across space and time (Garofalo, 1987:26). Specifically, lifestyles influence a person's exposure to places and times with differing risks of victimization and frequency of associations with potential offenders. A similar theoretical model developed by Kennedy and Forde (1990a:209, 211) suggests that background characteristics affect time spent in risky activities that lead to dangerous results (i.e., criminal victimization).

Major Findings

A large body of research illustrates relationships between routine activities, victim lifestyles, and criminal victimization. In the original study of routine activity theory, Cohen and Felson (1979:600) find that daytime burglaries increased over time along with time spent outside of home during the day. Additionally, Miethe, Stafford, and Long (1987:192) find that persons with low daytime and nighttime activities outside of the home have the lowest risk of property victimization, and people who find themselves away from the home due to daytime and nighttime activities have the highest risks of crime victimization.

Overall, the findings from routine activity research indicate that the risk of criminal victimization varies "among the circumstances and locations in which people place themselves and their property" (Cohen and Felson, 1979:595). Specifically, Cohen and Felson (1979:596) claim that victimization rates vary inversely with age and are lower for people with "less active" statuses such as keeping house, being unable to work, being retired, and so forth. However, Cohen and Felson did not actually measure activity levels associated with each status. In fact, lifestyles or routine activities of potential victims are typically inferred from demographic variables; they are rarely directly measured (Akers, 1994; Kennedy and Forde, 1990; Maxfield, 1987; Miethe, Stafford, and Long, 1987; Moriarty and Williams, 1996; Sampson and Wooldredge, 1987). One study of note which actually measured routine activities directly through on-site observations found support for the proposition that increased activity around residences is associated with a lower risk of burglary victimization (Robinson, 1999).

Numerous studies have shown relationships between daily activities of individuals and their likelihood of criminal victimization (Riley, 1987:340). In other words, what people do and how they behave places them at either more or less risk of criminal victimization (Maxfield, 1987; Miethe, Stafford, and Long, 1987; Sampson and Wooldredge, 1987). According to Sampson and Wooldredge (1987:372), an active lifestyle increases victimization risk by increasing the likelihood that potential offenders will find suitable targets with low levels of guardianship. An active lifestyle may not necessarily increase one's risk of criminal victimization. For example, if there is a great deal of activity by residents, neighbors, or passersby around a residence, then this activity may serve to decrease the likelihood that a property offender will victimize a residence. In fact, many property offenders are nonconfrontational and want to avoid being seen by residents, neighbors, or passersby (Cromwell, Olson, and Avary, 1991; Tunnell, 1994; Wright and Decker, 1994).

Recent research is highly supportive of routine activity theory. Studies find that as time away from home increases, so too does the risk of household burglary (Groff, 2007). Generally, the more suitable opportunities present for offending, the higher the risk of criminal victimization. Some of the factors that make targets more attractive are physical (such as unoccupied residences), while others are social (such as unstructured socializing of young people). Studies show that if parents do not supervise their kids effectively (a form of guardianship), children are more likely to socialize with their peers in unsupervised settings, which is associated with rates of delinquency (Osgood and Anderson, 2004). Further, low levels of guardianship of youth are associated with higher risks of assault and robbery victimization among rural youth (Spano and Nagy, 2005). Even pleasant weather is found to be associated with higher rates of crime, for it presumably increases the suitability of targets for criminal victimization because people are more likely to be out and about (Hipp et al., 2004). This has been verified for virtually every type of crime, including crimes against agricultural equipment, crops, and livestock in rural areas (Mears, Scott, and Bhai, 2007). Similarly, the risk of criminal victimization is lower when targets are made less suitable due to factors such as heightened surveillability and occupancy (Coupe and Blake, 2006).

Both lifestyle/exposure and routine activity theories can be considered as subsets of a more general *opportunity model* (Cohen, Kluegel, and Land, 1981; Sampson and Wooldredge, 1987) and can be interpreted with *rational choice theory.* For more on these approaches, see the Focus On box. Garofalo (1987:27) pointed out the basic differences between the two approaches, noting that they "relate to how they were explicated by their authors rather than to difference in substance." For example, Cohen and Felson (1979) utilized aggregate measures of routine activities and linked them to changes in crime rates over time, while Hindelang, Gottfredson, and Garofalo (1978) related differences in lifestyles of population segments at one point in time to differential victimization rates.

FOCUS ON
OPPORTUNITY AND RATIONAL CHOICE THEORIES

Rational choice theory examines offender decision making and the factors that affect it such as assessments of risks, rewards, and morality of various behaviors (Clarke, 1983:232). The balance between likely risks and rewards influences offenders' target selections. According to Brantingham and Brantingham (1984), the level of risk is one of the factors that make a target "good" or "bad." Offenders plan to reduce the level of risk associated with committing criminal offenses through selecting the most suitable targets. Taylor and Harrell (1996:2) claimed that offenders often behave in a rational fashion, because they choose to commit crimes that require little effort, but which provide high rewards and pose low risks of painful consequences. Hickey (1991) and Wright and Rossi (1983) discussed how even violent criminals are selective in their choices of targets: Serial killers rarely choose weight lifters or martial arts experts as victims. Other violent criminals rarely choose armed victims; they pose too much of a risk (Siegel, 1995). The mere fact that victims are not chosen at random suggests a rational offender (Fattah, 1993:244).

Of course, to conclude that offenders are rational based on their behaviors, and then to utilize the concept of rationality in order to explain the same behaviors, constitutes the logical error of circular reasoning (e.g., see Akers, 1994:8). For instance, Jeffery and Zahm (1993:339) noted that the concept of choice "is neither empirical nor observable, and the investigator can only know when an individual has made a choice when he behaves in a given way. From the observed behavior, the investigator inputs a cause (such as rational choice or social control)." Jeffery and Zahm (1993:337) went on to note that because the heart of the rational choice model is focused on "an analysis of the thought or cognitive means by which individuals process information from the environment" (Jeffery and Zahm, 1993:337), it is not possible to test the theory directly. Thoughts cannot be studied directly, they can only be verbalized by offenders. As explained above, verbal statements constitute verbal *behavior*, not the thought processes they are portrayed to represent by rational choice theorists. These problems with rational choice theory make interpretations of findings within such a framework questionable at best.

Opportunity theory holds that criminal behavior most often reflects offenders' exploitations of perceived opportunities. Opportunity theory can generally be understood in terms of the number of targets available for crime (Fattah, 1993:248). Cook (1986) defined opportunity theory as "the interaction of victims and offenders in relation to targets" that are viewed by offenders as "opportunities" when they are "attractive because of a high payoff and little risk" (Jeffery and Zahm, 1993:335). Of course, much environmental research can be interpreted using both rational choice and opportunity theory, for "rational" involves evaluation of opportunity (Cornish and Clarke, 1986). The concept of opportunity is central to the rational choice perspective (Fattah, 1993:248); the rational choice perspective views crime as a function of opportunity, where the opportunity structure is determined by contacts in the physical external environment (Fattah, 1993:236, 239).

Interpretation of research findings with opportunity theory can be tautological, for they often translate into a statement such as "this victim was at higher risk because he or she or it offered a better or more suitable opportunity to the offender," where higher risks and better opportunity mean the same thing. This theory cannot *explain* why a particular offender thought the target was better or more suitable, or what caused the offender to have criminal motivations in the first place and then act on them. In Chapter 5, we turn to the issue of offender site selection.

Problems and Criticisms of Theory

Like situational crime prevention in practice, the routine activity theory on which it is partially based also neglects the criminal offender. Even though motivated offenders are part of the model, rarely do tests of the theory directly measure offender motivation.

Perhaps even more problematic is that there have actually been only a handful of studies that actually directly measure the key concepts of the theory (Robinson, 1999). In their original formulation of the theory, Cohen and Felson (1979:600) wrote, "The limitations of annual time series data do not allow construction of direct measures of changes in hourly activity patterns, or quantities, qualities and movements of exact stocks of household durable goods." In other words, Cohen and Felson did not find available data or collect new data that would allow them to test their theory directly.

These data are still not widely available today. Cohen and Cantor (1980:145) concluded that "many of the data needed to operationalize and rigorously test the routine activities approach to criminal victimization are not yet available." As a result, surrogate demographic variables are used in their place (e.g., see Messner and Tardiff, 1985). This led Massey, Krohn, and Bonati (1989:383) to conclude that previous research has relied too heavily on "social demographic factors as proxy indicators of 'suitable targets' and 'capable guardians.'" For example, Cohen and Felson (1979) used employment and marital status as indicators of routine activities rather than measuring them directly (Kennedy and Forde, 1990a:208). Cohen and Felson never measured the amount of time individuals spend in different types of places in order to relate it to lifestyle variations and risk of criminal victimization. Rather, they explained national crime trends with national trends in presumed places of routine activities.

Cohen and Felson created the "household activity ratio" as an estimate of the "proportion of American households in year 't' expected to be most highly exposed to risk of personal and property victimization due to the dispersion of their activities away from family and household and/or their likelihood of owning extra sets of durables subject to high risk of attack" (Cohen and Felson, 1979:601). The logic of this measure as an indication of a level of "guardianship" present in the home is that households in which someone is home most of the time are less likely to be victimized (Stahura and Sloan III, 1988:1107). This household activity measure was calculated as the number of married, husband-present female labor force participants plus the number of non-husband-wife households divided by the total number of households in the United States.

According to Massey, Krohn, and Bonati (1989:380), the "household activity ratio was intended to measure the dispersion of activities away from the household (guardianship) and/or the likelihood of owning extra sets of durable goods that would be suitable targets," or "the extent to which households are 'unprotected' by continuous occupancy" (Stahura and Sloan III, 1988:1107). Massey, Krohn, and Bonati (1989:380) referred to this measure as a "creative" one, but stated that it confounds the two dimensions of guardianship and target suitability.

Stahura and Sloan (1988:1102) measured criminal opportunities with aggregate measures of employment concentration and percentage of multiple housing, and guardianship with aggregate measures of police employment, police expenditure, and female labor force nonparticipation. Clearly, these measures are not direct measures of what they are intended to represent.

A study by Robinson (1999) measured routine activities directly by observing them on-site. Residents' schedules and traffic patterns were observed and related to criminal victimization risk. Surveys of people's activities and observations of pedestrian and automotive traffic patterns around their residences showed that there was an inverse relationship between levels of surveillability (potential witnesses to crime) and burglary rates; that is, the higher the levels of pedestrian and automotive traffic, the lower the risk of burglary. This study is the exception rather than the rule, however. Recall our earlier discussions of traffic patterns and burglary suggesting that less pedestrian traffic generally means higher risks of burglary victimization.

CRIME PATTERN THEORY

Major Hypotheses

Crime pattern theory is focused on the criminal event, which is "an opportune cross-product of law, offender motivation, and target characteristic arrayed on an environmental backcloth at a particular point in space-time" (Brantingham and Brantingham, 1993a:259). It is therefore an attempt to address and correct what Brantingham and Brantingham call "the primary weakness in most criminological theory," which is "a tendency to equate criminality with crime even when criminality is but one of the elements contributing to a criminal event."

Crime pattern theory is a combination of the complementary work of many parts of an alternative movement in criminology which focuses on the criminal event itself or on patterns of crime and criminal behavior including: rational choice theory; routine activity theory; environmental criminology (e.g., Brantingham and Brantingham, 1981, 1984, 1991a); strategic analysis (Cusson, 1983); and lifestyle/exposure theory. It also includes application of other ideas, such as CPTED, situational crime prevention, hot spot analysis (e.g., Block, 1990), and opportunity theories.

The reason Brantingham and Brantingham (1993a:261–264) grouped together these "theoretical, research, and practical approaches to the study of crime," despite their variation in content and focus, is because of their commonalities. These include the following:

1. They view the criminal event as the end point in a decision process or sequence of decision steps;
2. The decision process or sequence of decision steps is rational;

3. The decisions themselves are neither random nor unpredictable (also see Brantingham and Brantingham, 1978; Clarke and Cornish, 1985; Cusson, 1983; Willmer, 1970);
4. The decision process begins with an offender who is ready for crime (who has sufficient motivation and knowledge to commit the crime);
5. Criminal motivations and states of readiness come from diverse sources;
6. Whether the offender's state of readiness leads to crime is a function of environmental factors, such as available opportunities;
7. The number and sequence of decision points in the process that lead to a criminal event vary with the type and quantity of crime (also see Brantingham and Brantingham, 1978), such that the decision process is crime-specific;
8. The level of crime readiness in any offender varies over time and place given his or her background and site-specific features;
9. Neither motivated offenders nor opportunities for crime are uniformly distributed in space and time;
10. Opportunities for crime are developed by routine activities of daily life (e.g., commuting patterns during the week and leisure activities on weekends);
11. How suitable a target is, is a function of the characteristics of the target and the characteristics of the target's surroundings;
12. The target identification process (e.g., what makes a good or bad target) is a multi-staged process contained within a general environment;
13. Individuals develop images about what surrounds them, which make up "templates," or "an aggregate, holistic image that is not always easily analyzed or understood by fragmenting it into discrete parts," and which is "formed by developing an array of cues, cue sequences, and cue clusters that identify what should be considered a 'good' target in specific cites and situations" (also see Brantingham and Brantingham, 1978; Cromwell, Olson, and Avary, 1991; Macdonald and Gifford, 1989);
14. These templates vary by specific crimes, offenders, and the general context for the crime, such that what makes a good target for one type of crime and offender may not for another; and finally,
15. Each of these approaches sees crime as complex, but still "finds discernible patterns both for crimes and for criminals at both detailed and general levels of analysis." Thus, they all see that "Crimes are patterned; decisions to commit crimes are patterned; and the process of committing a crime is patterned."

Brantingham and Brantingham (1993a:266–268) developed crime pattern theory in order to describe the process whereby a criminal event occurs. Essentially, it starts with a person acting or behaving in some manner (including engaging in legitimate acts or behaviors). With the presence of some event, the desire or willingness to engage in crime is "triggered." This triggering event leads to an offender search, which can be minimal or broader depending on such factors as how well the offender knows the area. This search, depending on the availability of suitable targets, may result in the criminal event. For example, a person (e.g., a potential offender) walks through a neighborhood and sees that no one is home in the entire area. In this case, the offender noticing that no cars are parked in the driveways of any of the houses is a triggering event. This triggering event leads the potential offender to conduct a cursory search of various homes for signs of easy access and signs that there will be valuable yet transportable property inside. When the potential offender sees such a target, he or she then commits the crime.

The three main concepts of crime pattern theory are nodes, paths, and edges. *Nodes* refer to where people travel to and from (e.g., home, work, store, etc.). *Paths* are the main areas of travel between these nodes (e.g., the streets and sidewalks on which people travel to and from home and work). Finally, *edges* are the boundaries of areas where people engage in their activities (e.g., the neighborhoods and cities where people spend their time). These terms are diagramed in Figure 4.6. Imagine how nodes, paths, and edges affect crime risks. Their relation to offender site selection is discussed in Chapter 5.

According to Brantingham and Brantingham (1993a:268), the criminal event process "rests on a general backcloth formed by routine activities and on a template that

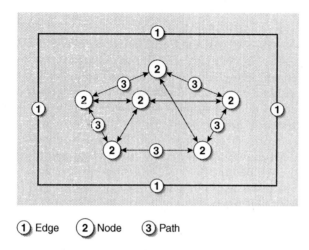

(1) Edge   (2) Node   (3) Path

FIGURE 4.6   Crime Pattern Theory

helps identify what a 'great' chance is or what a 'good' opportunity would be or how to search for chances and opportunities." Because virtually everyone develops "activity routines," or "a set of repetitive processes that organize most of life's actions," they form a "patterned backcloth on which criminal events are played out." This makes it understandable why Eck and Weisburd (1995:6) claimed that the "crime pattern theory" is a combination of rational choice and routine activity theory in an attempt to explain how and why crime is distributed across places.

According to Brantingham and Brantingham (1993a:269), the activity routines of people help shape their activity space, and from that, people develop an *awareness space* ("formed by past activities and shapes the time and location of future activities"). The activity routines of potential offenders define the search patterns of potential offenders, such as burglars (e.g., see Brantingham and Brantingham, 1975; Carter and Hill, 1979; Cromwell, Olson, and Avary, 1991; Maguire, 1982; Rengert and Wasilchick, 1985). Search patterns of potential offenders help determine target selection by offenders. The target selection of offenders "depends on mental templates used to shape searches for targets or victims and to predefine the characteristics of a suitable target or suitable place for finding targets" (Brantingham and Brantingham, 1993a:269). For example, individuals create templates that they use to identify "good" or "bad" targets. In Felson's (1987) terms, a "suitable" target is a "good" target. Additionally, as discussed by Brantingham and Brantingham (1993a:287), templates are used by both potential offenders and all people in society for legitimate purposes such as "for identifying where they want to eat, to live, to shop," because daily "functioning within the infinitely complex cue-emitting environment involves the development of cognitive images and cognitive maps and the use of these images" (also see Garling and Golledge, 1989; Garling et al., 1986; Genereux, Ward, and Russell, 1983).

One factor in the template of the offender is the activity pattern of the victim. According to Brantingham and Brantingham (1993a:270), in order to understand crime patterns, we must at the very least understand these routine activities. The routine activities of potential offenders have effects on both spatial and temporal aspects of offending, because they "generally define both the areas where and the times when they are likely to commit a crime" (Brantingham and Brantingham, 1993a:269). Additionally, the routine activities of potential victims also shape the distribution of crimes by place and time (e.g., see Fattah, 1991; Kennedy and Forde, 1990; Lasley, 1989; Maume, 1989).

Eck and Weisburd (1995:6) noted that the way targets actually come to the attention of potential offenders will influence the distribution of crime over time, space, and among targets. Crime distributions or patterns by place and time can be described and explained by distributions of offenders, targets, handlers, guardians, and managers over place and time. A reasonably rational offender who is engaged in his or her daily routine activities will notice unguarded and unmanaged places where his or her own intimate handlers are not likely to be present, and will be most likely to offend in these areas (Eck and Weisburd, 1995:6).

Crime pattern theory claims that increased numbers of targets and increased attractiveness of those targets (due to decreased effectiveness or lack of presence of handlers, guardians, and managers) are due to changes in society (Eck and Weisburd, 1995:6). Crime pattern theory holds that as offenders go about their normal, legitimate activities, they discover opportunities for legitimate successes (e.g., criminal activity), as well.

Major Findings

According to Felson and Clarke (1998:16), "Crime pattern theorists have described offender movements in terms of a basic search pattern. Starting with a triangle, they consider offenders going from home to work to recreation. Around each of these three nodes and along each of these three paths, offenders look around for criminal opportunities. They may find these a little way off the path, but they usually do not go far beyond the area they know." Offender site selection is discussed more in Chapter 5.

Crime pattern theory can be applied to any crime. Brantingham and Brantingham (1993:276–284) utilized it to explain minor crime (pilfering of office supplies), property crime (household burglary), and violent crime (serial rape). Brantingham and Brantingham (1993:278–282, 288) also applied crime pattern theory to the crime of residential burglary. They started out by discussing the motives for burglary and concluded that it is committed for many reasons, "but thrill seeking and appropriation of goods appear to be the dominant goals behind most burglaries" (e.g., see Bennett and Wright, 1984; Cromwell, Olson, and Avary, 1991; Rengert and Wasilchick, 1985). They then went on to discuss how those potential burglars who are sufficiently ready to commit a household burglary "are often clustered in limited parts of town and have limited access to transport" (e.g., see Baldwin and Bottoms, 1976; Shannon, 1988), such that they have a limited awareness space out of which suitable target templates are constructed. However, Brantingham and Brantingham mentioned that changes in transportation in society should produce "a 'sprawl' of residential burglary" (e.g., see Brantingham and Brantingham, 1981; Brantingham, Brantingham, and Wong, 1991; Burgess, 1925).

According to Brantingham and Brantingham (1993:281), the triggers for crime will vary by the type of individual committing the crime, such that the triggers can be more situational or more planned: "For some, the crime will be immediately opportunistic, triggered by noticing an attractive possibility or by the urging of friends. For others, the crime is more firmly directed at getting money." The type of triggering event affects the type of search that is conducted: For the opportunistic group, the search will more likely be brief. For the other group, the search will be more predictable (e.g., see Brantingham and Brantingham, 1991; Capone and Nichols, 1976; Costanzo, Halperin, and Gale, 1986; Cromwell, Olson, and Avary, 1991; Rengert and Wasilchick, 1985). For more on the Brantinghams, see the Focus On box.

FOCUS ON

PAUL AND PATRICIA BRANTINGHAM

Paul J. Brantingham, B.A. and J.D. (Columbia), Dip. Crim. (Cambridge), a lawyer and criminologist by training, is Professor of Criminology at Simon Fraser University. He was Associate Dean of the Faculty of Interdisciplinary at Simon Fraser during the early 1980s and served as Director of the Simon Fraser Centre for Canadian Studies during 1992. Professor Brantingham was Director of Special Reviews at the Public Service Commission of Canada from 1985 through 1987. He has been a member of the California Bar since 1969.

(continued)

Professor Brantingham is author or editor of more than 20 books and scientific monographs and more than 100 articles and scientific papers. His best known books include *Juvenile Justice Philosophy* (1974, 2nd ed. 1978), and *Environmental Criminology* (1981, 2nd ed. 1991) and *Patterns in Crime* (1984) both co-authored with Patricia Brantingham.

Professor Brantingham has been involved in crime analysis and crime prevention research for more than 20 years. He is one of the co-developers of the primary/secondary/tertiary model of crime prevention now commonly used by criminologists and crime prevention specialists. He is well known for work on offender decision making and on the ways in which the physical environment shapes both the incidence and the fear of crime. He is an expert on legal aid and has served as a special consultant to the Canadian Department of Justice for more than a decade.

Recent research has included study of victimization on university campuses, study of the geography of persistent offending, and study of crime in complex urban ecologies. In 1978 he chaired the national program committee of the American Society of Criminology and has served on that committee several times since. He is currently serving on the executive board of the Western Society of Criminology. He taught at Florida State University prior to joining the School of Criminology at Simon Fraser University. Paul Brantingham is listed in *Who's Who in America*, *Who's Who in American Law*, *Who's Who in the West*, and *American Men and Women of Science*.

Patricia L. Brantingham, A.B. (Barnard College), M.A. (Fordham), M.S. and Ph.D. (Florida State), a mathematician and urban planner by training, is Professor of Criminology, Director of the Institute for Canadian Urban Research Studies, and Co-Director of the Crime Prevention Analysis Laboratory (CPAL) at Simon Fraser University. She served as Director of Programme Evaluation at the Department of Justice Canada from 1985 through 1988. During 1991–1992 she was one of the four members of the Government of British Columbia's special Task Force on Public Order. Dr. Brantingham has conducted fundamental research into the organization and operation of legal aid systems in Canada and elsewhere. Her evaluation of the experimental introduction of a public defender office in British Columbia has had impact throughout the British Commonwealth. Dr. Brantingham has been involved in the development and application of principles of environmental criminology and situational crime prevention for more than two decades. She worked with the Royal Canadian Mounted Police in the development of its standard training course on CPTED and has recently worked with the Architectural Institute of British Columbia and the City of Vancouver in the development of an environmental criminology course for architects and urban planners.

She is internationally known for her work on offender target selection processes and on the geography of crime. Her mathematical work on the distribution of crime in relation to the structure of neighborhoods is fundamental to the field of environmental criminology. Dr. Brantingham's advanced seminar on CPTED features field projects in which teams of students analyze and recommend solutions for discrete crime problems nominated by police departments and planning agencies throughout British Columbia. Recent projects have included redesign of a municipal downtown core; regulation of problems associated with bars and cabarets; reduction of problems associated with video game establishments; and reduction of problems associated with a major transit system. In addition to the *Western Criminology Review*, Dr. Brantingham serves on the editorial boards of many professional and scholarly journals, including the *Journal of Research in Crime and Delinquency* and *Criminometrica*. She has held many offices in the American Society of Criminology.

Dr. Brantingham is the author or editor of two dozen books and scientific monographs and more than 100 articles and scientific papers. Recent books of interest include *Environmental Criminology* (1991) and *Patterns in Crime* (1984). Recent research has looked at the patterns of crime at shopping malls and on transit systems, the distribution of crimes on road networks, and the location of crime in complex urban ecologies. She has been particularly interested in the problem of using computerized mapping techniques for crime prevention analysis. Patricia Brantingham is listed in *Who's Who in America*, *Who's Who in the West*, and *American Men and Women of Science*.

Source: http://wcr.sonoma.edu/eabios.html

Problems and Criticisms of Theory

The main limitation of crime mapping theory is that it has not widely been tested. Thus, its degree of empirical validity is not yet fully understood (Ratcliffe, 2006; Tita and Griffiths, 2005).

Some claim that both adult and juvenile offenders create and utilize holistic templates to help identify suitable targets (e.g., Macdonald and Gifford, 1989). Yet, understandably, no one can effectively describe how to empirically verify such mental templates, being that they apparently exist in the minds of offenders. The only way that they can be verified is through verbal discussions with offenders. As noted by Jeffery and Zahm (1993:337, 339), verbal behavior is just that—behavior. It is not the internal thought processes that the researcher thinks he or she is studying. Both the verbal behavior and the thought process of offenders are under the control of brain, making even the thought processes of offenders physical and not mental. Templates probably do exist, but they exist in the brains of offenders rather than in their minds. In this sense, templates would simply be seen as coded and stored information (i.e., memories), which could be recalled or reconstructed by offenders during the course of a search for suitable targets.

Crime mapping software is potentially very useful for illustrating the key concepts of crime pattern theory. It is possible to map key nodes of activity and the paths of would-be offenders as they travel to and from these locations within the edges of their activity spaces. This is related to offender site selection (discussed in Chapter 5) and which helped lead to the capture of the Washington, D.C., area sniper mentioned in Chapter 1.

Figure 4.7 illustrates the shooting locations of the "DC sniper." The tight location of a large portion of the shootings suggested to law enforcement officials that the sniper

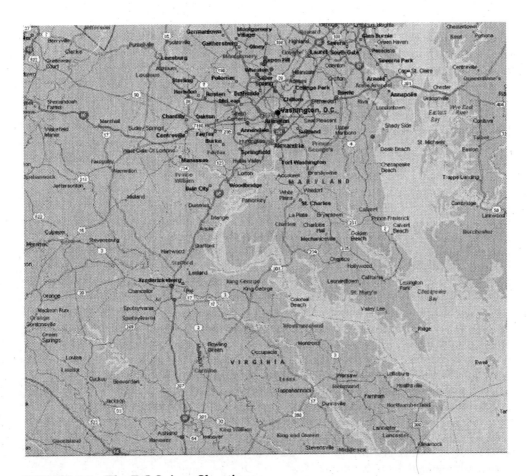

FIGURE 4.7   The DC Sniper Shootings

lived, worked, or would be found in the vicinity of these shootings. Specifically, the first eight shootings were all in the same vicinity, whereas shootings nine through 15 were more spread out, deliberately so. This suggested that the sniper was intentionally varying his shooting locations, moving from north to south, then back to north and to south again, in order to make his attacks less predictable. Ultimately, two men were captured at a highway rest area in their car to the Northwest of the first eight attacks.

SUMMARY OF MAJOR FINDINGS AND IMPLICATIONS

List of Major Research Findings Relating to Ecological Theories of Crime

In this chapter, you learned about several ecological theories and practical approaches to preventing crime. Some of the most important points include the following:

1. Defensible space, a concept put forth by Oscar Newman, is aimed at increasing territoriality and natural surveillance to prevent crime;
2. Territoriality can be understood as evidence that residents in a community care enough about their own place of residence to defend it against criminal intrusions;
3. Natural surveillance refers to the ability of residents to see potential criminality by going about their normal, everyday activities;
4. Surveillability is virtually synonymous with natural surveillance and refers to the visibility of a residence or potential crime target by residents, neighbors, passersby, and other users of a given space;
5. Scholars have posited that city streets are crime prone because they lack three primary qualities: a clear demarcation between public and private space, diversity of street use, and fairly consistent sidewalk use;
6. Defensible space is aimed at reducing crime and fear of crime through increasing a sense of community in a neighborhood, reducing opportunities for crime, and increasing surveillability;
7. Newman thought that criminal opportunities were thought to be most prevalent in areas characterized by neither high- nor low-intensity use, but rather in-between or moderate levels of use;
8. The theory of defensible space was tested by the Westinghouse Corporation, under a Law Enforcement Assistance Administration (LEAA) grant, at a school in Florida, a commercial mall in Oregon, a mixed land use area in Connecticut, and in numerous other settings including public housing, city streets, and entire neighborhoods;
9. Defensible space efforts are typically aimed at controlling access (or reducing accessibility), increasing surveillance, and generating activity support and reinforcement;
10. Target hardening is often used in conjunction with defensible space and can be understood as implementing any mechanism aimed at making it more difficult for an offender to gain access to a target or victim;
11. Studies of defensible space tend to offer very little in terms of evidence in support of the theory;
12. Studies of defensible space tend to find more evidence in favor of opportunity theories of crime including routine activity and lifestyle exposure theories;
13. Newman claims that some defensible space mechanisms are effective at reducing crime and/or fear of crime, including reducing pedestrian traffic, dividing residential areas into multiple spaces, improving lighting conditions, and increasing aesthetic qualities or reducing incivilities;
14. Defensible space continues to influence numerous projects in terms of how they are designed and built;

15. Crime Prevention Through Environmental Design (CPTED) is often confused with defensible space, and generally refers to changing the physical and social environment in order to prevent crime, fear of crime, and perceptions of crime risk, as well as to increase the aesthetic qualities of an environment;

16. C. Ray Jeffery, who coined the phrase CPTED, further developed his CPTED model to include efforts aimed at changing the internal environment of the offender in order to reduce the risk of criminality;

17. There are two environments that can be altered to reduce crime—the external environment of the place and the internal environment of the offender;

18. CPTED as it is practiced in the real world is very different from Jeffery's theory—common CPTED strategies include alterations to buildings, residences, neighborhoods, businesses, and so forth;

19. Jeffery's complete CPTED model has not been subjected to empirical testing;

20. CPTED projects subjected to empirical testing are typically defensible space projects in actuality;

21. The most effective CPTED strategies at reducing crime appear to be those that reduce opportunities for crime to occur and those that make people feel safer in their environments;

22. A thorough review of crime prevention programs aimed at places found that there are no such crime prevention programs proven to be ineffective, although most such programs are not well studied;

23. The program that is thought to be effective at reducing crime is nuisance abatement, and programs considered promising include multiple clerks in convenience stores and designing stores to reduce opportunities for crime, training bar and tavern workers to recognize signs of trouble, metal detectors and guards at airports, street closures, target hardening in public facilities, and situational crime prevention efforts aimed at reducing opportunities for crime;

24. Situational crime prevention, a term coined by Ronald Clarke, includes efforts to eliminate opportunities for crime by managing, designing, and manipulating the environment to increase perceived risks and reduce rewards of criminality;

25. Situational crime prevention is common across Europe and is increasingly being implemented in the United States, often under the term CPTED;

26. Situational crime prevention includes 16 different strategies for reducing crime, organized into four categories: increasing the difficulty of crime, increasing the perceived risks of crime, reducing the rewards of crime, and removing excuses for crime;

27. Clarke documents more than 100 successful case studies of situational crime prevention, yet most of these success stories are for relatively minor crimes;

28. Situational crime prevention efforts have shown that displacement of crime—the movement of crime from one place to another after crime prevention efforts have been directed at it—is rare and never enough to equal the benefits of crimes reduced;

29. Situational crime prevention efforts have also shown that diffusion of benefits—additional crime prevention beyond that which was planned—often occurs;

30. Routine activity theory shows that crime cannot occur without the convergence of three elements in time and space: a presence of likely or motivated offenders; a presence of suitable targets; and an absence of capable guardians to prevent the criminal act;

31. A likely offender includes anyone with an inclination to commit a crime;

32. A suitable target includes any person or thing that may evoke criminal inclinations, which would include the actual value of the target and the monetary and symbolic desirability of it for offenders, the visibility to offenders or their informants, the access to it, the ease of escape from the site, as well as the portability or mobility of objects sought by offenders;

33. A guardian is a person who can protect a target and includes friends and formal authorities such as police and security personnel, intimate handlers such as

parents, teachers, coaches, friends, employers, and place managers such as janitors and apartment managers;

34. An absence of capable guardians is often produced by average citizens going about their daily life;

35. The term routine activities means any recurrent and prevalent activities that provide for basic population and individual needs, whatever their biological or cultural origins including formalized work, leisure, social interaction, and learning, occurring at home, in jobs away from home, and in other activities away from home;

36. The acronym VIVA suggests there are four elements that influence a target's risk of being victimized by crime. They are value, inertia, visibility, and access;

37. Value refers to what the target is worth to the offender—items high in value are more attractive;

38. Inertia refers to the ability of a target to be taken—those that can be taken easier are more attractive;

39. Visibility refers to how easily targets are seen by offenders—more visible targets are more vulnerable;

40. Access refers to how easily targets can be accessed by offenders—more accessible items are more vulnerable;

41. Routine activity theory also points to factors unique to lifestyles or potential offenders and victims as these are affected by larger social processes;

42. Lifestyle/exposure theory posits that lifestyles that encompass differences in various demographic factors affect daily routines of people and thus increase vulnerability to criminal victimization;

43. Lifestyles are patterned, regular, recurrent, prevalent, or routine activities, consisting of the activities that people engage in on a daily basis, including both obligatory and discretionary activities;

44. Obligatory activities include all things (such as work) that must be engaged in while discretionary activities are pursued by choice (e.g., recreation);

45. There are clear relationships between routine activities, victim lifestyles, and criminal victimization;

46. Cohen and Felson found that daytime burglaries increased over time along with time spent outside of the home during the day;

47. Other studies found that persons with low daytime and nighttime activities outside of the home have the lowest risk of property victimization, while people who are away from the home due to daytime and nighttime activities have the highest risks of crime victimization;

48. Generally, people with less active statuses have lower risks of most forms of criminal victimization;

49. An active lifestyle generally increases victimization risk by increasing the likelihood that potential offenders will find suitable targets with low levels of guardianship, but an active lifestyle may not necessarily increase one's risk of criminal victimization;

50. Crime pattern theory, developed by considering and combining the main contributions from rational choice theory, routine activity theory, environmental criminology, strategic analysis, lifestyle/exposure theory, CPTED, situational crime prevention, hot spot analysis, and opportunity theory generally, is aimed at explaining why some places are more prone to serve as hosts to and targets of crimes;

51. According to crime pattern theory, the criminal event is triggered by the presence of an opportunity that an offender comes upon in the course of a search, which can be minimal or broader depending on such factors as how well the offender knows the area;

52. The three main concepts of crime pattern theory are nodes, paths, and edges;

53. Nodes refer to where people travel to and from;

54. Paths are the main areas of travel between these nodes;
55. Edges are the boundaries of areas where people engage in their activities;
56. Activity routines of people help shape their activity space, which refers to the places people normally travel to and from;
57. From the activity space, people develop an awareness space, which is the areas that people know best and are most comfortable in;
58. The target selection of offenders depends on mental templates used to shape searches for targets or victims and to predefine the characteristics of a suitable target or suitable place for finding targets;
59. Mental templates help offenders define targets as good or bad;
60. According to Brantingham and Brantingham, crime pattern theory can be applied to any crime; and
61. As of today, it is impossible to directly measure the mental templates used by offenders, though they certainly do exist; instead, researchers rely on self-report measures of mental templates by offenders.

Implications of Findings for Crime Mapping and Spatial Analysis

The main significance of ecological theories of crime is that they can be used, perhaps more than any other theories, to prevent criminal victimization and the tremendous harm it causes.

Although increasing territoriality and natural surveillance does not seem very effective at preventing crime, other than those benefits illustrated in a few studies, creating defensible space gives residents a greater sense of control over what happens in their community. Increased natural surveillance or surveillability will undeniably reduce some crimes because this makes crime more risky for offenders.

Using defensible space may also reduce fear of crime by making people feel safer to move about their familiar environments. Efforts to harden targets also reduce opportunities for crime and therefore undeniably prevent some crimes; they also can make people feel safer in their homes. CPTED initiatives are often successful at preventing crime, lowering fear of crime and perceptions of crime risk, and are usually built around the plan of increasing the aesthetic qualities of an environment. All of these are worthwhile efforts.

The most successful crime prevention initiatives seem to be situational crime prevention efforts aimed at increasing the difficulty of crime, increasing the risks of crime, reducing the rewards of crime, and removing excuses for crime. Studies show that these efforts tend to reduce crime, not lead to displacement of crime, and provide benefits beyond those that were expected.

A thorough review of crime prevention programs aimed at places found that there are no such crime prevention programs proven to be ineffective, and many programs are considered promising. These programs tend to cost far less than reactive mechanisms such as police, courts, and corrections.

Studies of routine activity theory and lifestyle/exposure theory may guide practitioners to lower the likelihood that motivated offenders will come into contact with suitable targets with no guardians capable to prevent crime. Logical, place-oriented crime prevention initiatives include reducing the suitability of targets and increasing guardianship by police and security personnel, parents, teachers, coaches, friends, employers, and place managers. To the degree that victims' lifestyles precipitate their victimization, efforts can be made to inform citizens of how they can protect themselves from criminal victimization by changing their lifestyles.

Because the value, inertia, visibility, and access of a potential target also influence its likelihood of being victimized, items high in value that are more easily transported, more visible, and more accessible to offenders can be identified and protected. Ideally, the presence of such items can be mapped in order to implement a well-designed program or policy. The key question is how to obtain such data from would-be victims in order to determine its effects on criminal victimization.

Crime pattern theory suggests that careful study of the nodes where people travel to and from, the paths of travel between these nodes, and the edges or boundaries of areas where people engage in their activities will result in a greater understanding of how criminal opportunities are created and can be changed to lower crime rates.

The main concepts of defensible space, CPTED, situational crime prevention, routine activity theory, and crime pattern theory can be mapped in order to explain why crime occurs more in some places than in others as well as to predict which areas of a place will likely be more subjected to criminality based on their characteristics. One difficulty in doing this is gathering data on variables to be mapped, such as territoriality, natural surveillance, accessibility, designation, definition, design, and opportunity. Data on such variables can be gathered from on-site observations of places such as city blocks, as well as from surveys of residents in those areas. When plotted against crime rates and risk of criminal victimization, crime mapping techniques allow criminologists to better understand why crime occurs in certain places more than others and how to better prevent crimes from clustering in certain spots.

CASE STUDY
ENVIRONMENTAL DESIGN IN THE NATION'S CITIES AND ARCHITECTURE

Although the original crime prevention programs based on defensible space are widely considered failures, governmental agencies currently utilize CPTED principles and architectural design projects continue to reflect them. The fact that CPTED studies and programs are deeply rooted in the national government of the United States serves as evidence of this (e.g., see Crowe, 1991:28). The National Crime Prevention Institute's CPTED studio and one- and two-week courses offered opportunities to organize workshops and classes related to CPTED for the corporate businessperson, planner, and designer. At lower levels of government, state-wide laws and city-wide ordinances aimed at CPTED are well known. For example, the state of Florida passed the "Safe Neighborhoods Act," and the cities of Gainesville, Florida, and Kent, Ohio, passed ordinances regarding changes at convenience stores aimed at reducing robberies (Crowe, 1991:4; Jeffery, 1990:415–416).

Additionally, virtually all law enforcement agencies in the United States of any decent size contain a crime prevention unit. These units often consult with businesses and builders in the design stages of various projects in order to assist with design strategies that will ultimately promote crime prevention and improve the quality of the built environment. Old buildings are frequently renovated or replaced; improvements of streets, walkways, courtyards, parks, and parking areas are made, not only to serve people during daytime working hours but also to promote hotel, dining, and entertainment activities during evenings, weekends, and holidays. The interrelated objectives of increasing aesthetics and preventing crime are routinely promoted as critical aspects of these projects. "City governments are finding out that it is a lot cheaper to design crime prevention into the way things are done than to hire extra police, or to pay for extra protection that can make the community look like a fortress instead of a nice place to live" (Crowe, 1991:27–28).

Based on CPTED research into areas such as defensible space and target hardening, various businesses have sprung up across the United States which do little more than provide CPTED consultation. For example, according to Smith (1996), consultants specializing in parking lot design have espoused the use of CPTED for over 20 years. Additionally, professional alarm companies call residents living in neighborhoods where recent burglaries occurred in order to recommend design changes such as installing electric eyes, burglar alarms, and other target-hardening mechanisms (Robinson, 1994). Almost every business utilizes some CPTED strategy, whether it be trimming the hedges near windows and doors to increase visibility or installing cameras to deter offenders from committing offenses. Such changes are rooted in common sense understandings about preventing crime (Crowe, 1991:105; Murray, 1994:349).

In fact, when businesses refuse to participate in CPTED activities, police officials voice concern about the continued crimes committed against those businesses. Crowe's CPTED strategies are suggested for numerous commercial establishments, as well as downtown streets and pedestrian areas, office and industrial systems, hallways and restrooms, malls and shopping centers, and convenience stores and branch banks.

Such strategies are being followed all over the United States and also around the world, including Canada, Japan, New Zealand, England, Australia, France, the Netherlands, and Germany, but under different names. For instance, Wekerle and Whitzman (1995) discussed examples of CPTED strategies being employed in transportation-linked spaces (e.g., public transportation and parking garages and parking lots), commercial areas (e.g., central business districts, commercial streets in neighborhoods, shopping plazas, industrial areas), and residential areas (e.g., residential streets, alleys, high-rise residential areas, interior spaces in multi-unit housing, parks, and university and college campuses). These CPTED initiatives are given a different name—the "Safe Cities" approach—which is focused on a "partnership between government and citizens . . . prevention of criminal behavior through environmental design, community development, education . . . social prevention . . . [and] urban safety as a catalyst for change" (Wekerle and Whitzman, 1995:8) but are very similar to CPTED as it exists in the United States. Unfortunately, very few of these CPTED and Safe Cities projects have been subjected to critical evaluation. Still, they are based on the assumption that changes to the physical environment at particular places can reduce crime. Crime mapping software allows such changes to be illustrated and carefully studied.

CHAPTER 5

Behavioral Geography and Criminal Behavior

This chapter provides a comprehensive discussion of behavioral geography as it relates to understanding criminal offender decision-making processes. Specifically, certain aspects of behavioral geography will be discussed as they relate to offender decision-making processes in terms of where offenders commit crimes. This chapter provides a sound understanding of the spatial processes at work in terms of criminal offender site and victim selection.

Chapter Outline

In the fall of 2002, the nation was riveted by the actions of the "D.C. snipers" and the seemingly random killings committed throughout Maryland, Virginia, and the District of Columbia. Throughout the entire length of the investigation, one of the main focuses of media coverage of the crimes was the various "new" technologies being employed by law enforcement agencies to catch the killers. One of the most talked about of these new technologies was geographic profiling, a technique that uses logic, principles, and ideas developed in behavioral geography to help narrow the search area of serial offenders. While for the majority of the public the extent of their knowledge of behavioral geography deals only with geographic profiling, there are several other areas within the field that are important to the study and understanding of crime and its patterns. With this in mind, Chapter 5 will focus on providing an introduction to the concept of behavioral geography and its application to crime and the actions of criminal offenders. Specifically, this chapter will discuss the areas of mental maps and awareness space, journey to crime research, and geographic profiling. While several of these concepts were introduced in Chapter 4 in a discussion of their role in crime pattern theory (awareness space, activity space, nodes, paths), Chapter 5 will provide a more thorough discussion of their development, patterns, and impact on criminal behavior.

INTRODUCTION TO BEHAVIORAL GEOGRAPHY

As a subfield of geography, behavioral geography began to develop into its own in the 1960s when researchers challenged existing theories of how people made decisions concerning travel and associated behaviors (Rengert, 1989). In particular, behavioral geography challenged existing theories concerning the decisions people made in regard to running errands, selecting houses, and other decisions involving rather mundane actions. Rengert (1989) defines behavioral geography as the spatial decision making of individuals that precedes their behavior. In simpler terms, behavioral geography can be thought of as a body of research in which researchers are interested in why and how people make decisions about where to go for everything from food to entertainment to criminal activities.

Not long after the development of behavioral geography, it began to be applied to research on spatial decision making in crime. In general, research in behavioral geography can be divided into two different areas, both of which have implications for crime and criminal justice. The first area of behavioral geography research is termed *behavior in space* (Rengert, 1989). As it relates to crime, Rengert (1989) defined behavior in space as a research approach that "considers the geographic distribution of opportunities for crime and the social, economic, physical, and physiological constraints on criminal spatial behavior." As implied from the definition, this area of crime research deals with how the spatial structure of opportunities for crime can shape the distribution of crime. Thus, behavior in space research is more place specific and looks at how the mix of opportunities and constraints within an area impacts patterns of crime. Criminological research that has been strongly influenced by this area of behavioral geography includes crime pattern theory and opportunity structure models of crime.

An example of how the geographic distribution of opportunities for crime affects crime patterns is the spatial distribution of shoplifting. In most cities, shoplifting patterns are highest in certain areas, specifically those areas with high concentrations of stores. Shoplifting hot spots tend to cluster in areas such as shopping districts and areas with high concentrations of malls and strip centers because shoplifting by definition requires shops and merchandise (see Figure 5.1). In analyzing how opportunity structures impact the distribution of burglary in Philadelphia, Rengert (1991) found that the number of residential housing units in an area was a strong measure of "criminal attractiveness." While this area of research may seem relatively obvious in its findings, opportunity structure and its impact on crime distributions are nonetheless important to criminal justice practitioners and criminologists alike. In particular, opportunity structures can foretell the spatial patterns of some crimes, and effective criminal justice policy can be created to deal with these issues.

The other general area of behavioral geography is *spatial behavior*. Spatial behavior focuses more on the individual as an active participant in crime rather than just a reactor to physical and social elements within the physical environment (Rengert, 1989). Whereas behavior in space research is more place specific and is concerned with opportunities and constraints, spatial behavior research looks at the role of the person in the geography of crime. Specifically, spatial behavior focuses on individual actors and their differences in terms of spatial knowledge and, in turn, their spatial activity. While criminological research dealing with behavior in space concepts has been rather limited, research dealing with spatial behavior concepts has been much more extensive. In particular, research dealing with spatial behavior concepts such as mental maps, awareness space, and journey to crime (JTC) is quite extensive and well established within both geographical and criminological literature. Because of the breadth of

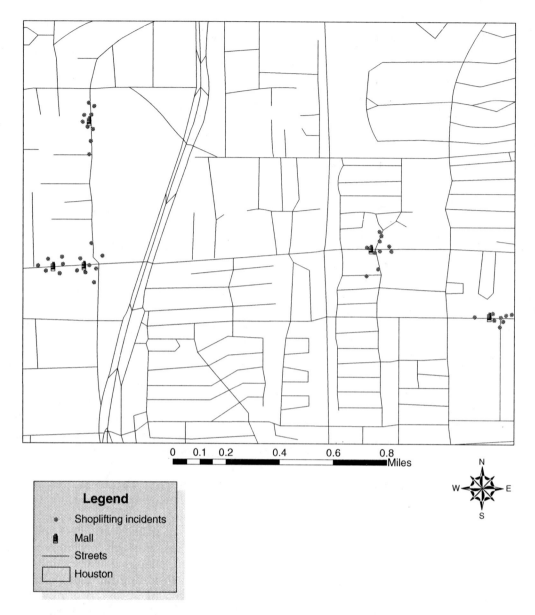

FIGURE 5.1   Shoplifting Incidents Near Malls/Shopping Areas. Shoplifting incidents are clustered closely around major shopping malls and high shopping areas.

criminological research on spatial behavior concepts and its impact on crime patterns and criminal justice policy, the remainder of the chapter will be devoted to discussing spatial behavior concepts.

MENTAL MAPS

An obvious starting point for a discussion of spatial behavior concepts is the *mental map,* also called a cognitive map. Although mental maps, awareness space, and JTC are all highly interrelated in terms of spatial knowledge, spatial activity, and criminal behavior, they will all be discussed individually. Smith and Patterson (198; p. 205) define a mental map as "a mental description of an environment" while Canter and Hodge (2000) define it as "those internal representations of the world that we all use to find our way around and make decisions about what we will do and where." In

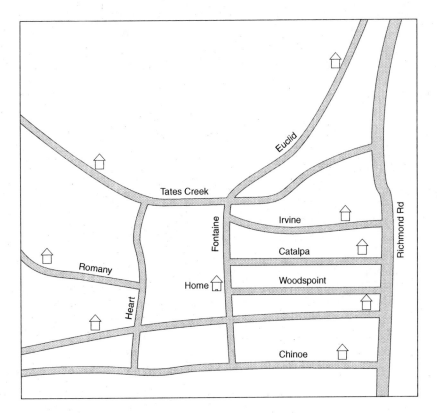

FIGURE 5.2 Offender's mental map displaying his or her home in relation to those of his or her victims.

general, a mental map can be thought of as a mental sketch of a place or area comprising an individual's knowledge about that place or area. Importantly, a mental map does not necessarily indicate that an individual has a detailed knowledge of an entire area, only that a person has a mental image of the geography of that area. Most often people have mental maps that are highly detailed in some areas and only vague understandings of other areas, largely due to the variation in the amount of activity they conduct in the different areas. These fragmented mental maps are the result of mental maps being created through an individual's experience, whether hands on (travel and interaction) or perceptual (media and friends). These mental maps are used to solve problems, form opinions about an area, and direct actions such as routes of travel and shopping habits. Figure 5.2 is a sketch of a mental map of a neighborhood showing where an offender committed his crimes in relation to his home. The simple sketch map is one of the most popular methods for understanding a person's mental perception of areas, with the route map sketch being another popular method for determining an individual's mental images of geographic areas (Canter and Hodge, 2000). While similar in style (sketching), they provide different bits of information about a person's perception of an area. Specifically, the simple sketch map provides information about a person's perception about an area as a whole, while the route map provides a view of a person's travel patterns, based on his or her mental maps.

Research Findings

While mental maps are not an inherently criminal concept, in that both criminals and non-criminals form mental maps, within criminological research they are of importance in several areas. One of the more important areas of mental map research involves perceptions of crime patterns within a city. As the simple sketch map above demonstrates, a mental map provides a look at a person's mental image of an area, one aspect of which is his or her perception of where crime occurs within that city. As you would expect, because mental maps are based on people's experiences, there are distinct differences in their mental map perceptions of crime within a city. Specifically, research has found that there are numerous differences in crime perception based on different social characteristics. In his seminal study of spatial perception of crime in Akron, Ohio, Pyle (1980) found that perceptions of high-crime areas varied according to different social characteristics:

- *Race:* Blacks had a more accurate perception of where crime occurred within the city as compared with white residents;
- *Gender:* Females tended to overestimate the amount of crime in city locations as compared with males;
- *Age:* Very young (16–19 years) and older (45–54 years) residents tended to overestimate the amount of crime in city locations as compared with other groups;
- *Income:* Wealthier residents tended to overestimate the amount of crime in the city center as compared with poorer residents;
- *Education:* Those with lower education levels had more accurate perceptions of city-center crime rates than those of higher education levels;
- *Tenure:* Those who lived in the area longer were more accurate in their perceptions of high-crime areas in the city center than those who were more recent to the area;
- *Suburban Residents:* Those who lived in the suburbs tended to have exaggerated perceptions of the levels of crime within the city center.

Overall, Pyle (1980) found that of all the characteristics analyzed in regard to spatial perceptions of crime within Akron, where the individual lived (city v. suburb) was the biggest factor in terms of the accuracy of his or her perception of crime in the city-center area. It was postulated that these differences were due in large part to familiarity with the area, with residents of the city being more familiar with the area in general and the crime levels within the area than those who lived in the suburbs.

In addition to citizens' mental maps, other researchers have studied the mental maps of police officers as they relate to crime patterns within a city. In looking at the perception of crime by police officers, Ratcliffe and McCullagh (2001) found that the accuracy of officers' perceptions varied by crime types. Officers were most accurate in their perceptions of where burglaries were concentrated and less accurate in their perceptions of other crimes such as auto theft and non-residential burglary. It was theorized that the geographic knowledge of burglary was attributed to the seriousness of this crime and the officers' increased desire to reduce and prevent these types of crimes over other crime types (auto theft and non-residential burglary). The importance of these incorrect perceptions lies in the increased use of community policing, a concept that relies heavily on problem solving by individual officers. If officers have incorrect perceptions of where crimes occur within a jurisdiction, it could significantly impair their ability to implement problem-solving strategies in places where they will effectively reduce crime. Ratcliffe and McCullagh (2001) note that at the time of the study crime maps were not distributed to officers and there is hope that in the future, crime maps may be able to improve the accuracy of officers' perceptions of crime distributions.

Finally, as would be expected, research has also been conducted on the mental maps of criminals. As opposed to research on the mental maps of citizens and police officers, research on the mental maps of criminals focuses on which areas of a city criminals feel are good for criminal activities. Overall, it was found that criminals and non-criminals have very similar perceptions of crime patterns, but that criminals view the city differently than non-criminals (Carter and Hill, 1978). Criminals' images of the city can best be described as divided into "dimensions of evaluation," in which criminals evaluate different areas based on their potential for criminal activity (Carter and Hill, 1980:200). In general, criminals evaluate areas differently than non-criminals, largely based on their "work"-oriented view of an area as either good or bad for criminal activity (Carter and Hill, 1980). Two key evaluative criteria are used by criminals in their mental maps of an area—familiarity with an area and potential strategy for an area (Carter and Hill, 1980). Familiarity involves areas suitable for crime based on in-depth knowledge and feelings of comfort, whereas strategy involves areas that are most attractive criminally. In terms of strategy, research into the mental maps of burglars found that burglars viewed more affluent areas as prime areas for criminal activities (Petersilia, Greenwood, and Lavin, 1977; Reppetto, 1974). Moreover, differences in mental maps were found to exist by both age and race (Reppetto, 1974). Specifically, younger criminals chose areas with higher amounts of multi-family housing, and racially criminals were decidedly intra-racial in the areas they chose, preferring to avoid areas where they might stand out (Reppetto, 1974). Furthermore, black criminals' mental maps were more heavily influenced by familiarity considerations, whereas whites' mental maps were found to be equally influenced by familiarity and strategy (Carter and Hill, 1980).

AWARENESS SPACE

As was mentioned previously, most individuals' mental maps will contain both areas where they have only vague geographic knowledge and those areas where they have more detailed geographic knowledge. In behavioral geography terms, those areas in which an individual has a more detailed geographic knowledge are called *awareness spaces.* Awareness space is a very important concept to spatial crime research and JTC in particular, because research has shown that an offender's main search area in terms of criminal activity is within his or her awareness space (Brantingham and Brantingham, 1991; see also discussion of crime pattern theory in Chapter 4). Figure 5.3 provides a graphic representation of the relationship between an individual's mental map and his or her awareness space, particularly how the more detailed awareness space usually lies within a more general mental map of an area.

Of utmost importance in a discussion of awareness space is how an individual acquires his or her awareness space. As with mental maps, awareness space is not an inherently criminal concept, and both criminals and non-criminals obtain their awareness spaces through the same general processes of conducting legitimate routine activities (Brantingham and Brantingham, 1993). The area in which an individual regularly travels for legitimate purposes is termed his or her *activity space,* and is contained within an individual's awareness space (Rossmo, 2000). Rossmo (2000:255) defines activity space as "Those places regularly visited by a person in which the majority of their activities are carried out." Thus, the activity space of each individual will vary in size and shape depending on the distance and direction of routine activities. Consequently, the areas where criminals will search for criminal activity will also vary in size and shape according to their individual activity space.

Central to the size and shape of an individual's activity space are the concepts of nodes and paths. As you saw in the last chapter, *nodes* are those places that are central to an individual's life, such as home, place of work, school, shopping areas, and favorite recreation spots (Brantingham and Brantingham, 1993). The places where individuals travel to and from essentially make up the extent of an individual's activity space and act as anchor points for an individual's legitimate *and* criminal activities. Specifically, nodes form mental boundary points within which criminal offenders will search for criminal opportunities.

In addition to central place nodes such as home, place of work, and school, two specialized types of nodes, crime attractors and crime generators, also play a role in shaping an individual's activity and awareness space. *Crime attractors* are those places, areas, or neighborhoods where criminal opportunities are well known, and to which

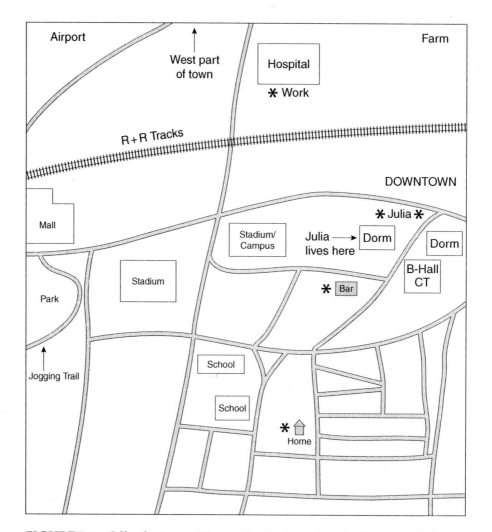

FIGURE 5.3   Offender's mental map displaying where he lives in relation to work, friends' homes, and recreation places. This awareness space makes up his most likely criminal hunting area.

motivated offenders are subsequently attracted as a source for criminal activity (Brantingham and Brantingham, 1993). Examples of crime attractors include red light districts, known drug markets, bar districts, and large shopping areas, all of which provide ample criminal opportunities for different offenders. Crime in these areas is often committed by people who live outside the area and who travel relatively long distances specifically because of the criminal opportunities that exist there (Brantingham and Brantingham, 1993).

In contrast to crime attractors, *crime generators* are particular places and areas to which large numbers of people are attracted for legitimate reasons, but which provide criminal opportunities because of the sheer number of potential victims (Brantingham and Brantingham, 1993). Examples of crime generators include shopping centers, entertainment districts, college campuses, and sports stadiums, all of which generate crime by providing large numbers of potential victims at specific times and within concentrated areas.

Complementary to the concept of nodes are *paths,* which are the everyday routes that people use to travel between different nodes of activity. While nodes act as anchor points for a person's activity space, paths determine the areas an individual will learn about through the routes he or she travels on a regular basis. Because people spend long hours in routine paths traveling to and from activity nodes, paths will determine the areas along which criminals will search for potential victims (Brantingham and Brantingham, 1993). Figure 5.4 provides an example of several different nodes and their resulting paths and also provides a visualization of their impact on the activity space and awareness space of an individual. In this example, the nodes and paths are in a triangular relationship and, thus, so is the activity space; in reality nodes, paths, and the subsequent activity space they create can be in any form or shape. As discussed earlier, these nodes and paths will form the basis for a criminal's search area in terms of criminal activities. Research has found that criminals choose to commit crimes in areas they know well because they feel they will not stand out as they belong in that area (Sacks, 1972).

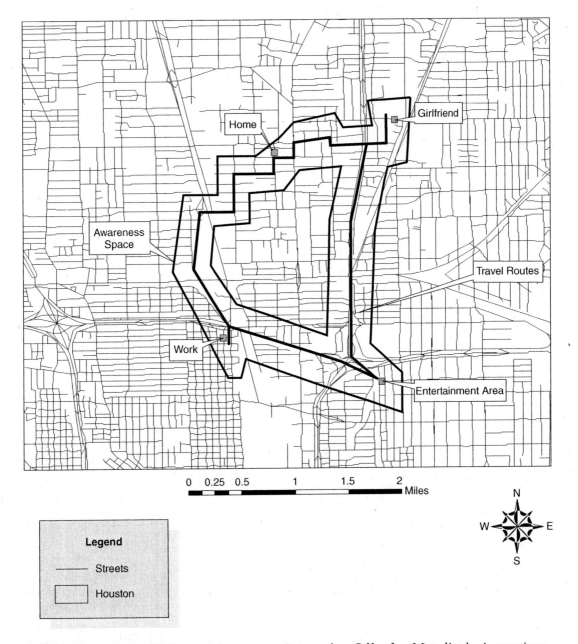

FIGURE 5.4   Nodes, Paths, and Awareness Space of an Offender. Map displaying various offender nodes and paths and their resulting impact on an offender's awareness space. This will in turn impact where an offender looks for victims.

Research Findings

Because of the interrelatedness of mental maps, awareness space, and JTC concepts, research involving one area is intrinsically related to the other areas. Moreover, because of this interrelatedness, research that deals *only* with one specific area such as awareness space is more limited in nature. This notwithstanding, important research has been conducted concerning awareness space, nodes, and paths, and their impact on crime. In looking at awareness space and its related concepts, research has focused on two different areas, differences in awareness space and the impact of awareness space, nodes, and paths on criminal activity.

Research involving differences in criminals' awareness space has found that awareness space varies depending on several factors:

- *Age:* Young people have a more limited awareness space than working-age people, largely due to transportation issues and younger people being more limited in their travel patterns (Ley, 1983). This can change for very old people as they may be limited in their ability to travel and thus have a more limited awareness space (Orleans, 1973);
- *Gender:* Females have a more limited awareness space than males (Rengert and Monk, 1982). This finding is largely due to the disproportionate number of women who are tied to home, often with children;
- *Race:* Black criminals were shown to have less spatial awareness than white criminals, largely due to access to transportation (Rengert and Wasilchick, 1985). Moreover, blacks were not likely to be familiar with white areas, and whites were not likely to be familiar with black areas (Carter and Hill, 1979);
- *SES:* Poorer people have more limited awareness space than people who are from wealthier areas (Orleans, 1973);
- *Employment Status:* Those who are unemployed have more limited awareness space than those who are working (Orleans, 1973). This is different from SES in that many who are unemployed may be stay-at-home parents;
- *Residential Status:* Inner-city youth have smaller awareness spaces than those who live in suburban areas (Orleans, 1968). However, inner-city youth have much more detailed geographic knowledge about their awareness space than do suburban youth.

As stated above, much of the awareness space differences can be attributed to differences in requirements and availability to transportation. Importantly, research has also shown that awareness space can change and evolve over time due to availability of new transportation (Brantingham and Brantingham, 1991), learning from more experienced criminals (Letkemann, 1973; Mack, 1964), and people's growing older and gaining experience (Brantingham and Brantingham, 1993).

In terms of how awareness space impacts crime patterns, researchers have consistently found that criminals tend to operate in neighborhoods they know well, despite the fact that they identified other neighborhoods as having better potential opportunity (Repetto, 1974). Rengert and Wasilchick (1985) found that burglars usually chose crime sites only a limited distance from their normal travel paths, usually along the path between home and place of work. Moreover, other research has found that nearly all robbery, burglary, serial rape, and serial murder are committed within the awareness space defined by offenders' nodes and paths (Alston, 1994; Canter and Larkin, 1993; Gabor et al., 1987; Maguire, 1982; Rengert and Wasilchick, 1985; Rossmo, 1994; Wright and Decker, 1994). Overall, research is consistent in the assertion that most criminals commit crimes within their awareness space, usually centered around the nodes and paths that make up their routine activities, and that spatial exploration for the purpose of criminal activity is a very rare phenomenon (Rengert and Wasilchick, 1985).

JOURNEY TO CRIME

The last of the interrelated behavioral geography concepts to be discussed is *journey to crime*. JTC is an area of criminological research in which researchers are interested in the distances that criminals travel to commit crimes, specifically the distance from their residence to the offense site. While the idea of criminals' journeys to crime is relatively simple, the implications of where and why criminals travel to specific places to commit crime impact the majority of criminological theories (Rengert, Piquero, and Jones, 1999). While criminals' journeys to crime are influenced by numerous different theories, including routine activity, rational choice, differential association, and crime pattern theory to name a few, in general criminals' journeys to crime are thought to be driven by one or more of three important spatial factors. Specifically, target attractiveness, spatial attractiveness, and target backcloth are all thought to have a major influence on criminal journeys to crime.

The *target attractiveness* of an area alludes to the amount of high-value targets that are available within a given area (Rhodes and Conly, 1991). Specifically, criminals will travel to areas with target attractiveness because of the perceived high value of criminal opportunities available in these areas. Theoretically, the higher the target attractiveness of an area, the more likely criminals will travel long distances to offend there. Examples of area characteristics that rate high on a scale of target attractiveness are areas with high income, high amounts of single-family dwellings, or large amounts of potential victims (Rhodes and Conly, 1991). In the previous discussion of activity nodes, both crime generators and crime attractors are examples of factors that can increase the target attractiveness of an area.

In contrast to target attractiveness, areas high on *spatial attractiveness* are areas that are spatially close to or well known to the offender, offering a short travel distance or relative comfort with one's surroundings. An area will not be victimized, even if it is high ranking in terms of target attractiveness, if it is unknown to criminals, or if it is in an area that is difficult to access without being noticed (Rhodes and Conly, 1991). The rationale behind spatial attractiveness relies on the least effort principle that all things being equal, criminals will choose to commit crime closest to home.

The last major influence on a criminal's decision process in terms of travel distances is termed *target backcloth*. Target backcloth, also called victim backcloth, is the spatial distribution of criminal targets or victims within a given area (Brantingham and Brantingham, 1991). The importance of target backcloth is that the locations of suitable victims may not be uniformly distributed within a criminal's hunting areas, particularly when a criminal is looking for a particular type of victim. In cases in which the criminal is seeking a specific type of victim, the JTC and offense locations will be influenced more heavily by the victim's activity spaces than by the offender's activity spaces (Rossmo, 1994). An example of how target backcloth impacts JTC would be a serial arsonist who only likes to burn warehouses. In the case of such an offender, those areas where there are suitable victims (warehouse districts) would define his or her target backcloth, and subsequent journeys to crime. By contrast, a serial arsonist who has no specific victim type would have a very different target backcloth and JTC. Figure 5.5 illustrates these differences, showing the crime site locations for a warehouse arsonist and an arsonist with no specific victim type. Target backcloth has been found to be particularly important in understanding the JTC of certain types of serial offenders, particularly serial murderers and serial rapists (Rossmo, 2000).

Research Findings

In comparison with research on mental maps and awareness space where the amount of research conducted is relatively modest, a considerable amount of research exists concerning criminals' journeys to crime. In general, research on JTC has produced a

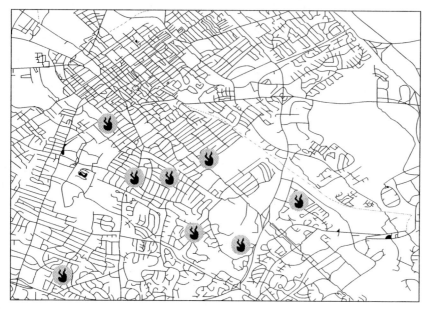

Random victim type arsonist

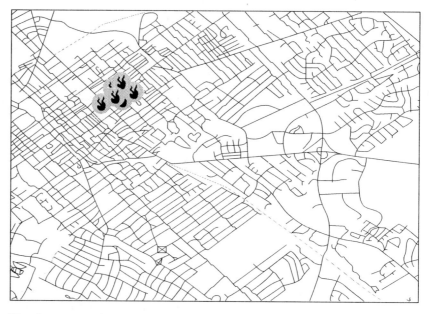

Warehouse arsonist

FIGURE 5.5   Target Backcloth for Two Different Types of Offenders. Two maps showing how target backcloth can impact the distribution of crime incidents. The random victim type arsonist has a much larger crime distribution compared with the warehouse arsonist whose victims are contained within a limited area within the city.

remarkably consistent body of findings indicating two overall principles concerning criminals' journeys to crime. The first major finding is that there is a definite distance decay factor at work in criminals' journeys to crime (Rengert, Piquero, and Jones, 1999). Simply defined, *distance decay* states that offenders generally select targets close to their homes and that the farther they go from the homes, the fewer crimes they will commit (Phillips, 1980). Importantly, Rossmo (1993) states there is a *buffer distance* around a criminal's home area where he or she will not commit crime in order to avoid detection. This buffered distance decay function is particularly acute in confrontational crimes such as robbery where criminals do not want to choose victims from their neighborhood for fear of being recognized and apprehended. Thus, after this buffer zone distance, crime decreases the further from home that a criminal travels. Figure 5.6 illustrates this distance decay and buffer zone effect. This finding is so consistent and robust that it forms the basis for criminal geographic targeting (geographic profiling) and plays an important role in the overall profiling of criminal offenders (Canter and Larkin, 1993; Le Beau, 1987; Rossmo, 2000).

Explanations for this distance decay function fall into one of two different categories—ease and local knowledge (Von Koppen and De Keijser, 1997). *Ease* refers to the nature of criminals to commit crimes that are easy and quick, and thus, criminals travel distances that are relatively close to home. Closely related, *local knowledge*

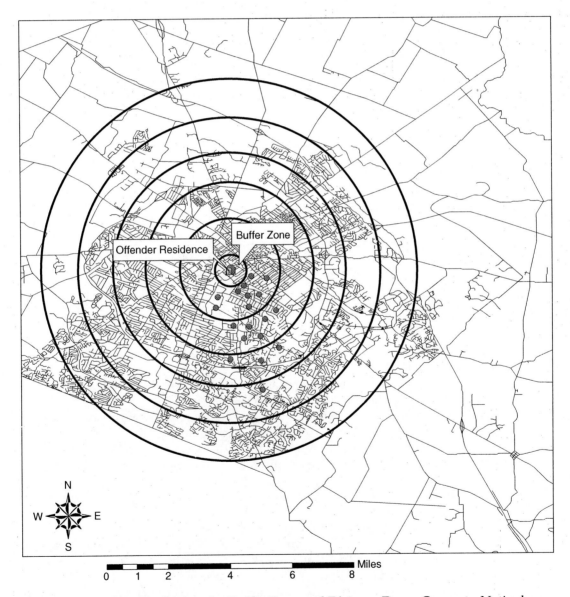

FIGURE 5.6   Map Illustrating the Buffer Zone and Distance Decay Concepts. Notice how no incidents occur within the buffer zone and that the distribution of incidents is highest closer to the offender's residence and decreases as the distance from the residence increases.

suggests that offenders are more familiar with areas close to home than those farther away, and thus commit crimes in areas they know well to reduce chances of capture.

The other major finding from JTC research is that the distances traveled by criminals vary greatly based on different offender- and offense-specific characteristics. In this area, findings indicate numerous offender- and offense-specific factors that impact JTC. In looking at offense-specific factors, findings include the following:

- *Property v. Personal:* Offenders travel longer distances to commit property crimes such as burglary and auto theft than to commit personal crimes such as homicide, robbery, or rape (Baldwin and Bottoms, 1976; Brantingham and Brantingham, 1991; Le Beau, 1987; Phillips, 1980; Pyle, 1974);
- *Individual Crimes:* Research has found that even among general crime categories, such as property and personal crimes, there are differences between specific crimes (Rhodes and Conly, 1991). Among personal crimes, distances have been found to be farther for armed robbery than for unarmed robbery (Nichols, 1980);
- *City Type:* In older cities that are more compact and have a more defined central core area, criminals should have shorter crime trips than criminals in newer, more spread out cities (Brantingham and Brantingham, 1991);
- *Rural v. Urban:* Criminals living in rural and mixed urban/rural areas have longer journeys to crime than those who live in purely urban areas (Barker, 2000); and
- *Neighborhood Type:* Distance traveled is positively related (longer) to the extent that an offender's surroundings consist of single-family dwellings, multiple dwellings, and small businesses (Rhodes and Conly, 1991). Conversely, travel distance is negatively related (shorter) to the extent to which the surrounding neighborhood is characterized as industrial, transitional, and mixed (Rhodes and Conly, 1991).

Turning to how offender-specific characteristics impact JTC distances, there are considerable findings as well. Specifically, findings related to individual offender characteristics include the following:

- *Gender:* Female offenders generally travel shorter distances to commit crimes than do males, although the distances traveled are not a great deal farther (Brantingham and Brantingham, 1991; Phillips, 1980; Rengert and Wasilchick, 1985; Repetto, 1974);
- *Race:* Black offenders tend to travel shorter distances to commit crimes than do whites (Carter and Hill, 1978; Nichols, 1980; Phillips, 1980);
- *Age:* Juveniles are more likely to commit crimes in their home areas and are less mobile than adult offenders (Baldwin and Bottoms, 1976; Gabor and Gottheil, 1984; Nichols, 1980; Repetto, 1974; Rhodes and Conly, 1991);
- *Income:* Those who are of lower economic status travel shorter distances to commit crimes than do those who are wealthier (Orleans, 1973);
- *Planned v. Unplanned Crimes:* Crimes that are more situationally induced, such as rape and homicide, occur closer to home than do crimes that involve more advance planning, such as robbery and burglary (Rhodes and Conly, 1991);
- *Victim/Offender Relationship:* Crime distances are longer when the victim is a stranger than when the victim and offender know each other (Le Beau, 1987; Rhodes and Conly, 1991);
- *Criminal Experience:* Offenders with criminal records travel farther than those without criminal records to commit crimes (Rhodes and Conly, 1991). Moreover, criminals tend to commit their first offenses closer to home and increase the distances traveled as they obtain more experience (Barker, 2000; Le Beau, 1987);
- *Hunting Type:* JTC distances differ according to the type of hunting method employed by the offender in acquiring victims. Le Beau (1987) found that rapists who employed a "capture the victim's confidence" hunting style traveled much farther distances than those employing other methods such as illegal entry or

even kidnap methods. Furthermore, Canter and Larkin (1993) found that rapists were more likely to employ a marauder hunting technique involving hunting from a home base, than a commuter hunting technique in which the rapist traveled far from home to commit crimes.

It should be noted that research has also indicated that the distance a criminal will travel to commit a crime changes over time and that criminals will travel farther distances as they grow older and gain more experience (Canter and Larkin, 1993; Carter and Hill, 1980). Overall, findings of JTC research provide relatively complete and important information pertaining to travel distances.

Criticism of Research

While the review of the literature concerning JTC made it clear that the research findings are well established and consistent, there are several important criticisms of JTC research, largely concerning the methods employed in the crime trips. The first criticism deals with the assumption that most crime trips began at home. When measuring JTC, almost all researchers measure the distance between an offender's home and the offense site location, assuming that the offender started the JTC from his or her primary residence. However, several researchers have found that criminals do not always start their journeys to crime from home. Specifically, Rengert, Piquero, and Jones (1999) report that several burglars in their sample started their searches from well over a mile away from home, a significant distance in urban areas. Moreover, Pettiway (1995) found that only 25 percent of crack users originated their drug-buying trips from home, with over 30 percent starting their trips from shopping, business, or other places. The impact of this assumption is that it may obscure the reality of how far criminals are really traveling to commit crime from when they first decide to commit a crime to when they arrive at the offense site. Based on this "domocentric" assumption, JTC research may more accurately be said to be measuring the distance from a criminal's home to the offense site. While this information is still valuable, it cannot accurately be called a JTC.

Closely related to the first criticism, the second major criticism also involves the methods used to measure the actual JTC trip. Specifically, even if we know the location where criminals originated their journeys to crime (which in general we don't), JTC researchers almost never know the exact route used to arrive at the offense site. Instead researchers use one of three different methods to estimate a criminal's journey to a crime site (Manhattan distance, Crow Flight, or Wheel Distance). While each of these methods calculates the distance between the offender's home and the offense site differently, none of them uses the actual crime trip involved. By not measuring the actual travel route used by the offender, JTC research again is only measuring the distance from an offender's residence to an offense site. While this may be important information, it is in no way synonymous with a criminal's trip to a crime site and may be either overestimating or underestimating the actual JTC of criminals.

A third major criticism of JTC research concerns the accuracy of the distance decay function discussed earlier. Specifically, criticism has stated that the distance decay function is a statistical artifact called an ecological fallacy, created by aggregating individual level crime data (Rengert, Piquero, and Jones, 1999). Using simulated data, Van Koppen and de Keijser (1997) were able to show that by aggregating individual level crime data they were able to produce a distance decay function, despite one not actually existing. While Rengert, Piquero, and Jones (1999) were able to convincingly argue against the points made by Van Koppen and de Keijser, questions still remain about the methods used in aggregating crime distances measured at the individual level.

The final criticism of JTC research involves its over-reliance on official data. With a few notable exceptions (Rengert and Wasilchick, 1985), almost all research on JTC involves only offenders who have been arrested and prosecuted for a specific crime. As numerous researchers have pointed out, there are serious problems that exist when using official crime data. First and most important is the fact that official data is not a complete recording of all crimes, but rather it is only a recording of all crimes known to the police (Robinson, 2002). Most crimes are not known to the police, leading to official data only being a partial indicator of the extent of crime in a jurisdiction. This unreported crime is commonly called the "dark figure of crime" and is considered to be a significant portion of all crimes committed within the United States each year (Robinson, 2002). Importantly, the Bureau of Justice Statistics reports that victims report only one in three property crimes and that victims are more likely to report crimes if they are violent in nature, where an injury results or where property loss is over $250 (1997). Moreover, of all crimes that are reported to the police few crimes are cleared (offender is arrested), further limiting the potential sample size used in JTC research. According to the Bureau of Justice Statistics (2000), in the year 2000 the clearance rate for violent crime offenses known to the police was 47.5 percent and only 16.7 percent for property crimes. Moreover, since 1971 the clearance rates for violent crimes have never been over 50 percent, while the clearance rates for property crimes have never been over 19 percent (Bureau of Justice Statistics, 2000). The impact of this reliance on official data is that researchers are making assumptions about criminals' travel distances based on small and most likely unrepresentative samples of the criminal population. In a sense, JTC research can best be described as research on the JTC of only the criminals who were bad enough to get caught and successfully prosecuted for a crime, a less-than-complete sample of all criminals.

GEOGRAPHIC PROFILING

The last section of this chapter provides a brief overview of geographic profiling, a practical application of the research on mental maps, awareness space, and JTC as well as several theories previously discussed in other chapters of the book. Geographic profiling is a tool used primarily in the investigation of serial offenses such as robbery, burglary, rape, or homicide (Rossmo, 2000). Although the concept of geographic profiling is relatively new, maps and crude spatial analysis have been used for years by law enforcement agencies to assist in the apprehension of suspects. In discussing the development of geographic profiling, Rossmo (2000) lists several major investigations in which mapping and spatial analysis were employed:

- *Hillside Strangler:* LAPD mapped the location of the abduction sites and body dump sites of the victims in an attempt to determine the locations where the killings were occurring. The results of this analysis were used to saturate a 3-square-mile area where police felt the offender lived. Although the analysis did not result in arrests, it was later learned that the focus area was close to killer Angelo Buono's auto shop;
- *Andrei Chikatilo:* Russian officials used geographic analysis to focus patrol efforts on several train stations where they suspected the offender would strike. The analysis led to the arrest and subsequent conviction of Andrei Chikatilo for the murders of 53 women and children; and
- *Railway Killer:* Academics and officials used spatial analysis to help narrow the list of individuals who would be tested for DNA in the Railway Killer investigation. The list was reduced from 5,000 to under 2,000, of which the offender was one. John Francis Duffy was arrested and subsequently convicted of the rape and murders of seven women in the London area.

While these early examples of using mapping and spatial analysis to assist in investigations were often crude and in many cases did not directly lead to the arrest of the offender, they laid the groundwork for the future development of geographic profiling.

Development of Geographic Profiling

While as early as 1986 Le Beau recognized the investigative potential of geostatistical analysis and crime pattern research for reducing offender search areas, it wasn't until 1990 that true geographic profiling was developed (Rossmo, 2000:195). The individual most recognized as responsible for the development of geographic profiling is D. Kim Rossmo, a former inspector for the Vancouver, Canada, Police Department who holds a Ph.D. in Criminology from Simon Fraser University. As stated before, the rationale behind geographic profiling comes from numerous sources including routine activity theory, rationale choice theory and research into mental maps, awareness space, and JTC. However, the biggest influence on geographic profiling can be most directly tied to crime pattern theory and research conducted by Paul and Patricia Brantingham (Rossmo, 2000). In their research, the Brantinghams have used an understanding of a criminal's activity space to predict where the offender will commit crimes. Geographic profiling essentially takes these ideas and inverts them (Rossmo, 1995a). Using information about where an offender has chosen to commit crimes, geographic profiling attempts to determine where the offender is most likely to reside. As Rossmo (2000) states, "while the two models have different purposes and inputs, their underlying concepts and ideas are similar."

One of the biggest misperceptions about geographic profiling involves what a geographic profile actually provides in terms of investigative assistance. Many people, both outside and within law enforcement, wrongly believe that a geoprofile tells law enforcement officials which exact houses to search for the offender, or that it puts an "X" on a map to show where the offender lives. In reality geographic profiling can best be thought of as a strategic information management system designed to support investigations into serial crimes, with the purpose of helping to narrow the search area for an offender (Rossmo, 2000). Rather than place an "X" on a map to show where the offender lives, geographic profiles provide output in the form of probability maps (called jeopardy surfaces or Q ranges) that indicate the areas within the search area where the offender is most likely to reside. Figure 5.7 provides an example of a geographic profiling output, with the areas darkest in color being the areas of highest probability of offender residence. This information is then used by law enforcement officials to develop new investigative strategies. Rossmo (1997) outlined several examples of how geographic profiling results can impact an investigation:

- *Suspect prioritization:* Based on the results, suspects who live in the areas of highest probability may receive additional investigative focus. Rossmo (1997) states that this is particularly beneficial when an investigation is suffering from "information overload" in which there are too many suspects;
- *Patrol saturation:* Police patrols can be increased in size in areas where the offender is thought to reside or search for victims;
- *Neighborhood canvasses:* Police can conduct door-to-door canvasses or mail information requests in areas where the offender is thought to live;
- *Police information systems:* Data contained within police databases such as probationer and parolee residences, known offender information, and criminal intelligence data can be overlaid with the profile results. Using this information, suspects may be added to the investigation; and
- *DNA searches:* Geographic profiles can be used to narrow the lists of individuals required to submit DNA samples, reducing the costs associated with these tests. This is an investigative technique that has been used numerous times in Britain.

It is also important to stress that a geographic profile alone cannot solve a crime; rather, geographic profiling is part of an overall investigative strategy. Geographic profiles should only be brought into an investigation after a series of crimes have been linked together through traditional police investigative techniques (Rossmo, 1997). As

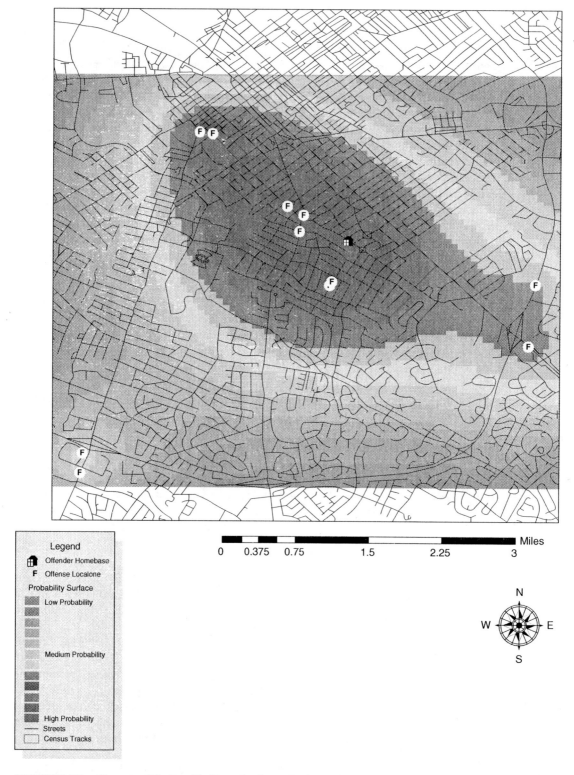

FIGURE 5.7   Geographic Profile Results for a Serial Rape Case. Map showing the results of a geographic profile. The dark shaded areas are the areas of highest offender residence probability, whereas the lighter shaded areas signify areas where the offender is less likely to reside.

with any investigative tool, geographic profiling has its limits and even its biggest proponents point out that there are numerous types of crimes that cannot be profiled and that only in appropriate cases can it produce beneficial results (Rossmo, 2000).

Profiling Models

While geographic profiling is still a relatively new field, there are now several well-established geographic profiling models currently used to assist in investigations. Currently, there are four main geographic profiling models: the Rossmo model, the Canter model, the Levine model, and the centrographic model, the first three of which have an associated software application—Rigel (Rossmo), Dragnet (Canter), and Crimestat (Levine). The commercialized nature of geographic profiling models may have actually served to limit the research surrounding the validity of these different models, as each organization wishes to avoid negative research results concerning the utility of its product. Specifically, research indicating that one model works better than another may result in decreased sales of these highly specialized and rather expensive programs. While all models are similar in their basic rationale and the Rossmo, Canter, and Levine models are similar in their underlying statistics, there are important differences in each different method that can impact their utility.

Rossmo Model.[1]   The Rossmo model, known as criminal geographic targeting (CGT), is based on research of serial offenders and applies the underlying principles of the Brantinghams' search model to locate an offender's residence (Levine, 2002b). In particular, CGT follows a distance decay function with criminal activity decreasing the farther you get away from an offender's house. Conducting a profile using the Rossmo model involves a four-stage process:

1. A rectangular search area is defined as one extending beyond the entire range of incidents in the series committed by the offender. This rectangular search area comprises a grid that is used to calculate distances;
2. Manhattan distance measurements are created between each crime location and each grid cell;
3. These distances are then compared to a buffer zone to produce numbers that correspond to each crime location and each grid cell. Thus, if there are nine crime locations, each grid cell will have nine numbers associated with it; and
4. Finally, these numbers are multiplied together to produce a single score for each grid cell. The higher the score, the greater the probability the grid cell contains the offender's residence.

Canter Model.[2]   The second model of geographic profiling was developed by David Canter and his colleagues at the Institute for Investigative Psychology at the University of Liverpool in England. As with the Rossmo model, the Canter model is based on the premise that most offenses will be committed near the home of the offender. Practically, there are two main differences between the Rossmo and Canter models (Levine, 2002b). First, while the Rossmo model focuses on determining the residence of the offender, the Canter model focuses on a practical search area for law enforcement. In particular, the Canter model provides a search strategy by providing output that gives probabilities of where an offender's home base is, not necessarily his or her residence. The second difference between the two models is a statistical or mathematical difference. Specifically, the two models use different distance decay functions to calculate distances between grid cells and crime locations (Levine, 2002b). Because of the similar rationale underlying the

---

[1]For a complete discussion of the mathematical and theoretical rationale behind this geographical profiling model, see Levine (2002b).

[2]For a complete discussion of the mathematical and theoretical rationale behind this geographical profiling model, see Levine (2002b).

models, the processes involved are fairly similar. Levine (2002b) describes the five-step process used by the Canter model to determine an offender's most likely residence as follows:

1. A rectangular study area is defined as one that is 20 percent larger than the range of the crime locations in the series. Over this search area, a grid of 13,300 cells is overlaid;
2. A distance decay coefficient is selected. Unlike the Rossmo model, the Canter model uses a series of distance decay coefficients to estimate the sensitivity of the model. This equation indicates the likelihood that any grid cell is the home base of the offender on one crime;
3. In order to account for different search areas used by criminals, the distances between each grid cell and each crime are divided by a normalization coefficient. Canter employs two different coefficients, the MID point and the Q range;
4. A calculation is created for each grid cell measuring the distance between each cell and each crime, and a likelihood estimate is created for each grid cell; and
5. A search cost index is defined as the proportion of the study area that has been searched to find the offender.

Levine Model.   The third geographic profiling model is that created by Levine for the Crimestat spatial analysis software. The Levine model differs from the two previous models in that it is not strictly speaking a geographic profiling model, but rather a JTC model (Levine, 2002b). In discussing the difference between a JTC model and a geographic profiling model, Levine (2002b:344–345) states,

> . . . journey to crime estimation follows a much simpler logic involving the distance dimension of the spatial patterning of a criminal. It is a method aimed at estimating the distance that serial offenders will travel to commit a crime and, by implication, the likely location from which they started their crime trip. In short, it is a strictly statistical approach to estimating the residential whereabouts of an offender compared to understanding the dynamics of serial offenders.

Thus, the main difference between a geographic profiling model and a JTC model is that the JTC model is a strictly statistical model and largely ignores the conceptual framework of geographic profiling. This is not to say that the two models are dissimilar in their calculations and basic assumptions. In fact Levine (2002) states that his JTC model builds on the Rossmo model and extends its modeling capability. To this point, conducting a geographic profile with the Levine model involves four stages similar to those of the Rossmo model:

1. A grid is overlaid on top of the study area. Unlike the Rossmo and Canter models, there is no optimal study area and so the user must be cautious when selecting a study area (Levine, 2002b);
2. The distance between each crime location and each cell is calculated. Importantly, whereas the Rossmo model uses Manhattan (indirect) distances to calculate the distance between each crime and each grid cell, the Levine model measures the distance between each crime and the centroid of each grid cell. Levine (2002b) states that this is usually a more appropriate method as routes of criminals are rarely known;
3. A distance decay function is then applied to each grid cell crime pair, and it sums the value over all crime incidents (Levine, 2002b). The Levine model then allows the user to decide whether to use one of five mathematical functions or an empirically derived function to model the travel distance of the offender (Levine, 2002); and
4. Finally, using the distance decay function, one can create a likelihood estimate for each grid cell. This grid cell output is a probability surface showing the areas of highest and lowest likelihood of offender residence in the study area.

Centrographic Model. The final geographic profiling model is known as the centrographic model and is probably best associated with research done by Derek Paulsen and the National Law Enforcement Corrections Technology Center-Southeast (NLECTC-SE), although several other researchers have also worked with centrographic methods. Although theoretically all four geographic profiling models are similar in their assumptions about offender awareness space and JTC, the main difference between the centrographic model and the other geographic profiling models is the method employed for the calculation of the top profiling region. In particular, centrographic models employ the use of centrographic statistics (center of minimum distance, mean center) to create a seed point around which a top profiling region is created. Thus, rather than use a complicated distance decay function to estimate an offender's anchor point and subsequent profile area, centrographic models use simple centrographic statistics to estimate the anchor point and create a top profiling area. Although there are different centrographic models, the model developed by the NLECTC-SE works in the following manner:

1. The center of minimum distance is determined for all crimes in the series. The center of minimum distance is the single point that is closest to all locations, or the point that minimizes the distance between all locations.
2. A top profile area is drawn based on a radius that is the median distance between each crime location and the center of minimum distance.
3. The profile area is prioritized based on quadrants, in which the quadrant that has the most crimes occurring within it is given the highest priority.

Criticism of Geographic Profiling

While the benefits of geographic profiling are admittedly powerful in that it can help drastically reduce the amount of time and energy expended in a serial crime investigation, there are several problems with the concept of geographic profiling. First, while geographic profiling is admittedly based on empirical research, the general field of *profiling* has been sharply criticized for lack of validity, reliability, and theoretical basis (Bartol, 1996). Most damning of the criticism comes from the American Psychological Association, which found that the FBI Behavioral Science Unit's famed psychological profilers were lacking concern over reliability and validity issues when it came to the assertions of their profiles (Poythress et al., 1993). Moreover, the FBI even admits that the process of profiling is more art than science (Hazelwood and Douglass, 1980). Although geographic profiling is based on theoretical principles and grounded in research findings concerning the spatial actions of criminals, issues surround making inferences about individual behavior based on aggregate research still exist (Van Koppen and de Keijser, 1997).

FOCUS ON
NEXT EVENT FORECASTING

One area of spatially related crime research that has increased over the last five years is the field of crime series analysis. This field of research is primarily concerned with providing both theoretical and practical understanding of spatial and temporal patterns of serial crime. A primary goal within the field of crime series analysis research is gaining a better understanding of the spatial aspects of serial offending in order to develop investigative tools to aid in the apprehension of serial criminals. While geographic profiling is the best known crime series analysis technique, next event forecasting (NEF) is equally as beneficial a crime series analysis tool and is starting to gain ground in use and utility in serial crime investigation.

(continued)

NEF and geographic profiling are both built off the same theoretical model developed by the Brantinghams, yet NEF uses it for a slightly different investigative purpose (Paulsen, 2005). As with geographic profiling, NEF builds on the foundation that in general offenders commit crimes where there is an overlap between suitable targets and their personal awareness space. However, whereas geographic profiling uses the locations of crimes to infer an offender's anchor point, NEF uses the locations of crimes to try and infer the offender's awareness space. In combining the locations of known crimes with the temporal order of the crimes in the series, NEF attempts to determine the area where an offender will commit their next crime. Once the known offenses are mapped, the temporal order of the crimes in the series is used to help determine where in the offenders' awareness space they are likely to offend next. JTC research has shown that most offenders travel a relatively short distance to commit their crimes; thus, the distribution of crime locations is a proxy for the offenders' awareness space. Importantly, this awareness space is fairly stable indicating that once it is established, criminals will offend mostly within this area. When temporal analysis is performed on the known offense locations, it provides a sound indicator of where within the offenders' awareness space their offenses have concentrated most recently. In a sense, NEF provides an indication of the offenders' spatial trend within their criminal awareness space, so that areas of the most likely next offense can be determined.

While the theoretical ground underlying NEF is fairly well established, only recently is there beginning to be agreement as to the best method for which to perform NEF. In particular there are four main methods currently used for conducting NEF of crimes: standard distance deviation rectangles (also called Gottleib rectangles), a two standard deviation rectangle drawn around the mean center of the incidents, Jennrich–Turner ellipse, a two satandard deviation ellipse drawn around the mean center of the incidents, minimum convex-hull polygon, a method in which a polygon is drawn in "dot to dot" around the incidents to create a small bounding rectangle, and time-weighted kenral density interpolation, a kernel smoothing technique that uses time as a weighting variable. In addition to these four main methods of NEF, there are also countless other homegrown methods used everyday by crime analysts to perform tactical crime analysis, such as correlated walk analysis, centrographic analysis, and human judging. In research conducted by NLECTC-Rocky Mountain as part of crime series analysis project, researchers found that the method most commonly used by police for forecasting of next event locations was "other" followed by standard distance deviation rectangle, minimum convex-hull polygon, Jennrich–Turner ellipse, and finally time-weighted kernel density interpolation. While these findings point to the relatively nascent nature of NEF, they also point to the general lack of research and dissemination into the accuracy of NEF methods. As of now, only one real study has been conducted comparing the accuracy of different NEF methods against each other and necessary control methods (Paulsen, 2005). Research results indicated that the time-weighted kernel density interpolation methods was significantly more accurate while still reducing the search area to a level that is practically useful (Paulsen, 2005). Although these results were significant and provide an indication of the potential of NEF to assist in serial crime investigation, more research needs to be done to determine both when these techniques can best be used as well as

A second problem with geographic profiling involves the data used to create and test the profiling algorithms that produce the profiles. As discussed when critiquing JTC research, the statistical computations and algorithms are based solely on research involving offenders who have been arrested, a less than complete selection of all criminals. Canter et al. (2000:467) actually mention this as a potential problem:

> The limitations on the results presented are a function of the data set used. Only offenders who have been caught were included in the sample, so it is an open question whether their parameters of movement are the same as those of offenders who evade detection. Similarly, the models apply to offenders who come to police attention due to discovery of the locations where the victims' bodies have been disposed of.

Moreover, the models base their calculations on samples that are particularly small. In the case of the Canter model, the mathematical function relating to site selection behaviors of serial offenders is derived from a sample of only 79 serial offenders who dumped their victims' bodies in locations different from their residences (Canter et al., 2000). Thus, serial killers such as John Wayne Gacy, who killed 29 victims, were excluded from the analysis because he buried his victims in his own basement. Levine (2002b:343) goes further and states that the empirical model used in the Canter model is strictly pragmatic and without theoretical basis. Overall, the possibility exists that the mathematical reasoning used to inform these geographic profiling packages is severely limited due to the databases used to create the equations. [3]

Finally, the previous research on the accuracy of geographic profiling calls into question the accuracy of geographic profiling in general and the comparative accuracy of the more mathematically complicated methods. In particular, several research articles written in the past few years have found that simple centrographic models as well as human judges are as accurate as the more advanced (Rossmo, Canter, and Levine) geographic profiling models (Paulsen, 2006a, 2006b; Snook, Canter, and Bennell, 2002; Snook, Taylor, and Bennell, 2004; Snook et al., 2005). While the research that has been published casts serious doubt onto the improved accuracy of advanced geographic profiling models over more simple models, questions as to the veracity of these claims still linger because of methodological issues in the comparative research (Paulsen, 2006b). Unfortunately for the field of geographic profiling, the majority of researchers appear to be more interested in arguing over issues of accuracy than in attempting to find solutions to the other problems facing geographic profiling (Paulsen, 2007). Specifically, the issues of determining a commuter offender from a marauder offender and determining linked crimes in a series are both highly important to accurate geographic profiling and both seriously under-researched (Paulsen, 2007).

SUMMARY

List of Major Research Findings

1. Spatial behavior focuses on the role of the individual and his or her spatial knowledge in determining crime patterns;
2. Mental maps are mental sketches of a place or area comprising an individual's knowledge about a place or area;
3. Mental maps are created through individual experience, whether it is hands on (travel and interaction) or perceptual (media and friends);
4. Perceptions of crime patterns vary by race, age, gender, income, education level, tenure in residence, and suburban/urban;
5. Individual perceptions of crime patterns are not very accurate when compared with official crime patterns;
6. Awareness space is those areas in which an individual has a more detailed geographic knowledge;
7. Activity space is those places regularly visited by a person where the majority of his or her activities are carried out;
8. Activity space varies in size and shape depending on the distance and direction of routine activities;
9. Nodes are those places that are central to a person's life (home, work, recreation area) and make up the extent of an individual's activity space, acting as anchor points for both legitimate and illegitimate activities;

---

[3]For a complete discussion of the computational weaknesses in the different geographical profiling models, see Levine (2002b).

10. Crime attractors are those places such as red light districts, drug markets, and nightclub areas where criminal opportunities are well known and to which motivated offenders are subsequently attracted as a source for criminal activity;

11. Crime generators are places such as shopping centers and entertainment districts to which large numbers of people are drawn for *legitimate* reasons but which provide criminal opportunities because of the sheer numbers of potential victims present;

12. Paths are everyday routes that people use to travel between activity nodes. Criminals often choose victims that are along paths because they are within areas the criminal knows well;

13. Awareness space varies based on age, gender, race, class, employment status, and residential status;

14. Most criminals commit crime within their awareness space, usually centering around the nodes and paths that make up their routine activities;

15. Journey to Crime (JTC) is the distance a criminal travels to commit a crime. JTC is usually measured from an offender's residence to the crime location;

16. Criminals will travel to areas with target attractiveness because of the perceived high value of criminal opportunities;

17. Criminals favor areas that are spatially attractive (close by or well known to the criminal) over areas that have high target attractiveness but are unknown to the offender;

18. Target backcloth refers to the spatial distribution of criminal targets or victims within a given area. Target backcloth can significantly impact the distribution of a criminal's offending;

19. JTC exhibits distance decay in that criminals select targets closer to home, with criminal victimizations declining the farther they travel from their residences;

20. Buffer zones exist around criminals' residences, in which offenders will not offend in order to avoid detection;

21. JTC varies by crime type, city type, and offender characteristics such as gender, race, age, income, hunting type, criminal experience, and victim/offender relationship;

22. Research on JTC suffers from numerous problems including: assumptions that crime trips begin at home, not knowing the actual routes taken by criminals, and an over-reliance on official data;

23. Geographic profiling works by taking information about where an offender has chosen to commit crimes and trying to determine where the individual lives;

24. Geographic profiling is used as part of an overall investigative strategy to help narrow the search area for an offender, not to place an "X" on a map where the criminal lives; and

25. Research into geographic profiling has yet to conclusively show whether or not geographic profiling is more accurate than traditional investigative techniques at resolving serial crimes.

Implications of Research for Crime Mapping and Spatial Analysis

The implications that behavioral geography has for crime mapping and spatial analysis of crime are probably more powerful than in any other chapter in this book. Through the study of behavioral geography we can better understand, on an individual level, why criminals choose to commit crimes where they do. Specifically, behavioral geography informs us that criminals' choices about where to commit crimes are not random, but are guided by their awareness and activity spaces, concepts that are heavily influenced by an individual's nodes (home, work, recreation area) and paths (travel routes between nodes). Furthermore, JTC research has shown that criminals travel relatively short distances to crime, preferring to stay in areas where they have spatial knowledge and feel comfortable, even if it means forgoing more attractive targets. However, despite this tendency to commit crimes closer to home, offenders rarely if ever commit crimes in areas directly surrounding their homes (own neighborhood) for fear of identification by those who could recognize them.

As the development of geographic profiling has shown, behavioral geography can help us to better understand and possibly predict where offenders' live based on where crime occurs. Through crime mapping and crime pattern analysis, we can generate numerous hypotheses about where offenders may reside, work, and travel and in turn develop more effective policies and police practices to prevent crime in the future. Moreover, through the synthesis of behavioral geography and crime mapping, we can determine areas that are crime attractors and crime generators and take appropriate action to monitor these more closely. Overall, the intersection of crime mapping tools and behavioral geography knowledge holds a great promise to lead to the further understanding of criminal victimization and potential crime reduction.

CHAPTER 6

Epidemics, Diffusion, and Displacement of Crimes

The purpose of this chapter is to provide a comprehensive discussion of the spatial processes of epidemics, displacement, and diffusion as they relate to crime. In this chapter, we examine these three vitally important spatial processes and their implications for crime mapping and crime prevention.

Chapter Outline

INTRODUCTION TO EPIDEMICS, DIFFUSION, AND DISPLACEMENT

EPIDEMICS
  Types of Epidemics
  Crime and Epidemics
  FOCUS ON: Media Coverage of the
    "Crack Cocaine Epidemic"

DISPLACEMENT
  Types of Displacement
  Crime and Displacement

DIFFUSION
  Types of Criminal Diffusion
  Crime and Diffusion

SUMMARY
  List of Major Research Findings Related
    to Epidemics, Diffusion, and
    Displacement
  Implications of Findings for Crime
    Mapping and Spatial Analysis
  CASE STUDY: The Place of School Violence

INTRODUCTION TO EPIDEMICS, DIFFUSION, AND DISPLACEMENT

According to *Merriam-Webster's Collegiate Dictionary* (2007), an *epidemic* means "affecting or tending to affect a disproportionately large number of individuals within a population, community, or region at the same time." Something can be described as an epidemic if it is "excessively prevalent" or "contagious." When you hear words like epidemic or contagion, you likely think of medical conditions such as HIV/AIDS, cancer, obesity, or other illnesses and conditions studied by the Centers for Disease Control and Prevention (CDC). According to the CDC, "an epidemic occurs when the incidence of a condition is higher than normal or higher than what health officials expect" (reported in Jacobs and Henry, 1996:367). In addition to these illnesses, crime is often considered to be an epidemic or at epidemic levels. As you will see in this chapter, crimes such as homicide, rape, gang violence, drug use and abuse, school shootings, and similar crimes have been described as epidemic in the United States.

Displacement refers to being physically moved out of position (*Merriam-Webster's Collegiate Dictionary,* 2007). For example, when an object is dropped into a bucket filled with water, the water that overflows from the bucket has been displaced. In crime research, displacement refers to the movement of crime from one area to another, after efforts to prevent crime in the area have been initiated. If police focus their attention on an area infested with drug dealing activity, a possible outcome is that drug dealers will simply move to another area where police presence is not so high.

Diffusion can be understood as having been poured out and permitted or caused to spread out freely. It is synonymous with scattering or becoming transmitted especially by contact (*Merriam-Webster's Collegiate Dictionary,* 2002). In terms of crime, diffusion is relevant in at least two ways. First, the term *diffusion* is usually used to refer to the spreading of crime, from one area to another over time. Second, the term *diffusion of benefits* is used to describe how the benefits of crime prevention tend to be even greater than those that are intended. For example, a program aimed at preventing underage drinking on a college campus may also reduce the incidence of rape on campus, even if unintended, because alcohol consumption is related to rape victimization (Robinson and Roh, 2007).

In this chapter, we discuss the spatial processes of epidemics, displacement, and diffusion as they relate to crime. We show that crime can be studied as an epidemic specific to particular places and times, that crime can be displaced by crime prevention efforts (although crimes displaced rarely are as frequent as those prevented), and that the diffusion of crime and crime prevention has significant implications for crime mapping.

EPIDEMICS

In the introduction to this chapter, we briefly discussed some illnesses that people tend to think about when they hear the word epidemic. In many ways, crime is like an illness. Like some illnesses, crime

- Tends to appear in the presence of some environmental characteristics more than others (like tuberculosis, or TB, which is more prevalent in crowded areas without access to clear air);
- Tends to affect some people more than others (like sickle cell anemia, which is the most common single-gene illness among African Americans);
- Tends to be spread from one area to the next through movement patterns (like HIV/AIDS, which spreads through sexual contact, shared needles, blood transfusions, and other unsafe contact with bodily fluids);
- Can be moved from one place to another without completely preventing it (like measles, or rubeola, which is contracted via the airborne route, and most often in schools because of recirculated air from ventilation systems).

Interestingly, we can compare these illnesses with crime. For example, the same environmental conditions that have been claimed to produce high rates of street crime are also associated with increased rates of TB (recall the factors of high population density, urbanization, immigration, and so forth, discussed in Chapter 3 on social disorganization and crime). Thus, efforts to control the spread of TB in America early in the twentieth century were also used to prevent TB. During this time, both crime and TB were viewed as problems of the poor, and efforts to control crime and TB were aimed disproportionately at poor immigrants in large cities (del Carmen and Robinson, 2000). According to the World Health Organization (WHO, 2002), TB "kills approximately 2 million people each year. The global epidemic is growing and becoming more dangerous. The breakdown in health services, the spread of HIV/AIDS, and the emergence of multidrug-resistant TB are contributing to the worsening impact of this disease." In 1993, the WHO declared tuberculosis "a global emergency" and yet it is feared that between 2002 and 2020, approximately 1 billion people will be newly infected, over 150 million people will become ill, and 36 million will die of TB. Street crime is down in the United States, but it has spread to areas across the globe as countries have experienced growth and increased globalization (recall the discussion of crime trends and international crime rates in Chapter 2 on crime and place). So, in many ways, crime is epidemic, as well.

Additionally, serious street crime victimization is more prevalent among African Americans than other groups, much like sickle cell anemia. According to the American Sickle Cell Anemia Foundation (2002), the disease affects millions of people throughout the world and "is particularly common among people whose ancestors come from sub-Saharan Africa; Spanish speaking regions (South America, Cuba, Central America); Saudi Arabia; India; and Mediterranean countries, such as Turkey, Greece, and Italy." In the United States, nearly 72,000 people, most of whose ancestors came from Africa, have the condition. Another 2 million Americans, or 1 in 12 African Americans, carry the sickle cell trait.

In terms of criminal victimization, the Bureau of Justice Statistics (2006) reports that in 2005, African Americans were more likely to be victimized by violent crimes. For every 1,000 African Americans, 27 were victimized by violent crimes in 2005 versus 20 Caucasians and 14 persons of other races. Blacks and whites experienced similar rates of simple assault, rape/sexual assault, and robbery, but the FBI's Uniform Crime Reports (UCR) tend to show that African Americans are disproportionately likely to be murdered. The 2005 UCR, for example, showed that blacks made up about 49 percent of murder victims, even though they accounted for only about 12 percent of the U.S. population. Thus, the murder rate for black victims was 20.6 per 100,000 people, versus only 3.3 per 100,000 for whites. We do not think that there is anything about being black that explains higher rates of violent crime (see Robinson, 2004); instead, we hold that living in certain environments, such as in the inner city in conditions of concentrated poverty, increase the risk of violent victimization. Similarly, this explains why African Americans are disproportionately likely to be victimized by burglary and motor vehicle theft.

Finally, like with HIV/AIDS, oftentimes victims of crime are victimized by their own actions. According to the Office of the U.S. Surgeon General (2002), the research is clear that the spread of HIV/AIDS can be reduced significantly by using protection during sexual activity and by reducing or eliminating exposure to bodily fluids.

The same is true with many street crimes. People can reduce their risk of robbery, assault, and murder, for example, by staying away from or at least reducing the amount of time they spend in or near bars. This is not to say that AIDS victims are to blame for their illnesses, or that crime victims are to blame for their victimization (recall the discussion of the lifestyle/exposure theory in Chapter 4 on ecological theories of crime). We are simply pointing out the very strong research that suggests that potential victims have the best chance of any group of preventing victimization.

Types of Epidemics

There are many examples of epidemics that can be discussed from the medical literature. The CDC recognizes chronic diseases and illnesses as types of epidemics and discusses historical occurrences across the globe of bubonic plague, smallpox, measles, influenza, yellow fever, cholera, typhoid, polio, tuberculosis, ebola, hepatitis, sexually transmitted diseases, and so forth.

The Head Injury Center at the University of Pennsylvania adds traumatic brain injury (TBI) to the list of epidemics in the United States. They call it a "silent epidemic" because, despite the prevalence of TBI, only one in three Americans are familiar with the term *brain injury* and people do not typically associate TBI with the most common form of injury—concussions. According to the Center:

- Each year, an estimated 2 million Americans suffer some form of TBI; TBI is the leading cause of death and disability in persons under 45 years of age;
- Brain injury is suffered by someone in America every 15 seconds;
- Each year, nearly 100,000 people die from TBI and 500,000 more are permanently disabled;
- Each year, about 80,000 people experience the onset of long-term disability following a severe brain injury;
- Approximately 5.3 million Americans—more than 2 percent of the U.S. population—are living with a disability that results from TBI; and
- The costs associated with treatment, rehabilitation, and care for TBI sufferers are about $30 billion each year in the United States.

According to Stevenson (2001), there are two main types of epidemics. They include (1) common source epidemics; and (2) propagated epidemics. *Common source epidemics* infect many people from a single contaminated source. It is characterized by a rapid onset and a " 'sharp' peak and rapid decline in incidence." *Propagated epidemics,* in contrast, occur after an infected person is introduced to a susceptible population. It is characterized by a slow onset and a " 'blunted' peak and slow decline in incidence."

Bugl (2001) also labels two types of epidemics: common source and host-to-host. *Host-to-host epidemics* are the same as propagated epidemics. Bugl writes, "common source epidemics usually produce more new cases earlier and faster than host-to-host epidemics. Once the infected source is closed, sealed, or removed, the common source epidemic usually abates rapidly. Host-to-host epidemics are slower to grow and slower to diminish." Figure 6.1 illustrates the incidence and life course of a fictional common source and host-to-host epidemic.

The steps in the origin and development of any disease, or *pathogenesis,* are very similar to the origin and development of crime in any area. Stevenson suggests that to cause disease, bacteria, viruses, or any other *pathogen* must contact the host, colonize the

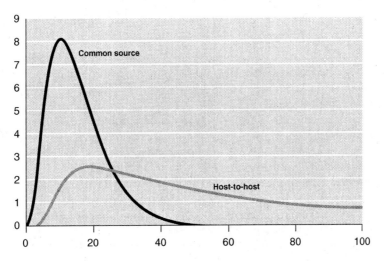

FIGURE 6.1   Incidence and Life Course of a Common Source and Host-to-Host Epidemic

Source: Bugl (2001). "Epidemiology." [On-line]. http://uhaweb.hartford.edu/BUGL/epidemiology.htm

host, infect the host, evade the host defense system, and damage host tissues. This is much like how crime invades a neighborhood, when criminals move in, make contact, colonize, infect, evade, and cause damage.[1] The notion of *contagion* underlies any epidemic. A contagion is a contagious disease, something that is spread by contact, whether direct or indirect in nature.

Crime and Epidemics

It is hard to say exactly how many true crime epidemics there have been in American history and across the globe, although many claim juvenile and violent crimes were epidemics in the 1980s and 1990s (Cook and Laub, 1998; Jones and Jones, 2000; Loftin, 1986; Marcus, 1996). Many so-called epidemics turn out to be false, socially constructed by powerful institutions such as religion and the media. One notable example of a false crime epidemic goes all the way back to the Massachusetts Bay Colony, which found itself suddenly confronted by dozens of witches committing crimes against religion (Erikson, 1966). Other so-called crime epidemics include use of illicit drugs such as methamphetamine (Feldkamp, 1996), rape and child sexual abuse in the United States (Russell and Bolen, 2000), and hate crimes (Byers and Zeller, 2001). Research on the hate crime "epidemic," however, shows that it is without real evidence and was socially constructed by the media (Jacobs and Henry, 1996).

The same can be said for many of the nation's drug war "epidemics." For example, Robinson and Scherlen (2007) show that the crack cocaine epidemic of the 1980s was blown way out of proportion to the small threat posed by the drug, being used by a very small segment of the population, mostly in the nation's large cities.

An example of a crime epidemic that seems to be real is the homicide epidemic of the late 1980s in the United States, committed disproportionately by young, inner-city males with guns, as part of gang activity and the illicit drug trade (Baumer, Lauritsen, and Rosenfeld, 1998; Blumstein, 1995, 1996; Cohen et al., 1988; Hamid, 1992; Johnson, Golub, and Fagan, 1995; Klein, Maxson, and Cunningham, 1991; Zimring, 1996). Figure 6.2 illustrates homicide trends in the United States since 1960.

According to the Bureau of Justice Statistics (2002), "The homicide rate doubled from the mid 1960s to the late 1970s. In 1980, it peaked at 10.2 per 100,000 population and subsequently fell off to 7.9 per 100,000 in 1985. It rose again in the late 1980s and

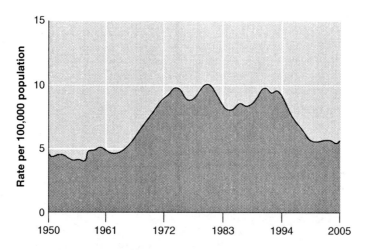

FIGURE 6.2   Homicide Victimization, 1950–2005

Source: Bureau of Justice Statistics (http://www.ojp.usdoj.gov/bjs/homicide/hmrt.htm)

---

[1]Compare these to the processes of *invasion, domination,* and *succession* discussed by Robert Park in Chapter 3 on human ecology.

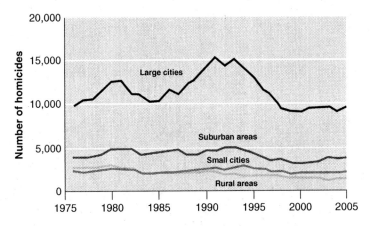

FIGURE 6.3 **Homicides in Urban, Suburban, and Rural Areas, 1976–2005**

Source: Bureau of Justice Statistics (http://www.ojp.usdoj.gov/bjs/homicide/region.htm)

early 1990s to another peak in 1991 of 9.8 per 100,000. Since then, the rate has declined sharply, reaching 5.7 per 100,000 by 1999." As of 2005, the rate of homicide in the United States was 5.6 per 100,000 people.

The increases in homicide are not easily seen in Figure 6.2. When separated out by city size, however, one can see that the increases came mostly in the nation's largest cities, just as expected given our examination of crime facts in Chapter 2. Figure 6.3 shows homicide trends in large cities, small cities, rural areas, and suburbs. Without question, homicides increased dramatically in the nation's large cities in the 1980s. Cohen and Tita (1999:373) suggest that in the fields of mathematics and biology, the term epidemic is "a formal term describing both unexpected nonlinear growth in some phenomenon and some process of mechanism of spread across or within populations." They add that in public health, the term means "the existence of a greater than expected—based on prior trends—number of events." Homicide increases in large U.S. cities in the 1980s seem to fit each of these definitions.

Perhaps just as telling are trends in homicide by weapon type. Figure 6.4 conclusively shows that homicide increases in the 1980s were almost entirely due to

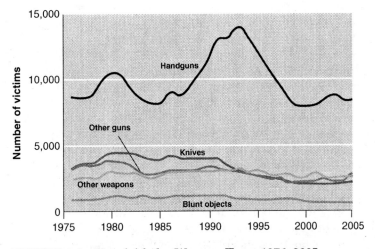

FIGURE 6.4 **Homicide by Weapon Type, 1976–2005**

Source: Bureau of Justice Statistics (http://www.ojp.usdoj.gov/bjs/homicide/weapons.htm)

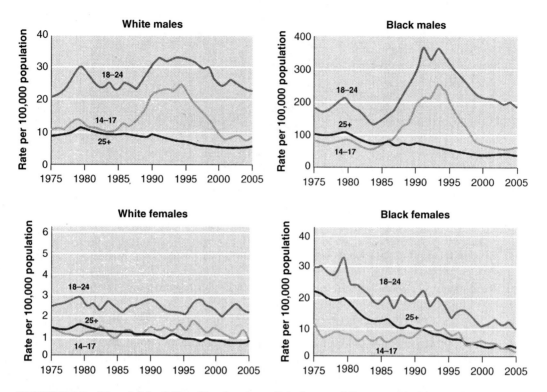

FIGURE 6.5   Homicide Offending by Age, Gender, and Race, 1976–2005

Source: Bureau of Justice Statistics (http://www.ojp.usdoj.gov/bjs/homicide/ageracesex.htm)

homicides by handguns. Homicides by other guns, knives, blunt objects, and other weapons either did not increase in the 1980s or did not increase as rapidly as homicides with handguns.

Finally, Figure 6.5 shows homicide trends by age, gender, and race. These data clearly show that the homicide increases in the 1980s were mostly attributable to young males between the ages of 14 and 24 years, particularly black males between these ages.

All of these data support the notion that a violent crime epidemic swept through America's large cities in the 1980s, especially homicides committed with guns by young minority and white males. These homicide increases were preceded by the invasion of crack cocaine into the nation's cities. As discussed in Chapter 1, our goal with theory is to explain why the epidemic occurred. As you will see in this chapter, crime maps can help us understand this particular crime epidemic. The "crack cocaine epidemic," as it has been called, is discussed in the Focus On box.

We discuss the media coverage of this crack cocaine event not to draw attention away from the very serious nature of illicit drugs such as crack, but rather to point out that oftentimes crime epidemics are overblown in the media. With crack cocaine, the media clearly got their coverage wrong. Yet, this does not change the fact that the arrival of crack cocaine into the nation's cities resulted in the prevalence of numerous guns, easily accessible to young people in gangs and not in gangs. These guns were used in homicides, often in gang warfare and to assure a share of the illicit drug market. The result was a contagion of homicide (Blumstein, 1995).

One source of "contagion" of violent crime may very well be poverty, supporting the main propositions of theories such as social disorganization (discussed in Chapter 3). Some studies, for example, find that levels of deprivation of one community tend to predict the levels of violence that will occur in neighboring areas (Bhati, 2005).

Eck (1997) relates the concept of contagion to crime by focusing on criminal offenders: "Contagion suggests that when offenders notice one criminal opportunity they often detect similar opportunities they have previously overlooked. Crime then spreads. The broken-windows theory (Wilson and Kelling, 1982) is an example of a contagion theory." The broken windows theory, first introduced in Chapter 1, is related directly to the notion of *incivilities* and suggests that when conditions of any environment are left to deteriorate, they will attract crime. More specifically, small signs of disorder or minor crimes, if left unchecked, will eventually breed serious crime (recall the discussion of incivilities as "untended property" and "untended people and behavior" in Chapter 4 on incivilities and crime). Messner et al. (1999:424) also explain that violence can be transmitted through contagion because they are "mutually reinforcing. As information about violent events is transmitted through social networks and other media of communication, the probability of subsequent violence is likely to increase."

FOCUS ON
MEDIA COVERAGE OF THE "CRACK COCAINE EPIDEMIC"

The Community Epidemiology Work Group (CEWG) was established by the National Institute on Drug Abuse (NIDA) to provide community-level surveillance of drug abuse in 20 metropolitan areas. Claims by field sources show concern about crack cocaine in America's inner cities in the early 1980s:

- Boston: Cocaine is a massive problem;
- Miami: Cocaine is more available than ever before;
- Newark: Cocaine is gaining rapid popularity;
- New Orleans: Cocaine appears to be dominating the drug scene;
- Philadelphia: There is a significant increase in availability and use;
- Phoenix: Large quantities are available through Miami, prices have dropped;
- Seattle: Cocaine is the county's most important problem;
- Buffalo: There has been a marked increase in cocaine use;
- Chicago: Cocaine is the only drug to have shown consistently increasing patterns of abuse;
- Denver: It is the major drug of abuse in the state;
- Detroit: Cocaine use continues to increase;
- Los Angeles: Cocaine use has reached epidemic levels;
- New York City: Cocaine activity continues to increase;
- St. Louis: Cocaine is readily available throughout the metropolitan area;
- Washington, D.C.: Cocaine use continued to rise;
- Dallas: Pushers were selling cocaine in capsules in African-American lower-income communities. Cuban cocaine traffickers were arrested; and
- Newark: African Americans were dealing large amounts of cocaine (reported in Robinson, 2002).

Reinarman and Levine (1989) outline the 1980s crack cocaine drug scare, where all sorts of societal problems were blamed on the substance crack. They argue that media portrayals of crack cocaine were highly inaccurate. The scare began in 1986, as *Time* and *Newsweek* magazines ran five cover stories each on crack cocaine. *Newsweek* and *Time* called crack the largest issue of the year (Beckett, 1997). In the second half of 1986, NBC News featured 400 stories on the drug. In July 1986 alone, the three major networks ran 74 drug stories on their nightly newscasts (Potter and Kappeler, 1998). Drug-related stories in the *New York Times* increased from 43 in the second half of 1985 to 92, and 90 and 220 in the first and second halves of 1986, respectively (Beckett, 1997), and thousands of stories about crack appeared in magazines and newspapers (Reinarman, 1995).

As media coverage of drugs increased, people were paying attention. This is because consumers of media information are more likely to recognize issues as the most important problems when they receive a lot of notable attention in the national news. Drug coverage in the media was more extensive in the 1980s than at other time periods. For example, the CBS

(continued)

program "48 Hours on Crack Street" obtained the highest rating of any similar news show in the early 1980s (Reinarman and Levine, 1989:541–542). The most startling thing about all of this news coverage is that it did not reflect reality, as crack cocaine use was actually quite rare during this time period (Walker, 1998). Research from NIDA showed that crack use was in fact declining during this time period. According to NIDA, most drug use peaks came between 1979 and 1982, except cocaine which peaked between 1982 and 1985 (Jensen and Gerber, 1998:14).

Media coverage of cocaine use increased in the late 1980s even after drug use already began to decline. Jensen and Gerber (1998:17) suggest that President Reagan's declaration of war against drugs in August 1986 created an "orgy" of media coverage on crack cocaine. Public opinion about the seriousness of the "drug problem" changed as a result. In mid-August 1986, drugs became the most important problem facing the nation in public opinion polls. And by late August, 86 percent of Americans said "fighting the drug problem" was "extremely important" (Robinson and Scherlen, 2007).

DISPLACEMENT

As we mentioned in the introduction to the chapter, displacement of crime typically refers to the movement of crime from one place to another in response to crime prevention efforts (Farrington et al., 1993; Laycock and Tilley, 1995). Scholars who have asserted that displacement makes crime prevention impossible assume several things about criminal offenders and about crime. For example, Eck (1998) writes, "Fear of displacement is often based on the assumption that offenders are like predatory animals (they will do whatever it takes to commit crimes just as a rat will do whatever it takes to steal food from the cupboard)." Clarke (1998:2) adds that some feel crime prevention is not a worthy pursuit because of displacement: "Since the motivation to commit crime remains untouched, reducing opportunities is seen to be a largely futile exercise."

Felson and Clarke (1998:26) also discuss the faulty assumptions of the offender's underlying the fear of displacement. Those who fear displacement view the offender not only as a predatory animal, but also as someone who has a propensity to commit crimes that

> builds up and must be discharged, in the same way that sexual release is sought. In other cases, the drive to commit crime is seen to be so strong and persistent that, like a flood tide, it will break through any barriers. In yet other cases, it is assumed that "professional" criminals or drug addicts must obtain a certain income from crime to maintain their lifestyles or their habits.

Felson and Clarke reason that these assumptions of the offender ignore the critical role that temptation and opportunity play in criminal offending. Many offenses, they contend, are committed because of immediate and passing temptations that can easily be prevented by reducing opportunities for crime. Weisburd (1997:4) calls such offending "situational, often serendipitous" in character. The key is that when simple opportunities for crime are eliminated, most offenders will not purposely seek out other targets to victimize, but instead will only commit future crimes if they again happen on convenient and easy opportunities.

It turns out that this is even true with regard to some forms of suicide. Clarke and Mayhew (1989) showed that, following the detoxification of the domestic gas supply in England and Wales during the 1960s and 1970s, suicides by gas decreased greatly. Furthermore, total suicides decreased, as other forms of suicide did not increase. Other studies of suicide and gun availability have followed (Carrington and Moyer, 1994).

Historically, criminologists have assumed that there are simply too many opportunities for crime in existence to effectively prevent motivated offenders from finding suitable targets or victims (Weisburd, 1997). Although early studies tended to confirm this (Chaiken, Lawless, and Stevenson, 1974; Lateef, 1974; Mayhew et al., 1976; Press, 1971; Trypak, 1975), it appears that for many types of crimes, this is not correct. Weisburd (1997:3) concludes that displacement is "seldom total and often inconsequential." This is because crime opportunities are differentially distributed by time and space and are not readily available everywhere and at any time.

Types of Displacement

According to Clarke (1998:2), the following types of displacement have been identified: displacement of crime from one place to another; displacement of crime from one time to another; displacement of crime from one target to another; and displacement of crime from one kind of crime to another. Similarly, Felson and Clarke (1998:25) identify five types of displacement: *geographical displacement*, where crime moves from one place to another; *temporal displacement*, where crime moves from one time to another; *target displacement*, where crime moves from one target or set of victims to another target or set of victims; *tactical displacement*, where one method of committing a crime is replaced by another; and *crime type displacement*, where one type of crime is replaced by another.

Crime and Displacement

According to Clarke (1998), the Ministry of Justice of Holland examined 55 studies of displacement (Hesseling, 1994). In 22 of the studies, there was no evidence of displacement. In 33 studies, some displacement was found but tended to be small in size. "In no case, did the crime displaced elsewhere equal the crime prevented" (Clarke, 1998:14).

According to Eck (1998), there have been four empirical reviews of the displacement phenomenon over the past decade. He writes,

> Theoretical explorations based on a rational choice perspective . . . find no basis for believing offenders always completely displace if they cannot attack their favorite targets. . . . Reviews of empirical studies examining place-focused prevention, police enforcement, and other preventing tactics in the United States, Canada, Great Britain, continental Europe, and Australia, find that there is often no displacement, but when displacement occurs it does not overwhelm other gains from blocking crime opportunities. . . .

Eck concludes, "Concern about displacement is usually based more on pessimism than empirical fact." Felson and Clarke (1998:26) add, "Those who assume that displacement is inevitable overestimate its capacity to occur."

Felson and Clarke (1998:27) provide several examples of studies that did not find evidence of displacement. They include the following:

- Check frauds in Sweden were reduced with new identification procedures, with no displacement to other forms of property crimes;
- Target hardening of Australian banks resulted in lower robbery rates, and areas surrounding the banks did not see subsequent increases in robbery;
- Thefts at a marketplace decreased when the stalls were rearranged and lighting was improved, with no displacement to nearby markets;
- Improved security to a parking deck in England did not result in increased thefts to other parking decks that did not change their security precautions; and
- Efforts to control prostitution in a park through street closures and increased police patrols decreased prostitution but did not lead to increases in prostitution in nearby areas.

Perhaps the one type of crime where we should expect displacement to be common is with drug crimes, although Weisburd (1997) cites several studies that do not find this to be the case. Some experimental studies do find evidence of displacement in drug markets after a community policing intervention (e.g., Mazerolle and Green, 2000). With regard to policing illicit drug markets, Robinson (2008) contends that there are only three possible outcomes of policing a neighborhood with the goal of ridding it of drugs: *subterfuge*, where the offenders hide and defend their territories from the police; *replacement*, where offenders are arrested but replaced by new offenders willing to take the risks of arrest; and *displacement*, where offenders leave the area and set up shop somewhere else. None of these amounts to a success in terms of crime prevention. Yet, most crime prevention efforts result in little displacement and rarely if ever displace more crime than is prevented. Figure 6.6 shows an example of how a targeted crime

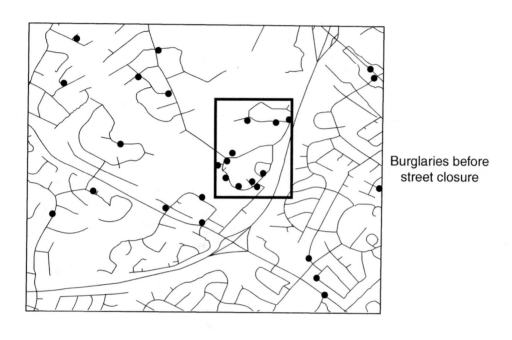

Burglaries before
street closure

Burglaries after
street closure

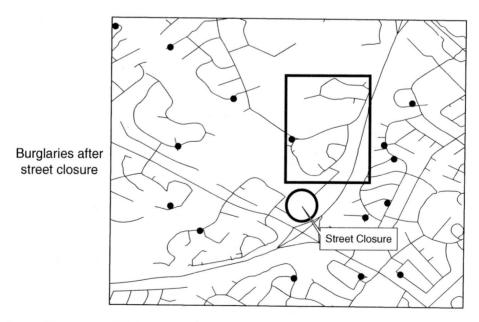

Street Closure

FIGURE 6.6   Street Closures and Crime

prevention initiative led to crime reductions without spreading crime to new areas. In this case, a street to a neighborhood with a burglary problem was closed based on speculation that a particular band of burglars was driving into the area along this route. The result was reduced burglary with no evidence of displacement.

DIFFUSION

In Chapter 2, we discussed theories such as modernization theory, also known as anomie theory, which attributes higher crime rates to sudden changes in society and communities. In Chapter 4, we also discussed opportunity theories such as routine activity and lifestyle/exposure theory that link higher crime rates to increased opportunities for crime created by changes in society's structures, institutions, culture, and social processes. Additionally, in Chapter 2, we saw that cultural theories attribute crime rate differences to differences in belief systems, attitudes, values, norms, and ways of life of unique groups. We also saw that strain theories, also known as economic deprivation and social stratification models, posit that frustration—usually caused by economic conditions—leads to higher crime. Finally, in Chapter 3, we examined social disorganization and social control theories that attribute higher crime rates in any area to a breakdown in the bonds that normally hold citizens to society and its laws. Each of these theoretical approaches can be applied to the process of diffusion, when crime spreads from one place to another.

Types of Criminal Diffusion

As we mentioned in the introduction to this chapter, there are two main types of diffusion relevant to crime: (1) criminal diffusion and (2) diffusion of benefits. *Criminal diffusion* refers to the spreading of crime from one place to another. This type of diffusion can be divided into: (a) contagious diffusion and (b) hierarchical diffusion. *Contagious diffusion* depends on direct contact and occurs between adjoining areas, such as neighboring cities or counties, whereas *hierarchical diffusion* "spreads broadly through commonly shared influences" (Cohen and Tita, 1999:451). The latter type does not require direct contact and tends to emerge through spontaneous innovation or imitation. For example, crack cocaine spread through the inner cities of the United States in numerous ways that were unconnected to other areas. Contagious diffusion can further be divided into: (a1) *relocation diffusion* and (a2) *expansion diffusion*. The former refers to when crime emerges in one place and spreads outward from that point, whereas the latter is similar but the original area where the crime wave began continues to experience high rates of crime (Cohen and Tita, 1999).

The *diffusion of benefits* refers to additional benefits of crime prevention beyond what were expected (Clarke and Weisburd, 1994). Clarke (1998:14) calls diffusion of benefits "the reverse of displacement"—"wider reductions in crime beyond the reach of the prevention measures." Diffusion of benefits has also been referred to as the "multiplier" effect (Chaiken, Lawless, and Stevenson, 1974), the "halo" effect (Scherdin, 1986), the "bonus" effect (Sherman, 1990), and the "free rider" effect (Miethe, 1991).

Crime and Diffusion

There is growing literature on criminal diffusion. Studies have examined diffusion and motor vehicle theft (Rice and Smith, 2002), robbery (Smith, Frazee, and Davison, 2000), drug use (Frischer et al., 2002), and other serious street crimes. Smith, Frazee, and Davison (2000) found that robberies near a face block (both sides of a city block between two intersections) in a medium-sized city in the southeast United States increase the likelihood of robberies occurring on a face block. This study suggests that both social disorganization of a neighborhood and routine activities of offenders increase the likelihood that robbery will occur on a given face block.

Other studies of criminal diffusion attempt to explain how crime can grow from one area to another, for example, within a city or county. Morenoff and Sampson (1997) show how violent crime and disadvantage grow from one area to another, resulting in population loss. In their study of homicides in Chicago, the movement of homicide is found to follow a pattern very similar to the movement of socioeconomic disadvantage. One result is that people who can move do move, in order to get away from the dual tragedies of economic disadvantage and homicide risk. This process is known as *out-migration* and is thought to worsen conditions of social disorganization, leaving behind people who are less able and willing to impose informal social control. Social isolation can be forced by discrimination (e.g., red lining by banks) that can ultimately lead to crime clusters and can even limit the diffusion of crime (Cohen and Tita, 1999). This would explain why homicide rates are often found to be highest in areas inhabited by poor, isolated, minority groups (Rosenfeld, Bray, and Egley, 1999).

Much of the research into criminal diffusion concerns serious street crimes such as murder. This should not be surprising given the "epidemic of youth homicide in the late 1980s and early 1990s" that we demonstrated earlier (Cohen and Tita, 1999:373). According to studies, explanations of why some places have higher homicide rates revolve around "age distribution (an overabundance of youth), and/or the economic and social turmoil in neighborhoods with the highest concentration of the most susceptible urban underclass population." It appears that movement of these factors account for diffusion of homicide, as do "the organizing features of crack markets and urban youth gangs and their impact on the escalation of gun carrying" (Cohen and Tita, 1999:374).

Cork (1999), for example, examines the spread of crack cocaine, homicide, and the emergence of gang activity in large cities. His work is based on claims by Blumstein (1995) that the illicit crack cocaine markets led to an infusion of guns in the inner cities and subsequently increased homicide rates. Cork finds that crack markets tend to emerge about two to three years earlier than homicide increases among youth. He writes, "in most large American cities, the diffusion process for crack cocaine experienced an onset of dramatic growth that was followed by a similar, slightly slower growth in gun homicides committed by juveniles" (p. 379). Importantly, he concludes that "little to no clear growth was discernible in juvenile nongun homicide . . . reinforcing the claim that the spike in homicide among juveniles owed to new-found guns in impulsive hands" (p. 403). Because Cork finds that homicide tends to begin as intergang activity and spreads to nongang youth, it is possible that an increased availability of guns spread to areas outside of traditional gang areas. Finally, Cork finds that increases in homicide in the United States started in cities on the East and West coasts and then spread inland.

Studies by Mencken and Barnett (1999) and Messner and colleagues (1999) at the county level are inconclusive but do find evidence of some diffusion of homicide from urban areas to rural areas in some counties. Mencken and Barnett (1999:408) expected to find diffusion in five southern states given that "many of the predictors of county violent crime and homicide rates, such as household poverty, income inequality, urbanization, and population dynamics" will have effects on crime not only in any county but also in adjoining counties, based on social disorganization theory.

Messner et al. (1999:423) write, "The possibility that homicides can spread from one geographic area to another has been entertained for some time by social scientists, yet systematic efforts to demonstrate the existence, or estimate the strength, of such a diffusion process are just beginning." The research by Messner and colleagues of the distribution of homicides in 78 counties in and around St. Louis during two time periods finds that homicides are distributed nonrandomly. The authors also find evidence of diffusion of homicides from hot spots (high rates of homicide) in and around the urban core of St. Louis, as well as evidence of clustering of cool spots of homicides (low rates of homicide) away from the urban core. The existence of homicide clusters, both hot and cool spots of murder, is suggestive of contagious diffusion of the past. And the fact that a new hot spot of homicide emerged in the second time period of study suggests hierarchical diffusion where homicide moved from major metropolitan areas to smaller urban areas. Finally, Messner et al. (1999) find barriers to homicide of diffusion in rural and agricultural areas, suggesting natural constraints to the growth of some crimes.

Cohen and Tita (1999) examine homicides among youth gangs across neighborhoods in a city. They find contagious diffusion of homicides between neighboring census tracts only during the peak growth year of homicides, "when high local rates of youth-gang homicides are followed by significant increases in neighboring youth-nongang rates . . . [which] is consistent with a spread of homicides from gang youth to nongang youth. All other increases in homicide are found to occur simultaneously in nonneighboring tracts" (p. 451). Cohen and Tita suggest this result "is compatible with youth both in and out of gangs increasingly relying on guns for protection and settling disputes" (p. 481), which is consistent with hierarchical diffusion.

Diffusion of crime is a process that can be readily mapped. Figure 6.7 illustrates an example of diffusion. In this figure, you see the growth of drug crimes over a two-year period, spreading outward in a concentric pattern.

In terms of diffusion of benefits in crime prevention, there are numerous examples from research to verify its existence. Scherdin (1992), for example, found that the use of magnetic book tags by a university library not only reduced book theft, but also reduced thefts of audio- and videotapes even though they were not tagged. Other examples are similar:

- Poyner (1997) showed that the installation of a closed-circuit television camera (CCTV) in a parking lot on a university campus in England not only reduced thefts from the three parking lots where the camera was functional, but also in a fourth parking lot not being watched by the camera. Clarke (1998) reasons that because car thieves did not know how the camera worked and which lots it protected, they must have decided to avoid the university all together;
- Felson et al. (1996) examined 63 interventions made to the New York City Port Authority Bus Terminal, including cleaning the area, restricting access to spaces, improving opportunities for legitimate uses such as shopping, increased enforcement, and other measures aimed at facilitating natural surveillance by users. Not only did robberies and assaults decline in the station, they also declined around the station. One possible interpretation of this finding is that would-be robbers left the area completely—not only the station but also the neighborhood surrounding it;
- LaVigne (1994) examined restricting inmate access to phones at the Rikers Island jail, aimed at controlling costs of fraudulent calls. Phone costs declined, but so did phone-related fights among inmates. A possible interpretation of this finding is that inmates who normally would have come to blows over the phone were restricted from using the phone and therefore did not fight; and
- Poyner (1992) studied the effects of CCTV installations on the top deck of two buses in England. Dummy cameras were applied to three other buses. One bus was also brought to local schools to illustrate how people could be seen if they decided to vandalize the buses. Vandalism of the buses declined not only on the buses with the CCTV cameras but on all of the 80 buses in the fleet.

January–July 2001

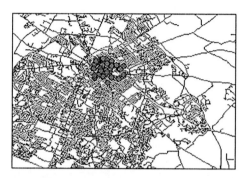

August–December 2001

January–July 2002

August–December 2002

FIGURE 6.7   Diffusion of Drug Crimes

Felson and Clarke (1998:30) add the following examples, as well:

- A New Jersey electronics store began counting highly sought-after merchandise daily in its warehouse in order to reduce theft, and not only did theft of those items decrease but so did theft of other, noncounted items;
- Efforts aimed at reducing burglary in homes that had been burglarized in England resulted in reductions in burglary to other homes not targeted by the crime prevention measures; and
- Vehicle tracking devices implemented in six American cities resulted in declines of car thefts across the cities, not just for the owners who had the tracking devices.

It is presumed that offenders become aware of changes made to potential targets of crime and then change their behaviors as a result. The above examples suggest that offenders can be deterred from committing crimes with simple environmental alterations. However, it should be pointed out that experts believe that the benefits of diffusion of crime prevention efforts decay over time as offenders learn that the risks have not increased as much as they originally thought they had. If true, many benefits of crime prevention diffusion will be shortlived.

SUMMARY

List of Major Research Findings Relating to Epidemics, Diffusion, and Displacement

In this chapter, you learned about several important place-related phenomena, including epidemics, diffusion, and displacement. Some of the most important points are as follows:

1. An epidemic is something, usually bad or harmful, that affects a disproportionately large number of individuals within a population, community, or region at the same time;
2. Displacement refers to being physically moved out of position, as when crime moves from one area to another, after efforts to prevent crime in the area have been initiated;
3. Diffusion can be understood as having been poured out and permitted or caused to spread out freely, as when crime spreads from one area to another over time or when the benefits of crime prevention tend to be even greater than those that are intended because they spread to other types of crime;
4. Crime is much like an illness in several ways: It appears in the presence of some environmental characteristics more than others, it tends to affect some people more than others, it tends to be spread from one area to the next through movement patterns, and it can be moved from one place to another without completely preventing it;
5. There are at least two types of epidemics, including common source epidemics and propagated epidemics/host-to-host epidemics;
6. Common source epidemics infect many people from a single contaminated source and are characterized by a rapid onset and a sharp peak and rapid decline in incidence;
7. Propagated epidemics occur after an infected person is introduced to a susceptible population and are characterized by a slow onset and a blunted peak and slow decline in incidence;
8. Pathogenesis refers to the process by which a pathogen contacts the host, colonizes the host, infects the host, evades the host defense systems, and damages host tissues, and is similar to the processes of invasion, domination, and succession that characterize the introduction of crime into a neighborhood;
9. One of the most studied crime epidemics is the homicide epidemic of the late 1980s in the United States, committed disproportionately by young, inner-city males with guns, as part of gang activity and the illicit drug trade;
10. Most of the increases in homicides in the 1980s were due to murders committed in the nation's largest cities with handguns, which were preceded by the invasion of crack cocaine into the inner cities;
11. Epidemics rely on contagion, or the spreading of disease or crime by one host to another;
12. Broken windows theory—an example of a contagion theory—suggests that when conditions of any environment are left to deteriorate, they will attract crime;

13. Types of displacements identified by scholars include geographical displacement, temporal displacement, target displacement, tactical displacement, and crime type displacement;
14. Geographical displacement is when crime moves from one place to another;
15. Temporal displacement is when crime moves from one time to another;
16. Target displacement is when crime moves from one target or set of victims to another target or set of victims;
17. Tactical displacement is when one method of committing a crime is replaced by another;
18. Crime type displacement is when one type of crime is replaced by another;
19. Scores of studies of displacement find either no evidence of displacement or small amounts of it that do not equal the crime prevented;
20. Some studies of crime do suggest displacement, such as in drug markets after community policing interventions and raids by police on drug-selling areas;
21. Criminal diffusion includes contagious diffusion and hierarchical diffusion;
22. Contagious diffusion depends on direct contact and occurs between adjoining areas, such as neighboring cities or counties;
23. Hierarchical diffusion spreads broadly through commonly shared influences, does not require direct contact, and tends to emerge through spontaneous innovation of imitation;
24. Contagious diffusion can further be divided into relocation diffusion and expansion diffusion;
25. Relocation diffusion occurs when crime emerges in one place and spreads outward from that point;
26. Expansion diffusion also occurs when crime emerges in one place and spreads outward from the original point, but the original area where the crime wave began continues to experience high rates of crime; and
27. There have been numerous studies to document the realities of diffusion of crime and diffusion of crime prevention benefits, although studies of homicide diffusion do not provide complete evidence of this phenomenon.

Implications of Findings for Crime Mapping and Spatial Analysis

The main significance of the phenomena of epidemics, diffusion, and displacement of crime is that they allow researchers to visually depict and thus "see" how crime moves from place to place on a map. Careful study of these processes allows scholars and practitioners alike to more fully understand how and why crime occurs and is likely to occur in the future at a given place. Ultimately, studies of epidemics, diffusion, and displacement of crime will also allow us to better prevent criminal victimization based on our understanding its spatial dynamics.

Learning that criminality operates much like illness is a major discovery. And it is likely that this is true with regard to all forms of criminality, including corporate and white-collar crimes. Imagine being able to study, using crime mapping software, how crime spreads from room to room, floor to floor, and office building to office building, among business executives. While this may seem like science fiction or the story of fantasy writers, crime mapping software is quickly approaching this ability. As of today, most studies using crime mapping techniques are aimed at street crimes such as homicide, burglary, and even drug offenses. The spread of homicide, drug dealing, and even the movement patterns of a burglar throughout a city or group of neighborhoods, can be plotted using crime mapping software. We saw a recent example of this with the recent sniper attacks in the United States that killed 13 people. Ultimately, this allowed police to zero in on the suspected killer(s). Thus, crime mapping also holds great promise for use as an apprehension tool.

Studies showing the minimal impact of displacement of crime and the diffusion of crime prevention benefits should strengthen the case for all crime prevention initiatives. Being able to visually depict these social facts using crime mapping software provides practitioners with valuable evidence to justify increased funding of crime prevention initiatives that will benefit us all. Maps of areas depicting the presence of crime and any criminogenic conditions can be generated before, during, and after a crime prevention initiative is implemented. Imagine being able to show, through careful evaluation, that crime rates have decreased in the targeted area, as well as in another areas and for other types of crimes, while also finding little or no evidence of crime displacement. Crime mapping is the best tool available to visually depict such welcome changes.

CASE STUDY
THE PLACE OF SCHOOL VIOLENCE

Based on increased fear of crime at school and increased media coverage of school crime through the 1990s, many thought school crime was increasing. In fact, schools were safer in 1998, the year of the mass murder at Columbine High School, than they were at any other time in the 1990s. Some statistics bear this out. Between 1991 and 1998, the number of murders at schools declined, as did the percentage of students involved in physical fights, the percentage of students injured in physical fights, and the percentage of students who carried weapons to school (Brener et al., 1999).

Figure 6.8 shows some of the highly publicized cases of school violence in the United States. Because of the intensive media coverage of these cases, particularly the mass murder at Columbine, students report being more afraid of school violence and more likely to avoid certain places at schools, and schools have begun forcing children to walk through metal detectors and carry see-through book bags.

Fortunately, schools are relatively safe places (*Indicators of School Crime and Safety*, 2006), even with the large numbers of guns brought to school each day. As stated by the *Annual Report on School Safety* (1999:iv), "The vast majority of America's schools are safe places. In fact, notwithstanding the disturbing reports of violence in our schools, they are becoming even safer." And as measured by serious violent crimes at our nation's schools in the report, *Indicators of School Crime and Safety*, 2006, they are safer today than they used to be. The rate of violent acts at schools and away from schools per 1,000 people has slightly declined over time. School shootings each year have also declined.

The realities of school crime in America include the following:

- The most common type of school crime is a physical attack or fight without a weapon;
- The least common type of school crime is a murder;
- One's chance of dying at school is roughly 1 in 2 million; and
- Just over 1 percent of killings of juveniles occur at schools.

Additionally, surveys of American schools show that only about 10 percent of schools report having at least one serious violent crime. Almost half of schools in America report that they experienced no incidents of serious crimes. Even most violent crimes committed at schools *do not* result in any actual injury to anyone. Further, less than 1 percent of students aged 12–18 years report experiencing a serious crime while at school and less than 5 percent report experiencing any crime. Additionally, less than 10 percent of teachers are threatened per year and less than 5 percent are actually physically attacked.

Despite this good news, surveys of schools do find that

- 900 teachers are threatened per hour in the United States;
- 20 percent of high school seniors report being threatened with violence every year;
- 2,000 students are actually attacked per hour;

(continued)

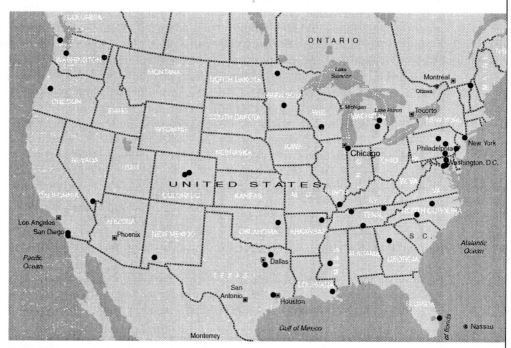

FIGURE 6.8   School Shootings

Source: "U.S. School Shootings." [On-line]. http://www.cbsnews.com/htdocs/guns_in_america/
html/school_shooting_map.html

- 40 teachers are attacked per hour;
- 100,000 guns are brought to school every day; and
- The ratio of students to counselors in elementary and secondary schools in the late 1990s was 513:1 (Robinson, 2002).

When one considers how many students and teachers are in American schools, it is easier to get a proper perspective on the problem. In 2004, for example, there were more than 26.4 million students aged 12–18 years. These students suffered 1.45 million crimes including only 582,000 violent crimes and 107,400 serious violent crimes. Thus, 22 per 1,000 students were victimized by violent crime and only 4 per 1,000 were victimized by serious violent crimes.

Despite the rare nature of school violence, acts of violence at schools trigger great alarm and worry because schools are supposed to be safe places. From the above figure on school violence, it is clear that most have occurred on the East coast of the United States, particularly the Southeast.

Studies of school violence also show that acts of violence at school are more likely to occur in rural areas where rates of gun ownership are high. In terms of campus location, certain places are more prone to acts of school violence than others. For example, public places where a lot of students and teachers congregate at predictable times each day are most prone to school shooting attacks.

Based on these data, crime mapping allows us to:

- Visually diagram locations of school violence so that consumers of criminal justice data get a better understanding of where such acts have occurred; and
- Attempt to predict where acts of school violence are more likely to occur.

School administrators have used data generated from crime mapping studies to assess their own campuses in order to make environmental alterations to lessen the likelihood that school violence will occur on their campuses. Most school-level approaches deal with alterations to the physical environment of campus, including:

- Controlling access to outsiders;
- Diverting traffic flows away from risky areas;
- Scheduling routine activities such as lunch;
- Arranging supervision based on space use patterns;
- Prohibiting students from congregating in common areas;
- Creating a constant adult presence in common areas;
- Staggering dismissal times, lunch periods, gym periods;
- Monitoring school grounds;
- Eliminating "incivilities"; and
- Creating an effective communication system.

Crime mapping software allows administrators to see the areas where such modifications are necessary, and ultimately to see whether such changes are effective at reducing signs of trouble, including incidences of violence. The result is safer schools.

PRACTICE

CHAPTER 7

Mapping in the Criminal Justice System

The purpose of this chapter is to provide an overview of the many ways in which GIS and crime mapping are used within the criminal justice system. Specifically, this chapter will provide a survey of the current uses of GIS and crime mapping within law enforcement and courts and corrections along with their problems and benefits. Moreover, future developments in the use of GIS and crime mapping will also be discussed.

Chapter Outline

INTRODUCTION

The popular image of crime mapping today is that of a highly trained crime analyst hunkered down in a computer-filled office using advanced and expensive computer programs and even more advanced and expensive computer hardware to create digital maps of crime distributions. While this view, popularized by television shows such as "The District," may provide a more accurate picture of the future of crime mapping than its current reality, crime mapping has definitely established itself as a valuable tool within the criminal justice system. However, this road to acceptance among criminal justice professionals has been a long, hard road filled with many potholes along the way. This chapter traces the development of crime mapping from its earliest historical uses to the current state of crime mapping in policing, courts, and corrections, finishing with a discussion of some future uses of crime mapping in criminal justice.

HISTORY OF MAPPING IN CRIMINAL JUSTICE

While computerized crime mapping is a relatively new phenomenon, the use of maps to visualize crime patterns dates back to the early 1800s. As with many new techniques, mapping of crime patterns was first conducted by researchers and was only later adapted by practitioners. As you saw in Chapter 3, the first known instance in which mapping was used to analyze crime distributions was conducted by the French lawyer Andre-Michael Guerry (1833). Guerry was interested in how patterns of criminality varied across France, and using demographic data from the French census as well as official crime statistics, he created several maps of property crime and crimes against the person. The maps revealed several important findings, most notably that areas with high property crime had low crimes against person rates and that areas of high property crime had higher education levels than low property crime areas. Guerry's early work succeeded in intriguing many researchers, and in 1842 further analysis of French crime patterns was conducted by the Belgian astronomer and statistician Lambert-Adolphe Quetelet. Whereas Guerry's work was largely concerned with simply mapping out crime patterns and provided no theoretical explanation for these patterns, Quetelet was more interested in explaining the reasons behind these patterns. In particular, Quetelet felt there was a correlation between crime rates and social factors such as education levels, ethnicity, race, and income levels. As with Guerry, several important findings resulted from Quetelet's research:

Crime was highest in southern areas of France;
Crime was highest among heterogeneous populations;
Crime was highest in areas with high population density;
Crime was highest in areas with high levels of poverty and low levels of education; and
Crime was fairly stable over time in its distribution.

This work by Quetelet not only helped influence the development of the social disorganization school of crime (see Chapter 3), but it also touched off a series of geographic studies of crime conducted in England and other European countries. While several studies replicated the work of Guerry and Quetelet by analyzing spatial patterns of crime on a national level across census tracts and counties, other researchers began to look at spatial aspects of crime patterns within cities. One study conducted by Glyde (1856) looked at crime among a variety of towns and villages across the English country-side. Glyde (1856) found that the highest levels of crime were reported in middle-sized towns, violent crimes were more common in the countryside than in towns, and towns situated along major highways had higher crime rates. Other research by Mayhew (1860) found several important findings concerning the distribution of crime within the London metropolitan area, specifically the location of high-crime areas or "rookeries" where criminals lived. First, these areas were located within the city so as to best take advantage of the distribution of possible victims. Second, these areas were most likely to be in places where policing was low in quality, such as on jurisdictional boundaries. Finally, these areas persisted over time, remaining problem areas for most of the 1800s and even into the 1900s in some cases.

While these early European studies would eventually influence criminologists in America to begin analyzing spatial aspects of crime patterns, this influence was not felt until the early 1920s with the work of the Chicago School. Although the Chicago School is best known for its development of the social disorganization perspective on crime (Chapter 3), it also helped influence modern crime mapping through its innovative use of mapping in analyzing spatial patterns of crime. Several of the mapping techniques developed and used by the Chicago School are still used today by both researchers and practitioners. Thrasher (1927) was the first researcher to map gang locations and distributions, a practice that is still in use by many police departments today to assist in gang suppression. Another innovation was the use of home addresses to analyze crime patterns, first used by Shaw and Myers (1929) when they mapped home locations of over 9,000 juvenile delinquents to determine correlates of crime. The mapping of offender residences is still a common practice among police departments to assist in determining areas to focus intervention efforts. A final innovation attributed to the Chicago School is development of neighborhood analysis. In their pioneering work, Shaw and McKay (1929) used social and ethnographic research to create community area boundaries that were approximates of neighborhoods and cohesive communities. These community areas were created as an alternative to using census tracts for analysis, which are rarely aligned with true community boundaries. In using these community areas, Shaw and McKay were better able to understand the level of crime associated with real communities rather than just artificially created boundaries. This practice of analyzing crime using community boundaries, rather than artificial boundaries such as census tracts or police beats, is still used today in many police departments that practice community policing.

THE DEVELOPMENT OF MAPPING IN AMERICAN POLICING

While sophisticated use of mapping to analyze crime in America truly began with the research conducted by the Chicago School, simple maps were already in use by select police agencies to assist in analyzing crime problems. Police agencies such as the New York Police Department claim to have been using some form of mapping to track crimes since 1900 (Harries, 1999). Admittedly, the mapping that was being done by police agencies in the early 1900s was very basic, a type of mapping that is often termed *pin mapping.* This most basic form of spatial analysis of crime simply involves placing pins in a jurisdictional map to designate locations where crimes have occurred.

Despite the ability to visualize basic crime patterns with pin maps, Harries (1999) points out several major problems that limited pin map use in analyzing crime and effectively slowed the growth of crime mapping as an effective tool for crime analysis. First, as crime maps were updated the old map data was lost. The only way to preserve the information from prior time periods was through taking a photograph of the crime map, an expensive and time-consuming exercise. The second problem with pin maps is their inability to be queried or manipulated. While different colored pins can be used to denote different crime types, analyzing changes in crime types over time is difficult if not impossible on a pin map. The third major problem with a pin map is that as crime gets added it gets increasingly difficult to read the maps. As crimes occur, increasing numbers of pins are necessary and the map gets progressively more jumbled and difficult to interpret for analytic purposes. Moreover, pin maps have difficulty showing locations where multiple crimes have occurred, an issue that is very real for most police departments. Finally, depending on the size of the jurisdiction, pin maps can take up an extraordinary amount of wall space, with pin maps in some jurisdictions covering up to 70 feet of wall space.

By the 1960s pin maps were still the dominant form of crime map used by police agencies, although computerized crime mapping was beginning to make inroads into policing largely because of its superior query and visualization abilities. Yet despite their potential, computerized crime maps were limited in their use by several technological and logistical problems. First and foremost, there was little understanding by police executives of how to integrate mapping into the management decision process. Because the maps that could be made were so simplistic, little relevant information could be gained from them, making them of little use in making management-level decisions such as patrol decisions, beat redistricting, and manpower decisions. Moreover, little help was available from either the government or academia, as both groups had lost favor with spatial analysis of crime and saw it as of little use for policing (Weisburd and McEwen, 1997).

A second problem was the expense involved in purchasing the hardware necessary for conducting computerized crime mapping. At this point in the evolution of computers the desktop computer revolution had yet to occur and the only computers available for use in crime mapping were expensive mainframe computers. Adding to the computer problems, these mainframes were very large and difficult to program and enter data, requiring the use of punch cards for all data entry needs. Thus, few if any departments could afford the expense involved in purchasing, housing, and manning these mainframe systems for what was essentially a "neat" but relatively useless crime mapping system.

The final limiting factor in the adoption of computerized crime mapping in the 1960s was the lack of accessible crime data. Automated data gathering and storage of calls for service and arrest information as well as other relevant crime data were nonexistent at this point in time. Data gathering was conducted solely using paper with little analysis of reports other than general summary statistics. Furthermore, processed reports were generally recorded after much delay, making crime information historically and virtually useless in terms of analytical ability.

However, by the mid-1980s the tide had turned in computerized crime mapping as several key factors combined to provide a surge of activity in the use of computerized crime mapping. Foremost in the rise of the use of computerized crime mapping was the advent of cheap, powerful, reliable (somewhat), and easy-to-use (somewhat) personal computers. Ushered in by the Apple computer in the early 1980s and kicked into high gear by Windows in the 1990s, personal computers became good enough and affordable enough that virtually any police agency could afford a powerful desktop computer.

Closely paralleling the development of the personal computer, GIS software became much powerful, easy to use, and capable of running on personal computers. While GIS software still required advanced training for competent use, the level and scope of training necessary to use the software for crime mapping dropped significantly, as did its price. When this was coupled with an increase in the automation of relevant crime data, it made crime mapping much easier and time efficient for agencies.

The final two factors that led to the explosive growth of computerized crime mapping were more philosophical than the tangible changes in computer hardware and software they accompanied. Specifically, research into crime and policing began to take on an increasing geographic focus as practices such as problem-oriented policing (POP) began to show promise in reducing crime and disorder within communities. Led by researchers such as Paul and Patricia Brantingham, Keith Harries, John Eck, David Weisburd, George Rengert, and others, geographic factors and the geographic analysis of crime became an important part of policing and crime prevention strategies within communities. This in turn caused more and more police agencies to incorporate spatial analysis of crime into their decision-making process.

Currently, over 16 percent of all local police agencies in the United States conduct computerized crime mapping to assist them in their decision-making process (Hickman, 2001). As with the adoption of any new technology, the rise in computerized crime mapping is largely driven by larger police agencies. In local agencies serving jurisdictions with over 250,000 people, over 90 percent of the agencies are currently conducting crime mapping. This compares to approximately 60 percent of agencies serving jurisdictions of 50,000–249,000 people and only about 14 percent of agencies serving jurisdictions of less than 50,000 people.

USES OF CRIME MAPPING WITHIN POLICING

As mapping has been used and accepted within the field of policing for a fairly long time, it stands to reason that mapping is integrated within police agencies more than any other section of the criminal justice system. Uses of mapping can be broken down into five main areas: crime analysts, patrol officers, investigation, police executives, and police/community relations. Each of these areas, while having different goals and needs, is highly related and necessary for the effective use of mapping within an agency.

Mapping by Crime Analysts

Within policing, one of the least talked about, but most essential positions within an agency is that of the crime analyst. Crime analysis is the "systematic study of crime and disorder problems as well as other police-related issues—including sociodemographic, spatial, and temporal factors—to assist the police in criminal apprehension, crime and disorder reduction, crime prevention, and evaluation" (Boba, 2005:6). In general, crime analysts are responsible for helping to determine what crime problems an agency is experiencing, where they are occurring, what the root causes of these problems are, and how effective the agency has been at reducing the problem and in developing new reduction strategies. In many agencies mapping and crime pattern analysis are conducted solely by crime analysts, although the degree of sophistication involved varies greatly from agency to agency. Because of this, crime mapping is most often associated with crime analysts. While data on the absolute numbers of crime analysts currently working within U.S. law enforcement are nearly impossible to find, estimates place the number in the thousands.

Crime analysis can be broken down into five different categories, intelligence analysis, criminal investigative analysis, tactical crime analysis, strategic crime analysis, and administrative crime analysis (Boba, 2005). While the duties of intelligence, criminal investigative, and tactical crime analysis are often shared or completely within other units depending on the agency, strategic and administrative analysis are pure crime analysis functions. Because of the crossover functions of intelligence, criminal investigative, and tactical crime analyss, they will be discussed in the Mapping for Investigations section, while strategic and administrative analyss will be discussed now. As mentioned before, crime analysis is one of the main areas within policing that truly necessitates the use of crime mapping and spatial analysis in order to truly accomplish its goals and objectives of understanding crime problems. In strategic crime analysis, analysts study "crime problems and other police related issues in order to determine long-term patterns of activity as well as evaluate police responses and organizational procedures" (Boba, 2005:15). Mapping and spatial analysis are essential to these tasks in order to get a better understanding of not only where crime problems are focused, but whether these locations have moved over time. In analyzing long-term crime problems, analysts often look to determine patterns of hot spots, repeat victimization locations, and persistently high crime rates by police beat or reporting district (Boba, 2005). In particular, analysts often create density maps to assess the highest density of incidents in a jurisdiction for a given period of time. Moreover, analysts also use density analysis to assess how crime patterns have moved or shifted over a given period of time. This type of analysis is also termed *dispersion analysis* and is discussed in-depth in Chapter 10 of the workbook. While assessing long-term trends is conceptually different than evaluating the effectiveness of police interventions and police responses, the tools used are often the same. Specifically, analysts often use density mapping and dispersion analysis to assess how crime patterns may have moved or altered their spatial patterns after an intervention or police response. In performing these types of analysis, it is important to remember that temporal aspects of the analysis are as important as locational aspects in determining change and relative densities of crime problems.

The final category of crime analysis is that of administrative crime analysis. According to Boba (2005:16), administrative analysis is mostly concerned with "the presentation of findings of crime research and analysis based on legal, political, and practical concerns to inform audiences within police administration, city government/council, and adapted citizens." Importantly, as opposed to other forms of crime analysis which are concerned with analytical techniques and problem solving, administrative analysis is more concerned with the presentation of research and analysis findings (Baba, 2005). In presenting these results, the audience can take on numerous forms: patrol officers, supervisors, command staff, city government officials, and citizens. Importantly, each of these different audiences of administrative analysis will be discussed more in-depth in the preceding sections.

Mapping for Patrol Officers

The heart of all law enforcement lies with the patrol officer, as it is through the patrol officer that all policing gets accomplished. While police executives are the ones responsible for dictating the strategies of a police department, it is patrol officers who are charged with implementing and putting into practice these often complex policies. Patrol officers are the most visible members of a police agency and are responsible for an agency's greatest success as well as its biggest failures. Duties of patrol officers range from arresting suspects, responding to calls for service, and controlling disturbances to providing funeral escorts, advice to community members, and other community service-oriented tasks.

Despite the supremely important role that patrol officers play in facilitating sound policing, it is only recently that patrol officers have been given an active role in defining what they do while on patrol. With the advent of police strategies such as community-oriented policing (COP), POP, and *COMSTAT*, officers are being asked to help solve community problems and devise strategies for crime reduction. In those agencies that have adopted computerized mapping, patrol officer maps have been used largely for the purposes of assisting patrol officers in both devising problem-solving ideas and understanding crime patterns within their beats. Maps provide valuable assistance to patrol officers in both of these duties through their ability to clearly display crime locations as well as locations of important aspects of a community or patrol area. Officers are able to quickly and easily assess crime distribution within their patrol areas as well as determine potential causes of crime problems.

While the purpose of computerized maps for patrol officers is fairly universal, the creation of computerized maps for patrol officers can be divided into those made *for* officers and those made *by* officers. These two different map formats have some important differences. Maps that are made for officers, or pre-made maps, are usually made by crime analysts or other trained personnel within a department whose major job responsibility is data analysis. Pre-made maps usually include spatial analyses such as hot spot analysis, time change analysis, and other useful analyses such as analyses using tabular data about recent crime events. These maps are created for all individual beats and are most often distributed to patrol officers in paper format before their patrol begins so as to inform them of recent developments. By contrast, officer-made maps are usually made using special mapping software that runs on a secure Internet or intranet connection. In making these maps, officers log onto the system and are usually able to customize the maps according to crime types, location, time period, and the amount of detail about the beat they desire, such as inclusion of gas stations, bars, and other important information.

Most agencies in which patrol officers use computerized maps opt to have crime analysts or other trained personnel make the maps for the officers rather than have the officers make their own maps. Importantly, both patrol map formats have associated costs and benefits that departments must weigh when deciding which format to use in their agency. In looking at pre-made maps, the benefits include competitive costs, less officer training, and the ability to conduct advanced analyses on crime patterns. However, cost and time issues can be very high in large police agencies as analysts are required to create daily crime maps for each different patrol section. These costs can be compounded if color maps are made or if large numbers of copies are required. In addition, the maps are not customizable to the officer and thus may not answer questions officers may have concerning their beats. By contrast, the biggest benefit of officer-made maps is that officers have complete control over the subject of the map. Thus, officers can create maps that may answer specific questions they have about things occurring on their beats, rather than try to figure out the answers by looking at pre-made maps. However, while customizable maps are very beneficial, in many cases the costs in terms of hardware, software, and training can make officer-made maps difficult to implement. Because officer-made maps utilize an Internet or intranet mapping system, the costs associated with implementing these systems are very high. Moreover, officers need to undergo much more thorough training in order to learn to use the system fully, whereas pre-made maps only require basic map-reading training. Finally, officer-made maps usually do not allow for officers to conduct any spatial analyses of crime patterns such as hot spots or change maps, something that is usually added to most maps made for officers. As of now mapping software used for customized officer-made maps has not advanced to the point where custom spatial analysis can be conducted.

It is important to reiterate that the format of the map is not nearly as important as the ultimate purpose behind the map. All patrol maps, regardless of whether they are pre-made or officer made, are designed to inform patrol officers of the extent of crime in their beats so that officers can adapt patrol strategies and assist in solving local community problems (see Figure 7.1).

Although there are differences in format as to how departments provide computerized maps for patrol officers, the content of patrol maps is fairly consistent across formats. Specifically, patrol maps focus on calls for service, arrests, criminal intelligence, recent crime series, known offenders, and information alerts. Regardless of the format of the patrol map, there are several important things to keep in mind when maps are being made for patrol officers. First, crime data should be as recent as possible in order for it to be effective. While historical data are important in determining beat design and manpower issues, patrol officers need recent crime data in order to make informed decisions about day-to-day patrol strategy. Importantly, getting up to date crime data is often the most difficult part of making good patrol officer maps. This problem is primarily a function of data collection schemes within police agencies that are designed more for storing and archiving crime data than for the rapid collection of crime data for analysis purposes. Currently, most agencies would be hard pressed to provide patrol officers with maps that have data that are less than three days old. However, as technology improves and more agencies put a premium on analysis of crime data, these issues will become less problematic.

Second, maps need to be specific to the areas that officers are patrolling. Thus, regardless of the map format, officers need crime pattern data that are specific to their beats and those that directly surround it. Too often officers are handed maps of an entire jurisdiction when what they really need is a more geographically specific map from which to make decisions.

Finally, patrol-oriented maps need to balance between too much and not enough information. Maps should have enough contextual information (street names, landmarks, etc.) that officers can readily understand where crimes are occurring, but not so much information that the maps become difficult to read. This also includes avoiding distracting colors and fonts as well as including the time period for which the map was created. Importantly, the only way to strike this correct balance is through the process of making maps and receiving officer feedback, as there is no gold standard format to follow. Chapter 3 of the workbook provides a more complete discussion of map-making tips.

In ending the discussion on computerized maps for patrol officers, a final comment must be made as to the utility of these maps. As stated above, patrol officer maps are designed to assist officers in devising problem-solving ideas and understanding crime patterns within their beats. However, recent research into the use of computerized crime maps by patrol officers calls into question how much these maps are used by the officers (Paulsen, 2003). Specifically, daily, weekly, and monthly crime maps showing the distribution of crime in a patrol sector had only marginal impact on officers' perceptions of where crime occurred in their jurisdictions (Paulsen, 2003). Moreover, when asked, most officers ranked crime maps below several other sources of information about crime patterns within their patrol areas (Paulsen, 2003). This seems to point to the fact that despite the promise maps have to facilitate changes in the nature of patrol work, many

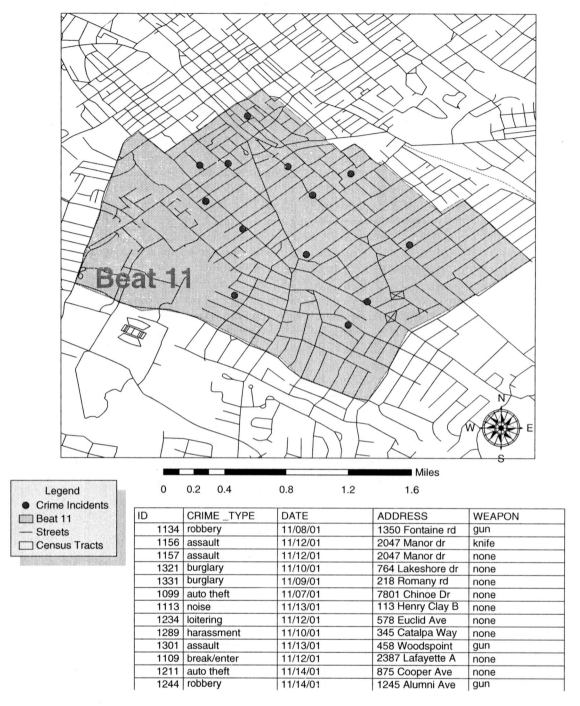

ID	CRIME _TYPE	DATE	ADDRESS	WEAPON
1134	robbery	11/08/01	1350 Fontaine rd	gun
1156	assault	11/12/01	2047 Manor dr	knife
1157	assault	11/12/01	2047 Manor dr	none
1321	burglary	11/10/01	764 Lakeshore dr	none
1331	burglary	11/09/01	218 Romany rd	none
1099	auto theft	11/07/01	7801 Chinoe Dr	none
1113	noise	11/13/01	113 Henry Clay B	none
1234	loitering	11/12/01	578 Euclid Ave	none
1289	harassment	11/10/01	345 Catalpa Way	none
1301	assault	11/13/01	458 Woodspoint	gun
1109	break/enter	11/12/01	2387 Lafayette A	none
1211	auto theft	11/14/01	875 Cooper Ave	none
1244	robbery	11/14/01	1245 Alumni Ave	gun

FIGURE 7.1   Beat 11 Crime Report 11/07/01–11/14/01. Patrol officer map showing crime distribution on a specific beat. The table included in the map provides officers with descriptive information about the crimes that occurred on their beats.

patrol officers choose to ignore the maps and the information they provide. Thus, in addition to the need to make well-informed, timely, easy-to-read crime maps, departments need to convince officers of the utility of computerized mapping. While computerized crime maps have the potential to change the nature of patrol work, unless they are being actively used by officers they are nothing more than a waste of an agency's resources.

Mapping for Investigations

Among members of the public, the most interesting and sought-after position within policing is that of detective. Based on what people have seen on television and in movies, the public believes that detective work involves roughing up "perps" for information, engaging in shootouts with robbery and murder suspects, and arresting criminal masterminds in their secret lairs. Unfortunately for undergraduate criminal justice students everywhere, investigation couldn't be much different from the fictionalized version we see in the media. Sound investigation work involves analyzing detailed case information, repeated questionings of witnesses, following up on leads, long hours spent checking alibis, and a moderate amount of luck. As computerized mapping has become more widely adopted within policing, investigations have increasingly turned to mapping for assistance. Because of its ability to link detailed information about a crime incident [suspect and victim information, modus operandi (MO), etc.] with location data, computerized mapping has developed several investigatory uses.

One particular use of mapping has been to identify the existence of *serial offense patterns by linking crimes to an offender or offenders.* Currently, one of the biggest limitations to using crime series analysis software (geographic profiling and next event forecasting) to assist in a serial crime investigation is not knowing that there is an active serial offender. By plotting the locations of crime incidents, such as burglaries, robberies, and sexual assaults, along with detailed suspect (MO, description, etc.) and case information (times, dates, etc.), investigators can determine the existence of possible serial criminals. Recent research indicates that one of the best methods for linking crimes is to analyze the locations of incidents (Bennell and Canter, 2002). Specifically, the distance between crimes has shown to be the best indicator of linked crimes, even better than MO factors such as entry method and goods taken (Bennell and Canter, 2002). Once these serial crime patterns are identified, police can then use crime series analysis techniques to assist in determining where and when to focus police resources in order to end the crime series. Detectives in Alberta, Canada, using spatial analysis of burglaries were able to direct patrol focus on a specific area, resulting in the arrest of two suspects and the clearance of 123 residential break-ins that resulted in over $500,000 being stolen (Warden and Shaw, 2000). While serial crime is not extremely common and all serial criminals are not as prolific as this Canadian pair, serial crime linkage is an issue that detectives can better determine and respond to through the use of computerized mapping.

One of the main duties of a detective during the process of an investigation is to check out the *alibis of suspects* to determine their validities. While often seen as a boring and mundane aspect of investigations, it is the checking of alibis and other basic facts of a case that often leads to a conviction. Here again computerized mapping can assist investigators by allowing them to visualize case-related data and information that may help prove the validity of an alibi. In gaining the conviction of two murderers involved in a string of car-jackings, investigators in South Africa used computerized mapping to track cell phone conversations between the offenders (Schmitz et al., 2000). Detectives were able to map the locations of cell phone conversations in relation to victims' bodies and stolen cars, directly contradicting the suspects' testimonies that they were someplace else at the time of the crime. Although most cases will not involve the mapping of such complex information, this example shows the power of computerized mapping to visualize and convey important information in an easily understandable form.

Another valuable use of computerized mapping for investigations is the *mapping of criminal intelligence* information such as known offender residences, probation/parole information, and gang territory information (see Figure 7.2). In many departments, in addition to being responsible for investigating crimes, detectives are responsible for gathering criminal intelligence information. Importantly, the focus on mapping, analyzing, and sharing of intelligence data has taken on new importance in the post 9/11 world, where intelligence analysis has gained in importance to police agencies. Criminal intelligence is

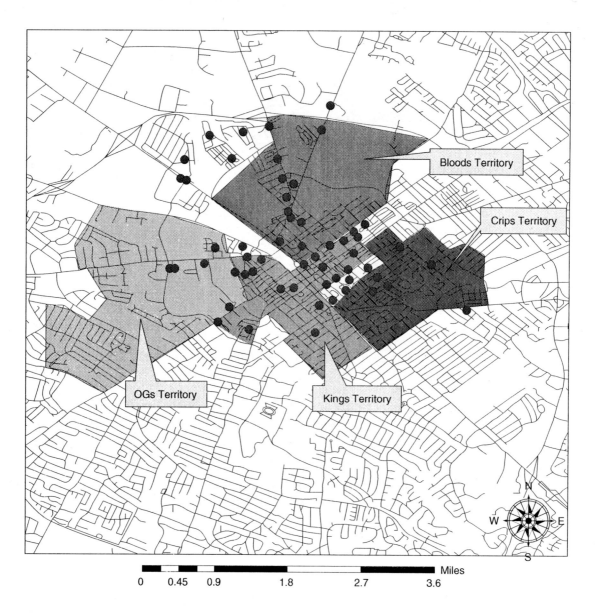

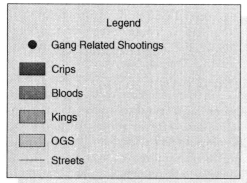

FIGURE 7.2   Known Gang Territories and Gang-Related Shootings. Criminal intelligence map showing known gang territories and gang-related shootings.

often a vital aspect of investigations, especially in developing suspect lists, as it provides detectives with a list of individuals from which to compare MO, descriptions, and other information. Mapping adds to this process by allowing criminal intelligence to be mapped and overlaid with crime information in order to facilitate the development of suspect lists and determine social networks of criminals. Specifically, departments can overlay maps of unsolved crime incident locations with information about known offender residences, probationers/parolees, and other pertinent information. Detectives can then conduct queries to develop suspect lists based on information such as residence proximity to crime, MO, physical description, social networks connections, and prior record. While many agencies are just in the early stages of mapping criminal intelligence data, the increased focus on fusion centers and intelligence analysis in a post 9/11 world will lead to increased advancements and utilization of intelligence mapping in the near future.

The final use of computerized mapping within investigations is through *crime series analysis* (see Chapter 5 for a more thorough discussion). As with other uses of computerized mapping for investigations, crime series analysis (geographic profiling and next event forecasting) is designed to assist in managing investigations and the creation of suspect lists and priority areas. However, as opposed to other previously discussed uses of computerized mapping, crime series analysis involves advanced spatial analysis based on criminological theory to help guide investigations. Specifically, using the locations of a series of connected crimes, geographic profiling, and next event forecasting can help determine the most likely area of offender residence or an offenders most likely next area of criminal activity.[1] This information is then used by investigators to help narrow suspect lists, determine interview schedules, direct police resources, and mail out information to citizens concerning crime incidents. Although crimes may appear to be random, serial offenders tend to commit crimes in areas where they feel comfortable, such as areas they frequently travel or near where they live. While crime series analysis is still a relatively new sub-field of crime mapping, research into new methods and better practical applications of the analytical methods is advancing rapidly. Unfortunately, advanced systems such as geographic profiling require extensive training for effective use and are extremely expensive to purchase, leaving these systems in the hands of only a select few large, well-funded departments. Yet, because of its potential to assist in investigations, work is currently under way to develop cheaper and easier-to-use crime series analysis systems for a wider audience.[2]

Mapping for Police Executives

One of the most important areas in which the use of computerized mapping has grown over the past decade is its use by police executives to assist in management-level responsibilities. Police executives, such as police chiefs, assistant chiefs, and other top level police officers, are similar to top executives in corporations, in that they are responsible for the overall health of the organization, from morale to performance to community relations. Major duties of police executives include such tasks as initiating new crime reduction and patrol strategies, determining manpower issues, and dealing with community members. Importantly, all of these activities can be enhanced through the use of computerized mapping.

One of the most important duties that police executives perform involves the initiation of effective *crime reduction strategies*. Fairly or not, the effectiveness of most police agencies is judged by the level of crime that occurs within a community, and thus the determination of effective crime reduction strategies is vitally important. As traditional models of policing have increasingly come under attack as being not only ineffective but also detrimental to the community, newer crime reduction strategies have begun to emerge. Two of the more popular strategies to develop over the last decade or so are POP and COMSTAT. While these two strategies are different in some respects, they share many things in common from a management perspective. Moreover, both of these strategies rely heavily on the use of computerized mapping to be successful.

First, both POP and COMSTAT rely on accurate and timely crime location data in order to determine areas that are in need of proactive police involvement. Computerized mapping enhances an agency's ability to scan for problem areas by not only allowing for the visual inspection of problem areas, but also allowing for statistical determination of high-crime areas. Spatial analysis techniques such as hot spot analysis and kernel density interpolation are often used by police agencies to determine areas that are most in need of proactive police involvement. In addition, computerized mapping can assist in determining the root causes of these problem areas by mapping contextual data such as abandoned housing, government housing, bar locations, and other important features near the problem areas. Once these areas are identified, police executives then work with patrol officers, community agencies, other government agencies, and community members to develop proactive solutions to these problem areas.

The other similarity between these two crime reduction strategies is the reliance on intensive assessment to determine the effectiveness of the solution that was implemented. In both POP and COMSTAT, strategies that are determined to be ineffective are stopped and new strategies are sought out. Here, as with determining problem areas, computerized mapping is relied on because of its ability to statistically determine reductions in crime in the effected areas. Importantly, statistical analysis techniques such as dual kernel density interpolation are excellent tools for determining whether crime is displaced to other areas. As discussed in Chapter 6, displacement of crime is one of the major issues surrounding the use of place-specific policing strategies. Figure 7.3 shows an example of a map of drug crimes in a high-crime area both before and after a police crackdown. In looking at the two maps, the benefits of mapping are readily apparent, as police executives can visually determine the effectiveness of implemented strategies.

One new tool that has been developed to assist police executives in better understanding community-level problems as they relate to crime problems, particularly juvenile crime issues, is the Socioeconomic Mapping and Resource Topography (SMART) system (Markovic, 2007). This new tool is an Internet-based GIS system that is "developed to support the early identification of emerging local issues and provide resources to assist decision makers with implementing both rapid response and long-term plans" (Markovic, 2007). The system makes it easy for agencies to visualize problem areas, community-level risk factors, and agency crime data (users can upload their own data) along with available resources to help solve these problems without the need for expensive GIS software or training. While this system is not as advanced as what can be done using a stand-alone GIS system, it is more than enough for the vast majority of agencies who have limited funding. Moreover, because the system provides community-level data for the entire United States, it facilitates regional analysis and potential data sharing between agencies. Although the system is designed for use by law enforcement and other local government agencies, registration is free and users are encouraged to explore the site (http://smart.gismapping.info).

Another major duty that police executives face involves *manpower issues* such as creating beat areas and determining shift-related resource requirements. Traditionally, police departments were very conservative in the way in which they managed police beats and shift-related resources (officers per shift). Oftentimes a police department would not redraw police beats or reallocate shift resources unless there was a major political outcry from the community. In many jurisdictions, police beats are in the exact same locations they have been in for 20 years or more, despite increases and decreases in demands within the community. However, with the changes that have occurred in government budgets, declining recruitment, and expanding police demands, many police agencies have been forced to place more of an emphasis on manpower issues. Computerized mapping assists police executives in manpower decisions by allowing them to geographically analyze demand for police resources. Specifically, police executives can analyze calls for service, arrests, and reported crimes, along with population and land use data to determine how to best draw police beats and allocate manpower based on community needs. Furthermore, these analyses can be conducted for each

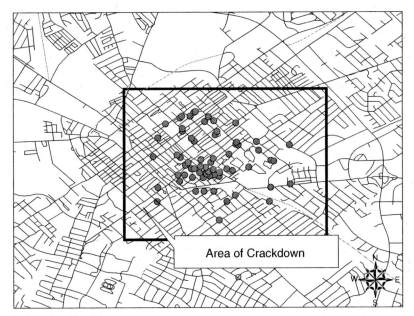

Before drug Crackdown

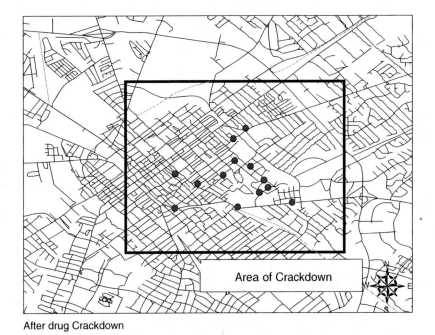

After drug Crackdown

FIGURE 7.3   Effects of a Drug Crackdown on Crime Incidents. Map showing the impact that a police crackdown had on the distribution of drug crime incidents.

different shift so that police executives can determine not only where but also when resources are most in demand and respond in the best manner. This type of analysis has become so popular that several different companies produce software to assist police executives in the creation of effective beats and shifts.

The last major duty in which computerized mapping has been increasingly used is in dealing with *community members*. With the increase in police agencies conducting COP community meetings and presentations have become a regular part of a police executive's duties. These meetings and presentations are often given to community groups and neighborhood associations in response to questions about police strategies or concerns with crime increases. Computerized maps have proven extremely beneficial in these meetings because they can more easily portray the nature and extent of crime in a selected area than charts, graphs, and statistics alone. In particular, density maps, hot spot maps, and maps that compare crime between different areas of a jurisdiction have proven effective. While in most cases maps have been well received by the public, there is the potential to confuse with poorly made maps. It is important that agencies that are going to use maps for community presentations make sure they are easily understood and that they do not mislead or distort the reality of crime in the community. Chapter 5 in the workbook provides a more thorough discussion of issues related to the design of maps for different audiences.

Mapping for Police/Community Relations

The final area in which computerized mapping is used within policing is in enhancing police/community relations. Since the early 1980s policing has seen a revolution in terms of how it is conducted, switching from the oft-criticized professional model toward a more community centered form of policing in COP. According to more recent figures, nearly 80 percent of all police departments are currently involved in some form of community policing (Trojanowicz, Kappeler, and Gaines, 2002). A key aspect of community policing is a more involved relationship with the community that is served. This more involved relationship ranges from increased involvement in problem determination and problem solving to better information sharing, especially where crime incidents are concerned.

It is in information sharing that computerized mapping has had the largest impact, particularly with regard to providing the public with improved access to information on both individual crime incidents and aggregate crime data within the community. One of the main ways that police agencies are increasingly sharing crime information with the public is through the use of interactive Internet crime maps. From an agency standpoint, Internet crime maps are an excellent method for sharing crime information because they free up officers from responding to individual requests for information while simultaneously satisfying public curiosity. Likewise, from the public's standpoint, Internet crime maps are beneficial because they allow citizens to create their own queries and answer questions on their own. Overall, both the police and the public reap real benefits from the use of Internet crime maps.

While similarities exist among agency websites in that they all provide basic information to the public about crime frequency and crime location, great differences exist about how agencies go about doing this. First, in terms of crime data, some agencies provide information about specific crime locations (1350 Fontaine Rd.), whereas others only provide crime data in aggregate form (police beat). Second, the amount of information provided about crimes also varies, with some agencies providing detailed information, such as victim and offender names, while others provide more general information such as reporting an assault occurred. Finally, the degree of customization of maps varies greatly, with some agencies creating advanced sites that allow users to determine search parameters such as data range and crime type, while others provide static maps that are not capable of query. Beyond the simple differences in the amount of information that is provided by agencies, these differences belie important ethical and legal issues. These ethical and legal issues will be discussed more completely in the next chapter.

An important development in community crime mapping has been the development of citizen-created crime maps. The last few years have witnessed a tremendous growth in the use and popularity of online mapping sites such as Google Maps, Google Earth, Microsoft Virtual Earth, Mapquest, and Yahoo Maps to name a few. While these sites are often used by citizens to find directions, restaurants, or businesses, the development of

Application Programming Interfaces (API) has allowed programmers to create what are termed "mash-ups". These mash-ups allow publicly available data to be easily geocoded and mapped for the world to view and use. One of the more popular crime-related mash-ups is "chicagocrime.org," which makes official Chicago crime data searchable and viewable on Google Maps. Although the data used in "chicagocrime.org" actually come from the Chicago Police Department public mapping system ICAM, chicagocrime.org has proven to be exceedingly popular because of its ease of use and its integration with Google Maps views. The importance of sites like chicagocrime.org cannot be underestimated as they provide an "alternative" view of crime in a community that allows citizens to see crime issues in their community without police assistance.

Mapping in Courts and Corrections

Despite the relatively wide acceptance of computerized mapping applications within policing, other aspects of the criminal justice system, such as courts and corrections, have been slower to adopt computerized mapping techniques. Because of this slow movement toward acceptance of computerized mapping as a valuable tool, the uses of computerized mapping within these two fields are much more limited.

In comparing courts and corrections, the more limited number of uses is within the court system, where the predominant use of maps has been in displaying evidence at trials. Trial maps are often used to display geographically complex evidence or information that is naturally best displayed geographically, such as routes that criminals traveled in committing crimes (see Figure 7.4). Examples of maps used at trials include maps showing cell phone use during a crime spree to indicate the routes used by the offenders and maps showing rape locations in the trial of a serial rapist.

Although maps have been used in court proceedings to display evidence for well over 100 years, few other uses of computerized mapping have been developed for the court system. Even as evidence at trials, computerized maps are not used heavily because of the expense involved in well-produced maps and the potential to confuse the jury with poorly made maps. It is the latter problem that has most limited the adoption of computerized mapping within the court systems, as maps that are made by inexperienced mapmakers are often more confusing than they are instructive. Tips for those making maps for trial use include keeping the maps simple, as complex maps will confuse rather than inform, using big and easy-to-read fonts, and using colors that are not too distracting. While it is true that a well-made map can help gain a conviction, poorly made maps can do more damage to a criminal case than the bumbling of even the most inept lawyers.

Although the court system has been slow to integrate computerized mapping technology, the field of corrections has been more willing to embrace mapping and the capabilities it brings with it. Within the field of corrections, mapping uses can best be broken down into applications involving probation and parole and those involving institutional corrections.

Probation and parole are services that are often termed *community corrections*. *Probation* is a form of punishment usually used in lieu of incarceration in a correctional facility, where offenders are allowed to remain living in the community under supervision of specialized correctional personnel. *Parole* is the supervision of offenders by specialized correctional officers *after* the conditional release of an offender from incarceration. The main distinction between probation and parole is that probation uses community supervision to attempt to avoid incarceration, whereas parole uses community supervision to ease the transition back to society of those released from incarceration.

Although the purposes and goals of probation and parole are different, they have several similarities, especially concerning crime mapping applications. The primary application of mapping in probation and parole has been the use of simple pin maps

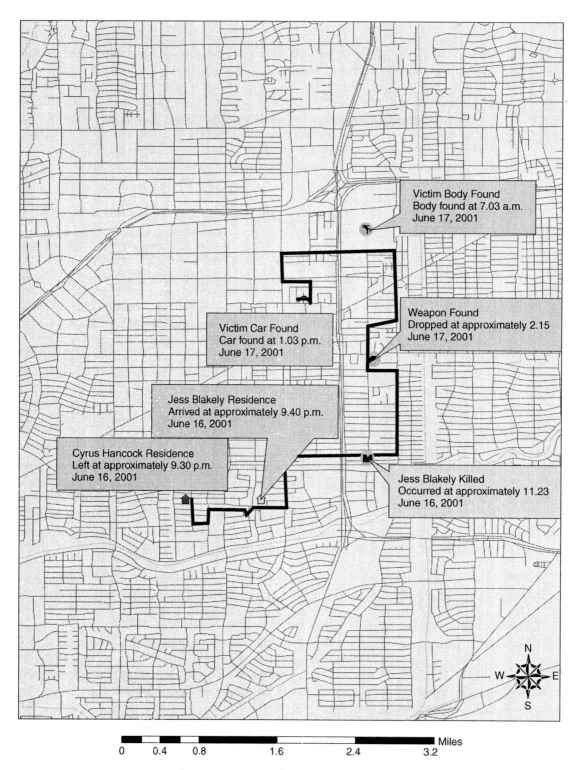

FIGURE 7.4 Route Traveled and Time Line of Cyrus Hancock during the Murder of Jess Blakely. Trial map indicating the route traveled and the time line of an offender during a murder.

to track the home locations of probationers/parolees. These pin maps have proved beneficial in several different ways such as service area allocation and management, investigation assistance to police, and the location of treatment centers.

Service area allocation and management involves the creation and management of probation/parole officer service areas. These service areas are similar to police beats in policing in that probation/parole officers are assigned probationers/parolees to supervise based on whether the residence of the offender falls within the officer's service area. As with beat redistricting in policing, probation/parole officers have been able to better manage officer caseloads by geographically assessing the distribution of offender residences and redrawing service areas to best match officer resources. In a pilot project in Wisconsin, two counties mapped and analyzed all offender residence locations in order to determine neighborhoods most in need of increased supervision and resources (Harries, 1999). Those areas that were targeted with increased officers and community resources had increased delivery of services as well as higher rates of completions of probation and parole (Harries, 1999). Mapping has also been used to assist officers in determining the most efficient routes to travel when making service visits. Several mapping software companies have route-finder extensions for their software which make route finding easy and efficient for officers.

Another major benefit of mapping within probation/parole has been in *investigative collaborations* between police agencies and probation/parole agencies. As more and more probation/parole agencies are beginning to map offender residences and associated criminal history data, more collaborations are taking place with the police. Residence location information of offenders is combined with information about open cases to help develop suspect lists as well as develop areas of increased concern for police (see Figure 7.5). In Knoxville, Tennessee, a serial rapist was captured after combining offense location information, victims' descriptions, and probationer/parolee residence information (Hubbs, 1998). First, a suspect list was generated from known sex offenders living near the offense locations. Officers then obtained pictures of known sex offenders, which they presented to the victims, who quickly identified the suspect. After the police approached the suspect, the suspect quickly confessed to the series of rapes. Increasingly, collaborations of this type are providing police with an extra advantage when approaching investigations of this type.

One specific type of police-corrections collaboration that has received a large amount of recent publicity has been in the area of sex-offender mapping. After the passage of Megan's law in the late 1990s, all individuals convicted of sex offenses had to register with local law enforcement. Under federal statute, this information is then provided to the public in order to notify them as to the residences of convicted sex offenders. Despite the controversy over the legislation, mapping has been beneficial to both the enforcement and dissemination of Megan's law information. From an enforcement aspect, agencies can use mapping applications to quickly determine whether or not registered offenders are living too close to restricted areas such as schools, churches, public parks, and libraries. On the other hand, maps have made dissemination easier by allowing agencies to create maps showing the location of offender residences throughout the community.

The final major benefit of mapping to probation/parole has been in the area of *location of treatment centers* and *halfway houses*. As a stipulation of many offenders' probation/parole conditions, offenders are required to reside for some period of time in a halfway house or treatment facility. Traditionally, the location of these facilities is based not necessarily on where they can provide the maximum benefit to those who need it, but rather political wrangling and the desire to keep these facilities out of certain communities. In particular, many communities do not want treatment centers or halfway houses located in their midst because of fear they will attract crime and other social problems. However, the advent of mapping has revolutionized the process of locating these facilities, making it far less political and more pragmatic. In some cities, agencies are mapping the locations of offenders' original residences in order to show residents' areas of greatest need. Other factors considered when locating facilities include access to public transportation, availability of job opportunities, and amount of known crime in the area. While mapping will not end the debate surrounding the placement of treatment facilities and halfway houses, it has made the process far less political and arbitrary.

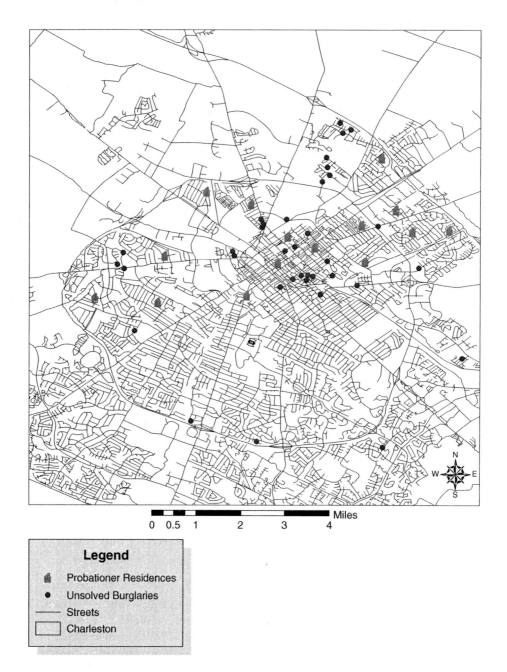

FIGURE 7.5   Unsolved Burglaries and Offenders on Probation for Burglary.
Probationer map showing probationer residences in relation to unsolved burglaries.

Despite the increased use of mapping by probation/parole agencies, several barriers still exist to its further acceptance and use. First, as with policing, cost is still an issue, especially for what many agencies feel is a tool that benefits law enforcement more than probation/parole. This is further compounded by the overall lack of funding to help improve mapping technology and training within the overall field of corrections. Second, ideologically, many probation/parole officers are unwilling to get involved in what they perceive as "community corrections," in which mapping is a major component. As with the resistance to community policing by police agencies, many corrections agencies feel that community corrections gets too far away from the original purpose of probation/parole.

As with probation/parole, institutional corrections has also slowly begun to incorporate the use of mapping into its decision-making process, largely in the facility location process, but to a lesser degree in sentencing decisions and analysis. Since the late 1980s and early 1990s, the building of prisons and other correctional facilities has skyrocketed, as federal and state governments have tried to keep up with ever-increasing prison populations. Because of the prison construction boom, prison facility location has become a much bigger issue within correctional circles. While prisons used to be considered a badge of scorn and ridicule for a community, prisons have come to be seen as a potential economic windfall for many small and rural towns.

As in locating treatment centers and halfway houses, *locating prison facilities* involves as much politics as it does anything. The benefit of mapping to this process is that it allows several different factors to be overlaid on a map in order to pragmatically determine the optimum location for a prison to be built, thus reducing the reliance on traditional political means of selection. Harries (1999) has identified several factors that are often considered when locating a new prison facility:

Terrain: Is the land flat, hilly, mountainous, swampy, etc.;
Prohibited land uses: Are any uses prohibited on the land;
Proximity of utilities: How difficult is it to obtain electricity, water, sewer, etc.;
Proximity of adequate transportation links: How close are major roads, airports, train lines, ports, etc.;
Availability of undeveloped land: Is undeveloped land available or must developed land be purchased and reengineered; and
Proximity to major cities and communities: How close is the land to major population centers.

The other major use of computerized mapping in institutional corrections is in the *analysis of sentencing decisions*. As the prison population exploded in the 1990s, so too did the controversy over the sentencing practices that led to this explosion. One particular area that drew a good deal of criticism was the sentencing of individuals to correctional institutions that were far from the communities in which they committed their crimes. The main controversy surrounded the potential detrimental effects that this distance would have on rehabilitation, particularly among juveniles who were sentenced to institutions far away from family. The argument is that juveniles who are sentenced to facilities far from home will be separated from family, making the maintenance of positive family relationships very difficult. In some states this sentencing practice has drawn the ire of politicians who have demanded study of sentencing practices to determine if, indeed, juveniles are being sentenced to facilities far from home and what, if any, potential effects this may have on rehabilitation. Figure 7.6 shows the results of research regarding juvenile sentencing practices in Texas. As indicated on the map, overall sentencing was found to be fairly well distributed, with most juveniles being sentenced to facilities near their home counties. While currently the use of computerized mapping to assess sentencing decisions is rarely employed, as prisons' populations continue to grow there is no doubt the use of mapping as a tool of assessment will grow as well.

FUTURE USES OF GIS AND CRIME MAPPING

Although use and acceptance of crime mapping have risen dramatically within the criminal justice system over the past 15–20 years, agencies of all types have barely begun to tap into the full potential of geographic information systems and crime mapping. While attempting to predict the future is never a wise proposition, discussing some emerging trends and uses of crime mapping provides a good

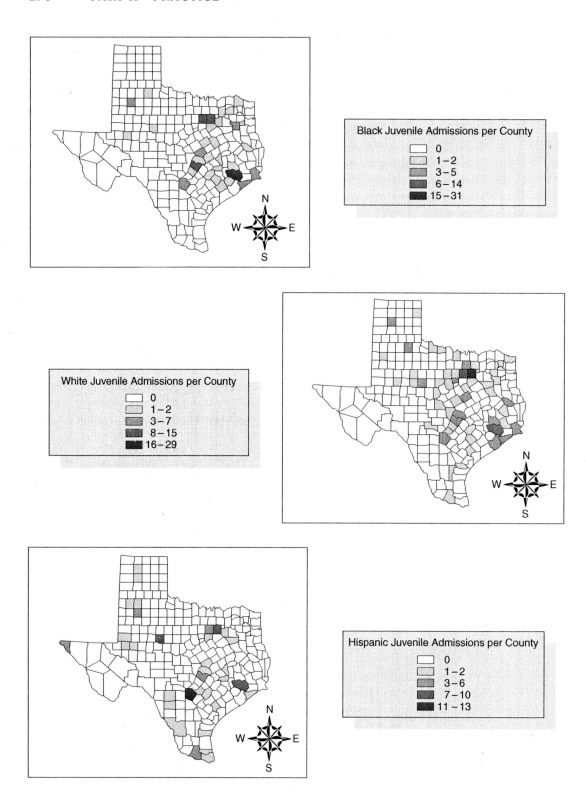

FIGURE 7.6   Racial Distribution of County Level Admissions for Corsicana RTC. Map showing the distribution of juvenile sentencing in Texas.

understanding of where crime mapping and GIS use are headed in the future. Several areas of emerging use in crime mapping include the integration of GIS and global positioning systems (GPS), high definition mapping, correctional facility mapping, 3-D mapping, regional mapping initiatives, and geosimulation and urban simulation of crime.

GIS and GPS

One of the latest technological wonders to infiltrate the consumer world has been GPS. First developed by the U.S. military as a way to accurately locate military hardware and personnel anywhere in the world, GPS works by triangulating a receiver's position using 24 earth-orbiting satellites. Used commercially for years by airline and other transportation industries, GPS has recently become a common option on higher-end automobiles and is often used by hunters, hikers, and fishermen to locate favorite spots. While levels of accuracy vary, GPS is capable of position accuracy down to one inch in some advanced modes.

The benefits to the criminal justice system of integrating an advanced location system like GPS with GIS are many. The most obvious benefit of GPS is its ability to provide extremely accurate location information, regardless of where a crime occurred. Traditionally, locating crime events has relied on geocoding (see Chapter 3 of Workbook for thorough discussion), which depends on crimes being committed at a specific street address. While many crimes do occur at specific addresses, many others do not. Thus, crimes that occur in vacant lots, street intersections, and highways can be accurately mapped for the first time. Moreover, environmental crimes such as wildfire arson, illegal dumping, poaching, and illegal timber harvesting can also be accurately mapped and analyzed using GPS. GPS is particularly useful to agencies that police large mostly rural jurisdictions where crimes often occur in places with poor residences or where accurate computerized street maps are lacking.

Another benefit of GPS is its ability to provide real-time location information of patrol cars by placing advanced GPS receivers in patrol cars. Called automated vehicle locators, or AVL, several agencies are currently experimenting with GPS in patrol cars in order to provide assistance in call response as well as officer management. While some officers have resisted GPS because of its ability to track their every move, overall reviews of its ability to provide assistance in call response have been positive.

In addition to near real-time officer tracking, the integration of GPS and GIS also opens up the possibility of near real-time crime data capture. One of the key complaints currently leveled at crime mapping is that the data are processed too slowly, and thus when maps are finally created the information is practically useless. From a management perspective, using weeks' old crime maps to guide daily patrol strategies is akin to using 20-year-old highway maps to guide you on a cross-country trip. However, using GPS with mobile data terminals or other technologies such as handheld computers allows for instantaneous crime data capture. A pilot program between the Kentucky State Troopers and Eastern Kentucky University in 2002 tested the usefulness of GPS and GIS. All troopers in one post were provided with GPS receivers and were instructed to radio basic crime and location information to their post after taking a crime report. These crime data were then used to create daily, weekly, and monthly tactical crime maps. Preliminary results have shown that crime data that used to take as long as 15 days to process and map are accurately being created and disseminated within a 24-hour period.

The last emerging use of GPS within the criminal justice system is surveillance and monitoring. Within the last few years, several probation and parole agencies have begun using GPS-equipped bracelets on probationers/parolees in order to monitor their movements. This monitoring by satellites has recently been commercialized for civilian use with the creation of "digital angel" to track and monitor the movements of children or elderly Alzheimer patients. Both the criminal justice and civilian models work similar to AVL systems, except that the receivers are small enough to be carried by the user. In an Orwellian twist, several companies are working on implantable GPS receivers that will allow the receivers to be virtually invisible to users. Other agencies have experimented with GPS bugs to track suspects rather than have officers trail them in cars. While many civil rights activists are worried about the potential abuses, GPS as a means of surveillance and monitoring will continue to grow in its use as GPS receivers drop in size and price.

Despite its potential to help revolutionize crime mapping, several problems currently limit the acceptance and usefulness of GPS. First, regardless of manufacturers' claims, GPS is often only accurate to within 100 feet. While this may not seem that bad, in practical terms this may result in a crime being mapped several houses away from where it actually occurred. Differential GPS can correct for these position errors, but is an expensive system to implement.

Another issue in the use of GPS involves the need to have a clear signal in order to receive satellite signals. This need for accurate "line of sight" with GPS satellites reduces the utility of GPS in large urban areas and densely wooded areas where buildings and trees can obscure satellite reception, and GPS is entirely useless for crime committed indoors. Moreover, unless officers have handheld GPS units, the accuracy of where a crime occurs will be limited by where an officer parks his or her patrol car.

A third problem involves officer error when recording coordinate data. Officers who are used to filling out reports by writing street addresses may have a difficult time adjusting to writing a string of meaningless numbers in the report, likely transposing the numbers. While misspellings of addresses can be easily handled in the geocoding process, transposed numbers require sending officers out to take a new GPS reading to prevent highly inaccurate data. In the Kentucky State Police study mentioned previously, officers incorrectly wrote down the coordinates in approximately 5 percent of all crimes, usually resulting in crimes showing up outside the jurisdiction (Paulsen, 2003).

The final problem with GPS is the associated costs. Although good handheld units are readily available for less than $150, when this cost is multiplied by the number of officers in a department the costs begin to add up quickly. As with all technology, the costs of GPS are continually dropping, especially as GPS becomes more ubiquitous in society.

High Definition Mapping

Another emerging use of GIS that is closely integrated with GPS is high definition mapping. Traditional mapping is an excellent tool for analyzing crime patterns and trends over large-sized jurisdiction areas, but is not as adept at analyzing patterns on smaller levels such as a specific community within a jurisdiction. High definition mapping allows for analysis of crime patterns in small areas through a two-step process. First, a highly detailed basemap of the area is created by rendering features of the built environment of an area to the map. In high definition mapping, the emphasis in creating the basemap is on including as much detail of the area as possible including adding all streets, buildings, sidewalks, fields, bushes, trees, shrubs, and other land-scaping features to the map. Next, crimes are mapped at their *exact* location. Exactness of the crime location is vital to high definition mapping including mapping a crime on the right side of a sidewalk, on a footpath between a sidewalk and some bushes, or on the right side of an alley. The more accurate basemap and crime location data allows for analysis that provides much more specific information about what may be causing crime. In 1998, Temple University implemented an experimental high definition mapping program in order to better analyze crime incidents on and around the university campus, with a special interest in reducing assaults and other violent behavior (Henderson and Lowell, 2000). Through the high definition mapping process, Temple University was able to identify several hot spots of activity and subsequently implement police practices and environmental changes that dramatically reduced crime in those areas (Henderson and Lowell, 2000). The success of the Temple program points out the benefits of high definition mapping to provide rich and detailed crime information for use in proactive policing, environmental design, and situational crime prevention practices. While high definition mapping is only now beginning to emerge as a vital new technology, the increased concern over analyzing crime at the community and neighborhood levels should ensure its rapid adoption in the future.

Correctional Facility Mapping

One of the emerging uses for GIS within the field of corrections involves mapping within correctional facilities. Despite mapping being used for other management related issues within corrections, mapping within correctional facilities has been slowed by the difficulty in dealing with 3-D space within GIS. In order to overcome the problems it has working in 3-D space, GIS is being integrated with computer-aided design (CAD), which offers a third dimension. Thus, through combining GIS and CAD, each prison cell can be mapped as an individual living space with information about each inmate being linked to his or her individual cell. Currently, the National Law Enforcement and Corrections Technology Center-Southeast (NLECTC-Southeast) and the U.S. Department of Energy's Savannah River Technology Center (SRTC) are developing just such a system called CORMAP (www.nlectc.org/assistance/cormap.html). In this new system, cells can be queried based on information about the inmates, such as offense history, race, gang affiliation, and other information essential to correctional facility management. Queries about gang membership would result in cells being colored differently based on whether the inmate resident is a known gang member. Moreover, crime and disciplinary incidents can be mapped within the facility to determine "hot spot" problem areas and areas in need of increased surveillance. While this system is currently only in development, this technology holds great promise for the future of mapping within correctional facilities and other enclosed spaces where crime occurs such as high-rise buildings and housing projects.

3-D Mapping

With the advancements in computer software and hardware throughout the last decade, increasingly complex map viewing, such as 3-D crime maps, has been made possible. Once the domain of video games and special effects-laden movies, with the advent of Google Earth and Sketch up, 3-D maps have started to become increasingly commonplace in viewing urban areas to assist in policy analysis. As these 3-D maps have become more common, they have increasingly become a valuable tool for criminal justice planning. 3-D maps provide criminal justice planners with realistic views of cities and towns capable of showing buildings and streets from almost any angle. One 3-D product developed by Harris Corporation acts as a virtual GPS receiver allowing users to virtually travel through a city while displaying their exact latitude and longitude information. Other software systems, such as Sketch-up, allow users to create their own buildings and even whole cities, and upload them to Google Earth where they can be combined with aerial photography, business data, crime data, and even traffic conditions. This combined view of an urban area allows users to get a more realistic image of an area than can be provided from viewing traditional static 2-D maps. Currently, 3-D maps are used primarily as tools for planning security measures and for viewing detailed building information, but future advancements promise enhanced crime mapping capabilities. Specifically, automatic vehicle location systems are already being developed to allow for vehicles to be tracked on 3-D city maps. Other advanced uses in development include the viewing and analysis of crimes in 3-D. Future work in 3-D mapping promises to allow users to view crime locations three-dimensionally to not only determine where hot spots are occurring, but to view the areas and their subsequent built environment in 3-D space. At this point the main limitations to 3-D mapping are the software and hardware requirements necessary for viewing as well as the exorbitant costs associated with developing accurate 3-D representations of cities. As with other emerging technologies discussed in this section, costs of 3-D technology should continue to drop as 3-D becomes more established.

Regional Mapping Initiatives

One of the peculiar characteristics about policing in the United States is that it is highly decentralized, with approximately 17,000 different law enforcement agencies existing on the local, state, and federal levels. In the normal course of events this doesn't lead to too many problems, yet when it comes to information sharing and cross-jurisdictional cooperation, problems exist. In terms of crime mapping, the biggest problem is that this decentralized police structure creates artificially boundaries. Although police officers may acknowledge jurisdictional boundaries such as city and county limits, crime and criminals do not, and crime often crosses over jurisdictional lines. When mapping crimes, this leads to incomplete pictures of crime patterns, with crime stopping at a jurisdictional line. Because of this problem, there has been a big push by federal and state agencies to encourage the creation of regional mapping initiatives, which would combine crime data from multiple jurisdictions. The benefits of such a system are obvious in that crime, particularly serial crime, can be tracked across jurisdictions. Moreover, smaller agencies that have had a difficult time acquiring computerized mapping on their own can now benefit from having their crimes mapped by other agencies.

Yet for all the promise that regional mapping initiatives hold for the future of crime mapping, early programs have produced problems that must be overcome if the full potential is to be realized. The most problematic involves creating general data agreements between all the agencies involved. Specifically, all agencies must agree to a common data structure (crimes to be recorded, how often, etc.) in order for these regional mapping initiatives to function correctly. A related problem involves simply determining what agency will act as a repository for the crime data and perform the necessary work to make the regional initiative function fully. A more troubling problem involves the lack of good information gathering systems by police agencies, inhibiting the ability of many agencies to provide accurate and timely data for analysis. Unless all agencies are capable of providing accurate and timely data in the agreed upon format, the regional analysis will be virtually worthless from a tactical point of view. The final, and potentially biggest problem facing regional mapping initiatives, is the natural tendency of police agencies to distrust each other and be unwilling to share information regardless of the potential benefits. If this and other problems can be overcome, regional mapping initiatives have a bright future ahead of them and can quite possibly revolutionize crime analysis.

Simulation

One of the main dreams of many crime analysts and police managers is to accurately predict which areas will experience increases or decreases in crime activity. The benefits of accurate crime prediction are many including more efficient staffing and manpower decisions, increased citizen satisfaction, potential decreased harm and property loss, and enhanced policy analysis. While prediction of crime events currently relies on clairvoyants and other dubious practices, recent advances have taken place that indicate that predicting crime may one day become standard practice. One of the most promising areas of study in predicting or modeling crime activities is the area of simulation. Simulation is a general area of study that involves trying to model or imitate natural or social processes such as urban growth and development, ant colony functioning, or social networking. There exists a long history of simulation research in fields such as economics, biology, and engineering, where simulation is a valuable tool in testing theories and understanding potential alternative outcomes. In terms of crime modeling and prediction, simulation work is primarily being carried out in the areas of geosimulation and urban land use modeling.

Geosimulation is a type of simulation modeling that focuses on modeling urban phenomena at the micro level such as individual household levels. In general, geosimulation differs from other types of modeling in that it views urban phenomena as "the result of collective dynamics of interacting objects" (Torrens, 2003). Current research involving the geosimulation of crime has focused on modeling how crowds behave in riot situations, the impact of police interventions on criminal activities, and offender mobility and burglary (Torrens, 2003; Malleson, 2007). The main goals of these models have been to better understand the actions of individual actors and to test theories of criminal movement and behavior. In contrast to geosimulation and its focus on micro-level processes of crime and criminal actors, urban land use modeling and simulation is interested in howchanges in urban growth and development impact the decline of neighborhoods and the change in crime patterns at the neighborhood level. In particular, research is being conducted by NIJ, which is working on developing models of urban crime that can be implemented with urban growth simulators for use in policy analysis, urban planning, and policing (Paulsen and Wilson, 2008). The goal of these models is to create easy-to-use tools to assist planners, policy analysts, and police executives in understanding potential changes in crime patterns based on changes in urban growth (sprawl, gentrification, infill). Importantly, these employ urban growth simulators, which have shown to be beneficial in understanding potential outcomes from urban growth decisions (zoning, urban service areas, etc.). While both of these simulation methodologies hold promise for better understanding of criminal processes, and in particular spatial aspects of crime, they are still at this point only in the alpha stage of development.

SUMMARY

List of Major Findings

1. The use of maps for understanding and studying crime has a long history, dating back to the mid-1800s;
2. Within policing, crime mapping can be traced back to at least 1900, with police departments using simple pin maps to analyze basic crime patterns;
3. The advent of affordable personal computers and easier-to-use GIS software ushered in modern crime mapping and helped lead to a major increase in the use of mapping throughout the criminal justice system;
4. Within policing, crime mapping has numerous uses including maps for patrol officers, investigations, and police managers;
5. It is important to remember who your audience is when making maps;
6. Patrol officer maps need to focus on informing officers about what is going on in their beats and should include the most recent data, be beat specific, and not include too much or too little information;
7. Maps for investigative purposes range from maps of criminal offense patterns to criminal intelligence, and geographic profiling of serial offenders;
8. Maps for police executives are designed to cover a range of issues including problem oriented policing maps, manpower allocation maps, and maps for community presentations;
9. Mapping within courts and corrections is far less advanced than in policing and mapping is still just beginning to find a use within decision making;
10. Within probation and parole, mapping is used most often for service area allocation and management, location of treatment centers and halfway houses, and in investigative collaborations with police;
11. Mapping within the CJS is still relatively new with far more advances yet to come in how mapping is both conducted and used by CJS agencies; and
12. Examples of future developments in mapping include the collaboration between GPS and GIS, high definition mapping, correctional facility mapping, 3-D mapping, regional mapping initiatives, and crime forecasting.

Implications for Crime Mapping and Spatial Analysis

As this chapter focuses on providing an overview of the uses of computerized mapping within the criminal justice system, its implications for mapping, although important, are not as extensive as in other chapters. It is important to learn from this overview that computerized mapping is still in its relative infancy in terms of uses within the CJS, but that computerized mapping has a bright future ahead of it. As can be seen from the discussion of future uses, integration of computerized mapping with other emerging technologies such as GPS and 3-D technology holds great promise for future applications within the CJS.

Perhaps the biggest implication in terms of crime mapping and spatial analysis from this chapter is the need to focus on the specific purpose and audience when making maps. For example, within policing computerized maps have numerous different applications ranging from patrol maps to criminal intelligence maps to manpower allocation maps. Importantly, the end users of each type of map have very different needs and very different requirements for these maps. Thus, when making maps for these different purposes you need to keep in mind the audience as well as the main purpose of the map and tailor the map to meet those specifications. Put another way, maps are not "one size fits all." Spatial analysis and crime mapping should not be entered into without a sense of purpose and a clear understanding from both the end user and the person making the map of what is to be analyzed and the final product to be generated.

CHAPTER 8

Major Issues in the Practice of Crime Mapping

The purpose of this chapter is to provide an overview of the different issues involved in the implementation and use of computerized crime mapping within law enforcement. Specifically, this chapter will discuss barriers to mapping, data-related issues, and ethical and legal issues in computerized crime mapping.

Chapter Outline

INTRODUCTION

As Chapter 7 illustrated, computerized mapping is undergoing major growth in use within the entire criminal justice system. Currently, over 16 percent of all local police agencies in the United States use computerized crime mapping in some capacity (Hickman, 2001). Moreover, recent advances in mapping technology and use indicate that computerized mapping will continue to be a major component of policing, courts, and corrections in the near future. However, with the increased use of computerized mapping, several major issues have arisen surrounding both the implementation and use of mapping within the criminal justice system. Chapter 8 provides a discussion of these major issues, including barriers to mapping, data issues, critical issues concerning the use of computerized mapping, and ethical and legal issues in mapping.

BARRIERS TO THE USE OF COMPUTERIZED MAPPING

A sound discussion of the barriers associated with implementing and using computerized mapping has been swept away in the rush by many criminal justice agencies to adopt computerized mapping technology within their agency. Too often academics, trade publications, and software companies have provided a one-sided view of computerized mapping, that of problem-free implementation and use by criminal justice agencies. However, a closer look at the overall use of computerized mapping within law enforcement indicates that there are many agencies struggling to implement and use computerized mapping effectively. Specifically, the use of computerized mapping in law enforcement is increasingly becoming limited to large police departments that make up only a fraction of the total number of law enforcement agencies nationally (Hickman, 2001). While 90 percent of agencies serving populations over 250,000 and approximately 60 percent of agencies serving populations between 50 and 250,000 are currently using computerized mapping, only approximately 14 percent of the nearly 13,000 departments serving populations less than 50,000 are currently using computerized mapping (Hickman, 2001). Moreover, the number of small departments using computerized mapping actually declined between 1997 and 1999 (Hickman, 2001). This is all the more striking given that small departments comprise approximately 90 percent of all law enforcement agencies nationally. These numbers appear to indicate that there are definite barriers to not only implementing computerized mapping, but also its continued use within an agency.

For the vast majority of agencies, the biggest barriers to successfully implementing and maintaining a computerized mapping system are the two interrelated problems of *cost* and *department need*. There is a tendency within criminal justice agencies, and law enforcement agencies in particular, to desire the newest "toys and gadgets" available regardless of whether or not they need or can afford them. Importantly, the trend for adoption of new technology usually flows downward with very large agencies being the earliest adopters of new technology and small and rural agencies being the last to adopt new technology. While there are always exceptions to this rule, such as small but wealthy agencies, it is usually the small and rural agencies that are the last to adopt new technology, if they adopt it at all.

Unfortunately for many software companies, most law enforcement agencies are simply too small to fully utilize a computerized mapping system. Specifically, most small and rural agencies do not have enough crime to justify the high costs associated with implementing and maintaining a computerized mapping system. While police agencies that serve jurisdictions with populations under 25,000 account for approximately 90 percent of all law enforcement agencies, they account for only approximately 16 percent of all reported crime, and only 11 percent of all serious violent and property crime (Pastore and Maguire, 2000). Crime issues in these small and rural agencies are usually easily understood without the aid of computerized mapping. In a survey of North Carolina police chiefs, Paulsen (2001b) found that most small town police chiefs thought that mapping was not necessary, as they already knew where crime occurred in their jurisdictions. Moreover, even if these agencies desired to conduct computerized mapping, almost all lacked sufficient funds and manpower to acquire and maintain a computerized mapping system.

When planning to implement a computerized mapping system, carefully and thoroughly weighing the perceived need against the costs associated with acquiring and maintaining the system cannot be emphasized enough. While it is true that the costs associated with computerized mapping have dropped significantly in the last ten years, it is still a prohibitively expensive proposition for many agencies. Costs associated with implementing and maintaining a computerized mapping system include software, hardware, training, and data.

While there are numerous companies that produce GIS software for use in computerized mapping, all with varying degrees of functionality and costs, most software prices start in the $1,000 range. Costs associated with the initial purchase of GIS software can increase or decrease depending on the number of licenses an agency purchases and the level of customization needed. Importantly, too many departments fail to consider all of the other costs associated with GIS software purchases. One additional cost is the annual maintenance fee that most software companies charge in order for an agency to receive the ever valuable customer support and upgrades that are constantly necessary. While software can always be purchased without the maintenance agreement, it is usually a wise purchase for new adopters of the software who may need a lot of assistance from customer service. Although prices of maintenance agreements vary widely among software providers, this fee can add significantly to the cost of the software purchase. Other software costs surround the options or add-ons that increase the functionality of the GIS software. These add-ons range from database extensions that allow communications between databases and GIS software, and Internet extensions that allow publishing of maps to the Internet, to crime mapping extensions that provide analysis functions like hot spot mapping. Importantly, while these extensions can increase efficiency, they can also considerably increase costs for an agency.

After the purchase of software, the second most important purchase is *hardware* on which to run the GIS software. Although cost is often the most important consideration for an agency, the main concern should be that the hardware meets the necessary requirements of the software to run efficiently. As a general rule, hardware should never be purchased without first consulting with the software vendor about hardware requirements for the software to run efficiently and effectively. Common problems that agencies experience are using existing (older) computers to run new software and purchasing hardware at the lower limits of the software requirements, limiting the functionality of the software. Luckily for criminal justice agencies, and all consumers, the cost of powerful computer hardware has dropped dramatically in the last few years to a point where excellent systems can be purchased for less than $1,000. Other hardware purchases that are often overlooked when acquiring computerized mapping systems but are often necessary include printers, scanners, and large screen monitors. As with software, all of these different hardware needs can add significantly to the costs of a computerized mapping system.

After the purchase of the software and hardware, one of the other most important costs associated with computerized mapping systems is the *cost associated with training* on the software. As with software and hardware purchases, the costs associated with software training vary greatly depending on the level and source of training. Training options include software vendor provided training, software vendor approved training, training by third party consultants, and training by universities, colleges and technical schools. In addition, training vendors will offer a range of different classes from beginning classes dealing with understanding GIS principles to classes covering advanced crime mapping concepts. While training needs for an agency will depend on each unique situation, it is suggested that at the very least basic training in the software be undertaken, with more advanced classes being dictated by agency needs. In addition to the cost of the actual training class, most agencies will also have to factor in travel costs associated with attending the training. With the exception of agencies in or near large urban areas, most agencies will have to travel to receive training, which can significantly increase the costs associated with training. Importantly, the availability of good, affordable, and geographically close training is one of the problems that agencies often express as preventing them from implementing their computerized mapping systems in a timely manner.

The final, but no less important, cost associated with implementing and maintaining a computerized mapping system is the *cost of acquiring basic jurisdictional data.* These basic jurisdictional data are generally limited to basic street maps and jurisdictional maps but can include data on businesses, churches, restaurants, and bars, and other social data within a jurisdiction that may relate to crime analysis. While many departments will be able to get this basic street and social data free from other government agencies within their jurisdiction, many departments will not. The necessity of good street maps cannot be overstated, as it is street maps that contain the addresses that are used in geocoding and entering crime data (see Chapter 2 of the workbook for a complete discussion of geocoding). Thus, if an agency has a poor street map, they will have poor crime maps, which will make the expensive computerized mapping system basically worthless. As with everything else, the costs of commercially available street maps will vary depending on the location, size of jurisdiction, and level of data desired. Generally, rural areas will have a harder time acquiring accurate street maps as these areas are given low priority by commercial firms who derive the majority of their profits from large urban areas.

Another related problem with data when implementing computerized mapping systems involves the inability of agencies to export data from a record management system (RMS) in a format usable by the GIS. Police agencies are notorious for collecting huge amounts of crime-related data, the majority of which is recorded and stored within an agency's RMS. Owing to the critical nature of RMS, these systems are very expensive to acquire and maintain, often being one of the most expensive purchases that an agency makes, and are thus not easy to replace or upgrade. Unfortunately for most agencies, many RMS systems were not designed to export data to other programs, only to record and store data. Paulsen (2000b) found that among police agencies that had implemented computerized mapping systems, the single biggest problem they experienced was integrating their RMS data with their GIS. Importantly, this data integration issue was even more of a problem than software and hardware costs, manpower, or training issues. There are numerous cases in which police agencies have purchased an expensive computerized mapping system (GIS software, hardware, etc.) only to find out after the fact that they cannot export any of the data from their RMS. Agencies are then faced with issues such as purchasing a new RMS, entering all RMS data into the GIS by hand, or not using the GIS at all, making it a rather expensive paperweight. While data integration is a potentially fatal barrier to computerized mapping implementation, this problem is easily avoidable through sound planning before implementation and discussing these issues with software vendors before purchase. Moreover, many GIS software vendors have begun to offer services in which they will assist in integrating an agency's RMS with the new GIS software. Thus, while data integration is a serious and potentially fatal barrier to implementing a computerized mapping system, it is a problem that can best be avoided through sound planning.

A final barrier that criminal justice agencies often face when trying to successfully implement and maintain a computerized mapping system involves *planning* for its integration and use within the department. Without proper planning about how crime maps will be integrated into both management-level decisions and patrol functions, computerized mapping is almost certain to flounder from a lack of direction. Oftentimes agencies implement a computerized mapping system because they want to be seen as using the latest technology and ignore issues of how the system will be used by both managers and patrol officers.

In his article describing the implementation and use of crime mapping in the "Western" police department, Manning (2001) cites the lack of a clear identifiable purpose for using mapping as the biggest reason for its being unsuccessful. In the department Manning studied, this lack of a clear purpose for using mapping affected both police managers and patrol officers. Despite being generally in favor of implementing a computerized mapping system, the police managers at the Western police department rarely if ever used crime maps in any management-level decisions. While one captain used maps extensively in his reports, maps were not systematically used for strategic planning, resource deployment, or any other management-level decisions.

Similarly, the crime maps that were given to patrol officers in Western were largely ignored as well. Patrol officers were not involved in the development of crime maps (areas analyzed, crime types, time periods, etc.) and thus were given maps that were essentially useless to them. Moreover, officers received no training in how to interpret the maps or how to use them to conduct any problem solving, despite that being the stated purpose for the maps. In order for a computerized mapping system to be successful beyond implementation, planning must occur as to how maps will be used in both management-level decisions and everyday patrol functions.

DATA ISSUES

One of the most important adages about computers and analysis is "GIGO" or garbage in–garbage out. If you analyze bad data, then your results will reflect that bad data. In order for any type of analysis to be successful, the data used must be clearly understood and must be chosen based on its utility in answering the questions that are asked. Suffice it to say, the selection and use of data is of vital importance to successful crime mapping applications, yet complete discussions of all the issues surrounding data are few and far between. This section will explore the various issues surrounding the data used in crime mapping, including discussions of the different types and sources of data and their associated benefits and problems.

In general there are two different types of crime data used in crime mapping, the first of which is commonly referred to as *point* data. Point data are crime data with a locational component, usually a specific street address of a crime location, although it can also be the coordinates of a crime location as well (Brantingham and Brantingham, 1984). In addition to location data on crime incidents, point data can also consist of contextual data (see Sources of Data later in this chapter). When point data are used in crime maps, the maps are generally referred to as point or dot maps (Brantingham and Brantingham, 1984). This is one of the most popular methods for analyzing crime data because the results are fairly straightforward and patterns of crime distributions can be determined relatively easily. Figure 8.1 provides an example of a point map in which crime incidents for Lexington, Kentucky, are mapped so as to help understand patterns of crime in the jurisdiction.

In addition to its relative ease of use and interpretation, point data have several other benefits when making crime maps. First, mapping crime as point data is often regarded as the best method for determining the existence of spatial patterns in crime distributions. Point maps allow for the analysis of crime patterns on a large scale (small geographic area such as a neighborhood or city block), which is often beneficial in determining causes of crime (Harries, 1990). While much analysis of point patterns is done visually, numerous statistical techniques have been developed to assist in determining if there are statistically significant patterns of crime. Techniques such as hot spot analysis and kernel density interpolation (see Chapters 9 and 10 of the workbook) are particularly well suited for determining patterns of spatial clustering in crime incidents.

A second benefit of using point data is that they are not dependent on jurisdictional boundaries or reporting areas for analysis. As will be discussed more in-depth later, the results of aggregate crime data analysis are subject to the geographic unit to which data are aggregated (Brantingham and Brantingham, 1984). Specifically, results of analysis may vary depending on whether crime is aggregated at the census tract, police beat, or some alternative unit. However, because point data provide the absolute location of crime incidents, they are immune to problems that may arise from aggregation (Brantingham and Brantingham, 1984). Moreover, as discussed above, point data analysis allows for analysis of crime patterns on larger scales (neighborhood, city block) than aggregate analysis, which can lead to better understanding of crime patterns.

While point data are often extremely useful in the analysis of crime patterns, there are several problems associated with the mapping of crime at the point level. First, it is difficult to accurately make correlations between point data and other data such as

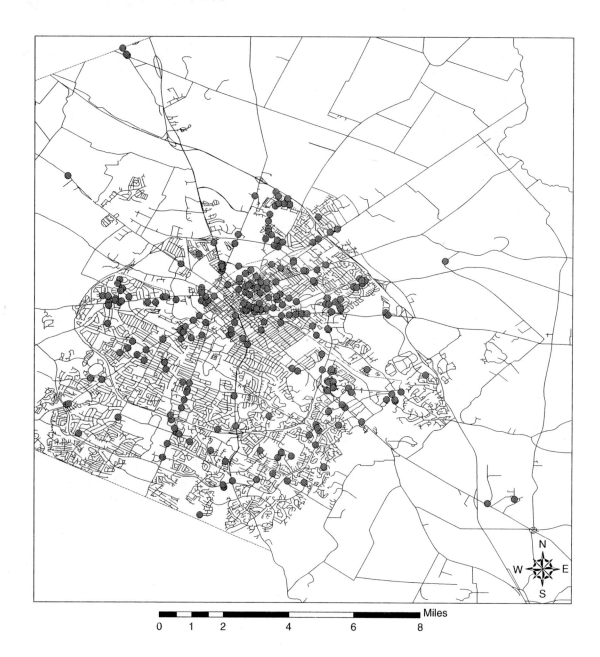

FIGURE 8.1   Gun Crimes in Lexington, Kentucky. Point map displaying gun crimes in Lexington, Kentucky.

income, poverty, and unemployment levels that are aggregated at the census tract. Although point data are often analyzed in this manner, the accuracy of such results is dubious. Without standardizing the point data, these types of analysis are at best only guesses about the relationships between incident locations and aggregated data.

Another related issue is the inability to accurately determine the magnitude of point data concentrations. While techniques such as hot spot analysis and kernel density interpolation can indicate if incident locations are closer than would be expected by chance (high concentrations of incidents), without knowing the underlying population data it is impossible to determine if these areas are unusually high areas. For example, if two different areas within a city both have clusters of 10 crimes but one has a population three times higher than the other, the magnitude of the crime concentrations is very different. Specifically, the less populous area would have a much higher magnitude crime problem despite both areas experiencing the same absolute amount of crimes. Thus, while point data are useful for determining "hot spots" of crime, this information alone is insufficient to determine the magnitude of a crime problem (see Figure 8.2).

A final problem with point data is the accuracy of the locational information. Locational information for point-level crime data is usually derived through a process called geocoding. *Geocoding* is the process of taking specific street addresses of crime incidents and matching them to a reference file containing a range of addresses for a given area such as a city.[1] Importantly, while geocoding can be a fairly efficient manner

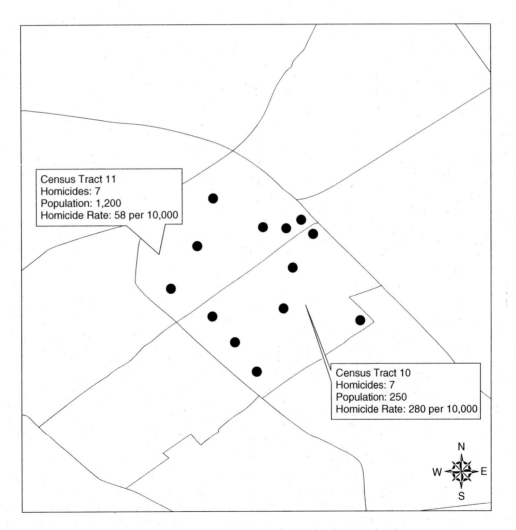

Census Tract 11
Homicides: 7
Population: 1,200
Homicide Rate: 58 per 10,000

Census Tract 10
Homicides: 7
Population: 250
Homicide Rate: 280 per 10,000

FIGURE 8.2   Map illustrating how point data can lead to misleading perceptions of the magnitude of crime.

---

[1]See Chapter 3 of the workbook for a complete discussion of geocoding and the issues surrounding geocoding.

for entering data, it is subject to several problems in terms of the accuracy of the locational data. Problems with geocoding include the following:

- Crime incidents that occur at locations where there are no specific street addresses, such as intersections, vacant lots, or fields.
- Poor data entry of crime location address, resulting in no match to a street address.
- Inaccurate street reference file resulting in crime incidents not matching real street addresses.

The cumulative effect of these and other problems with geocoding is that point data are often less than accurate in their location, resulting in analysis that is potentially biased and definitely misleading. This is not to say that geocoding is a poor method of data entry, simply that it is a process that is fallible and can lead to inaccurate point data.

In contrast to point-level crime data are *aggregate* crime data. Aggregate data are crime data that have been counted for a specific unit of geographic space such as a police beat or census tract. Thus, where point data show the exact locations of crime incidents, aggregate data provide a count of how many incidents occurred within a specific area such as a police beat. In general there are two basic types of aggregate-level crime data, the first of which is termed an *administrative unit* (Brantingham and Brantingham, 1984). Administrative units are defined as "spatial units designed primarily by government to organize the delivery of services, to provide common units for diverse reporting functions, and to provide an aggregate basis for government allocation and representation" (Brantingham and Brantingham, 1984). The two most commonly used administrative units for the aggregation of crime data are police beats and census tracts.

Police beats are best described as geographic units created by police agencies for patrol and administrative purposes. Most police agencies use police beats to manage and direct patrol officers' duties as well as for collecting and reporting crimes and calls for service. While there is no standardized method for their creation, police beats are usually created with several things in mind. First, determining size of the police beat is a balancing act. Police beats must be small enough that an officer can patrol the entire area without much difficulty, but not so small that patrol officers are used inefficiently. Beats that are too large in size would prevent officers from conducting meaningful patrol, while beats that are too small would require too many officers to be patrolling in a small area. Second, most police beats are drawn along the lines of existing geographic units or features such as census tracts, voting districts, zip code areas, neighborhood boundaries, or major streets. Thus, beats are often drawn based more on convenience than on either practical usefulness or social cohesiveness such as a uniform population base.

The other major type of administrative unit used for aggregating crime data is the *census tract,* as shown in Figure 8.3. Census tracts are administrative units that are drawn for purposes of counting the population of the country every ten years for use in numerous government administrative tasks. The foundation of the census tract is the census block, which is generally a unique city block (Harries, 1990). Information about households within this block area is gathered, and these blocks are in turn aggregated to the block group, which is a group of census blocks. Finally, groupings of census block groups are aggregated to create a census tract (Harries, 1990). Importantly, as a rule the smaller the administrative unit (census block), the less information about the households within this unit is released to the public (Harries, 1990). Thus, little information is available about households at the census block level, while all census data are available at the census tract level, giving rise to the popularity of aggregating crime at the census tract level. While the census tract and the smaller block groups and census blocks are unique to the United States, census geography is used to aggregate crime data in other countries as well. In Canada, Statistics Canada gathers census information, whereas in England the

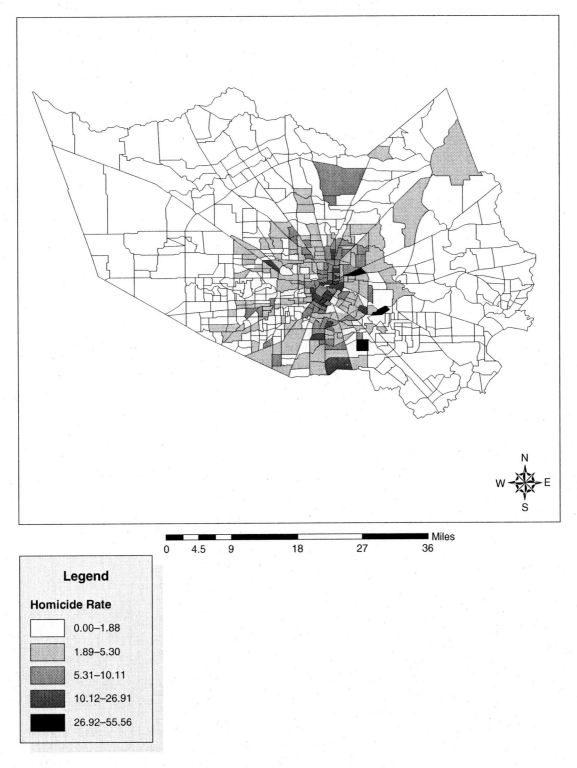

FIGURE 8.3   Houston Homicide Rate by Census Tract. Map detailing the homicide rate of Houston, Texas, by census tract.

agency responsible for gathering census data is the Office of Population Census and Surveys (Brantingham and Brantingham, 1984).

In addition to administrative units, the other main geographic unit used for aggregating crime data is called an *arbitrary coding unit* (Brantingham and Brantingham, 1984). An arbitrary coding unit is a geographic unit created only for the purposes of counting or aggregating crime data within a given area. Researchers and crime analysts who use arbitrary coding units for aggregating crime often use grids for counting crime data. In this process a grid is placed over an area and individual crimes that fall within each individual grid cell are totaled to create an aggregate count. Although grid cells can be of any shape that is desired, squares, hexagons, and triangles are most commonly used (Brantingham and Brantingham, 1984). Importantly, while crime incident data can be directly recorded to administrative units (police beats and census tracts), the aggregating of crime data in arbitrary coding units involves using a GIS to count point data within the user-created grid cells. While most GIS programs can easily count data in user-defined cells, it is a process that is slightly more difficult than other forms of aggregate data.

In terms of crime mapping, aggregated crime data have numerous benefits and problems. The clearest benefit for aggregating crime data is the ability to both create *rates of crime* and *compare crime data with other social data.* Both crime rates and comparisons of crime data with other social data are important aspects of crime mapping because they allow for more advanced analysis of crime problems. By creating crime rates, we are able to better understand differences in crime magnitude across jurisdictions than if we simply were analyzing individual crime locations only. Moreover, by comparing aggregate crime data with other social data such as income and unemployment levels, we can better understand root causes of crime distribution patterns. While creating crime rates and comparing crime incidents with other social data are difficult to do with point data, they are easily accomplished with aggregate data. Although it is admittedly easier to create crime rates and compare relationships between crime data and other social data with census tracts than with other aggregate data types, it can still be accomplished. Most GIS programs have functions that will merge data from one polygon source (census data) to another polygon source (arbitrary coding unit or police beat) allowing for data to be compared across different boundaries.

The other main benefit of aggregating crime data is that it provides crime information in a form that may have more *practical significance* to end-users than point data. While crime data aggregated to the census tract or arbitrary coding unit have some practical usefulness, it is crime data aggregated to the police beat that are most beneficial. Because beats are integral to both patrol and administration, making crime maps based on these geographic units makes a great deal of sense. Most officers and police managers think of crime and police work in terms of police beats, thus being able to view crime distributions according to police beats would be best for their daily functions. Other benefits include being able to compare aggregate crime data with other information collected at the police beat level, such as information related to shifts and manpower issues. While practical benefits associated with aggregate data are limited mostly to data aggregated to the police beat, this is certainly an important group where crime mapping is concerned. Thus, for strictly police uses, aggregating and analyzing crime by police beats is clearly beneficial.

Despite its clear benefits, aggregating crime data does pose some serious problems. First among these problems is the issue about how *boundaries* are drawn for the geographic units used in creating aggregate counts. Specifically, the manner in which these boundaries are drawn can have a significant impact on the crime totals for each different unit. While this is primarily a problem for both census tracts and police beats, which are created for administrative reasons, it can also impact arbitrary coding units despite their being created primarily for crime analysis purposes. Central to this problem is the fact that boundary lines for both census tracts and police beats often correspond with major city streets that, while convenient, often intersect crime distributions (Brantingham and Brantingham, 1984). The distribution of crime often clusters along major roadways; thus, what appears to be a cluster of crime incidents on a point map is often split up into different cells of an aggregate map (Brantingham and Brantingham, 1984). The effect is that the cluster of crime incidents is divided up into different cells and does not appear to have a high amount of crime. Figure 8.4 illustrates how the drawing of boundary lines can seriously impact the counts of crime and effectively make a real crime cluster disappear into an aggregate count of crime. While arbitrary coding units can be drawn in a manner that minimizes this problem, this is a problem that will always impact aggregate measures of crime.

Another related issue with the drawing of boundaries for aggregate crime units is the fact that they are often stable over time despite the growth and change of the city in which they are drawn. Specifically, boundary lines often don't change for 20 years or more, although the populations within the boundaries have changed dramatically. While the stability of boundaries can be beneficial for long-term trend analysis, changes within the population size and homogeneity can make statistical analysis difficult (Brantingham and Brantingham, 1984).

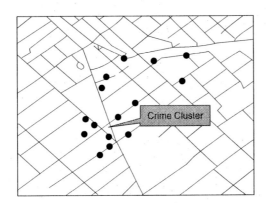

Natural crime cluster

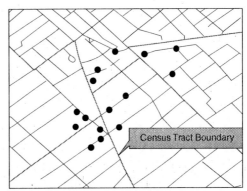

crime cluster is split
by census tract boundaries

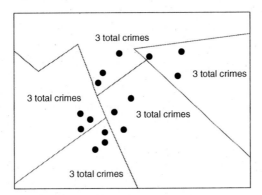

crime totals aggregated
to the census tract

FIGURE 8.4   Maps Illustrating How the Position of Boundary Lines Can Obscure Actual Crime Clusters.

A more serious problem with the drawing of boundaries involves differences in the size of the different cells used for aggregation. In particular, the relative *size and shape* of the cells used for aggregation directly impact the results of statistical analysis involving aggregate data. In general as the size of a cell increases, correlations become stronger, meaning it is more and more difficult to draw correct conclusions about the relationships between two areas as their sizes increase (Brantingham and Brantingham, 1984). This problem arises from the fact that crime data in aggregated units are averages of the individual points within each cell. Thus as you increase the number of incidents within each cell, the variability of the data becomes lost and data within differing cells become more similar leading to stronger correlations. It is important to underscore that these correlations are statistically true but practically invalid, in that the areas are more similar simply because there are more data and the data tend to create averages that are similar. Moreover, attempting to infer correct relationships between two different sized cells is particularly difficult, a problem that is especially important when analyzing census tracts and police beats that are of varying sizes. As a general rule, geographic units of vastly different sizes should not be used for comparison as the data within them are too different to accurately reflect real relationships (Brantingham and Brantingham, 1984). Importantly, collecting data in a standardized size, such as with arbitrary coding units, is a good way to prevent problems with incorrect correlations.

Another problem involving aggregate data involves attempting to *combine data with boundaries of differing shapes and sizes.* While census data and data collected at the police beat level are two of the more popular forms of data used in crime mapping, numerous other types of data are also available that may prove beneficial to understanding patterns of crime. Combining data is a process that is often used when overlaying data from different sources in order to create a new set of data that represents the two pieces of data that are of interest. The problem with combining data from different sources is that the boundaries may be different in shape and size, and thus the data may not combine as accurately as necessary for proper inference and analysis. While most GIS packages have methods for combining different shaped data, they do it in an arbitrary way that may not reflect the reality of the original distributions. Figure 8.5 provides an example of how combining school district data with crime data from census tracts in order to determine crime per school district can result in incorrect relationships. Notice how the distribution of point data is skewed when aggregating data to the census tract and how in turn these data are further skewed upon combining them with school district data. The resultant data provide a mistaken portrait of crime distributions in two different school districts. Although improvements in GIS software have helped to limit the problems with combining data of differing shapes, problems still exist that can lead to incorrect inferences about crime distributions. The problems are compounded when these data are then used to create policy, inform the public, or report research results.

The final problem associated with aggregated data involves how aggregate data are interpreted and is termed *ecological fallacy.* The concept underlying ecological fallacy is a relatively easy one, but one that is vitally important in terms of interpretation and understanding of aggregate crime data. Ecological fallacy is the idea that individual behavior cannot be inferred from aggregate data (Rossmo, 2000). In examining aggregate crime data, this is often a very attractive and common error, one that can lead to problems in both crime policy and public perception. An example of committing this type of error in reasoning would be to state that individuals who are high school dropouts are more likely to commit crime than high school graduates, based upon findings that there is a correlation between crime and high school graduation rates at the census tract level. This individual inference cannot be made simply because the relationship exits at the aggregate level. There is no way to infer individual behavior simply from relationships that exist at the aggregate level, and to do so is to invite problems concerning the validity of the

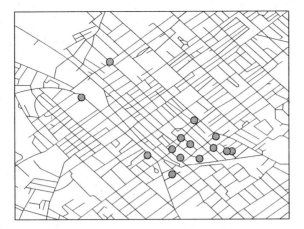

Natural crime distribution

Crime is aggregarted to
the census tract with 14 total
crimes being counted for
census tract 12.

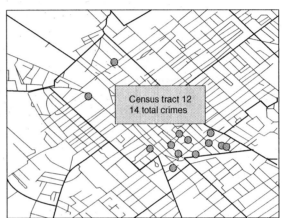

GIS software divides the
14 crimes evenly, despite
the fact they are heavily
concentrated in school
district 2.

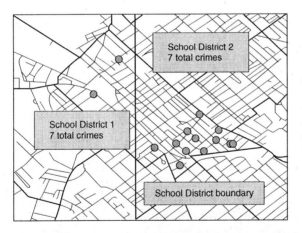

**FIGURE 8.5   Maps Illustrating How GIS Programs Can Combine Data in a Manner
That Obscures the Actual Distribution of Crime Incidents.**

researchers' work. The only way to prevent these types of errors in reasoning is to
report findings on the aggregate level as aggregate-level findings only and not to
attempt to make leaps to individual level behavior.

Sources of Data for Crime Maps

Integral to a discussion dealing with types of data used in creating crime maps is a
discussion of the issues surrounding sources of data commonly used in crime

mapping. As with types of data, there are several main sources of data used in creating crime maps, each with associated problems and benefits. The first and most important source of data for creating crime maps is *official crime data*. Official data are generally considered to be any data officially recorded by a law enforcement agency relating to the commission of a crime. In practical terms, official data usually center on calls for service and arrest data. *Calls for service* are reports taken when an individual calls a law enforcement agency in order to report a crime. When a call for service is received, an officer is usually dispatched to handle the call, resulting in a more detailed report of the offense type, victim, and other information pertinent to the incident. In contrast to calls for service are *arrest* data, which are data concerning individuals who have been arrested on suspicion of committing a crime. Arrest data are usually even more detailed than calls for service data, providing information about the offender, motive, and other pertinent incident level data. In combination these two sources of data are the most commonly used data for creating crime maps. It is important to note that this is pretty much the extent of data sources dealing with official crime as known to the police. While information concerning other aspects of policing such as investigations, gangs, and drugs are often mapped, the data are usually some variation of either calls for service or arrest information.

The most important benefit of official data is that they are the most *comprehensive* recording of crime information available for mapping. Currently, there is no more extensive recording of data about the nature and extent of crime available for use in mapping. The important part of these two prior phrases is "available for mapping." While other data sources exist about overall crime in the United States, in the form of self-report surveys and victimization surveys, none of these data sources can provide data (addresses) that can be mapped. Moreover, these other sources of information also are limited in their scopes, in that they are national in nature and thus are inappropriate for detailing the nature and extent of crime in states, counties, cities, towns, and neighborhoods. However, as we will discuss, while official data are the best source currently available for use in creating crime maps, they are far from a perfect source of data on the nature and extent of crime.

While there is largely only one major benefit to official crime data, there are two important problems associated with their use in crime mapping. First and most important is the fact that official data are not a complete recording of all crimes, but rather they are only a recording of all *crimes known to the police* (Robinson, 2002). Most crimes are not known to the police, leading to official data only being a partial indicator of the extent of crime in a jurisdiction. This unreported crime is commonly called the "dark figure of crime" and is considered to be a significant portion of all crimes committed within the United States each year (Robinson, 2002). Importantly, the Bureau of Justice Statistics reports that victims report only one in three property crimes and that victims are more likely to report crimes if they are violent in nature, if an injury results, or if property loss is $250 or more (Bureau of Justice Statistics, 1997). The importance of this is that official crime data only provide a partial view of the distribution of crime, a serious issue when the goal of crime mapping is to provide a picture of the crime problem for a jurisdiction. In making crime maps using official data, practitioners and researchers must remember that the maps are not comprehensive crime maps, but rather maps that reflect the distribution of crimes and how those crimes are reported.

The other major problem with official data centers around how patterns of crime are determined largely by using both the crime data collected and the information on areas that police patrol (Trojanowicz, Kappeler, and Gaines, 2002). Because of the way we *define and enforce laws*, crime is not equally distributed across time and space, but rather is clustered in areas where police activity is focused. In particular, official crime tends to focus on street crimes that occur in bars, certain apartment complexes, areas around liquor stores, and shopping malls, choosing to ignore crimes of a more white-collar nature (Trojanowicz, Kappeler, and Gaines, 2002). Were police to focus more heavily on crimes of the "suites" instead of crimes of the streets, patterns of crime would have a very different look, centering in wealthier areas, business districts, and corporate areas.

An example of how crime patterns are affected by how we define and control crimes is how the drug war has been framed. In both definition and control, the war on drugs has focused on illicit drugs such as marijuana, cocaine, and heroin, while ignoring the illegal use and abuse of prescription drugs. Importantly, this definitional and enforcement focus on illicit drugs over illegal use of prescription drugs occurs despite government statistics indicating that the abuse of prescription drugs is more prevalent than that of illicit drugs. The impact that this definitional and control focus on illicit drugs has on crime maps of drug crime is striking. Specifically, if hot spots of prescription drug crimes were created, they would most likely be in very different areas of a city than hot spots of illicit drug abuse. In general official crime and patterns of official crime are guided in large part by how we define and control crime and not so much by the occurrence of crimes. The importance of this criticism is that it brings to light the fact that official data are not free of political bias in either its definition or its enforcement and that this bias can significantly impact the patterns of crime.

This critical view of how the definition and the differential control of crime impact the geographic distribution of crime is termed the *geography of social control* (Lowman, 1986). Definitional research focuses on how crime definitions impact patterns of crime as well as the development of alternative measures of crime that are not dependent on official definitions of crime and patrol strategies, but rather reflective of more practical definitions of crime. While considerable research exists concerning the creation of crimes and the social construction of crime, almost no research has dealt with the spatial aspects of these issues (Lowman, 1986). Moreover, while alternative measures of crime are a goal of this field of study, little work has been done in this area to date (Lowman, 1986). Examples of alternative measures of crime include public perceptions of crime and media coverage of crime, both of which show spatial differences in comparison with official patterns of crime (see Figure 8.6). Research into how police practices impact geographic distributions of crime has also been scarce. Although researchers have largely ignored this field of study, the importance of geography of social control concepts cannot be ignored when considering official patterns of crime and the impact that both definitions and control practices have on its distribution (see Case Study on p. 202 for more on the geography of social control).

A second source of data for use in creating crime maps is *unofficial data*. Where official data represent crimes known to the police, unofficial data reflect measures of crime that are not reflected in official measures. Examples of unofficial measures of crime include maps representing public perceptions of crime and fear of crime for a jurisdiction, maps of media coverage of crime, and victimization survey data that are capable of being mapped. The key to all of these different measures is that they are different measures of crime and crime-related phenomenon and thus provide a different view of crime patterns. Although these measures will probably never supplant official data for use in driving criminal justice policy, they can provide powerful insight into how other aspects of crime work within a community. While research has thus far been limited in terms of exploring these alternative unofficial measures of crime, there is promise that this research will advance along with the advance of spatial statistics and data collection technology.

The final source of data for use in creating crime maps is *contextual data*. Contextual data fall into a catch-all category including all other types of data pertinent to analyzing crime patterns, but are not crime related. The importance of contextual data is that they provide a frame of reference for analyzing crime and assisting in the determination of the root causes of crime. Examples of contextual data include:

- Census data;
- Bar and restaurant locations;
- School district zones;
- Tax assessor and voting districts; and
- Sexually oriented business locations.

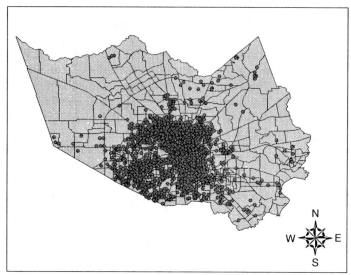

Total Houston Homicides

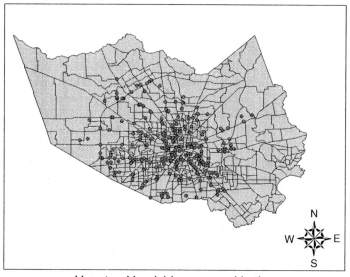

Houston Homicides covered in the
Front section of the Newspaper

FIGURE 8.6   Maps illustrating the difference in actual homicide locations and
the locations of those homicides covered in the front section of the newspaper.

The biggest problem with contextual data centers on the format in which most
contextual data is collected. Specifically, most of these data are in aggregate form and
thus all of the issues surrounding combining and analyzing aggregate data with
crime data apply. The problem with combining and analyzing data is particularly
problematic given that these contextual data are used to assist in policy analysis and
may have real impact on criminal justice policy. The problem is further aggravated
by the lack of knowledge about what types of data to select when conducting analysis
of crime data. Many practitioners conduct analyses of crime data with whatever
contextual data are easily available, irrespective of what data are necessary for a good
analysis. Thus, although contextual data is a potentially useful source of data, the
potential exists for policy to be based on analysis that is flawed due to aggregation
and data combining problems.

CRITICAL ISSUES CONCERNING THE USE OF COMPUTERIZED MAPPING

One of the presumed reasons for the increase in the use of computerized mapping within policing over the last ten years has been the increase in the adoption of community policing. Community policing is a policing philosophy that encourages police to no longer merely provide rapid response to calls for service, but to actually attempt to identify and reduce underlying causes of crime, fear of crime, and neighborhood disorder (Trojanowicz, Kappeler, and Gaines, 2002). At the heart of this focus on crime prevention is an increased effort by police departments to determine the root causes of crime, in which computerized mapping supposedly plays an integral part (Trojanowicz, Kappeler, and Gaines, 2002). Through computerized mapping, police departments can first identify hot spots of crime and then overlay contextual data in order to provide insight into the origins of the crime hot spots. Based on these analyses police departments then develop policies, increasingly of a non-law enforcement nature, that will attempt to reduce the amount of crime in that area. Moreover, computerized mapping can also be used to measure the "health" of a neighborhood through the analysis of crime data, citizen survey data, and other contextual data. These health forecasts can then be used to assist police departments and other government agencies in their delivery of services with the goal of preventing crime and fostering healthy communities.

While computerized mapping holds promise for helping to prevent and better understand causes of crime, it can also lead to problems concerning police strategies when police simply focus on "attacking the dots" on a crime map (Kappeler personal communication, August 19, 2002). *Attacking the dots* is when police use computerized mapping to identify areas of high crime, and then rather than use community policing principles to try to determine underlying causes of crime, they respond to the areas through traditional methods of policing such as directed patrol. In this sense police agencies are using crime maps merely to direct areas of attack, in which areas with a high number of dots (crimes) are the prime areas of targeted policing. The problem with this and other similar aggressive policing strategies is that they focus on immediate results and usually result in only short-term crime reduction due to crime displacement (see Chapter 6 for more in-depth discussion of displacement). Unfortunately, the "attack the dots" strategy of going after high-crime areas with traditional means is more likely to be the norm than the exception within departments using computerized mapping. First, many agencies that claim they are conducting community policing are doing so in name only. Trojanowicz, Kappeler, and Gaines (2002) state that "some police departments have used community policing as a cover for aggressive law enforcement tactics rather than serving the needs of their communities." Thus, for many police departments, computerized mapping was never intended for determining underlying causes of crime problems, but merely to help better direct patrols more efficiently. Further compounding this problem is the fact that most police have no understanding of theories of crime or how to test them, making analysis of underlying causes of crime nearly impossible (Manning, 2001). In talking about police officers' understanding of the causes of crime, Manning (2001:97) states,

> What causal forces are at work, underneath the dots, arrows, and signs? Western's officers, even those with college degrees, like officers in other police departments to my knowledge, have no generalized conception of the nature of crime, its causes, dynamics, or meaning.

The impact of this "attack the dots" mentality is that rather than use computerized mapping to further community policing principles and understand and prevent crime, mapping is primarily going to be used as a means of improving the efficiency of aggressive law enforcement. At the same time these aggressive tactics will be covered with the name of community policing and will be seen as impressive uses of emerging technologies, further lending legitimacy to questionable tactics. In the end rather than moving toward community policing and its focus on improving the community, computerized mapping may actually be reinvigorating aggressive law enforcement and the problems that it brings. The main way to combat the "attack the dots" mentality and the problems that lead to it is to improve officer education about causes of crime and research methods, as well as their importance in understanding and preventing crime.

ETHICAL AND LEGAL ISSUES IN CRIME MAPPING

As with the use of most new technology, legal and ethical issues concerning the use of the new tool begin to develop and take shape only after the technology has been used for some time and problems and issues arise. The same is true for the use of computerized mapping within law enforcement. While crime mapping has been around for well over a decade, it is only within the last two to three years that serious discussion of the ethical and legal issues surrounding the use of computerized mapping has begun to take place (Wartell and McEwen, 2001). Accordingly, because the discussion has now only just begun, little consensus exists as to how to handle the major ethical and legal issues confronting crime mapping. In fact, about all that can be said concerning ethical and legal issues involving crime maps is that there is a firm grasp of the nature of the issues, but only suggestions and conjecture in terms of how to handle them. Importantly, the major ethical and legal issues surrounding crime maps involve the balance between privacy and public access, sharing data with researchers, and liability issues. The remainder of this chapter will be devoted to exploring these issues.

Privacy v. Public Information

Perhaps no ethical or legal issue is more important to the continued use and support for computerized mapping than balancing the privacy needs of crime victims with the public's need for crime information. While this issue is certainly not new within law enforcement, it takes on a new face with the advent of crime maps and the ability to produce highly detailed maps of crime locations and their associated information. As almost any under-graduate student in criminal justice can tell you, police incident reports are public records virtually everywhere and as long as one has the time and desire they can go to a police department and view these records (Casady, 1999). As mentioned, crime maps add a new twist to information dissemination because of the ability to distribute highly detailed address-level information about crime incidents and more importantly the victims of crime. Moreover, with the surging use of the Internet among both law enforcement agencies and the public, crime maps are increasingly being published on the Internet for the public to access. In balancing the right to know and the right of victims' privacy, there are strong arguments both for and against the public dissemination of crime maps with no clear middle ground on which both are served appropriately.

In looking at the public dissemination of crime maps, there are numerous arguments in support of this practice. First, making crime maps available publicly can *increase collaboration* between the public and police agencies (Wartell and McEwen, 2001). By providing the public with information about where crime levels are highest, police have found that citizens may be more willing to work with them in collaborative crime prevention programs. Second, crime maps can increase the *public awareness* of crime patterns and help to increase citizens' own security (Wartell and McEwen, 2001). One of the main tenets of crime prevention is the idea that people who are informed of crime patterns can better protect themselves from criminal victimization. Through the dissemination of crime maps, the public knows where crime is highest and takes the necessary steps to ensure its own safety. A third benefit of distributing crime maps publicly is that it ensures that *crime data are accurately presented* to the public (Wartell and

McEwen, 2001). Increasingly newspapers and other news outlets are using GIS and police reports to create unofficial local crime maps, sometimes of suspect validity, for their readers and viewers. The obvious problem with these unofficial maps is that they may lead to incorrect perceptions of where crime occurs and subsequent misplaced fears of crime. In creating and distributing crime maps themselves, police agencies can ensure that the maps the public gets contain the most accurate data and potentially reduce misplaced fears of crime. A final benefit of publicly disseminated crime maps is that it can *reduce the workload of crime analysis sections* that often handle citizen requests for crime information (Wartell and McEwen, 2001). Crime maps that are placed on the Internet have the potential to reduce information requests in that the public may be able to answer its questions merely by looking at crime maps. Wartell and McEwen (2001) relate how the Tempe, Arizona, Police Department was able to reduce time and monetary costs associated with information requests by making constantly updated maps available on the Internet for the public to view.

Despite the benefits associated with the public dissemination of crime maps, there are numerous potential problems associated with their distribution and use. Foremost among these problems is the fear that the dissemination of detailed crime maps will *reduce the reporting of crimes by victims* (Anderson, 1999). Opponents of the public dissemination of crime maps fear that victims will be afraid of harassment or retaliation by their attackers and may not come forward to report crimes (Bueermann, 1999). Furthermore, the idea that victims of certain crimes can be further victimized by the public disclosure of their names, addresses, and other information has long been accepted within criminal justice and strengthens the argument against public disclosure of crime maps (Bueermann, 1999). In both instances, strong arguments can be made about how the need to protect the rights of the victim outweighs any right of the public to know the specifics of a particular crime.

Another argument against the dissemination of crime maps is the potential *misuse of the information* contained within these maps. In general, this misuse of information takes the form of either red-lining or commercial exploitation (Casady, 1999). *Red-lining* is said to occur when banks, mortgage companies, insurance agencies, or other such companies use crime information to guide decisions regarding loans, mortgages, or insurance rates. Thus, individuals who live in neighborhoods that have high crime rates might be turned down for a loan or mortgage or receive higher insurance premiums. In contrast to red-lining, *commercial exploitation* is where companies use information about crime victims to guide their sales pitches. An example would be an alarm company using detailed burglary maps to locate potential customers who will receive sales information (Wartell and McEwen, 2001). Both of these processes are made criminally easy when detailed crime maps with high crime areas denoted on them are made publicly available to employees of these companies. In fact, in many cases police departments have already done most of the work for these employees by creating detailed crime rate maps showing the neighborhoods with the highest levels of crime. While there have been no reported cases of red-lining or commercial exploitation, this may simply be a result of enforcement practices rather than the fact these actions haven't occurred.

A final problem with the public dissemination of crime maps is the potential for *misinterpretation of crime maps* (Wartell and McEwen, 2001). One of the main reasons that crime maps are employed is for their ease of interpretation and use, yet even well made crime maps can be difficult to understand, not to mention poorly made maps. The problem with misinterpretation of crime maps is that it can lead to irrational or misplaced fear of crime about an area. It is not out of the realm of possibilities that users of crime maps could get the completely wrong impression of where high crime areas are on a map. In general, interpretation problems involve poorly made map legends, crime symbol choices, aggregation of crime data, and labeling problems.[2]   These

---

[2]See Chapter 4 of the workbook for details about how to make effective maps.

misinterpretation problems can be aggravated by problems of inaccurately mapped crime data (Casady, 1999). Numerous problems can lead to inaccurate data, including misspelled addresses, poor street databases, new addresses, and other problems inherent in geocoding. It must be remembered that geocoding often involves the software making the best guess of where to place an address on a street, and thus is subject to imperfections (Casady, 1999). Casady (1999) points out that if a city has 100,000 incidents a year and geocodes at a 99 percent rate, which is reasonable to assume, then 1,000 incidents will be in the wrong place. Overall, inaccurate crime data aggravate the already existing problem of map interpretation, to the point that the public may have misplaced and unfounded fears of crime.

Issues and Guidelines

As a result of the problems associated with the dissemination of crime maps, much discussion has taken place concerning the creation of guidelines or standards for creating maps for public use (Wartell and McEwen, 2001). While there are no currently accepted standards or guidelines, numerous issues have been delineated concerning how to best present crime data in publicly disseminated crime maps. First among these issues involves the *data to be mapped.* While the public generally wants as much informa- tion as possible, privacy as well as time and money issues limits the mapping of all crime-related data. Although much of the data that departments collect is suitable for mapping (traffic accidents, calls for service, citizen complaints, etc.), making certain crime data publicly available may result in privacy problems. Specifically, most agencies are careful not to publicly disseminate detailed maps involving rapes, sexual assaults, domestic violence, or crimes involving juveniles. While state and federal law dictates what kind of information can be released publicly, each department has to make an individual decision about what information they feel is worth providing in map form to the public. Agencies are encouraged to first consult state and federal laws concerning more sensitive crime types, such as those mentioned above, and then decide what needs would be served in the mapping of these crime types. As a general guideline, not providing *detailed* (street addresses, victim names, etc.) maps of sensitive crimes (rapes, sexual assaults, domestic violence) is the best way to avoid problems involving privacy issues.

A related issue in creating publicly available crime maps involves the *level of data to be mapped* (Wartell and McEwen, 2001). Specifically, should crime data be mapped at the point or aggregate level? Although mapping crimes at the aggregate level avoids problems with providing sensitive information such as victim addresses, aggregate data are not free from problems. First, aggregating crime data can obscure patterns of crime within the aggregating unit (Wartell and McEwen, 2001). If crime is mapped at the census tract level, it may show a tract as having a high crime rate when in reality the crime problem is concentrated within a small section of the census tract. Although a solution to this problem is to aggregate crime at small levels, this may still engender problems with crime patterns. A second problem involves the creation of crime rates based on census data. Creating crime rates using census data can inflate a crime problem in an area that has few permanent residents but large daily populations. An example would be a shopping district that experiences a large daily influx of people and assorted crimes, but has few permanent residents. Creating rates for this area would make the crime rate appear to be much higher than in reality. In general, those agencies wishing to avoid problems of identifying victims should probably avoid creating point maps for public dissemination and instead make aggregate crime maps. Moreover, sensitive crimes such as rapes, sexual assaults, child abuse, and other such crimes should probably never be mapped at the point level as a precaution against problems with victim identification.

Another issue in the dissemination of crime maps is the *interpretation of these maps.* As mentioned above, one of the problems with crime maps is that many people have trouble correctly interpreting the data on the map and end up with inaccurate or confusing views of crime. In order to avoid problems with interpretation of map data, several different suggestions have been made concerning sound map creation and map composition (Wartell and McEwen, 2001). One area of confusion, and sometimes deception, within crime maps is in the choice of symbols used to represent crime incidents. Oftentimes symbols are chosen that are too large for the map scale, making the crime incidents look larger and more numerous than in reality and potentially leading to inaccurate perceptions of crime. Figure 8.7 illustrates how the use of overly large symbol sizes can make a crime distribution look worse than it really is. Other problems with symbol choices include poor color and shape choices that may serve to confuse and mislead those reading the maps.

Another source of confusion in map interpretation comes from poorly labeled and defined map data. Although police shows are very popular on TV, most people still do

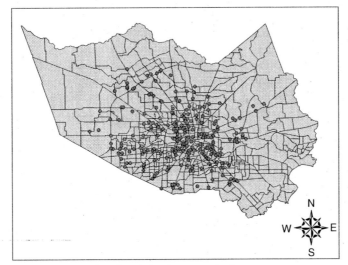

4 point crime symbols

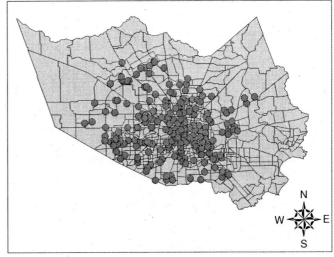

9 point crime symbols

FIGURE 8.7   Maps Showing the Same Crime Distribution but with Different Symbol Sizes in Order to Illustrate How Overly Large Symbol Sizes Can Distort the Reality of a Crime Distribution and Make Crime Appear More Dense Than It Really Is.

not fully understand the intricate police language surrounding differing types of crime data. Most of the general public does not know the difference between calls for service, crime incidents, and arrest data, nor would they know what different crimes compose index crimes (Wartell and McEwen, 2001). Because of this, those creating maps need to make sure they completely define *all* the different sources of data in a manner that lay people can understand. The best recipe for success in this is to think of oneself as completely ignorant of the criminal justice system and its practices when writing the definitions. Definitions should be written in plain English and be comprehensive enough to explain the nature of the data.

The final suggestion to avoid confusion in map interpretation is to make a comprehensive and easy-to-understand legend. A legend is designed as a method for informing the reader as to what all of the symbols and lines on the map represent. Problems of interpretation usually occur when crime symbols are poorly labeled, particularly when it comes to aggregate data. Specifically, aggregate data involving different colors or shades of color delineating different amounts of crime are often confusing for readers (Wartell and McEwen, 2001). Mapmakers need to clearly label and define all symbols, particularly different levels of aggregate information, to avoid problems with confusion.

A final issue in the dissemination of crime maps to the public is the use of *disclaimers.* A disclaimer is a statement about a product such as a map that is designed to help avoid liability from its use or misuse. In the case of crime maps, disclaimers are designed to avoid liability associated with the misuse and interpretation of crime data (Wartell and McEwen, 2001). A general rule about disclaimers is that they should state as thoroughly as possible what it is they do not want the creator to be held liable for (Wartell and McEwen, 2001). In the case of crime maps there are three specific areas that should generally be included in a map disclaimer: data accuracy, use and interpretation, and confidentiality. Data accuracy should state that the data are only "reported crimes" as well as discuss important issues about the geocoding of the data. When discussing geocoding, the disclaimer should at least report the geocoding accuracy for the data as well as explain how that can affect interpretation and use of the map. Alternatively, a definition of geocoding and the problems inherent with this process can be included somewhere on the map as well, although not necessarily in the disclaimer. The use and interpretation part of the disclaimer should generally state the purpose of the map, that being to inform the public of general crime patterns. Importantly, it should be stated that the map is not intended for commercial or illegal purposes. Finally, the disclaimer should contain a statement concerning the confidentiality of the data used in creating the map. Specifically, the disclaimer should note that every effort is being maintained to ensure the confidentiality of those whose victimizations are depicted in the map. While this statement will not prevent liability, it serves as a promise to the public that every effort is being made to maintain the privacy of those whom the data represent (Wartell and McEwen, 2001).

Sharing Data with Researchers

The relationship between researchers and law enforcement is a long and varied one, with some of the earliest crime maps being made by researchers interested in patterns of crime (see Chapter 7 for further discussion). While there are always exceptions, this relationship has generally been healthy and problem free, with both sides benefiting from the exchange of data. Researchers have benefited by being able to test theories of crime, whereas law enforcement agencies have benefited through the production of crime maps and other research products. Historically, much of this data exchange has been handled informally, but with the development of institutional review boards (IRB) and increases in concern over data confidentiality, this relationship has grown progressively more formal (Olligschlaeger, 1999). As with the public dissemination of crime maps, questions regarding victim confidentiality have taken center stage. Specifically, issues of victims' rights to privacy have led to concern over the sharing of data for purposes of academic research. Because of this concern, increased discussion has arisen surrounding the need for guidelines or rules regarding the sharing of data. The most comprehensive discussion of guidelines for sharing data was developed by Olligschlaeger (1999) as part of the Crime Mapping Research Center's (now the NIJ MAPS office) Data Confidentiality Roundtable, in which he outlines a 5-point model for data sharing. First, the two parties should determine the type, format, and nature of the data required for the research (Olligschlaeger, 1999). This involves making sure that the purpose of the research is sound and not detrimental or frivolous in nature, as well as determining if either the data or the results of the research are sensitive enough to warrant a privacy document to be signed. Moreover, the format of the data must be agreed upon, whether it is in raw paper format, geocoded digital format, or any combination in between.

Second, the two sides must agree upon how the research results will be presented (Olligschlaeger, 1999). This involves determining whether any of the data are too sensitive to be displayed on a map at the address level or if the data should be viewed at the aggregate level only. Importantly, this issue involves more than just victims' rights to privacy as the integrity of sensitive law enforcement information is also of paramount importance when reporting research results. Regardless of the nature of the data, both parties must agree beforehand about how the data will be presented when the finished research product is produced.

The third recommendation is to conduct a background check of the researcher (Olligschlaeger, 1999). While the mention of this would scare many a researcher, the background check to be performed is not one concerning criminal history as much as it is the reputation of the researcher. Specifically, law enforcement agencies should make sure that the researcher is not a "hack" out to do ambush research on the police, but rather is a serious researcher whose intent is to contribute to the academic literature. In most cases, requiring references as well as a vitae or list of publications will suffice to determine if the researcher is legitimate or out to cause problems.

The fourth recommendation involves deciding where the confidential data will be stored (Olligschlaeger, 1999). Whenever sensitive data are being given to an outside party, the security and integrity of the data is always an important issue, one that both parties must discuss before any data change hands. As hacking activity has increased, one of the primary targets has been the university setting and, in particular, the networks that researchers use to store and access data. In order to prevent data from being compromised, all data in which confidentiality is a concern must be kept on a secure server or local hard drive (Olligschlaeger, 1999). If secure data storage is not possible in the university setting, then the researcher should be given the opportunity to work at the police agency on their equipment (Olligschlaeger, 1999).

The final recommendation concerning data sharing involves the destruction of the data when the research is complete (Olligschlaeger, 1999). The primary purpose of this recommendation is to prevent sensitive data from either being used for other research later on or ending up in the hands of those who should not have it. Academics are notorious for being forgetful and overscheduled, both of which are likely to contribute to data being forgotten and ending up on other computers or in the hands of those who should not view it. To prevent any such problems, both parties need to agree in advance about the timeline of the research as well as what will become of the data when the research is finished.

Liability Issues

There is probably no other issue that causes police chiefs to lose more sleep than the issue of liability. To say that the United States is a litigious society is an understatement and police chiefs know about the hazards of liability as well as any trained lawyer. It is because of potential liability that many agencies are reluctant to get involved with crime mapping, particularly the public dissemination of crime maps. When dealing with public dissemination of crime maps liability concerns generally center on three issues: release of protected victim information, release of inaccurate data, and misuse of data. Although there is little to no existing case law dealing specifically with crime maps, there is existing case law concerning public records, which is highly applicable to a discussion of crime map liability (Meeker, 1999).

Of primary concern for most law enforcement agencies when dealing with the release of information such as the data contained in crime maps is whether or not this data are considered *public record*. In general, much of the data contained in arrest and calls for service records is considered public record, and thus releasing it in the form of crime maps will *not* incur liability (Meeker, 1999). While differences will exist by state, most states consider names, addresses, and circumstances surrounding both arrests and calls for service to be of public record and thus freely available to the public. Importantly, information regarding investigations is not generally public record and thus release of such information in the form of suspect maps may incur liability (Meeker, 1999). It is also important to note that while in many states victims of certain crimes (spouse abuse, child abuse, sex crimes, harassment) have the right to request that their names not be made public, court rulings seem to indicate that publishing crime maps that may allow for the determination of a victim's identity will *not* incur liability (Meeker, 1999). As a general rule, law enforcement agencies should review their state's Public Records Act to fully delineate the information that is considered of public record before disseminating any crime maps containing potentially sensitive information.

Another liability issue that keeps many law enforcement agencies from disseminating crime maps is the potential release of *inaccurate crime data* (Meeker, 1999). Data inaccuracy can come from several different means, such as incorrect crime data or incorrect basemap data (street data). Problems with inaccurate data arise when people rely on this information and make incorrect assessments or develop incorrect perceptions about an area based on inaccurate data. In general liability for the release of inaccurate data will not occur unless the data are intentionally released as inaccurate or there is negligence involved in the creation of the data (Meeker, 1999). Interestingly, most case law concerning public records data states that the purpose of the release of such information is so the public can determine if the data are inaccurate (Meeker, 1999). Meeker (1999) suggests that as a precautionary measure, law enforcement agencies should cite all sources of data not produced by them (census data) and/or use disclaimers about the accuracy of the data.

The final liability issue concerning the dissemination of crime maps involves the *misuse of the data*. As discussed earlier in this section, one of the potential problems with disseminating crime maps is that the information will be used for red-lining, commercialization, or criminal purposes. Interestingly, of all the potential liability issues involving crime maps, this issue is the most concrete and settled. In a nutshell, as long as the information is public record and of a nature that is required to be released, there is no limit on the use of the information (Meeker, 1999). Thus, agencies that disseminate crime maps containing valid public records cannot be held liable for the misuse of such information.

SUMMARY

List of Major Findings

1. The two biggest barriers to implementing a computerized mapping system are departmental need and cost;
2. Major cost issues encountered when implementing computerized mapping include software, hardware, training, and data acquisition;
3. One of the most overlooked issues when implementing computerized mapping is making sure that data from a department's Record Management System can be entered into a GIS. Without these data the GIS is virtually useless;

4. Data are most important in conducting sound analysis. Data must be clearly understood and must be chosen based on its utility in answering questions that are asked;

5. All data used in analysis have associated benefits and problems which need to be understood completely before a choice is made for analysis;

6. Point data are excellent for use in crime pattern analysis and are independent of jurisdictional boundary issues, but they are difficult for use in correlation analysis and in determining magnitude of a crime problem;

7. Aggregate data are excellent for making rates and comparisons and often have more practical significance than point data for police officers, but they are plagued by problems of artificial boundary drawings, which are often of various sizes, shapes, and underlying populations;

8. Ecological fallacy states that individual behavior cannot be inferred from aggregate data, a problem that is common within mapping and crime analysis;

9. There are problems associated with all sources of data (official and unofficial) that should be explored fully before mapping begins;

10. Official data only provide crimes known to the police and are not a complete measure of all crimes that have occurred in a jurisdiction;

11. Understanding the underlying causes of crime is the goal of computerized mapping, not simply creating short-term policies to move the dots off a map;

12. Those making maps must balance the public's right to know and the victim's right to privacy. Arguments for both sides must be weighed carefully before maps are released to the public;

13. As a general rule, don't provide detailed (street address) information of sensitive crime data (rapes, sexual assaults, domestic violence) to the general public;

14. Always use disclaimers when providing data to the public; and

15. A disclaimer should always address issues of data accuracy, use and interpretation of the map, and confidentiality of the information.

Implications for Crime Mapping and Spatial Analysis

After finishing this chapter, readers should be reminded of just how new a discipline computerized mapping is within law enforcement. Although crime maps of one form or another have been around for well over 100 years, many of the issues surrounding their use are just now beginning to be discussed. Issues regarding implementation and use, data concerns, and ethical and legal problems are all vitally important to the continued growth and use of crime maps in the future. In practical terms the biggest implication of this chapter is that those making computerized maps must be aware of all the issues surrounding the choice of data types, data sources, data analysis, and data dissemination before making any maps.

First, before making a map you should always consider all the benefits and problems associated with your choice of data type. Both point and aggregate data have numerous associated benefits and problems and the user must consider which data type is best for answering the questions they are asking. Second, one must also make determinations about whether or not to use official or unofficial data. While most people will only use official data, they must at least be cognizant of the limitations inherent in official data when making computerized maps. Third, those using maps to understand crime issues need to be aware of the host of problems that are inherent in map interpretation. Specifically, readers need to be sure to avoid ecological fallacy problems as well as tendencies to try to develop programs that focus on the crime incident locations without understanding why crimes are occurring where they are. Finally, when making and disseminating maps, one must always balance a victim's right to privacy and the public's right to know. Thus, as a general rule, you should avoid providing detailed information of sensitive crime data and provide disclaimers dealing with data accuracy, interpretation, and confidentiality on all maps disseminated to the public. Although there are currently no major issues with respect to liability for maps that are disseminated to the public, in a society as litigious as the United States, it is only a matter of time before case law develops.

CASE STUDY
THE GEOGRAPHY OF SOCIAL CONTROL

Examining the Spatial Aspects of Homicide Investigation and Prosecution
One of the lesser known areas of research within the general body of spatial aspects of crime is the geography of social control. The geography of social control is an area of criminological research that focuses on the geographic separation of crime from the control of crime. Most geographers have traditionally treated crime as a distinct behavior that is divorced from its political and legal context. Specifically, little attention has been given to social control or to the operation of the criminal justice system on the development or configuration of crime patterns. Importantly, both how we define crimes and how we enforce criminal laws significantly impact the distribution of crime.

As was discussed earlier in the text, an example of how crime patterns are affected by how we define and control crimes is how the drug war has been framed. In both definition and control, the war on drugs has focused on illicit drugs such as marijuana, cocaine, and heroin, while ignoring the illegal use and abuse of prescription drugs. Importantly, this definitional and enforcement focus on illicit drugs over illegal use of prescription drugs occurs despite government statistics indicating that the abuse of prescription drugs is more prevalent than that of illicit drugs. In terms of its impact on crime patterns, the definitional and control focus on illicit drugs is striking. Specifically, if hot spots of prescription drug crimes were created, they would most likely be in very different areas of a city than hot spots of illicit drug abuse. In general official crime and patterns of official crime are guided in large part by how we define and control crime and not so much by the occurrence of crimes.

In general, research into the geography of social control focuses on three different areas: the impact that definitions, differential control, and differential processing of crime have on spatial patterns of crime. The focus of this case study is on the potential differential processing involved in the investigation and prosecution of homicide incidents. Specifically, are there certain areas of a city in which homicides are less likely to be cleared and where murder charges are more likely to be filed?

Data for the analysis consisted of all 4,980 homicides that occurred in Houston, Texas, between 1986 and 1994. Of these 4,980 homicides, 78 percent were cleared (solved) and 49 percent resulted in a murder charge. In order to determine if there are areas in which homicide incidents were less likely to be cleared or if murder charges were more likely to be filed, a Risk Adjusted Nearest Neighbor Hierarchical Spatial Clustering (RNNH) analysis was conducted (see workbook Chapter 9 for a detailed explanation). This analysis allows for hot spots to be determined while taking into consideration an underlying variable. In a sense, RNNH hot spots are like hot spot rates in that the baseline variable controls for the differences in population where the incidents occur produce a more accurate depiction of high crime concentrations. Thus, when looking at homicide incidents with the baseline variable being population, RNNH would cluster homicide locations that are closer together than would be expected based on the underlying population where the incidents are occurring. Three separate RNNH analyses were conducted: one with homicides and the baseline variable being population, one with open (unsolved) homicides and the baseline variable being homicide rate, and one with murder charges and the baseline variable being homicide rate. These analyses will allow for the determination of whether both open cases and murder charges are closer than would be expected based on the underlying homicide rate.

Figure 8.8 provides the results of the analyses, which indicate that there are definite hot spots of open cases and murder charges. While homicides are also more concentrated than would be expected based on the underlying population, only one homicide hot spot overlaps with either an open case or murder hot spot. Although all three hot spot types are concentrated in the same general area, they are essentially in different neighborhoods. Thus, the

(continued)

CASE STUDY   CONTINUED

results indicate that there are definite areas where homicides are less likely to be solved and where homicides are more likely to receive a murder charge. Furthermore, these areas are largely independent of areas of high homicide, indicating these hot spots cannot be simply explained away by saying they are high-homicide areas. While this research does not provide any firm answers as to the causes of the open case and murder charge hot spots, it does provide evidence that these areas do exist. Moreover, this research gives support to the importance of geography of social control research in understanding crime patterns. Specifically, it underlies the fact that a simple analysis of crime patterns fails to provide a complete picture of what is actually occurring with respect to crime.

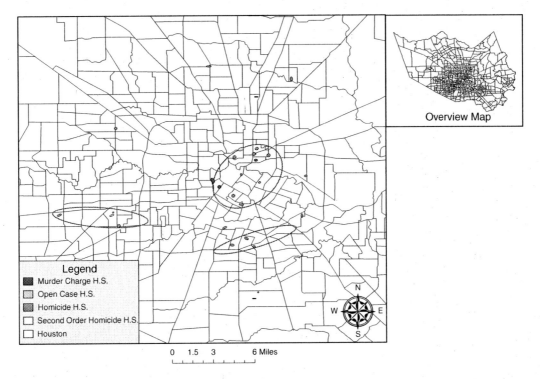

FIGURE 8.8   Overview of Homicide, Murder Charge, and Open Case Hot Spots. Maps illustrating the differences in hot spots of actual homicides, open cases, and murder charges.

CRIME MAPPING
WORKBOOK

PART III

ArcGIS Crime Mapping Workbook

We have now arrived at the workbook section of the textbook. The workbook is designed to provide students with a hands-on method for learning the basics of how to use ArcGIS to conduct crime mapping regardless of individual understanding or experience level with computers or GIS. The workbook is divided into four main sections with each section building on the knowledge learned in earlier sections. The first section, "ArcGIS Crime Mapping Workbook," takes the student through a review of the basic features of ArcGIS, data sources, data entry, data query, and map-making tips, all from a crime-mapping perspective. In the second section, "Basic Spatial Analysis," the student begins to conduct spatial analysis of crime data, using techniques such as buffer zones, spatial distribution measures, and distance analysis measures. Importantly, students will not only learn how to perform these analyses but also learn associated problems and limitations with each technique as well as how to interpret the results from both a theoretical and a practical standpoint. The third section introduces the student to more advanced spatial analysis techniques (using Crimestat 3.0) such as hot spot analysis, density analysis, spatial dispersion analysis, and geographic profiling methods. As with other sections, an emphasis will be placed not only on learning how to conduct these techniques but limitations of each technique and how to interpret the results logically. Finally, a new fourth section (Aggregate Data Analysis) will introduce the student to areal analysis techniques (using GeoDa) such as Moran's I and LISA statistics. While these concepts are more often associated with academic research, an effort will be made to demonstrate the use of these techniques for both practitioners and researchers. Each chapter is designed to incorporate hands-on exercises to facilitate learning and has accompanying sample data as well as accompanying Internet figures and resources for each chapter.

As briefly mentioned above, the workbook is highly integrated with the Internet. Specifically, software, sample data, figures, and resources for each chapter are available for student use. Importantly, because this book does not come with ArcGIS software, it is incumbent on the student to visit the textbook webpage in order to learn how to acquire a copy of ArcGIS and to download Crimestat 3.0 software, GeoDa software, and the sample data used in the workbook. Moreover, all figures referenced in the text of the workbook are viewable only on the textbook webpage. Finally, this workbook was written to work with ArcGIS 9.2 and should be compatible with recent versions of ArcGIS (9.0 and 9.1), but the authors offer no express guarantees. Importantly, as newer versions of ArcGIS are released and their adoption amongst users increases, newer versions of the workbook will be written and made available on-line. The webpage associated with the text is www.mappingcrime.org, and it provides a wealth of resources related to not only the workbook but also crime mapping and the spatial analysis of crime in general. Thus, before getting started with the workbook, it is strongly recommended that the student visit the textbook webpage and follow the instructions on how to download the sample data as well as any software (ARcGIS, Crimestat 3.0 and GeoDa) that the student does not already have access to.

Finally, it is important to state up front that this workbook is in *no way meant to substitute for an in-depth class on the use of a GIS or a class on spatial statistics*. While this workbook will provide students with an introductory understanding of how to use ArcGIS 9.2 for crime mapping purposes, it is by no means meant to be a comprehensive workbook on how to use ArcGIS and all of its features. Moreover, while the workbook will discuss spatial statistics techniques, it is designed to be an introduction to the use and interpretation of these techniques and not a comprehensive spatial statistics textbook. The primary purpose of this workbook is to provide students with an introductory hands-on experience in conducting spatial analysis of crime events using a GIS. At the end of each chapter are "Further Readings" sections that provide students with a list of books and articles that offer a more in-depth coverage of topics discussed in the chapters. It is recommended that students who wish to learn more about topics discussed in these chapters or about the full functionality of Arcview and other GIS products pursue these texts and articles.

Getting Started with ArcGIS

GOALS: 1. Accessing the textbook webpage.

2. Adding data to a view.

3. Examining basic ArcMap tools and features.

4. Saving your work.

GETTING STARTED

The first chapter will introduce students to ArcGIS ArcMAP and give them an overview of some of the basic functions and functionality of ArcGIS. Although this workbook was written using ArcGIS version 9.2, it should be compatible with recent versions of ArcGIS, though the authors offer no express or implied guarantees to this compatibility. The ArcGIS workbook was written in order to assist those people who have access to the cutting edge software from ESRI as to how to conduct basic crime mapping. While there are still some agencies that use the older Arcview 3.3, ArcGIS 9.2, and other recent versions have been widely adopted by those in the crime mapping field over the last few years. While not as ubiquitous as Microsoft Windows, ArcGIS is arguably the most commonly used GIS software in the world and in the field of crime mapping in particular. While other GIS software such as MapInfo is commonly used in crime mapping, ArcGIS has a very large and well-established customer base, and thus knowledge in how to use ArcGIS will serve students well in the professional world of crime mapping.

As for the content of Chapter 1, students will learn how to open ArcMAP (the mapping program within the ArcGIS program suite), open a view and add layers (map data), explore ArcMAP tools within a view, and save their work. Importantly, this chapter is designed **only** to give the student an introduction to ArcMAP and **some** of its basic features. This chapter is by no means a substitute for a comprehensive class or textbook explaining the complete functionality of ArcMAP. Students who desire a more in-depth instruction of ArcGIS and ArcMAP in particular are encouraged to review the "Further Readings" list at the end of the chapter as well as consult the online resources for each chapter on the text webpage.

Accessing the Textbook Webpage

In order for the students to use the workbook, they must first access the textbook webpage and download the sample data. The sample data and their accompanying codebooks are designed specifically for students using this text and are easily and quickly downloadable from the textbook webpage. In addition, the webpage also assists the student in downloading a free copy of Crimestat 3.0 and GeoDa, both of which will be used extensively in Sections III and IV of the workbook.

1. In the browser on your computer, type www.mappingcrime.org. This will bring you to the main menu of the webpage associated with Crime Mapping and Spatial Analysis: Theory and Practice.
2. On the main menu of the webpage, click on DATA. This will take you to the page dealing with downloading the data and its associated codebooks.
3. Follow the onscreen instructions in order to download and open the sample data.

Online Resources

In addition to the sample data and accompanying codebooks, there are also extensive online resources available to students and professors. Included in the online resources are links to related webpages, article downloads, and a PDF lab manual that provides step-by-step instructions with screen captures. In order to access these online resources, simply click on the appropriate buttons on the webpage (Links, Further Readings, and Lab Resources) and follow the onscreen instructions.

Obtaining a Copy of Crimestat 3.0 or GeoDa

Crimestat 3.0: On the main page of the textbook webpage, click on the main menu item labeled "Crimestat." Follow the onscreen instructions in order to download a free and fully functional version of Crimestat 3.0 and its accompanying manual.

GeoDa: On the main page of the textbook webpage, click on the main menu item labeled "GeoDa." Follow the onscreen instructions in order to download a free and fully functional version of GeoDa and its accompanying documentation.

Opening ArcMAP

1. On a Windows desktop, click on the Start button, go to the Programs folder, and look for the ArcGIS folder. For a typical installation of ArcGIS, the program is installed within a folder named ArcGIS.
2. Hold the cursor over the ArcGIS folder until ArcMap pops up, then move the cursor over ArcMap, and click on the program. This will bring up the welcome screen for ArcMap, giving you three options: (1) start using ArcMap with "a new empty map," the default option, (2) open a "Template" or a ready-to-use layout and base map for a certain geographic area, or (3) open "an existing map." Underneath the "An existing map" radio button is a window that shows a list of previously opened maps.
3. Select the default option "A new empty map" and click OK, which will take you to the main ArcMap application screen called the "Data View."

Adding Data to the View

In ArcMap, map data are called **Layers** and they can represent almost any type of data that has a geographic component. Examples of crime-related layers include individual crime locations, probationer and parolee home addresses, city streets, county boundaries, gang territories, satellite photos, and other images called orthophotos (discussed in Workbook Chapter 2). Importantly, until data are added to the Data View, the majority of buttons will not work.

1. In order to add a data layer, click on the button with the plus on it. Alternatively, you can click on the File menu at the top of the screen and select "Add data." After

clicking on the Add data button, the Add data dialogue box will appear. Scroll through the folders in the C drive until you come to the "CM Lab Exercises" folder and select this folder.

2. Within the CM Labs folder, click on the Chapter 1 folder. After opening this folder, you should see two different files: one named Houston.shp and the other named Homicides.shp. While these are Arcview shapefile, they are easily opened and used in ArcMap. Importantly, while Arcview 3.3 themes have three associated files (.shp, .dbf, and .shx), ArcMap layers save all relevant data in a Layer file (.lyr), making it easier to transfer data between computers and save for archival purposes.

3. Double click on the file named Houston.shp. This will add the theme to the table of contents of the Data View window. You will now see a map of Harris County Texas, the county that contains Houston Texas.

4. In order to make the data viewable (or not), move the cursor over the checkbox and click inside the checkbox to the left of the layer name. You will notice that by clicking in the box and removing the check mark, the data are no longer viewable.

Exercise 1.   Add and make viewable the Homicides.shp theme. You should now see a point theme depicting homicide locations in Houston Texas. Compare your map with Figure 1.1 (www.mappingcrime.org) to determine if your map is correct.

EXPLORING SELECTED ARCMAP TOOLS AND FEATURES

In this section, we will briefly explore the various functions of several of these buttons that are highly useful in crime mapping. Students are encouraged to explore other buttons on their own.

Editing the Legend

Editing the legend includes changing the color, size, fill pattern, and other factors relating to a theme's appearance. In this case, we will change the color of the Harris County map. This is a particularly important tool, in that it will help you make the map look nice and aesthetically appealing. Moreover, the size and color of symbols are essential in making a map understandable to your reader.

1. Make the Houston layer **active** by clicking on the file name. This should make the file name appear highlighted in the table of contents. Importantly, if a layer is not active you will not be able to edit its properties. Left click once on the colored box beneath the Houston layer, this will open the Symbol Selector box.

2. After the Symbol Selector box opens, you will have various options: the fill color, outline, shape, and size of the symbols on the map. In this case, because we are editing a polygon layer (see Workbook Chapter 2 for more discussion), we will only be altering the fill color and the outline of the polygon layer, not its shape as is routinely done with point data.

3. In order to change the color of the Houston layer, click on the "Fill Color" drop down menu and select a color of your choice. When you choose a color, the symbol color in the Preview box will change accordingly on the symbol selector main page. Importantly, in order to view the change, you must click "OK" on the Symbol Selector page.

4. In order to change the outline width of the layer, select either the up or the down arrows next to the Outline Width box. When you change the outline width

(either up or down), the changes will be viewable in the Preview box. As with changing the color of a symbol, in order to make the changes appear on the map you must click "OK."

Exercise 2.   Change the color and symbol type for Homicides to blue triangles. Check your work by looking at Figure 1.3 on the textbook webpage.

Zoom In and Zoom Out

Being able to zoom the view of the map in and out is essential while making crime maps because it allows you to control the viewable area of the map and helps to view the areas more clearly. Importantly, ArcMap has two different methods for zooming in and out.

1. On the right of the screen should be a floating menu labeled "Tools" containing eight rows of buttons in two different columns. This floating Tool menu contains some of the most often used and most important tools necessary to efficient map making and navigation. In the second row are two buttons: (1) the **Fixed zoom-in** button has arrows that point inward (left column) and (2) the **Fixed zoom-out** button arrows pointing outward (right column). When you place the cursor over either of these buttons, a yellow box will appear indicating the name of the button.
2. Click twice on the zoom-in button and the entire view will zoom in equally. In order to get the view back to its original view, you can either click twice on the zoom-out button or click on the **Full-extent** button (button that looks like the Earth). The zoom to full-extent button is similar to a home button on a web browser in that it will always take the map view back to the natural extent of the data. This is a particularly useful button when you are zoomed in on a specific feature and want to quickly look at the original view of the map.

Important Note: Importantly, clicking on either of these buttons will zoom in or zoom out the view at an equal rate. Thus, if you want to zoom in on a specific area or point, you will need to use the other two zoom control buttons. In order to zoom in on a specific area, you need to use the **interactive zoom-in** button that is on the first row of buttons (plus sign in a circle).

1. Click on the interactive zoom-in button to activate the zoom-in cursor. As you move the cursor over the map, the cursor will change to the button symbol (plus sign in a circle).
2. Place the cursor over the lone homicide incident in the extreme north northwest area of Houston. As you click on the homicide incident, the view will change its orientation completely, with the homicide being in the center of the view and the view being zoomed in. Click on the zoom to full-extent button to reset the view.

    In addition to being able to click and zoom in with this button, the interactive zoom-in button allows you to draw a rectangle around an area that you wish to zoom in on. This is particularly useful when you want to quickly zoom in on several crime incidents in an area.
3. With the interactive zoom-in button activated, click and hold the left button on your mouse and draw a rectangle around the two homicide incidents in the extreme northeast area of Houston. When you release the right button on your mouse, the view will zoom in on the two homicides that you selected.

Exercise 3.   Zoom in and return to the full extent on several different homicide incidents in the view.

Identify Features

One of the more helpful features that ArcMap offers is **identify features**. This button allows the user to look at the tabular data associated with any data on the map. This is particularly important for crime mapping where a user can use the identify button to have a quick view of the tabular data associated with a crime incident during spatial analysis.

1. Make the **identify** features button ("i" in a circle in the sixth row left column) active by clicking on it. As you move the cursor over the map, it will change to the button symbol ("i" in a circle).
2. Make sure that the Homicides layer is active (click on the name) and place the cursor over the lone homicide incident in the extreme north northwest area of Houston and click on the incident. **Importantly, the identify features button will only identify features of active themes.** You should see that the victim was a 32-year-old male Hispanic who was killed on July 24, 1992. Whatever information entered into the table will be viewable in the identify results window.

Exercise 4.   Try identifying homicide incidents in different parts of the city paying attention to the different motives, weapons used, and victim races.

Measure Tool

The last feature that we will discuss in this section is the measure tool. This tool is also especially useful for crime mapping in that it can be used to measure the distance between two crime incidents or any series of crime incidents, or measure the size of an area (such as a patrol area).

1. Make the measure tool (ruler with question mark over it in the bottom left corner of the floating toolbar) active. As you move the cursor over the view, it will change to a crosshair with a right angle on it.
2. Before using the measure button, it is necessary to change the measurement units for the map to Miles. Go to the View menu and select "Data Frame Properties."
3. Select the General tab, and in the Units box in the middle of the menu, scroll up in the Display box until you find "Miles" and select it. When you have selected miles, click on the OK button at the bottom of the menu. This will change the measurement properties for the map to miles.
4. Making sure that the Homicides layer is active, place the cursor over the lone homicide incident in the extreme north northwest area of Houston. Click the cursor once and draw a straight line to the northern most of the two homicides in the extreme northeast corner of Houston. When you get to the northern most homicide, click once and draw a line to the other homicide in this area and then double click on that homicide. The total length should be around 32.55 miles with the segment length being around 1.8 miles.

   Tip: Clicking on an area or incident once will mark a segment length whereas double clicking on an area or incident will stop the measuring completely.

Exercise 5.   Measure the distance from several homicides near the center of Houston. Importantly, you will probably have to use the interactive "zoom-in" button in order to get the view close enough to measure the distances accurately. Note how close together the homicides occur.

Saving Your Work

The last thing you will do before closing ArcMap is save your work as an ArcMap Document. All work done in ArcMap is saved in the ArcMap document files (.mxd files) much as Microsoft Word saves word documents as .doc files. Importantly, Maps will save any work done (such as editing and analysis) in data views, tables, and layouts. Saving your work as a Map allows you to open your work later without having to reopen layers or other files.

1. Go to the File menu and scroll down to "Save As."
2. Pick a destination drive and destination folder and save the project as something you can easily remember.

REVIEW QUESTIONS

1. What are map data called in ArcMap?

2. What is the difference between making a theme active and making a theme viewable?

3. When would it be useful to use the identify tool?

Understanding Data Sources

GOALS:

1. Learning the different types of data and their importance to crime mapping.

2. Learning about different sources for crime-related data.

3. Understanding the problems associated with crime-related data.

4. Classifying aggregate/polygon data.

5. Creating graduated symbols for point data.

INTRODUCTION

The second chapter is designed to provide students with a practical discussion of some of the issues discussed in Chapter 8 of this textbook. In Chapter 8 several important issues were discussed concerning crime data and the problems associated with it. In Workbook Chapter 2, we will explore, from a practical standpoint, how these data issues impact the making of crime maps. Specifically, this chapter discusses the different types of data used in crime mapping, different sources of crime-related data, and the problems associated with crime-related data. Finally, students will learn how to work with different data types in order to get the most out of their crime maps.

DIFFERENT TYPES OF DATA

In making crime maps, it is very important to incorporate different types of data and not just make simple point maps with only crime incident data. Too often crime maps are little more than just point maps depicting crime locations with the possible inclusion of jurisdictional boundaries and police beats. This misses the point of GIS analysis completely. The beauty of GIS and crime mapping is that it allows users to analyze complex spatial relationships that cannot be detected using point maps alone. If all you want to do is have a simple point map of where crime incidents are occurring in a jurisdiction, it would be far easier, and much cheaper, to avoid GIS and simply place pins in a wall map. Incorporating different types of data, such as contextual data about housing units, business locations, or population statistics, into crime maps allows users to understand more than just where incidents are occurring; it allows them to understand *why* crimes are occurring where they are.

Point Data

Point data are data that represent one place in geographic space, such as a physical address. The Homicides layer from Workbook Chapter 1 is an example of point data. While most point data usually represent one specific crime incident at an address, point data can also be used to show different levels of activity at a location, as when using graduated sizes of points. For example, larger sized dots can represent that multiple crime incidents have occurred at a location as compared with smaller dots that indicate only one crime has occurred at that location. Figure 2.1 (www.mappingcrime.org) is an example of how graduated symbols are used to represent different amounts of crime that have occurred.

The main type of data that most users will deal with when making crime maps is point data in the form of crime incident locations. However, it is important to know that there are many other types of point data that are also important to understanding crime patterns. These other point data are commonly called **contextual** data. Examples of some kinds of contextual point data include:

School locations
Bar locations
Liquor store locations
Sexually oriented businesses (SOBs)
Bus and train stop locations
ATM locations
Bank locations
Abandoned buildings
Check-cashing services

All of these data types are important to crime mapping in that they are places that are often related to where criminal events occur. By analyzing crime data in conjunction with contextual point data, users may see that a cluster of robberies occurring every Friday is occurring within a one block area of a check-cashing service see Figure 2.2 (www.mappingcrime.org). Thus, including these data into your maps can help understand why crimes are occurring, where they are occurring, and how to prevent further occurrences.

Exercise 1. List some other types of contextual point data.

Polygon Data

The other major data type that is used when making any kind of map is polygon data. Polygon data are data that represent areas, such as a county boundary, as opposed to a specific geographic location or addresses. In Workbook Chapter 1, the Houston layer that you added is a good example of polygon data, in that it is a county boundary for Harris County Texas broken into census tracts. As with point data, polygon data can contain both crime data and contextual data. Crime data in polygon form are usually aggregate or count data of crime events that occurred in certain areas such as police beats, police districts, census blocks, census tracts, or counties. In general, contextual data in polygon form are usually aggregate or count data of social variables such as population totals or total housing units at the census block or census tract level. The most commonly used contextual polygon data in crime mapping are census data but there are numerous other types of contextual polygon data such as:

Residential and business zone areas
Tax zone areas
Property value data
Neighborhood/community boundaries
Property ownership

All of these data categories are important to crime mapping in that they are often associated with crime and crime levels at the area level. By analyzing crime data in conjunction with contextual polygon data, users may see that the same cluster of robberies occurring every Friday near the check cashing service is also occurring in an area with high poverty see Figure 2.3 (www.mappingcrime.org). Thus adding contextual data, both polygon and point, provides a much richer view of criminal patterns by showing a more detailed view of the context in which crime is occurring. Importantly, we will explore ways to analyze this type of polygon or areal data in Section IV of the workbook.

Other Data Types

Two other forms of data that are often used in crime maps are **line data** and **image data**. While line data used in crime mapping are almost exclusively street data used for geocoding address locations and providing road information, it can also include rivers and stream information. While street data are essential for geocoding, it can also be important in analyzing why crimes are occurring in certain places. As research on routine activities, defensible space, journey to crime, and other place-oriented theories has shown, criminals are heavily influenced by street layouts and traffic networks. Adding detailed street data to the analysis of the robbery cluster example may show that the check-cashing service is located near a major on-ramp, facilitating escape for criminals see Figure 2.4 (www.mappingcrime.org).

Image data usually consist of satellite images of a place or area that have been georeferenced so that they can coordinate with other spatial data. While not necessarily essential to spatial analysis, adding images to a view can greatly enhance a user's understanding of the physical area that is being analyzed. In addition, adding image data is an excellent method for improving the attractiveness and comprehension of map data for a maps final audience. The same robbery cluster analysis example with image data added makes the map more easily understandable and also provides some other visual clues as to why crime is occurring in this location see Figure 2.5 (www.mappingcrime.org).

SOURCES OF DATA

While it is vitally important to understand the need for different types of data in conducting spatial analysis, equally important is knowing where to acquire these data as well as the potential problems associated with different data sources. Sources of data for crime mapping can be broken down into four general categories, self-generated, public agencies and universities, free resources, and private companies.

As discussed in Chapter 8 of the textbook, **self-generated** data in the form of crime incident locations and aggregated crime totals are the main source of crime data used in crime maps. Incident-level data usually consist of calls for service and/or arrest data, though these vary greatly by department. Some police agencies also create other data such as beat districts, station house locations, and jail locations. While self-generated crime data are the most commonly used data form for crime mapping, they are also the most problematic of data sources. As was discussed in-depth in Chapter 8 of this textbook, crime data have reliability problems because of issues related to geocoding of crime data and other issues. Specifically, addresses are not geocoded correctly because of problems such as officer misspellings, officer address gathering practices, and incomplete street files. Despite the potential problems associated with crime incident data it is the only method for gathering data and thus these problems must simply be worked around.

Other major sources for data used in crime mapping are **public agencies and universities**. Public agencies charged with gathering data are often excellent sources of data that can be used in crime mapping. Examples include agencies such as tax assessors, which gather data on property values and housing statistics. Other public agencies gather information on such things as zoning areas, liquor licenses, public assistance, abandoned buildings, and other data that can be important in analyzing crime patterns. Most important about public agencies is that the data they gather are usually available to police agencies and researchers at no cost. Universities are also an excellent source of data owing to their responsibilities as both data repositories and training areas. First, many universities have extensive amounts of geographical data, including satellite images, topographical data, census data, and other data available for use at no cost. Second, students are often available to help create and gather geographic data such as beat areas, street files, and other pertinent data for police agencies at no cost to the agency. The main problem associated with both public agencies and universities is their bureaucratic slowness. Public agencies and universities have a reputation for getting things done at speeds that can best be described as glacial. Thus, if data or assistance is needed quickly, these sources can often be problematic. However, because of their overall data quality and cost, public agencies and universities are both excellent sources of data.

With the advent of the Internet, many types of data can be acquired freely by simple download. The range of **free data** available from these services runs the gamut from satellite images and zoning data to census data and business locations. Sites such as ESRI's Geography Network (www.geographynetwork.com) and GIS Lounge (www.gislounge.com) are excellent clearinghouses of free GIS data. However, while the range of data available is often great, there are several potentially problematic issues involved with this data. The potential problem for free data sources is the accuracy of the data. The old adage of "you get what you pay for" is often true with free data, in that it is often missing vital information or is in an unusable format. Other problems include download problems inherent in all Internet transactions as well as the reputability of the individual or group offering the data. While free data is on the whole an excellent source of data, people must be wise consumers of data and be smart about where they get their data.

The final source of data for crime mapping is **private companies**. Companies such as GDT and Urban Data Solutions provide a range of GIS data for a fee. Data available from private companies range from enhanced street files, which are updated frequently, to business data detailing locations of all business in a given area to enhanced census data. Data from private companies are usually excellent, providing accurate, extensive customizable data for end users. The main problem is that to get this accuracy and customized data, end users will have to pay, and depending on the amount of data needed, the prices can be steep. However, if cost is not as much a concern as is accuracy and customization, then private companies are an excellent alternative data source to others mentioned above.

WORKING WITH DIFFERENT DATA TYPES

In this section, students will get a hands-on experience in using the different types of data discussed above, including point, polygon, street, and image data.

1. Open ArcMap. When the "ArcMap" screen appears, select "A new empty map" and click OK.
2. Click on the Add data button and maneuver on the C drive to the "CMLab Exercises" folder and then select "Chapter 2."
3. From the Chapter 2 folder, select Houston.shp. You should now be looking at a view with Harris County Texas as the basemap. The first type of data that we will work with is polygon data; in this case we are going to work with data that are at the census tract level.

4. Right click on the Houston layer and select Properties (bottom selection), opening the Layer Properties dialog box. Next select the "symbology" tab at the top. At the left in the Show box are listed different ways in which you can view the polygon data. These options include Single Symbol, Categories, Quantities, Charts, and Multiple Attributes. For the purposes of this lesson, click on Quantities.

5. After clicking on Quantities four different sub-fields should appear (Graduated Color, Graduated Symbols, Proportional Symbols, and Dot Density). Click on Graduated Colors.

6. Under the Fields menu you will see two scroll down menus, one for "Value" and the other for "Normalization." Under the "Value" field, scroll down and select the variable Homicide. This is a count of the amount of homicides that have occurred in each census tract in Houston between 1985 and 1994. You will notice that the legend has now changed into five categories of data with different symbol colors for each different category.

7. Click apply and close the legend editor. Figure 2.6 (www.mappingcrime.org) illustrates how the map has changed dramatically, with high homicide census tracts mostly concentrated near the center of the county.

This map is an example of a **choropleth** map. Choropleth maps are area maps that are shaded according to their level of some phenomenon, in this case homicide frequency (Harries, 1990). In making choropleth maps, there are five standardized options in ArcMap, each with a different method for creating classes of data and each producing a very different map. In addition, ArcMap allows the user to create their own categories with the "Manual" and "Defined Interval" methods. The method used to make the map before you is called **Natural Breaks or Jenks**, and it is the default method for choropleth maps in ArcMap. Natural breaks uses gaps in the distribution of data to establish categories (Harries, 1999). In the map before you, ArcMap split the census level homicide data into five categories based on what it perceived to be natural breaks in the distribution of homicides at the census tract level.

A second type of classification is **Equal Interval**. This method divides the distribution into groups with an equal range between the groups, such as 0–14.2, 14.2–28.4, 28.4–42.6, 42.6–56.8, etc.

Exercise 2. Right click on the Houston layer and select "Properties," opening the Layer Properties editor. Click on the Classify button opening the "Classification Menu." Under the Classification Method menu, scroll down to Equal Interval. Click OK and then click Apply and close the Layer Properties editor. Figure 2.8 (www.mappingcrime.org) illustrates again how the map has changed dramatically from the previous map. The majority of the map is in the lowest few categories with the highest areas of homicide being just a few census tracts that are confined to the center of Houston.

A third type of classification is called **Quantile** or equal count. In this classification method, approximately equal numbers of incidents are put in each category (Harries, 1999). Thus, in the case of the Houston data, approximately equal numbers of homicides are placed into each category. Importantly, this method is highly influenced by the number of categories selected. The default in ArcMap is five categories; however, this can be altered and will have significant impact on the map.

Exercise 3. Open the Layer Properties editor again and go back to the classify button (see above). Scroll down the Method category to Quantile. Click OK and then click Apply and close the legend editor. Figure 2.9 (www.mappingcrime.org) illustrates how the map is very different from the equal interval map and more similar to the equal area map, with a large number of census tracts being in the top groups.

The fourth type of classification is called **Standard Deviation**. This method is a statistical measure that classifies data based on the spread of data around the average score (Harries, 1999). First the average observation is determined for the distribution, and then groups are classified by how much above or below (1 standard deviation) from the mean they are. This method can be beneficial in displaying extreme scores both above and below the average of the distribution.

Exercise 4.   Open the Layer Properties editor again and go back to the Classify button (see above). Scroll down the Type category to Standard Deviation. Click OK and then click Apply and close the legend editor. Figure 2.10 (www.mappingcrime.org) displays the results of a standard deviation classification. The standard deviation map is probably the most different of all of the maps that have been made, but potentially the most beneficial as well. In this map, the darkest reds show the areas that are highest from the average number of homicides in Houston, while the blue areas are census tracts where homicide is below average in occurrence.

The final method of classification is called **Geometric Interval**. This last classification method is new to ArcGIS and not a method that is traditionally used in classifying data. This is not to say that it is necessarily a bad method, just that it is a new method. The geometric interval method breaks data into classes based on class intervals that have a geometrical series. This method determines these classes using a specially designed algorithm that ensures that each class has approximately the same number of values with each class and that change between intervals is fairly consistent (ESRI, 2007). This method was specifically designed to handle continuous data, such as population values or total number of crime incidents, and is designed to be both "visually appealing and cartographically comprehensive" (ESRI, 2007).

Exercise 5.   Open the Layer Properties editor again and go back to the classify button (see above). Scroll down the Type category to Geometric Interval. Click OK and then click Apply and close the legend editor. The geometric interval map is in many ways similar to the quantile map in its distribution of classes, with the exception being that the number of groups (census tracts) in each class is more equal.

While there is no one correct or best way to classify aggregate data in a choropleth map, there are some suggestions that can help users in making good maps.

SUGGESTIONS FOR CLASSIFYING DATA

1. Do not simply trust the default method of the computer (Monmonier, 1996).
2. Use not more than six and not less than four categories in choropleth maps (Harries, 1999).
3. When exploring the data use more classes, but as you move toward presentation use less categories (MacEachren, 1994).

CREATING GRADUATED SYMBOLS

One of the biggest problems with mapping crime data is that crime incidents often occur at the same location. The importance of this is that it makes it very difficult to determine locations that have a high number of incidents from those that have only one incident using standard pin map techniques. One of the best ways to overcome this visualization problem is to group incident by their location and symbolize them with graduate symbols. Mapping incidents using graduated symbols provides the ability to differentiate locations based on the size of the point symbol, with larger symbols having more incidents than small symbols.

Creating Graduated Symbols

1. Open ArcMap. When the "ArcMap" screen appears select "A new empty map" and click OK.
2. Click on the Add data button and maneuver on the C drive to the "CMLab Exercises" folder and then select "Chapter 2."
3. From the Chapter 2 folder, select both the Houston.shp and the Homicides.shp files. You should now be looking at a view with Harris County Texas as the basemap with approximately 536 homicide points on the map.
4. Open the ArcToolbox by clicking on the red Toolbox icon at the top of the screen. When the Toolbox menu opens, click on the Spatial Statistics toolbox, followed by Utilities and Collect events. Double click on the Collect icon.
5. When the Collect Events menu box appears click on the Open file icon next to Input Incident Features box, navigate to the Chapter 2 folder, and select Homicides.
6. In the Output weighted Point Feature Class box, click on the open folder icon, navigate to the Chapter 2 folder, and name the file "homicidecount."
7. Click OK and the process should begin running.
8. When the process has completed, close the Collect Events box and the ArcToolbox.
9. When you return to your open view, you should now have a new layer named "homicidecount."
10. Right click on the Homicidecount layer and select properties.
11. Once the Layer Properties box appears, select the Symbology tab and then under the show box select "Quantities" and then "Graduated Symbols."
12. Under the Fields area of the menu box, scroll down under Values and select the variable "ICOUNT." This should change the symbols at the bottom of the menu box. Importantly, as with the basemap, the number of breaks and the type of breaks can be edited by the user using the same classification schemes.
13. When the symbols are as per your choice (color and size), click OK. This will change their view on the Map. Now you should be able to see those locations that have a much higher number of incidents.

Tip: If you are having trouble determining the locations with one incident from those with multiple incidents, try changing the color of the single-incident locations to "no color." This will allow you to see where the single-incident locations occurred while making it much easier to see the multiple-incident locations.

PROJECT: CONTEXTUAL DATA ANALYSIS

The project for Workbook Chapter 2 is to combine different types of data to conduct a theory-driven analysis of homicide in Houston. Specifically, using theories discussed in the first part of the text and the sample data provided, students should attempt to conduct an analysis of homicide data in Houston.

Point Data

Homicides.shp: All homicides in Houston in 1992.
Bars.shp: All bars in Houston Texas.
Malls.shp: All malls in Houston Texas.
Liquor.shp: All liquor stores in Houston Texas.
Schools.shp: All schools in Houston Texas.

Line Data

Houstreet.shp: Street file for Houston Texas.

Polygon Data

Houston.shp: Polygon file containing census tract data.

Importantly, the accompanying "Houston" codebook will explain to the student the various census data that are contained within the Houston.shp file.

Examples of theory-driven analysis that can be done include testing social disorganization using social disorganization variables NDISADV or NINSTABL, which look at the amount of disadvantage and instability in a neighborhood.

REVIEW QUESTIONS

1. Why is it important to include other types of data besides crime data when making crime maps?

2. What is contextual data and what are some important types of contextual data for crime mapping?

3. Name the four main types of data.

4. What are the five main ways to categorize data in Arcview?

5. What benefit is there in using graduated symbols on crime incident data?

Entering Data

GOALS:
1. Learn the different types of data entry.
2. Learn about problems associated with data used for geocoding.
3. Learn how to geocode data as well as problems associated with geocoding.
4. Learn about GPS and how to enter GPS data.
5. Geocode sample data.

INTRODUCTION

One, if not the most important, part of mapping crime data is actually entering the data into the GIS. However, despite its importance to effective crime mapping, data entry and its associated problems receive little discussion in most crime-mapping texts. In Workbook Chapter 3, students will learn how to both geocode crime data and enter GPS coordinates of crime data as well as the problems associated with each method.

GEOCODING DATA

Geocoding is the process of taking specific street addresses in a table format and matching them to a reference file (street file) containing a range of addresses for a given area. When an address in your data table matches a range of addresses in the reference file, they are then given physical coordinates for that address (ESRI, 1998). Thus, in order to geocode crime data, you need both a table of crime incidents with associated addresses and a street file with address ranges for the area that contains the crime incidents. The benefit of geocoding is that it is a fairly quick and effective method for turning address-level crime data into points on a map that can then be analyzed.

While geocoding is by far the most popular method for entering crime data into a GIS, it is far from a perfect method. When geocoding, the accuracy of address matching is called the **hit rate**. A hit rate is the percentage of crime incidents that match to corresponding street addresses in the reference file. Importantly, the goal of geocoding is to have a 100 percent hit rate as unmatched addresses are not mapped, leading to inaccurate representations of where crime occurs. Missing crime data caused by low hit rates can lead to serious problems when mapping is being used for tactical or research purposes. However, due to the nature of where crime events occur and standard data gathering practices in police departments, geocoding can lead to low hit rates and inaccurate representations of where crime actually occurs. This is not to say that geocoding is a poor method of data entry for crime data, just that there are specific problems that need to be addressed in the data gathering stage that can help make geocoding more accurate.

One of the most common problems associated with accurate geocoding of crime incidents revolves around where crime incidents occur. Specifically, many crimes occur at places where there are **no associated street addresses**. Examples include crimes that occur in fields, on highways, at intersections, on railways, or on or near water such as a river, lake, or ocean (Gebhardt, 1999). While there is no one perfect solution for incidents that occur in these problem areas, suggestions include geocoding to the nearest actual street address, geocoding to the block instead of an address, and using GPS to get accurate coordinates (Gebhardt, 1999).

Another more common problem with data gathering involves **poor data entry** by officers in the field and data entry people. This problem takes on two different forms, officers using common place names instead of street addresses (Wal-mart instead of 1350 Fontaine Rd.) and officers and data entry people misspelling addresses. Because geocoding works by matching actual addresses to a range of street addresses in a reference file, misspellings and common place names will not match against the reference file, thus lowering the hit rate and leaving important crime data off of your maps. Several different solutions exist to this problem. One solution is to use **validated entry** for all addresses (Gebhardt, 1999). In validated entry, all addresses are checked against the reference file during the data entry process; if the address doesn't match an existing address in the reference file, the data entry person is alerted to a bad address. While this method makes data entry fairly easy, it requires a lot of advance work and programming to be effective (Gebhardt, 1999). Another solution is to use **forced entry** choices for all addresses (Gebhardt, 1999). Forced entry works by only allowing valid addresses to be entered through the use of drop-down menus of all valid addresses. While this method ensures 100 percent accuracy, it severely limits users and requires a lot of background programming and thus is not always recommended for large databases (Gebhardt, 1999). A final method is the use of **substitution tables** (Gebhardt, 1999). Substitution tables work by allowing programmers to create "other" address names for a valid address in the reference file, which the GIS then searches when looking for matches to addresses. Thus, common place names and common misspellings of addresses can be listed in the substitution tables, increasing the hit rate. This is the easiest of the three methods to implement as it has a standard part of all major GIS packages.

A final problem associated with low hit rates is **poor reference files** used for geocoding. This problem is most common in both rural locations, where street files are often poorly created and maintained, and urban areas that are constantly growing and adding roads. In addition, some software programs come with poorly equipped geocoding software, ill prepared to geocode many addresses that are valid (Levine, 2002b). Poor reference files make it difficult to match crime locations because they don't contain the full range of addresses for an area. The best solution for reference file problems is to update your reference file several times a year, either through manual updating or through the acquiring of reference files from government agencies or private companies.

PRACTICAL GEOCODING

1. Open ArcMap and select "A new empty map" and click OK.
2. Click the Add data button and maneuver on the C drive to the "CMLab Exercises" folder and than select "Chapter 3."
3. From the Chapter 3 folder, select the following layers:
   a. Houston.shp.
   b. Houstreets.shp

4. Open the ArcCatalog by clicking on the ArcCatalog icon at the top of the screen (looks like a file cabinet).
5. When ArcCatalog opens, double click the C drive icon and scroll to the CM Labs folder and Chapter 3. We are going to be creating an address locator and we are going to save it in the Chapter 3 folder.
6. Under the File menu, select New and Address Locator.
7. When the "Create New Address Locator" box appears, scroll down and select US Streets. Once it is selected, click OK.
8. When the "New US Streets Address Locator" box appears, name your Address Locator "Houston Geocode" by clicking in the box next to Name and editing the existing name. ArcGIS 9.2 will automatically save this new address locator in Chapter 3 if you have already navigated to that folder.
9. Under the Primary Table tab, click on the Open Folder icon and select the "Houstreets.shp" file. This is the street network file for Houston that we will be geocoding all of the addresses to. ArcGIS 9.2 should automatically have filled in all of the relevant fields necessary for geocoding in the "fields" section. These different fields indicate the different parts of the address and where they are contained in the data.

Once these first decisions have been made, there are several different things that need to be discussed more in-depth in order to prepare a street network for geocoding. Specifically, there are several decisions that must be made that will significantly impact the success of your geocoding of addresses. These decisions will be discussed more fully in the next section.

Matching Options and Setting Geocoding Preferences

In matching addresses, ArcGIS performs what is called a **batch match**, as opposed to earlier versions of Arcview where the user has the initial option of conducting either a batch match or an interactive match. In a batch match, ArcGIS will attempt to match as many addresses as possible based on geocoding preferences that the user sets before matching. By contrast, in an interactive match the user reviews each address individually and makes all decisions about whether to match an address or not. While batch matching is certainly faster at matching addresses, especially large datasets, it is potentially less accurate due to the setting of preferences.

As ArcGIS conducts a batch match, it is essential to set the **matching options** within the Address locator setup. This is important because how you set your preferences will help determine your hit rate. Importantly, hit rate is more than just getting a match for an address; it is about getting the *correct* match for an address. Thus, in this discussion of setting the geocoding preferences, emphasis will be on setting the preferences conservatively so as to make sure that addresses match correctly.

1. Under the "Matching Options," there are three preferences that we will be concerned with: Spelling sensitivity, minimum match score, and minimum candidate score.
2. **Spelling sensitivity:** This setting allows you to adjust how sensitive you want the spelling accuracy to be when looking for address matches. Importantly, 100 percent requires a perfect spelling match (almost unheard of) to match an address. Suggestions are given to leave the sensitivity at the default 80, in order to ensure correct spelling.
3. **Minimum candidate score:** This score is used to determine the minimum score needed for an address to be considered a candidate for matching. Scores can range from 0 to 100, with recommendation being to use the default value of 10 thus allowing a significant number of candidates to be considered.

4. **Minimum match score:** This setting determines the minimum score an address in the reference table has to have to be considered a match. For each address, ArcGIS creates a score from 1 to 100 showing how close to a match the address is. How you set this score will determine which addresses ArcGIS will automatically match. The higher you make the score, the fewer addresses will match automatically, but the greater confidence you will have in actually having a correct address. Importantly, unmatched addresses can be reviewed interactively after the batch match has concluded allowing you to interactively rematch addresses that fall below the criteria you set. Again the suggestion is to change the value to 100 in order to ensure data accuracy.

5. **Output options:** The Side Offset will move all geocoded points a fixed distance away from the street centerline. The benefit of this is that all residential crime incident locations will be moved away from the street to a location where the residence is more likely located. While not all crime incidents are at either residential or commercial locations, and the offset of residences varies greatly by neighborhood type, this will provide a better than most solution.

6. **Output Fields:** Before starting the geocoding process, the last thing to do is select the output fields that ArcGIS will create for the geocoded addresses. Given that the software we will use later in the workbook for analysis requires X and Y coordinates to work correctly, it is advised to select *X and Y coordinates* as an output field. Doing this will have ArcGIS attach the X and Y coordinates for each address that is geocoded.

7. After reviewing the matching options, output options, and output fields, click OK. This will start the process of creating the Address Locator and may take a minute depending on the speed of your computer.

8. When the address locator has been created, close Arc Catalog and go back to the ArcMap application.

Selecting File for Geocoding

1. Under the Tools menu again select "Geocoding"; however, this time when the options appear to the right of Geocoding, select "Geocode Addesses."

2. When the "Choose an address locator to use . . . " box appears, click on Add and navigate to the Chapter 3 folder and select the "Houston Geocode" address locator that was just created. When the "Choose and Address Locator . . . " menu appears, again click OK.

3. When the "Geocode Addresses: Houston Geocode" box appears, you will need to select the file that we are going to geocode. Next to the "address table" box, click on the open file button. This is where you will add the .dbf table to be geocoded.
   a. Go to Chapter 3 in the CM Lab folder and select Table A.

4. In the Street or intersection box, scroll down until you find the variable named INCADD and select it.

5. In the Output Shapefile or feature class: box, click on the open File icon and save the geocoded file as "incidents" in the Chapter 3 folder. When this is all completed, click OK.

This is the variable that contains the addresses for the incidents.

Interactive Address Rematching

1. After the batch matching is finished, the **Review/Rematch Address** box will appear. Click on the Match **Interactively** button, and the **Interactive Review** box will appear. This is where the user will go back and attempt to interactively rematch all of those address that failed to match in the batch match. Importantly, you can also perform a batch rematch, but unless you change your geocoding preferences, your results will not change.

2. When the Interactive Review editor appears, you will notice numerous buttons used in interactive rematching. Below is a description of the main sections of the Interactive Review editor:

> **Address Text Box:** This window located near the top of the editor displays the current address to be matched. Addresses that are being matched are highlighted.

> **Candidate Table:** This table at the bottom of the screen displays all of the candidates for the current address from the reference table. The table lists the score for each candidate as well as the address information for each candidate.

> **Match Button:** Allows you to match an address to a highlighted candidate from the candidate table. Click this button when you have selected a candidate from the candidate table.

> **Unmatch Button:** Allows you to "unmatch" an address that has already matched. Click this only if you feel that you, or the computer, have matched an address incorrectly.

> **Next Arrow:** Arrow next to the Record box that allows you to skip an address currently under review. Click this when there are no candidate addresses or no addresses you feel are correct.

> **Previous Arrow:** Arrow next to the Record box that allows you to go back to a previous address. This is similar to the back button on a web browser.

> **Search Button:** Allows you to enter changes you may have made to the address to be matched. When you click this button after making changes to the street address (spelling or street number), the program will attempt to match the newly changed address. Once the process is done, new candidates will be shown in the candidate box.

> **Geocoding Options Button:** Allows you to view the preferences that you established before the batch match.

> **Close Button:** Signifies that you have finished rematching the addresses. *Click this button only when you are finished with all of the addresses.*

3. When you have rematched all the addresses, click on the close button.
4. When the Review/Rematch box appears, again click on Done. This will create a new layer of the addresses that you just matched. The new layer will be named something similar to Geocoding results: Geocoding_result1.
5. To rename the Layer and save it in a file that you will remember, make Geocoding results: Geocoding_result1 active and right click on the Layer name and scroll down to "Save as layer File."
   a. Save the new file as something that you remember and in a folder where you will remember.

TIPS for Interactive Rematching

1. Try editing the spelling of the street name or number. Oftentimes addresses are spelled incorrectly.
2. Try editing the direction of the street, either adding or removing directions to a street. Sometimes streets have directions that are not added or street files have left the direction off of a street.
3. Pay attention to the score the candidates receive. If the score is high enough or the address appears to match the candidate's components despite a low score, you may want to match the address.
4. Whether you match an address interactively is completely up to you, as you *can* match almost any address if you edit it enough. Importantly, there are many ethical issues with how much editing you do in order to achieve a high hit rate.

ADDING GPS COORDINATES

One of the much-heralded suggestions for improving crime mapping accuracy is to increase the use of GPS measurements instead of relying on geocoding. GPS stands for *global positioning system*, a series of 24 satellites that orbit the Earth and provide exact coordinates for any position. Obviously GPS coordinates are an extremely attractive option because they provide exact position coordinates that do not need to be altered in order to put a crime location into a GIS. All an officer has to do to record a location is look at a GPS receiver and write the coordinates on an incident report. The coordinates can be in any coordinate system, such as decimal degrees or UTM depending on the coordinate system of your basemap. Once the reading has been made, the coordinates only need to be put into a table as a .dbf or .txt file so that they can be added to ArcMap. Importantly, GPS receivers have become increasingly cheap, small, and sophisticated, allowing better accuracy for less cost than five years ago. However, despite their appealing benefits, there are several problems with GPS receivers for use in gathering position data. First, for a position to be recorded, an officer has to actually be at the physical location to take a reading, as opposed to street addresses that can be recorded over the phone without the need of an officer. Second, despite improvements in GPS technology, reception can be impaired significantly by things such as weather, high buildings, tree coverage, and power supply. While there are technological means to deal with these problems, it increases the cost of GPS significantly. Despite the potential problems associated with GPS, it is definitely beneficial in situations where crimes occur on highways, fields, intersections, or waterways and will be increasingly used in the future.

Adding Event Themes

1. In the map that you currently have opened, go to the Insert menu and select "Data Frame." This will allow you to add a new set of layers.
2. Click on the Add Data button and from the Chapter 3 folder, add the Post7.shp theme. These data represent an 11 county area in central Kentucky.
3. Once you have added these data, click on the **Tools** menu and scroll down to **Add XY Data**.
4. When the Add XY Data menu opens, click on the open file button to the right of the "Choose a table from the map or browse for another table" box and proceed to Chapter 3 in the CM Lab folder and select **tableb**.
5. ArcMap will automatically place the variable "X_Coord" in the X Field box and "Y_Coord" in the Y field box. However, if for some reason, these variables do not show up in these field boxes, then scroll down and manually select them.
6. Click OK and the data should be added to the map of the 11 county area. Importantly, this new layer is not really a layer yet. In order to make this a true layer, we must save it as a layer.
7. Make "Table B events" active and right click on the Layer name and scroll down to "Save as layer File."
   a. Save the new file as something that you remember and in a folder where you will remember.

PROJECT: GEOCODING ACCURACY

1. Add the following themes:
   a. Lexington.shp
   b. Lexstreets.shp

2. Add the table Geocode.dbf and geocode all of the addresses. Remember to create and Address Locator the street file for geocoding (US Streets) and decide whether to use a batch match or interactive match.

3. Follow the instructions for creating a Address Locator in the workbook and use the practical geocoding directions to assist you in geocoding.

Project Answer: Check the accuracy of your geocoding against Figure 3.1 at www.mappingcrime.org

REVIEW QUESTIONS

1. What are the two main ways for entering crime data into Arcview?

2. List the associated problems with data used for geocoding.

3. What is a hit rate?

4. Name and explain the two methods for increasing hit rates.

5. Explain the difference between batch matching and interactive matching of addresses.

6. Explain the benefits and problems associated with using GPS for data acquisition.

FURTHER READINGS

Gebhardt, C. (1999). Geocoding: Improving Your Hit Rate. Presentation Given at the Crime Mapping Research Centers Annual Conference, Orlando, FL. Available on-line at http://iaca.net/resources/FAQs/hitrate.html

Querying and Joining Data

GOALS: **1.** Learn the importance of querying and merging data for crime mapping.

2. Learn the different ways to query and select layers.

3. Learn how to join data.

4. Query and join sample data.

INTRODUCTION

By now you have learned much about the basics of using ArcGIS for crime mapping, from how to use some of its basic tools to data quality issues to entering data into ArcGIS. In Workbook Chapter 4, we will focus on how to manipulate data for analytic and organizational needs. Specifically, you will learn how to query and merge data in order to create layers that contain only data that you need or want.

WHY QUERY AND JOIN DATA?

Most police reports contain numerous fields of information relating to the crime incident, including type of crime, date and time of occurrence, victim and offender information, weapon use and type, and incident location. While all of this information is extremely important to conducting analysis of crime series and crime patterns, unless it is manipulated correctly all of this information is potentially lost in crime-mapping applications. As we learned in Workbook Chapter 3, when crime information from police reports is geocoded and displayed on a map, it is based solely on the location of the incident, ignoring all of the other information contained in the report. When a month's worth of crime is geocoded and mapped, it only provides users with a point map view of all crimes in that jurisdiction for that month. Thus, if using this same map a user wanted to know the location of robberies only, or robberies in relation to drug crimes, the map would be virtually worthless. Importantly, maps based on information such as crime type, offender motive, and weapon use are vitally important to both criminal justice practitioners and researchers. Maps displaying spatial patterns of specific crimes are necessary for tactical planning and problem solving by practitioners and for research projects by researchers. Fortunately, ArcGIS makes the creation of these customized maps easy through the use of the **query** and **join** functions.

A **query** is a simple operation in which the user is allowed to define what features in a layer they want to display on a map. An example would be creating a query in which robberies are selected from a month of crimes in order to allow the user to see the location of all robbery locations. This function, which can be conducted on any information contained in a data table, is one of the more common functions used by crime analysts in their daily functions. Common queries relating to crime and crime reports include the following:

- Crime type
- Offender characteristics (race, gender, age range, etc.)
- Offender motive
- Weapon type
- Date of occurrence
- Time of occurrence

The other function that is commonly used in organizing and customizing data for crime maps is the join function. **Join** is a function that allows users to combine several different layers of the same type together to create a new layer. This type of operation is commonly used in crime maps when combining multiple crime themes from different time periods into one single theme for a longer period of time. An example would be joining robbery layers from each month in a given year to create a layer containing all robbery incidents for an entire year. It is important to note that only layers of the same type can be joined. Thus you can only join two point layers or two polygon layers, not a point layer and a polygon layer. In the context of crime maps, joining of layers is most commonly done to combine layers based on date of occurrence, type of crime, motive, or weapon used.

QUERYING LAYERS

1. Open ArcMap, select "A new empty map," and click OK.
2. Click the Add data button and maneuver on the C drive to the "CMLab Exercises" folder and then select "Chapter 4."
3. From the Chapter 4 folder, select the following layers:
   a. Houston.shp
   b. Homicides.shp
4. Make both layers viewable and make Homicides.shp active as well.
5. Under the Selection menu, scroll down to "Select by Attributes." This will open the Select by Attributes box, which will allow the user to perform various queries of the data.

Within the Select by Attributes box are several important areas. First is the **Fields** box, which lists all the different fields of information that you can choose to query. These different fields are the different variables within your data and their associated values. Second is the **Unique values** box, which contains all of the values of the selected fields. Specifically, when a field is selected, the values of that field will appear in the Unique values box. Third is the operator's area. This is the area underneath the Fields box and to the left of the Unique values box that contains the different operations that can be performed in the query. For example when querying months, you can choose all months greater than (>) 4 (April), all months less than (<) 4, or only incidents in the 4th month (=). The final area is the query text box, which shows the users the query that they are currently creating.

Creating a Query

1. After opening the Select by Attributes box, the first thing you need to do is select a **field** to query. In this example, we will select all female homicide victims. Importantly, all queries must contain three things: a field, an operator, and a value.

2. Scroll down the fields box until you find the field VGENDER and double-click on it, and it should appear in the "query text box" at the bottom. Importantly, you **must double-click** on the field name or else it will not appear in the "query text box" and will not be available for query.

3. Next we will pick an **operator function**, in this case the "equals." Click once on the "=" sign. When you click on the equals sign it should appear in the query text box after VGENDER.

4. Finally we will select the **value** for the query. In this case double-click on the "F" value. As with the fields, values must be *double-clicked* in order for it to be included in the query. The equation in the query text box should now read as follows:

"VGENDER" = "F"

Tip: If you click on a desired Field and no values appear in the Unique Values box, click on the Get Unique Values button. This will populate the Unique Values box with all of the different values associated with that field.

5. When your query is complete, click on the Apply button. This button will run your query for you, selecting all values that match your query and coloring them light blue on the map.

6. Figure 4.1 (www.mappingcrime.org) shows you how the map should look like if queried correctly. After you close the query text box, your map should have 71 incidents either colored blue or "selected". You can check if this is correct by opening the table (right click on the homicides layer and select "Open Attribute table"). On the bottom under the table it will indicate 71 of 536 selected, denoting that 71 of the 536 records were selected by your query. In lay terms, your query for female victims produced 70 incidents that had female victims.

Converting, Clearing, or Querying the Query

After you have conducted the query, you can convert the query to a layer, which will allow you to save it and manipulate it at a later date, clear the query allowing you to conduct a new query, or make a query of the selected features.

Convert the Query to a Layer

1. Right click on the Homicides layer and scroll down to Selection.
2. When the menu pops out to the right of selection, scroll down and select "Create Layer From Selected Features." You should now have a new layer entitled "homicides selection" added to your map.

Clear the query: Under the Selection menu, scroll down and select "Clear Selected Features." Alternatively, you can right click on the Homicides layer, scroll down to the Selection menu, and select "Clear Selected Features."

Query of the Selected Features (Query Results)

1. Open the Select by Attributes box and select a new field. Importantly, make sure that the layer selected for the query is "Homicides" (If you have cleared the previous query, then you will need to redo it for the rest of this exercise). If it is not selected, then go to the Layer menu at the top of the Select by Attributes box and scroll down to that layer. In this example, we are going to query white victims from the female homicide victims query to determine how many white female homicide victims there were.
2. Select a Field, in this case Vrace, for victim race.

3. Select an operator, in this case "=".
4. Select a value, in this case "W". Your equation should now look like the following:

$$\text{"Vrace"} = \text{"W"}$$

5. Before clicking on "Apply," go to the "Method" drop-down menu at the top and choose "Select from current selection." Once you have done this, click on Apply. This will make your selection from the selected features (female homicide victims). Close the Select by Attributes box after your query is complete.
6. Figure 4.2 (www.mappingcrime.org) shows how a correctly queried map should look like. The number of queries should have decreased significantly, so that only 22 incidents are selected. Again to check the queries, open the associated table.

JOINING LAYERS

1. With ArcMap already open, make all the current layers unviewable except for Houston (de-select the check boxes to the left of the layer names); add the following themes to the view:
   a. 1993.shp
   b. 1994.shp
2. Click on the red toolbox icon. This will open the ArcToolbox, which is designed to walk you through the process of joining layers (called merging layers in ArcGIS 9.2).
3. Click on the "+" next to "Data Management Tools" toolbox. This will expand to show you a list of different Data Management tools.
4. Click on the "+" next to the "General" tool. When this expands, double-click on the hammer that says "Merge." This will open the Merge dialog box.
5. At the top of the dialog box where it shows "Input Dataset," click on the down arrow and select 1993.shp. Repeat this process again and select 1994. This indicates that the 1993 and 1994 layers are to be joined together to form one new layer.
6. At the bottom of the dialog box where it shows "Output dataset," click on the open file icon and scroll to the Chapter 4 folder.
7. Name the new file 9394merge and click Save.
8. When you return to the Merge dialog box, simply click OK. When the merge process is complete close the append box.
9. Right click on the 9394merge layer and select "Open attribute table." As you scroll down, you will see that all of the 1993 homicides have been joined with the 1994 layer. Figure 4.3 (www.mappingcrime.org) shows you how a correctly merged map should look like.

Exporting the Layer as a .shp file

1. Right click on the 9394merge layer and scroll down to data and then Export data. When the "Export Data" dialog appears, click on the Open file box next to the "Output Shapefile or Feature class" box. Rename the shapefile "9394" and click save. When you return to the "Export Data" dialog box, click OK.
2. When the ArcMap dialog box appears, click Yes and you should have a new layer titled 9394 that contains all of the 1993 and 1994 homicides.

   Tip: While any two points or polygon themes can technically be merged, it is important to merge only those layers that share similar fields in order for all of the information to be included in the attribute table.

PROJECT: MERGE AND QUERY OF DATA

1. Create a new view and add the following themes:
   a. Houston.shp
   b. 1985.shp
   c. 1987.shp
   d. 1990.shp
2. Merge the three different point themes into one new theme and name it 8590.shp.
3. Query the new theme in order to find all **robbery homicides** committed during the **summer months** (May–September). In order to find out the Field and Value information to create this query, look into the "Homicides" codebook you downloaded from the textbook webpage.

Project Answer: To check the accuracy of your query, see Figure 4.4 on-line at www.mappingcrime.org

REVIEW QUESTIONS

1. What is a query and how is it important in crime mapping?

2. What is merge and how is it important to crime mapping?

3. What are the three necessary parts of a query?

4. How can you check as to how many incidents were selected by your query?

5. After you make a query, what are your main options as to what to do?

6. What happens if you try to merge two different types of themes, such as a point and a polygon theme?

Understanding Layouts and Map Design

GOALS: 1. Understand the importance of scale.

2. Understand how to use layouts.

3. Understand basic map composition.

4. Understand basic map design for crime maps.

5. Design, print, and export a map.

INTRODUCTION

While all of the previous chapters have been important in providing you with a basic understanding and sense of familiarity with ArcMap and making crime maps, none may be as important to your actual creation of intelligible maps as Workbook Chapter 5. In this chapter, we will explore the art/science of map design for making informative crime maps for audiences of different kinds. This chapter is so important for students because without a solid understanding of map design, your maps will be at least ineffective and at worst unethical and deceitful. Ultimately, how well a map speaks to the audience depends on how well a map is designed and produced.

SCALE AND MAP DESIGN

In map design, one of the more important factors to determine is the scale of the map. **Scale** is the degree of reduction in the map as compared to reality (Monmonier, 1993). Maps are designed to be miniature representations of reality, and the scale on a map is what tells us how much smaller than reality the map is. The scale of a map is usually expressed as a ratio of the distance measure on the map in relation to the distance measure on the ground (Monmonier, 1993). Thus, a scale with a ratio of 1:15,000 inches would indicate that one inch on the map is equal to 15,000 inches on the ground.

In general, there are two kinds of maps, **large-scale** maps, which show small areas and **small-scale** maps, which show large areas. An example of a large-scale map would be a map showing crime in a six-block area of a city, whereas a small-scale map would be a regional map of the United States showing crime victimization by state. The importance of scale to map design is the level of detail that is available in a map and its impact on the interpretation and meaning of a map (Harries, 1999).

Specifically, large-scale maps are capable of showing much more detail and are thus inherently easier to interpret, whereas small-scale maps have less detail and tend to be more abstract and difficult to interpret. Figure 5.1 (www.mappingcrime.org) shows the pattern of homicide incidents in relation to bar locations in Houston Texas from two different scales and illustrates the impact of scale on the level of understanding and detail in a map. The smaller scale map makes it appear that all homicides occur within feet of bars, whereas the large-scale map makes it clear that while there is a definite relationship between bars and homicide locations it is not as strong as it appears in the small-scale map.

From a practical standpoint when making a map, the level of scale used will depend largely on the purpose of the map and the subsequent data available for the map. For instance if you need to make a map showing the pattern of robberies for a six-beat section of a jurisdiction, your scale will be large by definition. This large-scale map will thus be able to show a great deal of detail of the six-beat area, including road names, bar locations, and ATM locations. By contrast, if you are showing the level of robbery victimization by county for an entire state, your scale will be small and your level of detail will be more abstract. If you were to try to show roads and road names in addition to bar and ATM locations, your map would be overwhelming and difficult to understand. Importantly, changing the scale of your map in ArcMap is very easy, as the "zoom in" and "zoom out" buttons control it. As you zoom in on a map location, the scale, which is displayed in the right corner of the view, gets larger.

MAP ELEMENTS

Before we discuss how to design and print a map using a "Layout," we need to discuss the four necessary elements of a map. While arguments can be made that certain maps do not need to contain all four elements of a map, in general these four simple elements improve the effectiveness and comprehension of a map. First, every map must have a **title**. Titles can vary from basic to complex, but serve the purpose of informing the reader of the purpose and content of the map. A second necessary element is the **legend**, which acts as a table of contents for the reader listing the different data and graphical features of the map. In general legends contain the symbols and colors that are used to define geographic features in the map as well as a text definition of what the symbol or color represents. A third necessary element is a **scale**. As discussed above, a scale is important because it tells the reader the relationship between the map measurement units and the measurement units in the real world. Importantly, scales also allow readers to measure distances on a map, which can be a primary function of some crime maps dealing with journeys to crime and travel distances. A final necessary map element is a **compass**, which informs the reader of the orientation of the map (North and South). Other elements of a map that are not necessarily essential but can be beneficial are **credits**, which inform the reader where the data came from, and **neatlines**, which surround the body and other elements of the map to give it a cleaner appearance.

MAP LAYOUT

1. Open ArcMap and select "A new empty map" and click OK.
2. Click the Add data button and maneuver on the C drive to the "CMLab Exercises" folder and then select "Chapter 5."
3. From the Chapter 5 folder, select the following themes:
   a. Houston.shp
   b. Homicides.shp

4. Make both of these viewable and edit their appearance. Make the Houston layer clear and make the Homicides into red stars at 12 pt size. In ArcMap, map design takes place in a Layout.

5. Under the View menu, select **Layout View**. This will bring up the Template Manager box. Alternatively, you can select the page button in the bottom left corner of the map (next to the small globe).

EDITING MAP ELEMENTS

Adding a Legend

When looking at the layout, you should instantly notice that none of the map elements that should be included with a good map are on the layout. In ArcMap, the user is charged with adding all of the different map elements that they want. Importantly, this allows the user the complete control of customizing the appearance of the map.

Legend Items

1. Under the Insert menu, select "Legend." This will bring up the Legend Wizard, which will guide you through designing an effective and attractive looking legend.

2. First you will choose the map layers that you want to include in your legend. In the left column are *all* of the layers that are in the data map that you are working on, while the right column shows the Legend items you have chosen to include. As a rule every layer that is visible on the finished map should be included in the legend. In this case there are only two layers on the map (homicides and Houston), both of which have been included in the legend.

3. If for some reason you want to remove a layer from the legend, simply click on it and then click on the arrow pointing toward the Map layers column. Conversely, if there are map layers you want to add to the legend, click on them and then click the arrow pointing toward the Legend column.

Legend Tips

A. **Legend Order:** The order of the legend can be altered by simply clicking on the Legend item and clicking either the up or down arrow to the right of the Legend Item column until the item is in the desired position. In crime maps, point layers (crime incidents) usually are at the top of the legend followed by line layers (roads) and polygon layers (jurisdiction boundaries).

B. **Items included in the Legend:** Only items that are "viewable" in the view mode are included in the legend.

C. **Layer names:** If the name of the layer is not as per your choice, then you need to return to the Data view and change it. Once in the data view, click on the Layer name until it is highlighted and then simply rename it to whatever you want. In all cases, Layer names should be capitalized.

Legend Title

1. Once you have all of the Legend items you want and in the order you want, click on the Next button at the bottom of the page. This will take you to the Legend Title page of the legend wizard.

2. In general, the legend is best left named "Legend," but if for some reason you want to rename it simply highlight the word legend in the "Legend Title" box and type in whatever you want as a title.

3. If you want to change the font and the justification (alignment) of the legend, that can also be easily done in this section of the Legend wizard.
4. Once you have finished with the Legend Title, click on the Next button.

Legend Frame

The legend frame gives the user the option of creating a frame around the legend that will set it apart from the rest of the map. Importantly, ArcMap gives the user several customization options.

Border: This is the outline around the legend. To add a border, click on the drop-down menu and select a border size that you find attractive.

For this exercise, select the 0.05 Point option.

Background: This is the background color/shading of the legend. To edit the background, simply click on the drop-down menu and choose a color that you find attractive.

For this exercise, select Gray 10 percent.

Drop Shadow: This is the shading behind the legend that gives the legend a 3-D appearance. To edit the Drop Shadow, simply click on the drop-down menu and choose a color that you find attractive.

For this exercise, select Gray 20 percent.

Once you have made these changes, click on the Next button.

Item Size and Spacing

The last two sections of the Legend Wizard allow the user to further customize the appearance of the legend by editing the size and shape of symbol patches as well as the spacing of the items in the legend. While this is a great feature for the advanced user, for our purposes it is beyond the scope of our discussion. Thus, for these last two sections of the wizard, simply click on Next and then Finish.

Altering the Size and Location of a Map Element

Once your legend has been created, you will probably want to move it around the map to a place where it does not obstruct the view of the items on the map. Importantly, moving and altering the size of all of the map elements is easily done.

1. With the pointer tool, click **once** on any of the basic map elements (compass, scale, title, legend). Four squares should appear at the corners of the map element. These four squares represent the outline of the map element and can be re-sized as per your choice.
2. Place the pointer on any one of the squares. This should change the icon to a two-headed arrow.
3. Click and hold the square and move the square inward or outward to change the size to your liking.
4. Once you have the map element the size you want, you can change its location by clicking once on the map element and placing the pointer over the main body of the map element.
5. When the pointer tool changes to a four-headed arrow, click and hold to drag the map element to wherever you want in the map layout.
6. If you want you can also alter the size and location of the view frame (main map), using the same procedures described above.

   Tip: When trying to determine the correct size of a map element, remember that map elements should not be so large as to distract from the view frame, nor should they be so small as to be difficult to find or understand.

Editing the Scale

While in the data mode, we can alter the scale of the map, which is the only other map feature whose properties and appearance in the layout are controlled completely in the data mode.

1. Select the interactive "zoom in" button and click in the center of the view.
2. After the map has zoomed in, minimize the view and open up the layout for view 1. Notice how the legend and scale have changed in accordance with the alterations made in the view mode. Whatever scale you are in the data mode will be the scale for the layout.

Adding a Compass and Scale Bar

As with the legend, all of the other map elements must be added to the layout by going to the Insert menu and selecting a map element. Importantly, in creating a north arrow and scale bar, the user simply chooses a style that they like from the options available in the North Arrow or Scale Bar selector menus and clicks OK.

> **Tip:** There is no conventional scale bar or compass style, but try to choose a style that complements the map rather than distracts. Remember that scales and compasses are there to inform, not to look pretty or distract from the message that the map is trying to convey.

Adding a Map Title

1. Under the Insert menu, select "Title." A small title box should now appear at the top of the map layout with the word "Title" highlighted.
2. Simply type the name for your map into the title box and it should appear. When you hit "enter," the highlight color should disappear.
3. In order to alter the font type and font size, simply double-click on your title, brining up the properties box.
4. On the bottom right corner of the Text Properties, click on the Change Symbol button.
5. The user is now able to scroll through a variety of options for font types and font sizes.
6. When you have selected a font type and size that you like, simply click on the OK button, which will take you back to the Text properties box. Now click on OK and your new font type and font size should appear.

ADDING OTHER ELEMENTS TO THE LAYOUT

In addition to editing basic map elements, ArcMap also allows you to add other elements to the layout such as charts, tables, and pictures. These elements often help to convey complex or supplemental information not easily conveyed in the map. In crime mapping, these elements are used quite often. **Charts** are often added to provide tabular views of crime distributions that are being displayed in the map. An example would be a point map of all homicides for a 12-month period with a chart showing the monthly distribution of homicides. **Tables** are also used quite often in crime maps to provide detailed information about the map elements. An example would be a point map of robbery locations with a table providing detailed information about suspect information and motive. Finally, **pictures** are also used quite a bit in crime maps to give them a more professional appearance. An example would be including a .gif image of a department or universities logo above the legend to inform the reader of the source of the map. In addition to charts, tables, and pictures, ArcMap also allows you to add basic map elements such as data frames, compasses, scale bars, and legends. With the exception of adding a data frame to display another map, this is primarily used when a user wants to design a layout completely from scratch.

1. In order to add these other elements, select "Picture" or "Object" from under the Insert menu. **Picture** will allow you to add images to the layout, whereas **Object** will allow you to add charts and other documents to the layout.
2. For this example select Picture. This should take you to the Chapter 5 folder within the CM Lab exercises folder. However, if you are not immediately taken there, then maneuver to this folder.
3. Find HPD.gif and select it and then click OK.
4. An image of the Houston Police Department badge will now appear on the layout. In order to change its position and size, follow the directions above. Figure 5.2 (www.mappingcrime.org) provides an example of a map layout with the Houston Police Department badge contained within it.

PRINTING AND EXPORTING A LAYOUT

Once you have your layout like you want it, you are down to the printing or exporting stage. Most times you will simply print out the map, but there are times when you may need to export the map as an image for use on the Internet or in PowerPoint presentations. To **print a map**, all you need to do is simply click on the printer icon at the top of the page. This will allow you to print to your default printer or select another printer to print from.

Exporting a Map

1. Under the File menu, select "Export Map."
2. After you have selected a folder to save the image to, you need to select the image file type. The default file type is .jpg, but you can choose from a wealth of other options by clicking on the "Save as type" drop-down menu.
3. In the File Name box, type an appropriate name for the map and click "Save."

MAP DESIGN

The last section of Workbook Chapter 5 is designed to provide readers with a discussion of the major factors that need to be considered when designing a map as well as provide some suggestions for how to best design a map. It is important to note that this section is not a substitute for a more complete study of cartography and map design. Those readers interested in a more in-depth discussion of the topics discussed here are encouraged to read the books in the "Further Readings" section and seek out instruction at a local college or university.

Audience and Medium

The two biggest factors to consider when beginning your map design are your map audience and the medium that the map will be read in. Both of these factors should be considered in-depth before beginning map design because of their impact on color, symbolization, and labeling. **Audience** refers to the main readers of your map. Importantly, different audiences have very different needs, requirements, and levels of

TABLE A   Audience Impact on Map Design

AUDIENCE TYPE	MAP NEEDS	EXAMPLE MAP	COLOR	SYMBOLIZATION	LABELING
Research	—Theory and fact oriented —Complex concepts	Aggregate crime rates at the census tract level	—Grayscales —Blues to reds color ramps	Avoid excessive symbolization	Avoid excessive labeling
Public	Simple and easy for all kinds of people	Crime incidents by neighborhood	—Avoid controversial colors —Avoid confusing color scheme	Nonthreatening and non-controversial symbols	Label all major places and features for ease of understanding
Officer	Quick and to the point	Recent series of robberies	Black and white over color	Simple symbols	Minimal labels necessary
Police Manager	Combination of research and officer maps	Impact of intervention on crime in a beat	—Grayscales —Blues to reds color ramps	Simple symbols	Minimal labels necessary

comprehension of a map and thus map design will be different depending on your audience. Table A outlines the four major audiences for crime maps as well as basic needs and suggestions for color, symbolization, and labeling of maps for these audiences. As you can see, the needs of the map and the sophistication of the readers impacts color, symbolization, and labeling in different ways. **Research** maps are geared toward conveying complex theoretical concepts and facts and assume an audience that is sophisticated in terms of map comprehension. Because of their sophisticated orientation, research maps should avoid excessive symbolization and labeling and use grayscales and blue to red color scales to show differentiations. By contrast, maps for **Public** consumption need o be geared toward ease of understanding by anyone, a sort of least common denominator approach. Thus, these maps should emphasize non-confusing color schemes and labeling of major geographic features, with particular attention being paid to the size and shape of symbols so as to avoid offending, confusing, or misleading readers. Maps for **officers** present a different purpose, as they are designed to provide quick and easy depictions of crime series and patterns to officers who are busy yet knowledgeable of the geography of the area they patrol. Officer maps should thus focus on black and white color schemes, simple symbolization, and basic labeling to facilitate officer comprehension while patrolling. Finally, **police manager** maps are a combination of research and officer maps in that they are often portraying difficult concepts, but must do so in a quick and easy manner. Maps for police managers should use grayscales and blue to red color ramps as well as avoid excessive symbolization and labeling. While far from hard and fast rules, these suggestions should be reviewed before beginning map design and altered to fit your specific needs.

In addition to the above suggestion based on audience type, users should also consider the suggestions given in Table B which describes the impact of **medium** on color, symbolization, and labeling. **Medium** is the method in which the map will be read and consists of normal print, large print, overheads, and electronic media. As with audience, the medium in which the map will be read impacts color, symbolization, and labeling. Notice that maps that will be printed out on **plotters** need more intense colors,

TABLE B   Medium Impact on Map Design

MEDIA TYPE	COLOR	SYMBOLIZATION	LABELING
Normal Print	Don't use color if printer is black and white	Match scale of map and printer size	Avoid excessive labeling
Large Format Print/ Plotters	Make colors more intense	Use large and clear symbols	Labels need to be larger and more detailed
Overhead	—Use darker and more intense colors. —Avoid light colors	Use large and clear symbols	Dark and large labels
Electronic Media	Colors should be readable on standard monitor	Avoid very detailed or intricate symbols	Easy to read font type

larger symbols, and larger and more detailed labeling than maps printed on normal paper because of the large size of the final product. Similarly, maps that are printed out on **overheads** also need darker colors, larger sized symbols, and darker and thicker labels because of the tendency of light colors and lettering to wash out on overheads. By contrast, one of the major issues for printing a map out on **normal paper** is whether or not the printer is color and its subsequent impact on color choices. Specifically, if a map is to be printed out in black and white then the symbolization and color scheme should de-emphasize colors to avoid problems with differentiating between symbols. Finally, maps used in **electronic media** should use simple colors readable on different monitors and use easy to read fonts as labels may be difficult to read depending on monitor resolution.

Map Colors

In making crime maps, or any maps for that matter, the three biggest issues to deal with are choosing colors and symbols that fit best with your map as well as labeling geographic features on the map. **Color** is extremely important in map making because it allows the map designer to convey a host of information quickly and easily. Color has three basic components **hue**, which is the actual color of a color, **value**, which refers to the lightness or darkness of a color, and **saturation**, which refers to the colors intensity, brilliance, or purity of a color (Monmonier, 1996). Changing the hue, value, and saturation of a color can dramatically alter its appearance and its usefulness in a map. In crime mapping applications, color can be used to show crime intensity or density in an isoline map, to show different values in an area or choropleth maps, and to differentiate between incident types in a point map. However, while color can be beneficial to understanding differences and intensities on a map, it can also be used to mislead and confuse the reader. Harries (1999) suggests that color can be used to make dangerous or politically charged areas appear less threatening through the use of "cool" colors that make the reader think the area is non-threatening. Other examples include giving violent crimes such as homicide emotionally charged colors such as red, which is usually associated with blood (Harries, 1999). Finally, if color schemes are poorly chosen they can easily confuse the reader, making maps hard to understand. Examples include using bright multi-color spectrums to show differences in crime rates at the census tract level in an area map.

Suggestions for Color

- Do not go overboard with colors just because they are available in ArcMap.
- Use color ramps (blues to reds) to show differences in intensity in isoline maps.
- Use darker colors to denote high values and light colors to denote low values (Harries, 1999).
- Grayscales are always a good choice when unsure about color choices.

Symbolization

The other important factor that crime mappers will deal with in map design is the choice of **symbols** for their map. As with color choices, symbolization is vitally important because it allows a user to convey a large amount of information quickly and easily. There are three basic symbols in all maps, **points**, which are used to mark specific locations such as crime incidents, **lines**, which are used to symbolize roads or rivers, and **areas**, which are used to symbolize the form and shape of jurisdictions or boundaries. Symbolization can make things more clear for a reader such as when different symbols are used to denote different crime types or when graduated points are used to denote differences in amount of crimes at a location or in an area. However, symbol size and shape can also confuse and mislead just as easily. If symbols are used that are too big for the scale of the map, the reader will be mislead as to the location of the crime, the value of incidents being portrayed, or its importance in relation to other information on the map. Similarly, making all non-violent crime symbols larger than the symbols used for violent crimes can mislead readers into believing violent crime is not as big a problem. Other potential problems include the emotional connection to certain symbol types, such as using little chalk outlines to portray homicide locations as in Figure 5.3 (www.mappingcrime.org). Map makers must always be cognizant of the audience of their map and the potential to mislead, confuse, or disturb the reader through the choices they make as to symbolization.

Suggestions for Symbolization

- Symbol size should match map scale.
- Symbol shapes should be logical and not confuse or mislead.
- Use graduated symbols to denote differences in amount and different symbol types to denote differences in crime types.
- Use color when necessary and make choices that are logical and not distracting.

Labeling

The last of the three major issues in map design is labeling. **Labeling** involves identifying places and geographic features on a map (Monmonier, 1993). As with color and symbol choices, label choices can help facilitate understanding of maps as well as confuse and mislead readers. The biggest issues with labeling revolve around font type and size, proximity to the place/feature, and the amount of labeling. Poorly chosen font size and font type can lead to reader confusion as when labels are too small to read or so large, they overlap different feature making it difficult to associate a label with the correct feature see Figure 5.4, (www.mappingcrime.org). This is closely related to proximity, which deals with the association of labels with their given place or geographic feature. If a label is too close or not close enough to a place or feature, it can lead to confusion as to the correct place that is being labeled. Figure 5.5 (www.mappingcrime.org) provides an example of how poor proximity labeling can lead to confusion in map interpretation. Finally, too much and too little labeling can also lead to confusion for readers. Too little labeling can leave readers wondering which places are which, whereas too much labeling can overwhelm a map and make interpretation next to impossible. Figure 5.6 (www.mappingcrime.org) provides examples of how too little and too much labeling can confuse the interpretation of a map. Importantly, as with choosing colors and symbols, labeling is part art, in that a map maker must attempt to get the right feel for how much, how close, and what size and type a label should be. In crime maps features that are usually labeled include major roads, jurisdictional boundaries (Counties), major cities and towns, landmarks, and in some cases specific incidents.

Labeling Suggestions

- Font size should fit with the scale of the map. The larger the scale, the more detailed labeling that is possible.
- Do not use strange looking fonts; stick with fonts such as Times New Romans.
- Labels should not be right on top of a feature so as to obscure the symbol you are labeling.
- Labels should not be on top of each other. Make sure that labels of different features do not overlap each other.
- Strike a balance between too much and too little labeling.

Other Issues in Map Design

In addition to color and symbolization choices, map makers must also consider several other important issues when designing a map. One important issue is internal organization. **Internal Organization** is the alignment of the different map elements in the layout. It should be remembered that the main focus of the map is the map itself and not the map elements. Thus, make the map elements complementary to the map frame and not distracting. A final important aspect is the **focus of attention** of the map. Focus of attention is the idea that people read maps as they would a page in a book, and thus the main focus of the layout should be the main map (Harries, 1999). Ideally the key issue to be addressed in a map would be closest to the center of the page as possible.

PROJECT: DESIGNING EFFECTIVE MAPS

1. Create a new theme and add the following themes:
   a. Houston.shp
   b. Homicides.shp
   c. Bars.shp
   d. Schools.shp
2. Create two different layouts, taking special consideration of the suggestions given in this section.

Map A: Portrait map showing point locations of all homicide incidents for August through December (Homicide Codebook from www.mappingcrime.org) and their relation to school locations. In addition you must insert the HPD symbol to the map. Refer to the suggestions in this section to help you in designing your map. Remember you must query the homicides theme to get only those incidents involving incidents from August through December.

> **Audience:** Public
> **Medium:** Large format print

Map B: Landscape map showing homicide rates by census tract for all of Houston and their relation to bar locations.

> **Audience:** Research
> **Medium:** PowerPoint presentation (electronic media).

Check your map design against the authors' maps on-line at www.mappingcrime.org

REVIEW QUESTIONS

1. Explain the difference between large scale and small scale and discuss their importance to map design.

2. Where does map design take place in ArcMap?

3. What two map features are controlled through a dynamic link to the view mode?

4. What four editing changes can be made to the basic map elements?

5. What are two of the most important things to consider when designing a map?

6. Audience and medium most directly impact what aspects of map design?

FURTHER READINGS

Map Design Readings

Dent, B.D. (1993). Cartography: Thematic Map Design. Second Edition. Dubuque, IA: William C. Brown.

Monmonier, M. (1993). Mapping it Out: Expository Cartography for the Humanities and Social Sciences. Chicago: University of Chicago Press.

Monmonier, M. (1996). How to Lie with Maps. Chicago: University of Chicago Press.

Basic Spatial Analysis

Now that you have a basic understanding of how to use ArcGIS to enter, query, manipulate, and display crime data you will begin to learn how to perform spatial analysis. While many researchers and police departments create maps that are little more than point maps of crime incidents when analyzing crime patterns, spatial analysis is vital to determining true spatial patterns. Specifically, in order to determine if crime incidents are truly random or clustered in space, spatial analysis must be conducted. Section II begins the process of informing students how to assess spatial patterns by introducing students to several basic spatial analysis techniques commonly used to assess spatial patterns. Workbook Chapter 6 discusses proximity analysis techniques such as buffer analysis and geographic selection. Workbook Chapter 7 introduces students to spatial distribution measures such as mean center, standard deviational ellipse, and spatial autocorrelation. Finally, Workbook Chapter 8 discusses distance analysis measures such as nearest neighbor analysis. As mentioned earlier, the workbook is not designed to be a comprehensive spatial statistics textbook as such an undertaking is far beyond the scope and purpose of this book. Rather, the workbook is designed to introduce students to spatial analysis techniques, their importance to crime analysis, when to use them, and how to interpret their results. For more comprehensive and technical discussions of the techniques discussed in these and subsequent chapters, students should pursue the readings in the "Further Readings" section of each chapter.

Proximity Analysis

GOALS: 1. Understand proximity analysis and its importance to crime mapping.

2. Understand how to conduct buffer analysis.

3. Understand how to conduct geographic selection.

4. Perform proximity analysis exercises.

INTRODUCTION

Up to this point, the workbook has focused almost solely on providing students with an understanding of how to use a GIS to enter, manipulate, query, and display crime data. While developing a basic understanding of ArcGIS is important to effective crime mapping, equally as essential is understanding how to perform spatial analysis of crime data to assess crime patterns and distributions. Workbook Chapter 6 introduces the student to basic spatial analysis through its discussion of proximity analysis techniques. Specifically, students will learn how to perform buffer analysis and geographic selection to answer specific questions about crime data.

WHAT IS PROXIMITY ANALYSIS AND WHY USE IT?

Proximity analysis is a term used to describe several techniques used to assess the proximity of crime incidents to other geographic features. Proximity analysis techniques are commonly used to determine how many crimes occur within a set distance of a specific location or class of locations. An example of this type of analysis is determining how many registered sex offenders are living within 500 feet of schools, an increasingly popular analysis with the increase in sex offender registration policies. While proximity analysis does not involve any spatial statistics and is rather basic in its creation and interpretation, it is an important part of spatial analysis because of its utility in answering everyday questions concerning crime incident locations and patterns. However, because proximity analysis is rather simple in its analysis functions, it is limited in its utility. Specifically, proximity analysis cannot determine randomness or clustering of incidents or provide any other useful statistical information, it is simply a set of techniques for determining the proximity of incidents to geographic features or locations.

The main methods of proximity analysis are buffer zones and geographic selection. **Buffer zones** are usually circles that are drawn around specific geographic features or locations at user-defined distances. The distance used for creating a buffer zone is not a constant and is usually dependent on either an investigative or analytical purpose (Harries, 1999). The example above involving sex offender zones around schools would

249

involve a buffer zone of 500 feet around every school in a jurisdiction, but this distance could easily be increased to any distance the user desired. Because the buffer zone distance is user defined and guidelines are non-existent for their creation, careful thought must go into the investigative or analytic purpose behind the creation of the buffer zone. As will be made clear in completing the exercises, the distance used in buffer zone creation greatly impacts the results of proximity analysis. Because of its ease of creation and interpretation, buffer zone analysis is one of the more common methods of basic spatial analysis. Specific examples of buffer zone analysis include:

- **Sex Offender Registration:** Used to determine if registered sex offenders are living too close to restricted areas such as school or parks.
- **Drug-Free Zones:** Used to determine if crimes are occurring within drug-free zones and are thus susceptible to stiffer penalties.
- **Alcohol-Related Crimes:** Used to determine the proximity of alcohol related crimes to alcohol-related establishments such as bars and liquor stores.
- **Probationers/Parolees:** Used to determine if probationer/parolee residences violate probation/parole conditions by being too close to specific locales (schools, bars, etc.).

The other major proximity analysis technique is geographic selection. **Geographic selection** is a technique that allows the user to select layer features that are within a specified distance of a different layer's features. Specifically, a user can select all homicides that are within 0.25 miles of a school or within 1,000 feet of a bar location. There are three main differences between geographic selection and buffer zone analysis. First, in geographic selection no graphic zones are actually drawn as with buffer zone analysis. While some find this beneficial because it makes it easier to analyze the selected features (they are highlighted as with a query), others would rather have the graphic zones for visual impact. A second difference is that as with queries (Workbook Chapter 4), a new layer can easily be created from the results of a geographic selection. This can be highly beneficial for analysis and visualization and is a feature that is often used by researchers. Finally, more advanced queries can be performed with the results of a geographic selection. Once a geographic selection has been conducted, further geographic selections can be conducted with the results or advanced queries can be conducted with the geographic selection results through the query builder (Workbook Chapter 4). For example if a user performs a geographic selection for all homicides within half mile of schools, they can then perform a query on the results in which they find all victims under age 18. This is a particularly valuable tool for looking at specific crimes or offender types in conjunction with proximity to specific geographic features.

BUFFER ZONE ANALYSIS

1. Open ArcMap, select "A new empty map," and click OK.
2. Click the Add data button and maneuver on the C drive to the "CMLab Exercises" folder and then select "Chapter 6."
3. From the Chapter 6 folder, select the following layers:
   a. Houston.shp
   b. Homicides.shp
   c. Bars.shp
4. Make all three of these layers viewable and edit their appearance to make the homicides easily distinguishable from the bars.
5. Click on the Arc Toolbox icon.

6. Click on the "+" sign next to Analysis toolbox, and then click on the "+" next to the Proximity toolbox.
7. Double-click on the "Buffer" tool.
8. Under the "Input Features," select "Bars" from the drop-down menu.
9. Under "Output Features," use the default path, which will save the buffers in the Chapter 6 folder as "Bars_Buffer.shp."
10. Make sure that "Linear field" is selected, and type a 1 in the open frame below it. This is the unit of distance we are going to make for our buffers around our bars.
11. Next. From the drop-down menu next to the distance field, select "miles."
12. Finally, under "Dissolve Type," select "All" from the drop-down menu.
13. Click on the OK button in order to calculate the buffers, which will appear on the screen when ArcMap is finished. Depending on your computer, the creation of the buffers and the dissolving of the buffer lines may take a few minutes. Figure 6.1 (www.mappingcrime.org) shows you how your map should look like when you have finished.

Interpretation: You should now see circles of 1 mile in diameter around every bar location in Houston. In order to use this analytically, you can zoom in on specific areas to count the number of homicides within the buffers. If you zoom in on the city center, you will notice that all homicides are within 1 mile of a bar and that the buffers are difficult to see because there are so many bars close together. This illustrates that importance of choosing a buffer distance wisely as this has little practical impact other than to tell the student that there are a lot of bars in Houston, so many that homicides are certain to occur near a bar.

Tip: You can edit the color and outline of the buffers in order to make it easier to interpret.

1. Click on the layer color in order to edit its appearance. Change the fill color to "no color," this will make the buffers clear.
2. Next increase the "Outline Width" to 2 by clicking on the up arrow next to the outline width. This will change the weight of the buffer zones making them darker in appearance.
3. Finally, in order to add color to the buffer zone lines, select a color of your choice in the "Outline Color" menu.
4. Once you are done with these three alterations to the buffer, click on the OK button. You should now be able to see the buffer much more clearly and thus be able to analyze the relationship of homicides to bars more easily.

GEOGRAPHIC SELECTION

1. Under the view menu, select "Data Frame" in order to create a new data view for which to conduct the next exercise. After you have added a new data frame, add the following layers from Chapter 6 in the "CMLab Exercises" folder.
   a. Houston.shp
   b. Homicides.shp
   c. Schools.shp
2. Make all three of these layers viewable and edit their appearance to make the homicides easily distinguishable from the schools.
3. Under the Selection menu, select "Select by Location."
4. When the Select by Location box appears, you will notice several drop-down menus that allow you customize your geographic selection. The first menu is the "I want to" menu, which determines what kind of location selection you will

be doing. For our purposes, and for most commonly conducted analyses that are performed, the operation conducted is "select features from." This operation simply allows you to select features from a current layer or layers based on some kind of geographic relationship.

5. The next menu is the "the following layer(s)," which lists all of the available layers that can be selected from. In this example, put a check mark in the box next to homicides.

6. The next drop-down menu is the "That" menu. This menu allows you to choose the geographic relationship that is to be selected on, such as "are within a distance of." Under this menu, there are 11 options allowing the user to have a wide range of choices in their selection methods. For this example, scroll down and select **"Are Within Distance Of."** Thus, for this example we are selecting all homicides that are within a specified distance of something, which will be determined in the next two menus.

7. The next drop-down menu is the **"the features in this layer"** menu, which allows the user to chose the layer that you want your active layer (Homicides) to be selected if they are within a specified distance of. In this case select Schools, because we want to select all homicides within a specified distance of school locations. Importantly, you can choose from any other layer that has been added to the view.

8. The final aspect of the geographic selection is the "apply a buffer to the features" menu, which allows the user to determine the distance to be used for the selection. In this case, type a 1 in the first box and scroll down to miles in the second box. Thus our query will select all homicides that occurred within 1 mile of schools. It is important to note that you can type smaller distances than 1 mile such as 0.1 mile. Moreover, you can also change the distance to any units you desire (feet, kilometers, etc.) simply by scrolling through the drop down in the second box.

9. When you are ready, click on Apply. This will select all of the homicides within 1 mile of schools and make them yellow. Figure 6.2 (www.mappingcrime.org) shows you how your map should look like after the theme selection is complete.

Options for Theme Select Results

A. Create new Layer: You can create a new layer of just the selected homicides by right clicking on the homicide layer and selecting "Create Layer from Selected Features" under the Selection menu (see Workbook Chapter 4 for more instructions). This will allow you to manipulate and edit a new layer and is beneficial if you need to analyze or view only these selected features.

B. Clear Selections: You can clear the current selections by clicking on the Selection menu and scrolling down to "Clear Selected features." This will clear all selected features, allowing you to return your view to the one before the selection process begun. This is recommended when you want to start the geographic selection process over from the beginning.

C. Advanced Query: You can perform a more advanced query by either using the Select by Attributes builder (see Workbook Chapter 4) or using the geographic selection option again. In order to query from the selected results, the user must choose the correct layer in the "the following layers" option. In this example, the layer would be "Homicides Selection." This is a particularly useful option as it allows the user to first select all incidents within a specific distance of a geographic feature and then query those results further based on some other important information such as offender type. An example would be to geographically select all incidents within 500 feet of schools and then query those results to find all drug-related crimes, thus providing information of all drug crimes within 500 feet of schools.

Interpretation of Geographic Selection Results: The results of a geographic selection are interpreted in the same manner as buffer zone results. In fact the results are easier to interpret simply because they are selected features and thus an accurate count of the incidents can be gained by simply right-clicking on the layer that was selected from and choosing the "Open Attribute Table" option after the geographic selection is complete and looking at the data line under the attributes table. In the example above, 296 of the 536 homicides that occurred in Houston occurred within 1 mile of a school.

EXERCISES

Buffer Zone Exercise: Conduct two different buffer zone analyses to determine the extent that homicides occur near bars.

> **Map A:** Buffer zone of 1 mile around bar locations.
> **Map B:** Buffer zone of 1,000 feet around bar locations.

Compare your results to the correct analysis on the textbook webpage www.mappingcrime.org

Geographic Selection Exercise: Conduct two different geographic selection exercises to determine the extent that homicides occur near schools.

Map A: Geographic selection of all homicides within 0.5 miles of schools.
Map B: Geographic selection of all homicides within 0.5 miles of schools *and* the victims below 18 years of age. See the Code Book in Appendix C for victim age information and see Workbook Chapter 4 for information on how to conduct queries.

Compare your results to the correct analysis on the textbook webpage www.mappingcrime.org

REVIEW QUESTIONS

1. What is proximity analysis?

2. How is proximity limited in its utility?

3. What are some common uses of buffer zone analysis?

4. List the three main differences between buffer zone analysis and geographic selection analysis.

Spatial Distribution Analysis

GOALS: 1. Understand spatial distribution analysis and its importance to crime mapping.

2. Understand mean center analysis.

3. Understand standard deviation analysis.

4. Understand spatial autocorrelation analysis.

5. Perform spatial distribution analysis exercises.

INTRODUCTION

While Workbook Chapter 6 introduced students to spatial analysis of crime data through a discussion of proximity analysis techniques, these techniques were fairly basic and without statistical significance. Workbook Chapter 7 however introduces students to more advanced spatial analysis through a discussion of first-order spatial analysis techniques. **First-order analysis techniques** are a group of techniques that describe the general spatial pattern of crime incidents such as where the distribution is centered, how far it spreads, and in what direction it disperses (Levine, 2002). Thus, first-order analysis techniques provide a good *general* description of the distribution of crime incidents as to its average location, movements, and directional change through time (LeBeau, 1987). Specific techniques to be discussed include centrographic measures such as mean center and standard deviation analyses as well as spatial auto-correlation analysis. As mentioned earlier, this chapter is not intended to provide an in-depth discussion of the assumptions and statistical methods behind each technique. Rather it is designed to provide the student a basic introduction as to how to use these techniques to analyze crime distributions. Students seeking more in-depth discussion concerning these techniques are encouraged to pursue the readings in the "Further Readings" section at the end of this chapter.

MEAN CENTER ANALYSIS

One of the most commonly used first-order techniques is **mean center** analysis. The mean center is by far the simplest technique used to describe a spatial distribution and is akin to the mean of a series of numbers in regular statistics (Levine, 2002). In technical terms, the mean center is the average location or center of gravity of the spatial distribution of a phenomenon (Levine, 2002). Le Beau (1987) describes the mean center of a distribution of incidents as "a synthetic point or location representing the average location of a phenomenon." In other words, the mean center provides the user with a point that is the approximate center of a distribution of crime incidents. The utility of mean center analysis is its ability to compare the distribution of different crimes or the same crime at different times. Figure 7.1 (www.mappingcrime.org) shows two different maps with the results of mean center analyses. Map A shows the mean centers for both robbery and burglary incidents in Houston. The mean center for robbery is close to the city center whereas the mean center for burglary is closer to the suburb area, indicating that the spatial distributions of robbery and burglary are very different. Map B provides the mean centers for robbery incidents for two separate months. In this case, the mean centers are almost on top of each other, indicating that the distribution of robbery incidents stayed fairly consistent spatially between the two months.

While the mean center is a good measure of the spatial distribution of incidents, it is subject to measurement problems based on the distribution of the incidents. Specifically, the mean center is prone to being influenced heavily by spatial outliers or odd-shaped incident patterns. Figure 7.2 shows two maps representing the results of two different mean center analyses (www.mappingcrime.org). Map A shows the results of a mean center analysis where the distribution of incidents is L shaped. In this analysis, the mean center is located in the middle of the L-shaped distribution outside of the actual incident pattern. Map B shows the results of a mean center analysis for a bimodal distribution of incidents, or incident pattern with two different areas of concentration. In this case, the mean center is in between the two clusters of incidents, which, while technically is the center of the distribution, is misrepresentative of the actual distribution of incidents. In both examples, the mean center results placed the mean center of the distribution outside of the actual distribution. This illustrates the point that users must be aware of the nature of their distribution for the mean center to be a credible measure (Stephenson, 1980). In the examples above, the user should possibly use a different spatial distribution technique or, in the case of the bimodal distribution, conduct mean center analyses on both parts of the distribution.

Performing Mean Center Analysis in Crimestat

The directions provided on how to conduct the various statistical analyses within Crimestat are abbreviated instructions. For a complete set of instructions as well as the rationale and theory behind each of the various techniques, download and read the Crimestat III manual from the textbook webpage (www.mappingcrime.org). Follow the directions in Appendix B in order to install Crimestat III on your computer.

1. Double-click on the Crimestat shortcut on your desktop or wherever you have placed the program. When the Crimestat splash screen appears, click anywhere in the screen to advance to the main menu.
2. When the main menu appears, you will see four main tabs, Data setup, Spatial description, Spatial modeling, and Options. These are the four main sections of Crimestat, each of which has numerous subheadings that will be explored more fully as necessary (for a full explanation of Crimestat and its many uses, download the Crimestat 2.0 manual from the textbook webpage, www.mappingcrime.org).
3. **Data Setup:** In order to conduct any type of analysis within Crimestat, you must first enter data in to the program. In the case of a mean center analysis, all that is necessary is data should be added under the **Primary File** tab.
4. With the Primary File selected, click on the Select Files button on the top right corner of the screen. This will allow you to navigate to the data file that you wish to use for analysis. In all analyses conducted in Crimestat, the Primary File is the default data file. Importantly, some analyses that will be conducted later in the workbook will require data to be entered into the secondary file as well as the Reference File.

5. Navigate on the C drive to the "CMLab Exercises" folder and then select "Chapter 7." Within Chapter 7, select "Homicides.dbf" and click OK, which takes you back to the main menu. Under the Variable column, all of the different variables will now have Homicides.dbf, and its path, as the file name. Notice that the default file type is .dbf, indicating that the file is a database file and not a shapefile that is used in Arcview and ArcMap. While .dbf is the default, if you scroll down the file type, you will see that Crimestat will allow you to input several file types as well as make connections to outside database managers.

6. In the variable section are four different columns, Name, File, Column, and Missing values. **Name** provides the name of the different variables in Crimestat, such as X, Y, Weight, Intensity, Time, Directional, and Distance. **File** provides the name of the file that is currently the primary file for the analysis. **Column** controls the selection of the variable within the file being analyzed and **Missing values** allows users to define how missing values are handled in their data.

7. **Defining Variables:** After selecting your data file to be analyzed, the next step is to inform Crimestat which variables within your data file contain the X and Y coordinates. This is an essential step as Crimestat uses X and Y coordinates to perform the analyses, and thus unless variables containing these coordinates have been identified, Crimestat will not be able to perform the analysis. In this example, for the X variable, scroll down in the column field until you find the variable named X_COORD, and for the Y variable, select Y_COORD.

8. **Setting Coordinates and Data Units:** The final step in setting up the Primary file is to select the coordinate system and data units. Crimestat is capable of performing analysis on data using several different types of coordinate systems including Spherical, Euclidian, and Angles and their corresponding data units such as decimal degrees, feet, and meters. For our purpose, make sure that spherical coordinates and decimal degrees are selected.

9. **Mean Center Setup:** Click on the Spatial Description tab and then click on the Spatial Distribution subtab. You should see that Crimestat provides several techniques that cover spatial distribution, more than will be discussed in this workbook (for more discussion on these other techniques, see the Crimestat manual).

10. Place a check mark in the box to the left of the line stating "**Mean Center and Standard Distance (Mcsd).**" This means that we have chosen to conduct a mean center and standard distance analysis. Importantly, in conducting this analysis, several centrographic analyses will be conducted, some of which will be discussed more fully in this chapter.

11. Click on the **Save Results To** button to the right of the check box. In the "Save Output to" box, select Arcview SHP and then click on the browse button (Crimestat lets the user select the method of the output from Arcview Shapefiles to Mapinfo MIF files; for our purposes always use Arcview SHP files). Navigate to the Chapter 7 folder within the CMLab Exercises folder and name the file **mean**. Click OK.

12. When you return to the Spatial Distribution screen, click on the Compute button in the lower left hand side. This will start Crimestat conducting the mean center analysis.

13. **Results:** When Crimestat completes the mean center analysis, a results screen will appear showing you in a text format the results of the analysis. Notice that Crimestat has computed several centrographic measures, including the mean center, geometric mean, harmonic mean, standard distance deviation (SDD), and the standard deviation of the X and Y coordinates (XYD). The geometric and marmonic means are two alternative centrographic measures that discount extreme values better than the mean center. They are not often used in crime analysis but are included in Crimestat and calculated when the mean center is calculated. The SDD and **standard deviation of X and Y coordinates** (XYD) are standard deviation measures and will be discussed more later in this chapter.

Tip: If you notice that there is no information for the mean or the results of the three different means are very different, then you probably have a problem with either your primary file setup or your data.

14. Close the results box by clicking on the close button, minimize Crimestat, and open ArcMap and select "A new empty map" and add the Houston.shp layer from Chapter 7 in the CMLab Exercises folder.

15. **Adding the Mean Center Shapefile:** Click on the **Add Data** button in the view and navigate to the Chapter 7 folder, where you saved the results of the mean center analysis. Look for a file named "**Mcmean.shp.**" The **MC** in front of the word mean (the name you used to save the results) stands for mean center. Every time Crimestat performs an analysis in which output is generated as a shapefile, it places a prefix in front of the name you use to save the results. This prefix is designed to make it easier for the user to identify results. Other prefixes generated during mean center analysis include:

   GM: geometric mean

   HM: harmonic mean

   XYD: standard deviation of the X and Y coordinates

   SDD: standard distance deviation

16. After you have added the Mcmean.shp file to the view, make it active. As Figure 7.3 (www.mappingcrime.org) illustrates, the mean center should be fairly close to the middle of the map near the city center.

   Interpretation of Mean Center Results: The mean center in the city center indicates that the approximate middle point of homicides in Houston is near the city center. Importantly, if we were to conduct mean center analyses for different crimes, we could determine how similar the distributions were. Moreover, mean center analysis could also be conducted on homicide distributions for other years in order to determine the degree that the distribution of homicides moves over time.

   Tip: The color, shape, and size of the mean center can be edited in the same manner as any other symbol within ArcMap.

STANDARD DEVIATION ANALYSIS

Another important first-order statistics used in analyzing crime distributions is the standard deviation. Measures of **standard deviation** are essentially two-dimensional versions of a basic standard deviation measure in statistics. The utility of standard deviation measures in analyzing crime distributions is that they can describe the dispersion, orientation, and shape of the distribution of crime incidents (Levine, 2002). As with mean center analysis, the main use of standard deviation analyses is to compare the distributions of different crimes or the same crime at different times. By using the various standard deviation analysis techniques, the user can compare the dispersion, orientation, and shape of different crime distributions. Crimestat calculates three different measures of standard deviation, the standard deviation of X and Y coordinates XYD, the standard distance deviation SDD, and the **standard deviational ellipse** (SDE), all of which will be discussed separately.

The XYD provides a simple measure of the dispersion of a crime distribution. Its output is a rectangle, with rectangles that are longer than they are tall having a more east–west orientation. Conversely output that is taller than it is wide has a more north–south distribution. Figure 7.4 shows the simulated results of XYD analysis for both auto theft and car jacking incidents in Houston (www.mappingcrime.org). The box representing the XYD results for auto theft is wider than that of the box representing the XYD results of car jacking, indicating that the dispersion of auto theft is more east–west than that of car jacking which is a more north–south dispersion. Unfortunately, one of the problems associated with XYD analysis is that it is unable to provide any information about the shape of the distribution, as it is solely a measure of the dispersion of a distribution.

A second measure of standard deviation is the SDD or standard distance as it is often called. The **standard distance (SDD)** is the closest to a two-dimensional equivalent to the standard deviation of the three standard deviation measures included in Crimestat. This measure is considered a more useful measure of the dispersion of a spatial distribution from the mean center than XYD analysis (Le Beau, 1987). Its main improvement of XYD analysis is that it provides a single summary statistic of the dispersion of crime incidents as opposed to two separate statistics that are created in XYD analysis (dispersion of X and dispersion of Y) (Levine, 2002). As with other standard deviation analyses, its benefit to analyzing crime distributions is that it can compare the dispersion of two different crime types or the distributions of the same crime at two different time periods. Figure 7.5 shows the simulated results of SDD analysis for both auto theft and car jacking in Houston (www.mappingcrime.org). As opposed to XYD analysis, the results of SDD analysis are ellipses that show the dispersion of the two distributions. In this case, auto theft with the bigger ellipse has a wider dispersion of incidents than does car jacking with its much smaller ellipse, indicating that car jacking incidents occur in a smaller area than auto thefts.

The final standard deviation measure to be discussed is SDE analysis. SDE is similar to standard distance (SDD) except that it is better able to represent distributions that are skewed in one direction or another, a common occurrence with crime patterns (Levine, 2002). As opposed to SDD, SDE analysis is capable of handling skewed distributions, thus providing a measure of the distributions shape and orientation. As we know, few crime distributions are perfectly symmetrical, most are skewed in one direction or another based on various factors such as built environment, criminal opportunities, and other factors. Thus, SDE is an excellent measure for assessing the spatial dispersion, orientation, and shape of crime distributions at different time periods or the distributions of two different crime types. Figure 7.6 (www.mappingcrime.org) shows simulated results of SDE analysis for car jacking and auto theft in Houston. The ellipse for the auto thefts is larger than that of car jackings and is pointed more in an east–west direction than the smaller more north–south ellipse representing car jackings. This indicates that the distribution of auto thefts is more dispersed and more differently shaped than the distribution of car jackings.

PERFORMING STANDARD DEVIATION ANALYSES

1. If you have left Crimestat open from performing mean center analysis, then go to the Spatial Distribution subtab under the spatial description tab. If, however, you have closed the Crimestat, then follow the directions above for performing the mean center analysis. Importantly, if you have already completed the above exercise, then the XYD and SDD analyses have already been completed and the results should be saved in Chapter 7.

2. Once you have selected "homicides.shp" for the primary file and completed the rest of the setup as described above for mean center analysis, go to the Spatial Distribution subtab and place a check mark in the box next to "Standard Deviational Ellipse." This will tell Crimestat to conduct an SDE analysis.

   Tip: If you still have a check mark in the box next to "Mean center and Standard Distance," you may want to deselect it. Crimestat is capable of running multiple analyses at once and will thus perform the mean center analysis again. While this is not a problem, it may take more time to complete the SDE analysis.

3. Click on the "Save Results to" box next to the SDE analysis and follow the instructions from above, saving the results as a .SHP file in the Chapter 7 folder. Importantly, save the file as "ellipse" in order to make it easier to identify the results when you add them to the view.
4. Click OK, and when you return to the main screen, click compute.
5. When the analysis is completed, close the results window and minimize Crimestat. Open ArcMap and create a new view and add Houston.shp (if ArcMap is already open from creating the mean center, then simply make the mean center not viewable).
6. Add the following layers, all of which should be contained in the Chapter 7 folder:
   a. Xydmean.shp: XYD
   b. Sddmean.shp: SDD
   c. Sddellipse.shp: SDE
7. As illustrated in Figure 7.7 (www.mappingcrime.org), as you make them viewable you will see that they overlap and are fairly consistent spatially. To make it easier to see the three different analyses, make all three themes clear and their outlines thicker and of different colors.

Interpretation of Standard Deviation Results: As discussed above, all three techniques provide a measure of the dispersion of the crime distribution, in this case homicides in Houston Texas. The different analyses all point to the fact that homicide is fairly dispersed in Houston with a slightly more east–west orientation than north–south. Moreover, the SDE analysis indicates that the shape of the distribution is slightly skewed but not much. Importantly, the SDE and SDD results are almost identical, indicating only a slight skew in the distribution toward the upper right corner.

SPATIAL AUTOCORRELATION ANALYSIS

The last spatial distribution methods that will be discussed are used for determining the degree of spatial autocorrelation present in a crime distribution. Spatial autocorrelation is an extremely important idea for the analysis of crime distributions, because it provides information on the degree to which the locations of crime incidents are related to each other (Levine, 2002). When the location of one crime incident (robbery location) is related to the location of another crime incident (separate robbery location), it is termed **positive spatial autocorrelation**. Generally, incidents that exhibit positive spatial autocorrelation are termed **clustered**. Thus robbery incidents that are clustered together in a specific section of a city exhibit positive spatial autocorrelation. Conversely, when the location of one crime incident (robbery location) is unrelated to the location of another crime location (separate robbery location), it is termed **negative spatial autocorrelation**. Crime incidents that exhibit negative spatial autocorrelation are termed **spatially independent** or **uniformly dispersed**. Thus, robbery incidents that are uniformly distributed throughout a city would exhibit negative spatial autocorrelation. It is important to note that in cities most social phenomenon such as restaurants locations, population centers, and ethnic groups exhibit positive spatial autocorrelation (Levine, 2002). This is important for crime research in that crime distributions may exhibit spatial autocorrelation simply because everything in the city exhibits positive spatial autocorrelation. While this measure is not used a great deal by practitioners conducting crime analysis, it is an important statistical tool for those conducting research into spatial patterns. Specifically, spatial autocorrelation measures are often used to determine the degree to which aggregate level data, such as crime rates at the census block or census tract level, are clustered within a city. In addition, these measures can also be used to determine the difference in spatial autocorrelation between two different crime types or the same crime at two different time periods.

The two main tests for spatial autocorrelation are **Moran's I** and **Geary's C**, both of which are used to determine the degree of spatial autocorrelation in aggregate data and both of which are included in Crimestat. Importantly, because these measures are for determining spatial autocorrelation in aggregate data, point data that have been used thus far for analysis will not work. Thus, in order to test for spatial autocorrelation using Moran's "I" or Geary's "C," incident level data must be aggregated to a zone level such as census tracts, police districts, etc. **Moran's I** applies to zones that have associated continuous variables attached to them (census tracts with homicide rates), and it works by calculating the value of the variable at one location with the value of that variable at all other locations (Anselin, 1992). The output of a Moran's "I" test is similar to a correlation coefficient, in that it varies from −1.0 to +1.0 where positive values indicate positive spatial autocorrelation and thus clustering, and negative values indicate negative spatial autocorrelation and thus spatial randomness (Anselin, 1992). When nearby values have similar values (high homicide rate next to high homicide rate), the "I" value is higher, conversely when nearby values have dissimilar values (high homicide rate next to low homicide rate), the "I" value is low (Levine, 2002). Thus, an analysis of homicide rates at the census track level that produced an "I" value of 0.875 would indicate very high positive spatial autocorrelation and thus clustering of census tracts with high homicide rates. Conversely, an "I" value of −0.236 would indicate negative spatial autocorrelation and that census tracts with high homicide rates were randomly distributed near census tracts with low homicide rates.

The other test for spatial autocorrelation is **Geary's C**. Although both of these tests provide accurate measures of spatial autocorrelation, Geary's C is more sensitive to differences in small neighborhoods and works by looking at the squared deviations of observations (Levine, 2002). Because the measures are determined using different methods, the output and subsequent interpretation are also slightly different. Geary's C ranges from 0 to 2 with values of less than 1 indicating positive spatial autocorrelation and values greater than 1 indicating negative spatial autocorrelation. Thus if an analysis of homicide rates at the census tract level produced a "C" value of 0.658, it would indicate positive spatial autocorrelation or clustering of census tracts that have high homicide rates. Conversely if the same analysis produced a "C" value of 1.034, it would indicate negative spatial autocorrelation, or that census tracts with high homicide rates where near census tracts with low homicide rates.

PERFORMING MORAN'S I AND GEARY'S C

Because these measures are so similar in their analysis, how to conduct and interpret them will be discussed together.

1. Open Crimestat and add as the primary file Houston.shp from the Chapter 7 folder within the CMLab Exercises folder. This is the basemap for Houston, Texas, which contains various amounts of data that have been aggregated at the census tract level.
2. For the X and Y values, scroll down and select X_Coord and Y_Coord, respectively. In this case the X and Y coordinates are for the center of each census tract, as opposed to the actual location of each incident as in all other analyses performed so far.
3. **Intensity Variable:** Unlike other analyses, both Moran's "I" and Geary's "C" require what is called an **intensity variable** in order for them to be calculated correctly. As mentioned in the explanation of these statistics, both techniques work by analyzing values at the zone level. The intensity variable serves as the value for this analysis. For this example, scroll down and select **Homrate** (directly after Dblack). This variable is the homicide rate for each census tract in Houston, Texas.

4. Click on the Spatial Distribution subtab under the spatial description tab. Click in the boxes next to both Moran's "I" and Geary's "C." When you do this, you will notice that two boxes named "**Adjust for small distances**" become active with check marks. This is a statistical weight that attempts to ensure the statistical validity of the measures by taking into account the small distances between the zones. It is recommended that adjustment for small distances be used when analyzing zones that are very close together such as census tracts.

5. After this is complete, click the Compute button.

Interpretation of Moran's "I": In looking at the results, the two main things to be concerned with are the Moran's "I" and the normality significance (Z) scores. In this case the Moran's "I" is 0.075480 with a Z score of 31.749654, indicating positive spatial autocorrelation. As mentioned before high and positive "I" values indicate positive spatial autocorrelation. Thus according to the Moran's "I" with adjustment for small distances, homicide rates at the census tract level **are** clustered. In practical terms, census tracts with high homicide rates are near census tracts with high homicide rates and census tracts with low homicide rates are near other census tracts with low homicide rates.

Interpretation of Geary's "C": As with the Moran's "I" results, the two key values to consider in interpreting Geary's "C" are the "C" value and the Z value. As mentioned before, values under 1 indicate positive spatial autocorrelation, while values over 1 indicate negative spatial autocorrelation. Thus according to Geary's "C" with adjustment for small distances, homicide rates at the census tract level **are not** clustered. Rather, in contrast to the results of the Moran's "I," census tracts with high homicide rates are not near other census tracts with high homicide rates. The differing results between the Moran's "I" and the Geary's "C" can probably be attributed to the more sensitive nature of Geary's "C" at the neighborhood level. As mentioned above, Geary's "C" is more sensitive to small neighborhood differences and is probably picking up some of the census tracts with high homicide that are near census tracts with low homicide rates (see Figure 7.8 for visual inspection of the distribution).

> **Tip:** In determining spatial autocorrelation in aggregate level data, it is always wise to run both Moran's "I" and Geary's "C" and to thoroughly analyze the distribution you are analyzing. Analyzing the spatial differences **visually** can help with the interpretation of the results when there are disagreements between the measures (see Workbook Chapter 2 to learn how to create maps using aggregate data). In the example above, Geary's "C" appears to be more sensitive to the neighborhood differences in homicide rates at the census tract level.

EXERCISES

1. *Mean Center Analysis:* Conduct two different mean center analyses to determine the extent that the distribution of homicide changed between 1989 and 1991.

   Themes required: Houston.shp, 1989.shp, 1991.shp

   Map Product: Mean center for both 1989.shp and 1991.shp.

   Compare your results to the correct analysis on the textbook webpage www.mappingcrime.org

2. *Standard Deviation Analysis:* Conduct two different standard deviation analyses using all three different standard deviation techniques (XYD, SDD, SDE). Determine the degree to which the distribution of homicides changed from 1989 to 1991.

Themes required: Houston.shp, 1989.shp, 1991.shp

Map Product: XYD, SDD, and SDE analyses for both 1989.shp and 1991.shp. It may be visually easier to create three separate maps one for each different standard deviation analysis.

Compare your results to the correct analysis on the textbook webpage www.mappingcrime.org

3. *Spatial Autocorrelation Analysis:* Conduct two Moran's "I" and Geary's "C" analyses, one on adult homicide rates and one on juvenile homicide rates (see Appendix C for code book information for Houston.shp).

Themes required: Houston.shp

Map A: Adult homicide rate with Moran's "I" and Geary's "C" values

Map B: Juvenile homicide rate with Moran's "I" and Geary's "C" values

Compare your results to the correct analysis on the textbook webpage www.mappingcrime.org

REVIEW QUESTIONS

1. Define what the mean center is and list its benefits as well as its associated problems.

2. List the three different types of standard deviation analysis and discuss their differences.

3. Define spatial autocorrelation and discuss the difference between positive and negative spatial autocorrelations.

4. How do the uses for each of the spatial analysis techniques differ?

FURTHER READINGS

Cliff, A. and J. Ord (1973). *Spatial Autocorrelation.* London: Pion.

Cressie, N. (1991). *Statistics for Spatial Data.* New York: John Wiley and Sons, Inc.

Ebdon, D. (1988). *Statistics in Geography.* Oxford: Blackwell.

Langworthy, R. H. and E. Jefferis (1998). "The utility of standard deviational ellipses for project evaluation." Discussion paper, National Institute of Justice: Washington, DC.

LeBeau, James L. (1987). "The methods and measures of centrography and the spatial dynamics of rape." *Journal of Quantitative Criminology*, 3 (2), 125–141.

Levine, N. (2002). *Crimestat: A Spatial Statistics Program for the Analysis of Crime Incident Locations (v2.0).* Ned Levine and Associates, Houston, TX and the National Institute of Justice, Washington, DC. Available online at: http://www.icpsr.umich.edu/NACJD/crimestat.html

Stephenson, L. K. (1980). Centrographic Analysis of Crime. In Georges-Abeyie, D. E., and Harries, K. (eds.), *Crime: A Spatial Perspective.* New York: Columbia University Press, pp. 146–155.

Distance Analysis

GOALS: 1. Understand distance analysis and its importance to crime mapping.

2. Understand nearest neighbor analysis.

3. Understand edge effects.

4. Understand K-order nearest neighbor analysis.

5. Perform nearest neighbor analysis exercises.

INTRODUCTION

The final analysis technique that will be discussed in the basic spatial analysis section is distance analysis. Distance analysis is in a class of techniques called second-order techniques. Whereas first-order statistics such as the mean center and standard deviations informed users as to the shape, orientation, and dispersion of a distribution of crime incidents, second-order statistics provide information on the clustering of crime distributions. Specifically, second-order statistics provide information about whether or not there are areas within an overall distribution of crime incidents that are more concentrated or clustered than other parts of the distribution (Levine, 2002). These measures are most commonly used in crime mapping to compare the clustering of the distributions of two different crime types, to compare distributions of the same crime at two separate time periods, or as a precursor to hot spot analysis.

NEAREST NEIGHBOR INDEX

One of the most popular and easier to use distance analysis measures is the **nearest neighbor index**. The nearest neighbor index compares the distance between actual crime locations and the distances of a random distribution to determine if the incidents are closer than would be expected by chance (Levine, 2002). The actual index is a comparison of the average distance between a crime incident and its closest neighbor, with a distance between two incidents that would be expected by chance (Levine, 2002). When an Nna is conducted, it does not produce any output that can be plotted on a GIS, but rather produces an index value based around a value of 1.0. Those crime distributions where incidents are clustered more than would be expected by chance have Nna index values less than 1.0, with values closer to 0 showing increased clustering. Conversely, those crime distributions that are spatially dispersed or non-clustered would have Nna values above 1.0. Importantly, Nna analysis alone cannot show you which areas of the distribution may be clustered, only that there are areas where incidents are closer than would be expected by chance. As discussed above, Nna analysis is primarily useful in determining the difference in the clustering of two different crime types or the difference in clustering of the same crime at two separate time periods.

For example, a crime analyst wanting to determine if assaults are more clustered in January than in February could use Nna to give a measure of both crime distributions. If the January assaults have an Nna value of 0.3584 and the February assaults have an Nna value of 0.5691, then it would appear that January assaults are more concentrated than February assaults and are thus more likely to have "hot spots."

While Nna analysis can be useful for understanding the amount of clustering within a crime distribution, there are two main problems associated with it. The first problem relates to the method for which nearest neighbors are selected and is termed **edge effects**. In the real world, crime is often committed on the border of artificially created police jurisdiction, yet when it is analyzed rarely are crime data from two or more jurisdictions analyzed. The impact of this is that the nearest neighbor of a crime incident may be across a jurisdictional border where no data exists, causing the Nna program to select another incident from within the study area that may not be as close. Figure 8.1 (www.mappingcrime.org) illustrates this problem of edge effects. This is termed the edge effect in that crime incidents that are near a study area's border may increase the nearest neighbor index value artificially (Levine, 2002). A solution to this problem is to use a modified search area that limits the area searched to just the study area. Crimestat solves this problem by providing two different edge effects search options, which will be discussed more fully in the next section.

The other problem with Nna analysis is that it is only an indicator of first-order randomness, or the distance between one crime location and its nearest neighbor. Thus, Nna ignores the possible importance of the distance between a crime location and its second nearest neighbor, the third nearest, etc. or what is called **K-order nearest neighbor** (Levine, 2002). This is an important issue because it limits the ability of Nna analysis to that of just first-order analysis and prevents it from being useful in judging the degree of spatial randomness of the entire distribution. On the other hand, K-order nearest neighbor analysis allows for just such a use, providing an indication of the degree of clustering for the entire distribution and in essence a measure of spatial randomness for a distribution (Levine, 2002). Thus, the main benefit of K-order Nna is that it provides a more complete picture of the entire distribution than a simple Nna analysis. K-order Nna is used in the same manner as a simple Nna, in that it is useful in comparing the distribution of two different crime types or the distributions of the same crime at two different times. As with edge effects, Crimestat allows for the computation of K-order Nna, the interpretation and analysis of which will be discussed more in the next section.

Performing Nearest Neighbor Analysis

1. Open Crimestat and proceed to the Data setup tab and the primary Field subtab. Navigate to the Chapter 8 folder within the CMLab Folder and add Homicides.shp as the primary file (see Chapter 7 for more assistance).
2. Click on the Spatial Description tab and the **Distance Analysis** subtab.
3. Put a check mark in the empty box next to the **nearest neighbor analysis (Nna)**. Below this box are several other boxes related to both edge effects and K-order Nna. For our purposes, edge effects will be discussed now, with K-order Nna being discussed later in this section.

Border Correction: By default, Crimestat does not take into account edge effects, thus the None option is selected in the border correction section. However, Crimestat allows the user to choose from two different edge effects search methods, Rectangular and Circular. *The default uncorrected method is fine for most calculations;* however, if you feel your distribution may be subject to edge effects, it is suggested that you try computing the Nna values with and without considering edge effects.

4. After you have determined whether or not to use any border correction method, click on the Compute button.
5. Crimestat calculates ten different statistics in performing the Nna analysis; the most important for interpretation is the nearest neighbor index, which is at the bottom of the output.

Interpreting Output: For the sample data of Houston homicides, the nearest neighbor index was 0.43001, indicating that the distribution of homicide incidents in Houston is more clustered than would be expected by chance. Thus, if this analysis was to be used to determine if "hot spot" analysis should be conducted, it should be conducted because it is likely that there are homicide "hot spots" in Houston. Moreover, this Nna result could now be used as a baseline for comparison to other crime distributions or the distribution of homicide at a different time period to determine if it is more or less clustered.

K-ORDER NEAREST NEIGHBOR ANALYSIS

There are two main differences in conducting a K-order Nna and a first-order Nna, the number of nearest neighbors to be computed and the output created by the analysis. In order to fully analyze the output of K-order Nna, it is recommended that the output be exported to a spreadsheet program and a graph of the data made.

1. With the Homicides.shp as the primary data, click on the distance analysis subtab within the spatial description tab.
2. Put a check mark in the empty box next the **Nearest Neighbor Analysis (Nna)**.
3. Under the Nna box is a box that says "number of nearest neighbors to be computed." Replace the default "1" with "100." While any number of nearest neighbor analyses can be conducted, Crimestat recommends that no more than 100 be computed. Importantly, anything over "1" nearest neighbor calculation is technically a K-order Nna.
4. Click on the "Save Results to" box and save the output as a .dbf file. Navigate to the Chapter 8 folder within the CMLab folder and name the file K-order.
5. Click OK, and when you return to the main distance analysis screen, click the Compute button.

Analyzing the output: The main difference between the output of a Nna analysis and a K-order Nna analysis is that in a K-order analysis you have 100 different Nna index values instead of just one. As you scroll down through the Nna index values, you can see that the first Nna index value is identical to that produced in the simple Nna analysis (0.43001) and that the other 99 values range from 0.51840 to around 0.56120, indicating that there is clustering throughout the entire distribution. In order to make analysis and interpretation easier, we are going to import the results into Microsoft Excel and graph the Nna index values.

6. Open a spreadsheet program such as Microsoft Excel. When Excel opens, click on the Open File button and navigate to the Chapter 8 folder within the CMLab exercises folder.
7. Change the file type to be opened from "All Microsoft Excel Types" to **.dbf** files by scrolling down the file type box. Double-click on **Nnakorder** file to open the K-order output in Excel. You should now see four different columns of data 101 rows in length: ORDER, NNDISTANCE, EXPECTEDNN, and NNINDEX.
8. Highlight the **NNINDEX** column by clicking on the "D" above NNINDEX.
9. With the NNINDEX column highlighted, click on the **Insert** menu and select **Chart**.

10. When the Chart Wizard appears, select "Line" under Chart type, which will change the chart sub-type views on the right. Select the chart sub-type from the upper right corner and click Next.

11. The next window will provide you with a preview of the chart; click Finish to complete the chart.

Interpretation of Results: The graph shows a line representing the Nna index values over the 100 nearest neighbors that were computed. Figure 8.2 (www.mappingcrime.org) shows how the graph should look like. The line of Nna values starts out at around 0.4000 and immediately jumps up to over 0.5000, and then makes a fairly steep climb to over 0.5500, where it then smoothes out for the rest of the distribution. Because all of the values are below 1.0, it indicates that there is clustering throughout the entire distribution. Thus, the graph reinforces the analysis that the distribution of homicides exhibits spatial clustering on a whole.

EXERCISES

1. *Simple Nna:* Conduct two different Nna analyses to determine if there are differences in the clustering of homicides between 1989 and 1991.

   Themes required: Houston.shp, 1989.shp, 1991.shp

   Compare your results to the correct analysis on the textbook webpage www.mappingcrime.org

2. *K-order Nna:* Conduct two different K-order Nna analyses to determine if there are differences in the clustering of homicides between 1989 and 1991.

   Themes required: Houston.shp, 1989.shp, 1991.shp

   Compare your results to the correct analysis on the Textbook webpage (www.mappingcrime.org).

REVIEW QUESTIONS

1. Explain what distance analysis is.

2. How is distance analysis beneficial to crime mapping?

3. What does nearest neighbor analysis determine?

4. How is nearest neighbor analysis useful in analyzing crime distributions?

5. What are edge effects?

6. What is K-order Nna analysis and how does it differ from a simple Nna analysis.

FURTHER READINGS

Clark, P. J. and F. C. Evans (1954). "Distance to nearest neighbor as a measure of spatial relationships in populations". *Ecology*, 35, 445–453.

Cressie, N. (1991). *Statistics for Spatial Data*. New York: John Wiley and Sons, Inc.

Ebdon, D. (1988). *Statistics in Geography*. Oxford: Blackwell.

Levine, N. (2002). *Crimestat: A Spatial Statistics Program for the Analysis of Crime Incident Locations (v2.0)*. Ned Levine and Associates, Houston, TX and the National Institute of Justice, Washington, DC. Available on-line at: http://www.icpsr.umich.edu/NACJD/crimestat.html

Advanced Spatial Analysis

The third section of the workbook is devoted to providing the student with an introduction to more advanced spatial analysis techniques. The techniques discussed in Section II provided information on the shape, orientation, and dispersion of distributions as well as the general clustering of crime distributions. While this information is of primary importance in assessing spatial patterns of crime, in many situations we need to see where clusters of incidents are occurring. It is this clustering of incidents that Section III will primarily focus on. Specifically, the chapters in this section will provide students with an understanding of the primary techniques used in determining where high concentrations of crime are occurring and if these areas are experiencing change over time. Chapter 9 discusses "Hot Spot" analysis in general covering the main issues involved in this type of analysis as well as several major techniques used for determining "Hot Spot" locations. Chapter 10 introduces students to density mapping and kernel density interpolation, one of the best methods for determining high concentrations of crime. Finally, Chapter 11 discusses spatial dispersion mapping and duel kernel density analysis, techniques used for assessing changes in spatial patterns of crime over time. As mentioned several times throughout the text, the workbook is not designed to be a comprehensive spatial statistics textbook as such an undertaking is far beyond the scope and purpose of this book. Rather, the workbook is designed to introduce students to spatial analysis techniques, their importance to crime analysis, when to use them, and how to interpret their results. For more comprehensive and technical discussions of the techniques discussed in these and subsequent chapters, students should pursue the readings in the "Further Readings" section of each chapter.

Hot Spot Analysis

GOALS:

1. Understand hot spot analysis and its importance to crime mapping.

2. Understand major issues surrounding hot spot analysis.

3. Know the different methods of hot spot analysis.

4. Understand the fuzzy mode analysis technique.

5. Understand the nearest neighbor hierarchical (NNH) analysis technique.

6. Understand the risk adjusted NNH (RNNH) technique.

7. Perform hot spot analysis exercises.

INTRODUCTION

One of the more popular current trends in policing is the use of hot spot analysis to assist in management decisions. Specifically, hot spot analysis has become a vital aspect of problem-oriented policing strategies and is used by many police agencies to help direct increasingly scarce resources and prioritize patrol function so as to target areas of increased need. Other uses of hot spot analysis included determining the differences in concentrations of different crime types and changes in concentration of a crime at different points in time. Despite increased use by police agencies in designing patrol strategies and resource allocation, much confusion exists as to what a hot spot really is. Harries (1999) defines a hot spot as ". . . a condition indicating some form of clustering in a spatial distribution." By contrast, Sherman and Weisburd (1995) defines hot spots as "small places in which the occurrence of crime is so frequent that it is highly predictable, at least over a 1-year period." A more statistical definition of hot spots comes from Levine (2002), who states that hot spots are groups of crime incidents that are spatially closer than would be expected by chance. While there is no widely accepted definition of a hot spot, most crime analysts and academics would agree that hot spots are areas where crime is more concentrated than in the rest of a crime distribution. These hot spots can be either places (building or bar location) or spaces (census tract or neighborhood) and are usually consistent over some period of time (Block and Block, 1995).

While confusion is rampant about the theoretical definition of a hot spot, even more confusion exists as to the practical definition of a hot spot, or how to define a hot spot for analysis purposes. Much of the confusion surrounding the practical definition of hot spots revolves around the impact of time, scale, number of crimes, and risk in determining if a hot spot actually exists. **Time** is a key element in hot spot determination as a unit of analysis. Specifically, how long of a time period will you analyze to determine if an area is a hot spot and how long must an area be hot to be considered a hot spot? Is a bar that has a brawl resulting in 12 arrests a hot spot although there has never been any arrest at the bar before or after the brawl, or must there be sustained problems at the location over a longer period of time for it to be a hot spot? Moreover what period of analysis do you use in determining hot spots, one day of data, one week, one month, one year? The length of time that is analyzed will significantly impact the determination of a hot spot. As the bar example from above shows, if you were to use one day or one week of crime data, the bar would probably be a hot spot, but if you were to use a month or a year's worth of data, it may not be. Most jurisdictions require an area to be an active problem area for at least two weeks and sometimes longer before it is considered a hot spot. As for the length of time used for analysis, jurisdictions vary greatly and most are impacted in part by the amount of crime they have. Those with more crime use shorter periods of analysis than those with smaller crime amounts. As there is no standard procedure for determining a hot spot, the best suggestion is to use your own knowledge and experience with the crime distributions you are analyzing to assist in time-related issues.

A second major issue in the determination of hot spots is the impact of **scale** on hot spot identification. As Figure 9.1 shows, when scale is smallest (county level) all crime incidents appear to be a hot spot, yet as scale increases (individual address) crimes become more dispersed and hot spots dissolve (www.mappingcrime.org). Many jurisdictions use the neighborhood or block level to determine hot spots. In this scheme if a given number of crimes occur within a one or two block area, they will consider it a hot spot, but if it is more spread out, they will not. While this method may work fine for large cities, rural areas, and small towns and cities that are more spread out will have to modify their scale or search area for hot spot determination. As with the impact of time on hot spot determination, the best suggestion is to use local knowledge and experience to guide the determination of the appropriate scale for analysis.

A third key element in hot spot determination is the **number of crimes** necessary for an area to be considered a hot spot. As with time and scale, number of crimes can have a significant impact on the determination of hot spots especially when considering jurisdiction size and crime frequency. With crime frequency being much lower and search areas much smaller in small and rural jurisdictions than in large urban jurisdictions, the threshold for an area to be considered a hot spot is also much lower. While in large cities a minimum of ten incidents for a hot spot may be appropriate, it is too high a minimum number for most small and rural jurisdictions. As Paulsen (2001) demonstrated, ten crime incidents represented approximately 24 percent of the average weekly number of crime incidents in a small town, far more than is necessary for an area to be considered a hot spot. By contrast, ten incidents represented only around 3 percent of all weekly crimes in a larger jurisdiction, a more reasonable percentage of total crimes for a hot spot. Thus, when determining the appropriate number of crimes necessary for a hot spot, individual jurisdictions need to analyze their crime distributions and establish minimum amounts that will show true clusters of crime.

The final key issue in determining hot spots is the ignorance of **risk** when determining hot spots. Hot spots are generally determined based solely on the volume of crime incidents in a geographical area, ignoring the importance of the relative number of victims/targets in those areas (Levine, 2002). High-volume crime areas, especially in large cities, are often a function of high population densities, meaning these areas may not really be experiencing an increased risk of crime. High-volume areas of crime may be high simply because there are more people living/working in those areas, and in fact they may be less risky than other areas with fewer crimes but also less people. The danger in using measures, based solely on volume, is that police may focus interventions in areas where crime volume is high but crime risk isn't, leaving areas with a higher crime risk devoid of police interventions. Importantly, one of the methods that will be discussed in this section is a risk-adjusted measure for determining hot spots of crime.

Overall in coming up with a practical definition for hot spot determination, the best suggestion is presented by Harries (1999), who suggests that "jurisdiction specific procedures to define hot spots make the most sense because they will fit local conditions." Importantly, in creating these local specifications, practitioners and researchers *must* be careful to consider the impact that time, scale, crime amount, and risk have on their creation of hot spots. A sound definition will factor in all of these key elements along with fitting local crime distributions in order to maximize valid hot spot identification. For a more complete discussion of both theoretical and practical considerations dealing with hot spots, the National Institute of Justice has recently published "Mapping Crime: Understanding Hot Spots." This freely available publication provides an in-depth discussion of different techniques for identifying hot spots as well as theoretical considerations as to the underlying causes of hot spots. For more information, see the Further Readings section at the end of this chapter.

HOT SPOT METHODS

Almost as problematic as the confusion over the definition of a hot spot is the number of methods used to determine if and where hot spots exist in spatial distributions. While an exhaustive discussion of the various methods used for hot spot determination is beyond the scope of this book, most methods can be grouped into one of five categories. Research conducted by the Crime Mapping Research Center (now called the NIJ MAPS Office) found that hot spot analysis techniques fall into five basic categories: visual interpretation, choropleth mapping, grid cell analysis, point pattern analysis, and spatial autocorrelation (Jefferis, 1999). Of these five methods, the most simplistic is the **visual** method. The visual method involves officers/crime analysts simply looking at point maps and determining areas that appear to be hot spots. While this is obviously the cheapest and quickest method, problems exist such as subjective interpretation by analysts and overlapping of points, both of which lead to problems with validity of hot spot locations (Jefferis, 1999).

The second method commonly used is termed **choropleth mapping** and involves aggregating crime data to beats or census tracts and creating color-shaded maps based on either crime frequency or crime rates (see Workbook Chapter 2). While this method can be useful for showing areas where crime is high in the aggregate, many of the problems discussed in Workbook Chapter 2 regarding the making of choropleth maps will impact its utility for hot spot analysis.

The third method for determining hot spots is termed **grid cell analysis**. Grid cell analysis works by placing a grid of equal size cells over the study area and aggregating the crime locations within each cell with cluster analysis then being performed on the aggregated cell counts (Jefferis, 1999). This type of analysis is often termed *density mapping* and will be discussed more in-depth in the next chapter on density maps and kernel density interpolation.

The fourth method commonly used for determining hot spots of crime is **spatial autocorrelation** and is generally conducted on crime data aggregated to block groups. Anselin and Bera (1998) define spatial autocorrelation as "the coincidence of value similarity with locational similarity." In other words, areas of similar crime totals will be clustered together spatially. The main difference between this type of analysis and choropleth mapping is that clustering is determined by statistical means such as Anselin's Local Moran statistic (see Crimestat manual for further discussion of Anselin's Local Moran).

The final method used for hot spot analysis is termed **point pattern analysis** and is one of the more common statistical methods used for determining hot spots (Mamalian and La Vigne, 1998). Point pattern analysis methods generally involve the analysis of the proximity of points from an arbitrarily placed seed point (Harries, 1999). These techniques seek to determine if crime locations are closer together than would be expected by chance. Numerous different programs exist for analyzing point patterns including STAC, SaTScan, Geographic Analysis Machine (GAM), and of course Crimestat, which includes six different point pattern techniques. Because of their combination of popularity, statistical inference, and visual output, the discussion of hot spot techniques will focus on these point pattern techniques. Specifically, we will focus on the fuzzy mode, NNH clustering and RNNH methods.

FUZZY MODE

Within point pattern analysis, there are several different types of methods; the simplest and most intuitive is the point location method, of which the fuzzy mode is one type (Levine, 2002). Point location analysis works by counting the number of incidents occurring at different locations; those locations with the most incidents are defined as hot spots (Levine, 2002). Thus, if looking at a distribution of robberies, those locations where multiple incidents occurred will be defined as hot spots. The major problem with standard point location methods, such as the mode, is that they are very limited in the hot spots they find. In particular, hot spots are really hot locations or specific locations with more than one incident. While this is useful in many situations, for certain crime types few incidents occur at the same location, but they do occur very near each other. An example would be burglaries. If all six houses in a neighborhood were burglarized in the same week, point location analysis would not classify this as a hot spot despite it being a higher than average incidence of burglary. In order to deal with some of the problems of the mode and other point location methods, the **fuzzy mode** was created. The fuzzy mode is a variation of the point location method in that it allows "users to define a small search area around each location to include events that occur around or near that location" (Levine, 2002). Thus, the user can define a search radius of 100 meters (or whatever they choose), and the routine will find all incidents that occurred at each location *and* within 100-meter radius of each location. In using the fuzzy mode, the user must be careful how they select the search radius, as increasing it too much (1 mile) will make many hot spots because of points being counted multiple times.

Performing a Fuzzy Mode Analysis

1. Open Crimestat, and proceed to the Data setup tab and the primary Field subtab. Navigate to the Chapter 9 folder within the CMLab Folder and add Homicides.shp as the primary file (see Chapter 7 for more assistance).
2. Click on the Spatial Description tab and the "**Hot Spot" Analysis I** subtab.
3. Put a check mark in the empty box next to **Fuzzy Mode (F-Mode)**. Below this box are two other boxes out to the right of the word "Radius" that are used for defining the search radius used in the fuzzy mode.
4. **Radius:** The first box is the distance box and is used for defining the distance of the search radius. For this discussion, type 100 in this box. Importantly, you can select any number and distance unit you like, but the larger the search radius, the less utility the fuzzy mode has.
5. **Distance Units Box:** The second box is the Distance Units box, which allows the user to select the distance units that they wish to use for the search radius. The choices include miles, nautical miles, feet, kilometers, and meters. For this discussion, select meters.
6. After you have set the search radius parameters, click on the "Save result to" box. Save the output as a .dbf file (your only choice) and name the file fuzzy and save it in the Chapter 9 folder. Click OK when finished.

7. When you are done, click Compute. Crimestat will create a .dbf file that contains four different variables:
   a. **Rank:** This is the rank order of the hot spot, those with the most incidents being ranked first followed by the second ranked location, etc.
   b. **Hits:** This variable tells you the number of incidents contained at each location.
   c. **X:** The X coordinate of the hot spot.
   d. **Y:** The Y coordinate of the hot spot.
8. **Adding Output to ArcMap:** Open ArcMap and add Houston.shp to the data view from the Chapter 9 folder.
9. Under the Tools menu select "Add XY Data."
10. When the add XY Data menu opens, click on the Open file button to the right of the blank box at the top. Navigate to the Chapter 9 folder within the CMLab Exercises folder (where you saved the fuzzy analysis) and add the "Fmodefuzzy.dbf" file.
11. When you return to the Add XY Data menu, make sure that X is in the X Field and Y is in the Y Field boxes and then click OK.
12. You should now see approximately 469 points added to the view. In order to tell which are the hot spots, we need to change these points to graduated symbols.
13. Right-click on Fmodefuzzy Events, scroll down, and select "Properties"
14. Click on the "Symbology" tab and then choose Quantities from the categories on the left hand side. Under Quantities, select "Graduated Symbols." In the Fields Value menu, scroll down and select Freq. This should make five classes of symbols of varying sizes (4–12 point sizes). Click apply, and you will now be able to see the hot spots on the map. Figure 9.2 (www.mappingcrime.org) shows how your map should look like upon completing the analysis.

Map Tip: In order to make the hot spots stand out more, change the colors of each different category so that they are all in different colors.

Interpretation of Output: Interpreting the output for the fuzzy mode, and most point pattern analysis, is very simple and straightforward. Those circles that are largest are the areas that have the highest concentration of crime. In this case, they represent the specific locations and areas within 100 meters that have the highest incidence of homicide in Houston. On this particular map, the two top hot spots are in the Southwest area of Houston (see Figure 9.2).

NEAREST NEIGHBOR HIERARCHICAL CLUSTERING

The second point pattern hot spot analysis method we will discuss is NNH clustering, which is a type of hierarchical clustering method (Levine, 2002). Hierarchical clustering methods work by grouping incidents together based on some criteria, and then grouping them again and again into second- and third-order groups until all the points are grouped together or the grouping criteria fail (Levine, 2002). In the case of NNH clustering, there are two criteria for grouping crime incidents. The first criterion is the nearest neighbor distance, which is set by using a confidence interval. This criterion works by the user selecting a desired confidence interval (0.10, 0.05, 0.01, etc.) to ensure that the points are not grouped by chances. Thus, a user selects a desired confidence level in order to ensure that points are not grouped together based on chance, with this confidence interval determining the size of the search radius. The smaller the confidence interval (0.01, 0.001), the smaller the search radius used for the clustering and the lower probability that crime incidents are grouped by chance. The second criterion is the minimum number of crime incidents necessary for the formation of a hot spot. Here the user defines the minimum number of points necessary for a hot spot to be found. Thus in NNH clustering, hot spots are created when a minimum number of points cluster together at a better rate than the user defined criteria for chance. For example, if the confidence interval was 0.01 and the minimum point was 10, then any hot spots that were found would indicate that we are 99 percent sure that 10 incidents were clustered together not by chance but by some real spatial association.

This method has both advantages and disadvantages as compared with other point pattern methods. In terms of advantages, NNH is able to determine small concentrations of incidents based on the ability to control the confidence interval level. Smaller confidence intervals (0.01, 0.001, etc.) create smaller grouping areas and are thus able to more clearly cluster small concentrations of crime (Levine, 2002). Second, groupings of hot spots can be found through the second and third-order clustering that occurs in NNH (Levine, 2002). In reality hot spots are often close together in space, with NNH analysis clusters of hot spots can be found indicating not only small areas of crime concentration but more global indicators of crime concentrations. In terms of disadvantages one of the biggest problem with NNH analysis is, it is subject to manipulation by users through the selection of confidence intervals and minimum points (Levine, 2002). When users alter these two criteria very different results can be created, leading to inconsistent results in analysis.

Performing NNH Analysis

1. Open Crimestat, and proceed to the Data setup tab and the primary Field subtab. Navigate to the Chapter 9 folder within the CMLab Folder and add Homicides.shp as the primary file (see Chapter 7 for more assistance).
2. Click on the Spatial Description tab and the **"Hot Spot" Analysis I** subtab.
3. Put a check mark in the empty box next to **Nearest Neighbor Hierarchical Spatial Clustering (NNH)**. Below are several boxes related to setting up the search radius (confidence interval) and the minimum points per cluster.
4. **Setting the Confidence Interval:** Setting the confidence is vitally important to NNH analysis because it will determine the size of the search radius. As the confidence interval gets smaller (sliding the arrow to the left toward 0.00001), the search radius gets smaller and the chance of grouping crime incidents together by chance gets smaller. However, along with the chance of grouping points by chance getting smaller, the chance of finding real hot spots decreases with a smaller search radius. Moreover, the size of the hot spots that are found will also decrease in size with the selection of smaller confidence intervals. Thus, users should think carefully of the consequences before choosing the confidence interval. For the purposes of **this exercise**, select the 0.05 confidence interval (fifth notch from the left).
5. **Setting Minimum Points:** As with setting the confidence interval, selecting the minimum points per cluster is vitally important to your final output. As discussed earlier in this chapter, the number of crimes in a hot spot is a dependent on several factors such as crime frequency and jurisdiction size. Ultimately, the decision on the minimum number of points per cluster is one that is based on local judgment and knowledge of the data being analyzed. It is important to remember that the goal of this type of analysis is to create hot spots that are meaningful in size and thus not simply two incidents that are close together. Levine (2002) suggests that users start with the default setting (ten points) and alter the setting if there appears to be too many or too few clusters. For the purpose of this exercise, leave the minimum number of points at the default ten incidents.
6. Click on the "Save ellipses to" box and navigate to Chapter 9 folder. Save the results as a .shp file and name the results homicide. Click OK when you are done.
7. When you return to the "Hot Spot Analysis" I screen, click Compute.
8. When the analysis is finished, scroll through the results to see how many, if any, hot spots were found and what order they are. In this case seven hot spots were generated, six first-order clusters and one second-order hot spot. In looking at

the results of the individual hot spots created, if you scroll to the right you can see how many crime incidents are within each hot spot.

9. **Adding the Output to ArcMap:** Open ArcMap and add the following layers from the Chapter 9 folder.

   a. Houston.shp

   b. Nnh1homicide.shp: first-order hot spots

   c. Nnh2homicide.shp: second-order hot spots

Map Tip: In order to make the hot spots more appealing visually, follow the following steps:

1. Click on the desired hot spot layer symbol to open up the Symbol Selector editor.
2. Change the fill color to "No Color." This will make the symbol empty and colorless on the view.
3. Change the Outline Width to 2.0. This will increase the size of the lines around the hot spots.
4. Change the Outline Color to red. It is important to choose a color that will stand out, such as red to make interpretation easier.
5. When you are done with your changes, click OK.

Interpreting the Output: Figure 9.3 (www.mappingcrime.org) shows you how your map should look. As with Point location analysis results, hot spots created by NNH analysis is fairly direct and easy to interpret. In the exercise at hand, there are six first-order hot spots (clusters of crime incidents) that are centered mostly around the city center, with the exception of one hot spot in the southwest area of Houston. There is also a second-order hot spot that encompasses parts of five of the hot spots in the city-center area, indicating that there are not only individual concentrations of crime in this area, but also a generally higher concentration of crime than the rest of Houston.

RISK ADJUSTED NNH ANALYSIS

While NNH analysis is an improvement over the fuzzy mode method of hot spot analysis, it still suffers from the ignorance of risk in its creation of hot spots. As discussed earlier in the chapter, NNH analysis is a hot spot method that creates hot spots based only on volume and not on any actual increased risk of victimization. Thus, NNH hot spots may be a function of high population density and may not represent the most criminally risky areas of a city, just the area of a city where most of the activity, both criminal and non-criminal occurs. While the volume method of hot spot creation is fine for many police patrol practices, dealing with increased risk of victimization is of primary concern in many police interventions. Thus, RNNH is an important analysis for understanding the relative volume of crime incident hot spots in relation to a baseline variable such as the underlying population of a city. RANNH works by combining a kernel density interpolation (to be discussed in-depth in Workbook Chapter 10) with an NNH analysis to produce clusters of points that are closer than would be expected on the basis of a baseline variable such as population or total crimes (Levine, 2002). It creates these risk-adjusted clusters by adjusting the search radius based on the distribution of the baseline variable (Levine, 2002). Thus, when looking at robbery hot spots with the baseline variable being population, RNNH would cluster robbery locations that are closer together than would be expected based on the underlying population where the incidents are occurring. In a sense, RNNH hot spots are like hot spot rates in that the baseline variable controls for the differences in population where the incidents occur to produce a more accurate depiction of high crime concentrations.

Performing RNNH Analysis

1. Open Crimestat and proceed to set up the primary file just as you did for the NNH analysis, *including checking the NNH box for analysis and setting the preferences, the same as for the NNH analysis.*

2. In addition to setting up the primary file, a secondary file and a reference file must be set up for an RNNH analysis to work. Thus click on the Data Setup tab and the **Secondary File** subtab.

3. For the secondary file, navigate to the Chapter 9 folder and select the Houston.shp file. Set the X and Y variables as you did the primary file and for the **Intensity** variable scroll down and select population. This intensity variable is what will serve as the baseline variable for the RNNH analysis.

4. Click on the Reference file and type the following coordinates in the Grid Area boxes.

	X	Y
Lower left	−94.91	30.20
Upper right	−95.95	29.51

5. When you are finished typing in the coordinates, click on the save button and name the grid file "**Houston.**" We are saving this file for later use in Chapter 10 and Chapter 11, where we will use grid cell analysis extensively.

6. Return to the Hot Spot Analysis I subtab under the Spatial Description tab and place a check mark in the box next to **Risk-adjusted**. This makes the NNH analysis a risk-adjusted analysis instead.

7. Click on the **Risk Parameters** box and place a check mark in the box next to Use Intensity variable. This tells Crimestat which variable to use as the baseline variable in the analysis. Leave all of the other settings at the default (for a more complete discussion of these different settings, see Chapter 10).

8. Click OK on the settings of the risk parameters box and then click on the "Save Results to" button when you return to the main Hot Spot Analysis I menu. Save the file as a .shp file in the Chapter 9 folder and name it **risk**. Click OK and then click Compute at the main menu.

9. When Crimestat has finished computing the RNNH, scroll through the results to see the number of hot spots that were created. Notice that **no hot spots were created with the preferences set as they were**. This means that there were no homicide hot spots of when clustering incident locations on the basis of the baseline variable of population.

10. Reset the preferences so that the minimum number of points per cluster is five and then click Compute. After Crimestat is finished, you will see that one hot spot has been found this time with six incidents.

11. Open the output in ArcMap as you did the NNH results. The prefix for RNNH output is RNNH. Figure 9.4 (www.mappingcrime.org) shows you how your map should look like for the RNNH analysis.

Interpretation of Results: As Figure 9.4 illustrates, only one hot spot was found using the RNNH method of hot spot analysis. The small single hot spot is in the southwest corner of Houston, contained within the lone hot spot in the southwest part of Houston from the NNH analysis. The results indicate that there is only one area where homicides are more concentrated than would be expected on the basis of the population distribution.

EXERCISES

1. **Fuzzy Mode Hot Spot Analysis:** Conduct two different fuzzy mode analyses to determine if there are differences in the clustering of homicides between 1989 and 1991. Use 100 meters as the search radius.

Layers required: Houston.shp, 1989.shp, 1991.shp

Compare your results to the correct analysis on the textbook webpage www.mappingcrime.org

2. **NNH Analysis:** Conduct two different NNH hot spot analyses to determine if there are differences in the clustering of homicides between 1989 and 1991. Use the following settings. Try adjusting the minimum number of points to both higher and lower numbers and see how it impacts the number of hot spots created.

   Search radius: 0.05 level

   Minimum Points: 10

   Layers required: Houston.shp, 1989.shp, 1991.shp

   Compare your results to the correct analysis on the textbook webpage www.mappingcrime.org

3. **RNNH Hot Spot Analysis:** Conduct two different RNNH hot spot analyses to determine if there are differences in the clustering of homicides between 1989 and 1991.

   Search Radius: 0.05 level

   Minimum Points: 5

   Risk Parameters: Select use intensity variable and use default for other settings.

   Layers required: Houston.shp, 1989.shp, 1991.shp

   Compare your results to the correct analysis on the textbook webpage mappingcrime.org

4. **Hot Spot Comparison:** Compare the results of the hot spot analysis for the 1989 data using the three different techniques to determine how much difference there is in how they create hot spots.

   Compare your results to the correct analysis on the textbook webpage www.mappingcrime.org

REVIEW QUESTIONS

1. Define what a hot spot is.

2. What are some of the major issues in determining where hot spots are occurring?

3. List the main ways in which hot spots are determined and some of the associated problems with each of them.

4. What is the best way to determine hot spots?

5. List the different methods for determining hot spots from point data.

6. Briefly describe the way in which point locations methods determine hot spot locations.

7. Compare fuzzy mode analysis with NNH analysis of how they create hot spots.

8. How does a RANNH analysis differ from a standard NNH hot spot analysis?

FURTHER READINGS

Block, C. R. (1994). "STAC hot spot areas: A statistical tool for law enforcement decisions". In *Proceedings of the workshop on Crime Analysis Through Computer Mapping*. Chicago, IL: Criminal Justice Information Authority.

Block, R. and C. R. Block (1995). "Space, place and crime: Hot spot areas and hot places of liquor-related crime". In John E. Eck and David Weisburd (eds.), *Crime Places in Crime Theory*. Rutgers Crime Prevention Studies Series. Newark: Criminal Justice Press.

Buerger, M. E., E. G. Cohn, and A. J. Petronison (1995). Defining the "hot spots" of crime: Operationalizing theoretical concepts for field research. In: John E. Eck and David Weisburd (eds.), *Crime and Place*. Monsey, NY: Criminal Justice Press; and Washington, DC: Police Executive Research Forum, pp. 47–62.

Eck, J., S. P. Chainey, J. Cameron, M. Leitner, and R. E. Wilson (2005). Mapping Crime: Understanding Hot Spots. Mapping and Analysis for Public Safety. Washington, DC: National Institute of Justice. Available on-line at: http://www.ojp.usdoj.gov/nij/maps/ncj209393.html

Grubesic, T. H. and A. T. Murray (2002). "Detecting hot spots using cluster analysis and GIS." Paper presented at Annual Conference of the Crime Mapping Research Center, Dallas, TX. Available on-line at: http://www.ojp.usdoj.gov/cmrc/conferences/01conf/Grubesic.doc

Harries, K. (1999). Mapping Crime: Principle and Practice. Available on-line at: http://www.ncjrs.org/html/nij/mapping/pdf.html

Jefferis, E. (1998). "A multi-method exploration of crime hot spots." Crime Mapping Research Center. Washington, DC: National Institute of Justice. Available on-line at: http://www.ojp.usdoj.gov/cmrc/whatsnew/hotspot/intro.pdf

Knox, E. G. (1988). "Detection of clusters." In P. Elliot (ed.), *Methodology of Enquiries into Disease Clustering*. London: London School of Hygiene and Tropical Medicine.

Levine, N. (2002). *Crimestat: A Spatial Statistics Program for the Analysis of Crime Incident Locations (v2.0)*. Ned Levine and Associates, Houston, TX and the National Institute of Justice, Washington, DC. Available on-line at: http://www.icpsr.umich.edu/NACJD/crimestat.html

Sherman, L. W. and D. Weisburd (1995). "General deterrent effects of police patrol in crime 'hot spots': A randomized controlled trial." *Justice Quarterly*, 12 (4), 625–648.

Wesiburd, D. and L. Green (1995). "Policing drug hot spots: The Jersey City drug market analysis experiment." *Justice Quarterly*, 12 (4), 711–735.

Density Mapping

GOALS:
1. Understand density mapping analysis and its importance to crime mapping.
2. Understand the kernel density analysis technique.
3. Understand the dual kernel density analysis technique.
4. Perform kernel density interpolation analysis exercises.

INTRODUCTION

An alternative method to "hot spot" analysis for determining areas with high concentrations of crime is to create a density map or kernel density interpolation map of crime. Kernel density interpolation is one of the new cutting edge spatial statistical techniques for analyzing point patterns in order to determine high-crime areas (Levine, 2002; McLafferty, Williamson, and Mc Guire, 2000). Whereas hot spot analysis techniques work by clustering incidents together that are closer than would be expected by chance, kernel density interpolation works by using grid analysis to estimate the density of crimes across an entire surface area. The first step in kernel density interpolation is to place a grid with equal-sized cells over the entire study area. A circular "kernel" with a constant search radius is placed over the center of each grid cell and crime incidents are weighted based on their distance from the center of this kernel. Those incidents that are farther away from the center are weighted less than those closer to the center. Using this analysis technique, users can weight crime incidents within each grid cell in the entire search area providing a measure of crime density for the entire search area. Thus, every grid cell has a respective crime density measure regardless of whether or not an incident has occurred in the grid cell, providing a smooth and constant picture of crime density for an entire area. The results for each grid cell (Z value) can then be easily visualized using contour maps, 3-D maps, or surface maps (Levine, 2002).

This method of determining high concentrations of crime holds several advantages over other "hot spot" techniques, the first of which is the constant density map that is created (Levine, 2002; McLafferty, Williamson, and McGuire, 2000). Whereas hot spot analysis techniques such as NNH provide information about crime incidents themselves (their relative spatial relationship to each other), interpolation provides information about an entire study area. Thus, through interpolation you can get a complete picture of the density of crime for each and every location within a search area, not just a picture of which incidents are most closely related. A second advantage of kernel density interpolation is the output that is generated. In hot spot analysis techniques such as STAC, NNH, RNNH, and others, ellipses are drawn around the crimes that have been determined to be closer than would be expected by chance. The problem with this is that few crime distributions are elliptical and thus these hot spots are not the true shape of the high concentration areas but merely convenient output methods. However, with kernel density interpolation, high-crime areas are represented in their true shape, which is often odd shaped and irregular. Thus, kernel density interpolation can provide a much more accurate visualization of true high concentration areas of crime. A final advantage of kernel density interpolation over other high concentration of crime methods is that it is statistically a better "hot spot" identifier than other techniques (Levine, 2002). As Levine states (2002), "the kernel estimate. . . is a continuous surface; the densities are calculated at *all* locations; thus, the user can visually inspect the variability in density and decide what to call a 'hot spot' without having to define arbitrarily where to cut-off the 'hot spot' zone." While kernel density interpolations are still subject to the subjective setting of several different parameters, they provide a more objective and statistically valid measure of high concentrations of crime than other measures.

PERFORMING A SINGLE KERNEL DENSITY INTERPOLATION

1. Open Crimestat and proceed to the Data setup tab and the Primary File subtab. Navigate to the Chapter 10 folder within the CMLab Folder and add Homicides.shp as the primary file (see Workbook Chapter 7 for more assistance).
2. Select the **Reference File** subtab. If you saved the reference file coordinates during the RNNH analysis setup, then simply click on the **Load** button, select the Houston file, and click Load. If you did not save the reference file coordinates from the RNNH analysis, then enter the following coordinates:

	X	Y
Lower Left	−94.91	30.20
Upper Right	−95.95	29.51

3. When you have finished entering the coordinates, click on the **Spatial Modeling** tab and then select the **Interpolation** subtab and place a check mark in the box next to the word **Single**.

Selecting Parameters for Kernel Density Interpolations: As with NNH and RNNH analyses, there are several different parameters in conducting a kernel density interpolation that have an important impact on the final output. In the case of an interpolation, the parameters of importance are the **interpolation method** and **bandwidth** selection and size.

Interpolation Methods: Crimestat contains five different interpolation methods—normal, uniform, quartic, triangular, and negative exponential. These methods of interpolation are the methods used for creating the kernels used in weighting the crime incidents within each grid cell. As there are advantages to each of these different methods, selection of an interpolation method is going to be based on the spread of the crime distribution as well as trial and error. Levine (2002) suggests that the user should start with the default method and then adjust according to how the density surface looks in relation to the actual crime distribution. The following descriptions of these methods are from the Crimestat manual (Levine, 2002).

> *Normal:* Weighs all points in the study area, with near points being weighed more highly than distant points. Produces a smoother distribution. This is the default for Crimestat.

Uniform: Weighs all points within the circle equally. Produces a smoother distribution.

Quartic: Weighs near points more than far points, with a gradual fall off of far points. Produces a smoother distribution.

Triangular: Weighs near points more than far points, but the fall off is more rapid than with quartic. Produces a spikier distribution by emphasizing the peaks and valleys between crimes.

Negative Exponential: Weighs near points much more highly than far points. Produces a spikier distribution by emphasizing the peaks and valleys between crimes.

***For the purposes of this exercise, we are going to use the default **normal** distribution. As mentioned above, trial and error and analysis of your crime distribution are the best methods for determining the correct interpolation method.

Bandwidth Selection: The other major parameter in conducting interpolations is the choice of a bandwidth. The bandwidth is the search radius that is used in determining how close crime incidents are to the kernel function. In general, larger bandwidths will create a smoother distribution whereas smaller bandwidths will create a spikier distribution that emphasizes the peaks and valleys between crime incidents. As with interpolation methods, selecting a bandwidth is not standardized and depends a lot on trial and error and how much emphasis a users wants to place on differences between points. Crimestat contains two different bandwidth choices, fixed and adaptive. The following descriptions of these bandwidths are from the Crimestat manual (Levine, 2002).

Fixed Interval: In this method, the user selects the exact bandwidth size they want to use in the analysis. If a user chooses to use a fixed interval bandwidth, they must select the measurement unit (squared miles, squared nautical miles, squared feet, squared kilometers, and squared meters) as well as actual measurement distance. Once this interval has been chosen, it will be used in each grid cell.

Adaptive Bandwidth: In contrast to fixed intervals, which use the same search radius throughout the analysis, adaptive bandwidths adjust the radius so that a minimum number of points are found, thus providing constant precision over the entire study area. Thus, in areas with many crime incidents a small bandwidth will be used, whereas in areas with few crimes a large bandwidth will be used. In selecting an adaptive bandwidth, the user has the option to change the minimum number of points selected by the bandwidth radius. As with choosing a fixed interval distance, smaller numbers of points will create a spikier distribution and larger numbers will create smoother distributions. Figure 10.1 shows how changing the minimum number of points affects the distribution, with the 25-point interpolation being spikier than the 100-point interpolation. In Crimestat, the default bandwidth is adaptive with a minimum number of points of 100.
   ***For the purposes of this exercise, we are going to use the default **adaptive bandwidth** with 100 minimum points selected. As mentioned above, trial and error and analysis of your crime distribution are the best methods for determining the correct bandwidth.

Output Units: This parameter allows the user to select the output units for the density estimate. The default is squared miles and in most situations this is the correct output unit to use. For the purposes of this exercise, we will use **squared miles**.

Calculate: The final parameter that the user must select is how the density will be calculated. There are three options that are provided in Crimestat, absolute density, relative density, and probabilities. The following descriptions of these three different methods are from the Crimestat III manual (Levine, 2002). **Absolute density** provides a measure of the density of crime over the study area. By contrast, **relative density** divides the absolute density by the area of the grid cell, providing a measure that is in the units of measurement (points per square mile) (Levine, 2002). Finally, **probabilities** renders the output as a probability that a crime will occur at any one location. Importantly, the selection of this parameter has no impact on the way the distribution will look visually, it only impacts the interpretation.

For the purposes of this exercise, we will select the default **absolute densities.

4. Once all of the parameters have been selected, click on the **Save Results to** button. Name the file **density** and save the file as a .shp file in the Chapter 10 folder.
5. After you return to the main Interpolation screen, click on Compute. After Crimestat has finished computing the Interpolation results, close the results window and open ArcMap.
6. After you have created a new view, add the interpolation output .shp file from the Chapter 10 folder. The prefix for all single interpolation outputs is K. Thus the output should be kdensity.shp. The output should appear as a big grid that covers the entire Houston area. In order to view the density results, we have to change the variable that is being viewed to the **Z value**.
7. Right-click on the kdensity layer and scroll down and select Properties. Select the symbology subtab and then select "Quantities," and under quantities, select "Graduated colors."
8. Under the fields menu, scroll down the Value drop-down menu and select Z and click OK. This variable contains the values for each grid cell and will reveal the density of crimes for the Houston area.

Map Tip: In order to make the grid lines disappear, click on each individual color symbol and change the outline color to "No color." After doing this for each different color in the grid, it should eliminate the annoying grid look to the results.

Map Tip: In order to see the basemap over the interpolation results, drag the basemap (Houston) layer above the interpolation result layer (kdensity) in the table of contents.

Interpretation of Results: Figure 10.2 (www.mappingcrime.org) shows how your results should look like for the kernel density interpolation. The darker the color on the map, the higher the concentration of crime incidents. Thus, in the example the highest area of homicides is in the city center area. Importantly, the distribution is almost like a bulls eye with lower areas of homicide density radiating out from the city center.

DUAL KERNEL DENSITY INTERPOLATION

In addition to a single kernel density interpolation routine, there is a second interpolation method called a dual interpolation. **Dual kernel density interpolation** works in the same manner as a single kernel density interpolation, with the exception that in a dual kernel density interpolation a secondary file containing other point data is also used. However, while single kernel density interpolations provide information about the volume of crime incidents, dual kernel density interpolations provide information about crime risk density and changes in crime density. Similar to a RNNH analysis, a dual kernel density interpolation can be used to create a measure of the density of crimes based on an underlying variable such as population in order to show the risk of that crime occurring. As with RNNH analysis, this type of analysis is very useful in many police interventions as it provides a more accurate measure of the true risk of crime occurrence and not just a measure of crime volume.

The other main use of a dual kernel density interpolation is for measuring changes in crime patterns over time. Importantly, this dual kernel density interpolation routine will be discussed in-depth in Workbook Chapter 11 on Spatial Dispersion mapping.

Performing a Dual Kernel Density Interpolation

1. Set up the primary and reference file exactly as you did for performing the exercise above for the single kernel density interpolation. As stated above, the vast majority of a dual kernel density interpolation analysis is identical to a single kernel density interpolation.
2. Click on the Secondary File tab. Navigate to the Chapter 10 folder and add the **Houston.shp** file. Set the coordinate values and make "**population**" an intensity value. Population will thus be the variable used to create the risk-adjusted density map for homicides showing the density of homicide risk in Houston.
3. Click on the **Spatial Modeling** tab and select the **Interpolation** subtab.
4. Place a check in the box next to the word **Dual**. By default, the primary file will be the first file and the secondary file will be the second file, but this can be changed for analysis purposes.

Setting of Parameters: The setting of parameters is identical to that for single kernel density interpolation, with the exception of the Calculation parameter. Thus, the only discussion of setting parameters will be of the calculation parameter. *For this exercise*, leave the interpolation method and bandwidth as the default measures.

Setting the Calculation parameter: As opposed to a single density interpolation where there were three calculation options, a dual kernel density interpolation gives the user six separate options. The different calculations include ratio of densities, log ratio of densities, absolute differences in densities, relative difference in densities, sum of densities, and relative sum of densities.

Ratio of Densities: First file divided by the second file. Can be used to provide an estimate of risk for a crime if the first file contains crime locations and the second file contains census data with population as an intensity variable.

Log ratio of Densities: This calculation takes the natural logarithm of the density ratio. This is used primarily when the majority of study cells have very low densities but a few have very high densities (Levine, 2002). The result will be one in which the spikes will not be as pronounced.

Absolute Difference in Densities: First file minus the second file. This method can be useful for looking at the differential effects in population and other aggregate level data (Levine, 2002).

Relative Difference in Densities: First standardizes the densities of each file by dividing the grid cell area, then subtracts the secondary file from the first. This method of calculation is useful in assessing the change in crime densities between two time periods (Levine, 2002). The result will be a density map showing where crime has decreased and increased between the two time periods.

Sum of Densities: The density estimate for the first file plus the density estimate for the second file. This is used for combining the density estimates of two separate crime distributions (Levine, 2002).

Relative Sum of Densities: First standardizes the densities of each file by dividing by the grid cell area and then subtracts the secondary file relative density from the primary file relative density. This is most often used for determining the total effect of two crime types on an area (adding burglary and robbery) (Levine, 2002).

***For the purpose of this exercise, select ratio of densities, as we want to create a density estimate of homicide risk in Houston.

5. Click on the **Save Results to** button and navigate to the Chapter 10 file. Save the file as a .shp file and name it **dual**.
6. When you return to the main interpolation menu, click the Compute button. When Crimestat finishes with the calculations close the results window, minimize Crimestat and open ArcMap.
7. Add the following layers to the view.
   a. Houston.shp: Basemap of Houston found in the Chapter 10 folder.
   b. DkDual: dk is the prefix for dual kernel density interpolation output.
8. Make dkdual viewable and follow the same procedure for making the density map as with the single density interpolation map. Figure 10.3 (www.mappingcrime.org) shows how your map should look like for the dual kernel density analysis. Don't forget to use the map tips from above in order to make the density map easier to view.

Interpreting of Results: As with a single kernel density interpolation, the darker the color, the higher the risk of a homicide. Figure 10.3 shows the results of the single kernel density estimate next to the risk estimate created through the dual kernel density estimate. Notice how the area of highest concentration of crime has changed shape, becoming more teardrop shaped. In addition, the rest of the distribution has also changed to reflect the impact of population on the risk of homicide victimization.

EXERCISES

1. **Single Kernel Density Interpolation:** Make two different maps of the 1989 homicide distribution with two different bandwidths in order to see how bandwidth impacts density maps.
   a. Map A: Use an adaptive bandwidth with a sample size of 100.
   b. Map B: Use a fixed interval bandwidth with an interval of 200 meters.

   Compare your results to the correct analysis on the textbook webpage www.mappingcrime.org

2. **Dual Kernel Density Interpolation:** Make two different risk maps, one for 1989 data and one for 1994 data to assess the difference in homicide risk between the two years. For both maps, choose the interpolation and bandwidth method of your choice using your knowledge of the crime distribution and kernel density methods.
   a. 1989 Map:
   b. 1994 Map:

REVIEW QUESTIONS

1. How is kernel density interpolation used in crime mapping?

2. Briefly describe the process of how kernel density interpolation is conducted.

3. List and explain the advantages that kernel density interpolation has over other techniques.

4. List the different interpolation methods that can be used in performing a kernel density interpolation and briefly describe the distribution that each creates.

5. Explain the differences in the two bandwidth options in Crimestat. Why would you use one over the other?

6. What are the two ways a dual kernel density interpolation can be used for crime mapping?

FURTHER READINGS

Farewell, D. (1999). "Specifying the bandwidth function for the kernel; density estimator". Available on-line at: http://www.iph.cam.ac.uk/bugs/documentation/coda/node44.html

Kelsall, J. E. and P. J. Diggle (1995). "Kernel estimation of relative risk". *Bernoulli*, 1, 3–16.

Levine, N. (2002). *Crimestat: A Spatial Statistics Program for the Analysis of Crime Incident Locations (v2.0)*. Ned Levine and Associates, Houston, TX and the National Institute of Justice, Washington, DC. Available on-line at: http://www.icpsr.umich.edu/NACJD/crimestat.html

Mc Lafferty, S., D. Williamson, and P. G. Mc Guire (2000). *Identifying Crime Hot Spots Using Kernel Smoothing*. In V. Goldsmith, P. G. McGuire, J. H. Mollenkopf, and T. A. Ross (eds.), *Analyzing Crime Patterns: Frontiers of Practice*. Thousand Oaks, CA: Sage Publications.

Spatial Dispersion Mapping

GOALS: 1. Understand spatial dispersion mapping and its importance to crime mapping.

2. Understand map calculations with dual kernel density interpolation.

3. Perform spatial dispersion map exercises.

INTRODUCTION

The last chapter in this section will discuss one of the newer and more important crime mapping tools, spatial dispersion mapping. Spatial dispersion is important to both crime mapping practitioners and researchers because it lets them assess changes in crime density over time or differences in crime density between two different crime types. By measuring differences in crime density over time users can see how crime distributions are evolving within a jurisdiction, which is particularly useful for redrawing police beats and reassigning work load. Figure 11.1 (www.mappingcrime.org) shows the result of a spatial dispersion analysis of homicides committed in January compared with those committed in February. The blue areas show where homicide decreased in February compared with January, while the red areas show where homicide has increased from January to February. Common time periods for this type of analysis include yearly, seasonally, monthly, and weekly changes in crime densities, as well as analyzing differences in crime patterns based on the time of day of the crime. Spatial dispersion analysis is also beneficial in other types of analysis, particularly when assessing the impact of police interventions. Using spatial dispersion mapping users can assess how successful an intervention was at reducing crime in a specific area as well as showing areas where the crime may have diffused or spread to because of the intervention. Finally, this type of analysis can also allow users to make comparisons in the crime density patterns of two different crime types, showing where one crime type is denser than another crime type.

The process involved in creating a spatial dispersion map involves conducting a **dual kernel density interpolation** with two different distributions of crime locations. This is the same process that was discussed in detail in Workbook Chapter 10. Because the dual kernel density interpolation conducted in Workbook Chapter 10 was for producing maps of risk, there are some subtle changes that need to occur in order to create a spatial dispersion map. The main differences between using dual kernel density interpolation for producing risk maps and spatial dispersion maps revolve around the data calculations conducted. In using a dual kernel density interpolation to produce a risk map, the secondary file must contain census data on population and coordinate information on the median centers of the census data. By contrast, when performing spatial dispersion mapping, the secondary file must be point locations for a crime distribution. For example, when conducting a spatial dispersion analysis of the change in homicides from January to February, the primary file would contain February homicide data while the secondary file would contain the January homicide data. The other difference when using dual kernel density interpolation for spatial dispersion mapping involves the calculation used for the density map. In creating a density risk map, the calculation used is the ratio of densities, whereas in spatial dispersion mapping it is the **relative difference in densities**. The difference in densities subtracts the second file from the first file. In the above example, the difference would be subtracting the January homicide density from the February homicide density. Importantly, all of the other issues surrounding kernel density interpolations (interpolation method, bandwidth size) still apply to spatial dispersion mapping. Thus, when using dual kernel density interpolation to produce spatial dispersion maps, it is suggested that you review the discussion in Workbook Chapter 10 concerning these issues.

PERFORMING SPATIAL DISPERSION MAPPING USING DUAL KERNEL DENSITY INTERPOLATION

1. Open Crimestat and click on the Data Setup tab. For the **Primary file**, select jan-jun.dbf, which contains all homicides in Houston from January to June. Make sure to enter the X and Y coordinates for this file, and leave all other fields blank.
2. Click on the **Secondary File** tab and select the file julydec.dbf, which contains all homicides in Houston from July to December.
3. Click on the **Reference File** tab and load the Houston reference file. If you have failed to save the reference coordinates from previous exercises involving kernel density interpolation, see Workbook Chapter 10 for the correct reference grid coordinates.
4. Click on the **Spatial Modeling** tab and the **Interpolation** subtab. Place a check mark in the box next to the word "Dual."
5. **Setting the parameters:** As you have learned in the last two chapters setting the parameters for an interpolation involves much trail and error and a strong knowledge of your crime distribution. While students are encouraged to experiment with using different parameters to conduct interpolations, for the purposes of this exercise use the parameters specified below.
   a. *Interpolation Method:* Use the default Normal.
   b. *Bandwidth:* Use the default Adaptive with 100 minimum point sample size.
   c. *Calculation:* Use relative difference in densities.
6. Click on the "Save Results to" button and navigate to the Chapter 11 folder. Save the results as a .shp file and name it "change." The prefix for the output is dk. Thus, your output file for the spatial dispersion analysis will be **dkchange.shp.**
7. When Crimestat finishes computing the dual kernel density interpolation, close the results window and minimize Crimestat.
8. Open ArcMap and add the following layers:
   a. **Houston.shp:** Houston basemap
   b. **dkchange.shp:** Output file for change in density of homicide.
9. Right-click on the dkchange and select Properties. When the properties menu opens, click on the Symbology editor as in Lab 10 in order to add the Z value. **Importantly**, instead of using the usual red monochromatic color scheme, select a **Red to Blue color scheme** in the color ramp drop-down menu. This will make it easier to interpret the output. Remember to use the map tips from Lab 10 to remove the grid lines and overlay the Houston basemap on top of the density output.

Interpretation of Results: Figure 11.2 (www.mappingcrime.org) shows the results you should have achieved. The darker blue areas show the areas where homicide decreased the most from the period of January to June to the period of July to December. In other words, in the second half of the year homicide incidents decreased the most in the dark blue areas followed by the lighter blue areas. By contrast, the darkest red areas show where homicide incidents increased the most from the January to June period to the period of July to December. In other words, in the second half of the year homicides increased the most in the dark red areas followed next by the lighter red areas. Finally, the white area in between the two color extremes is where homicide stayed fairly stable between the two time periods.

EXERCISES

Spatial Dispersion Map: Perform a spatial dispersion analysis on the change in homicide density from the period of 1986–1989 to the period of 1990–1994 to determine if the pattern of homicide changed much. Use all of the default parameters for the analysis.

Compare your results to the correct analysis on the textbook webpage www.mappingcrime.org

REVIEW QUESTIONS

1. List the different uses for spatial dispersion mapping for both practitioners and researchers.

2. What type of calculation is necessary for conducting a spatial dispersion map using kernel density interpolation?

3. What is the main difference between conducting a dual kernel density interpolation to produce risk maps and one to produce spatial dispersion maps?

FURTHER READINGS

Farewell, D. (1999). "Specifying the bandwidth function for the Kernel; density estimator." Available online at: http://www.iph.cam.ac.uk/bugs/documentation/coda/node44.html

Kelsall, J. E. and P. J. Diggle (1995). "Kernel estimation of relative risk." *Bernoulli*, 1, 3–16.

Levine, N. (2002). *Crimestat: A Spatial Statistics Program for the Analysis of Crime Incident Locations (v2.0)*. Ned Levine and Associates, Houston, TX and the National Institute of Justice, Washington, DC. Available online at: http://www.icpsr.umich.edu/NACJD/crimestat.html

Mc Lafferty, S., D. Williamson, and P. G. Mc Guire (2000). *Identifying Crime Hot Spots Using Kernel Smoothing*. In V. Goldsmith, P. G. McGuire, J. H. Mollenkopf, and T. A. Ross (eds.), *Analyzing Crime Patterns: Frontiers of Practice*. Thousand Oaks, CA: Sage Publications.

Aggregate
Data Analysis

The last section of this workbook will provide readers with an understanding of how to acquire, manipulate, and analyze aggregate data for both policy/research and practitioner uses. The techniques discussed in the earlier section of the workbook deal almost exclusively with the analysis of point data. While data analysis of this type is highly useful to both practitioners and researchers, the analysis of aggregate or areal data provides an ability to analyze and understand the nature and scope of crime at the community level. In particular, analyzing aggregate data is essentially to understanding underlying social factors that influence crime patterns (such as social disorganization), changing demographic patterns that may indicate future crime patterns, and determining clusters of crime at a neighborhood level. The chapters in this section will provide students with a better understanding of how to acquire different types of aggregate level data as well as analyze the data to determine neighborhood level clustering and underlying causes of crime. Workbook Chapter 12 discusses aggregate level data in general and how to download aggregate data and integrate it with existing map data. Workbook Chapter 13 provides an overview of the GeoDa software used for analyzing aggregate level data as well as how to perform basic exploratory analysis of aggregate data. Finally, Workbook Chapter 14 provides a discussion of spatial autocorrelation and how to determine clustering at the aggregate level. As mentioned several times throughout the text, this workbook is not designed to be a comprehensive spatial statistics textbook as much as an introduction to advanced spatial analysis techniques. In particular, the workbook is designed to introduce students to spatial analysis techniques, their importance to crime analysis, when to use them, and how to interpret their results. For more comprehensive and technical discussions of the techniques discussed in these and subsequent chapters, students should pursue the readings in the "Further Readings" section of each chapter.

Working with Aggregate Data

GOALS: 1. Understand differences between aggregate and point data.

2. Understand benefits of using aggregate data in research and practical analysis.

3. Understand how to transform point data into aggregate data.

4. Understand how to find and download aggregate data and join it with map data.

INTRODUCTION

The first chapter in this section is designed to provide students with a better understanding of the differences between aggregate data and point level data and is for the most part a review of the concepts discussed in Chapter 9 of the textbook. As Chapter 9 discussed, there are two main types of data used in crime mapping, point data and aggregate data. Point data is crime data with a locational component, usually a specific street address of a crime location, although it can also be the coordinates of a crime location as well (Brantingham and Brantingham, 1984). In addition to location data on crime incidents, point data can also consist of contextual data. When point data is used in crime maps, the maps are generally referred to as point or dot maps (Brantingham and Brantingham, 1984). This is one of the most popular methods for analyzing crime data because the results are fairly straightforward and patterns of crime distributions can be determined relatively easily. In addition to its relative ease of use and interpretation, point data is often preferred because it is not dependent on jurisdictional boundaries or reporting areas for analysis.

While point data is often extremely useful in the analysis of crime patterns, there are several problems associated with the mapping of crime at the point level. Most important to the discussion of aggregate data is the difficultly of accurately making correlations between point data and other data such as income, poverty, and unemployment levels that are aggregated at the census tract. Although point data is often analyzed in this manner, the accuracy of such results is dubious. Without standardizing the point data, these types of analysis are at best only guesses about the relationships between incident locations and aggregated data. Thus determining potential causes and correlations between crime and social factors (poverty, inequality, opportunities) is very difficult.

In contrast to point level crime data is aggregate crime data. Aggregate data is crime data that has been counted for a specific unit of geographic space such as a police beat or census tract. Thus, where point data shows the exact locations of crime incidents, aggregate data provides a count of how many incidents occurred within a specific area such as a police beat. In general there are two basic types of aggregate level crime data, the first of which is termed an administrative unit (Brantingham and Brantingham, 1984). Administrative units are defined as "spatial units designed primarily by government to organize the delivery of services, to provide common units for diverse reporting functions, and to provide an aggregate basis for government allocation and representation" (Brantigham and Brantingham, 1984). The two most commonly used administrative units for the aggregation of crime data are police beats and census tracts.

Police beats are best described as geographic units created by police agencies for patrol and administrative purposes. Most police agencies use police beats to manage and direct patrol officers' duties as well as for collecting and reporting crimes and calls for service. While there is no standardized method for their creation, police beats are usually created with several things in mind. First, determining size of the police beat is a balancing act. Police beats must be small enough that an officer can patrol the entire area without much difficulty, but not so small that patrol officers are used inefficiently. Beats that are too large in size would prevent officers from conducting meaningful patrol, while beats that are too small would require too many officers to be patrolling in a small area. Secondly, most police beats are drawn along the lines of existing geographic units or features such as census tracts, voting districts, zip code areas, neighborhood boundaries, or major streets. Thus, beats are often drawn based more on convenience than on either practical usefulness or social cohesiveness such as a uniform population base.

The other major type of administrative unit used for aggregating crime data is the census tract. Census tracts are administrative units that are drawn for purposes of counting the population of the country every ten years for use in numerous government administrative tasks. The foundation of the census tract is the census block, which is generally a unique city block (Harries, 1990). Information about households within this block area is gathered, and these blocks are in turn aggregated to the block group, which is a group of census blocks. Finally, groupings of census block groups are aggregated to create a census tract (Harries, 1990). Importantly, as a rule the smaller the administrative unit (census block), the less information about the households within this unit is released to the public (Harries, 1990). Thus, little information is available about households at the census block level, while all census data is available at the census tract level, giving rise to the popularity of aggregating crime at the census tract level. While the census tract and the smaller census block groups and census blocks are unique to the United States, census geography is used to aggregate crime data in other countries as well. In Canada, Statistics Canada gathers census information, whereas in England the agency responsible for gathering census data is the Office of Population Census and Surveys (Brantingham and Brantingham, 1984).

In terms of crime mapping, aggregated crime data has numerous benefits and problems. The clearest benefit for aggregating crime data is the ability to both create rates of crime and compare crime data with other social data. Both crime rates and comparisons of crime data with other social data are important aspects of crime mapping because they allow for more advanced analysis of crime problems. By creating crime rates, we are able to better understand differences in crime magnitude across jurisdictions than if we simply were analyzing individual crime locations only. Moreover, by comparing aggregate crime data with other social data such as income and unemployment levels, we can better understand root causes of crime distribution patterns. While creating crime rates and comparing crime incidents with other social data are difficult to do with point data, they are easily accomplished with aggregate data. Although it is admittedly easier to create crime rates and compare relationships between crime data and other social data with census tracts than with other aggregate data types, it can still be accomplished. Most GIS programs have functions that will merge data from one polygon source (census data) to another polygon source (arbitrary coding unit or police beat) allowing for data to be compared across different boundaries.

The other main benefit of aggregating crime data is that it provides crime information in a form that may have more practical significance to end-users than point data. While crime data aggregated to the census tract or arbitrary coding unit has some practical usefulness, it is crime data aggregated to the police beat that is most beneficial. Because beats are integral to both patrol and administration, making crime maps based on these geographic units makes a great deal of sense. Most officers and police managers think of crime and police work in terms of police beats, thus being able to view crime distributions according to police beats would be best for their daily functions. Other benefits include being able to compare aggregate crime data with other information collected at the police beat level, such as information related to shifts and manpower issues. While practical benefits associated with aggregate data are limited mostly to data aggregated to the police beat, this is certainly an important group where crime mapping is concerned. Thus, for strictly police uses, aggregating and analyzing crime by police beats is clearly beneficial.

Despite its clear benefits, aggregating crime data does pose some serious problems. First, among these problems is the issue about how boundaries are drawn for the geographic units used in creating aggregate counts. Specifically, the manner in which these boundaries are drawn can have a significant impact on the crime totals for each different unit. While this is primarily a problem for both census tracts and police beats, which are created for administrative reasons, it can also impact arbitrary coding units despite their being created primarily for crime analysis purposes. Central to this problem is the fact that boundary lines for both census tracts and police beats often correspond with major city streets, which, while convenient, often intersect crime distributions (Brantingham and Brantingham, 1984). The distribution of crime often clusters along major roadways; thus what appears to be a cluster of crime incidents on a point map is often split up into different cells of an aggregate map (Brantingham and Brantingham, 1984). The effect is that the cluster of crime incidents is divided up into different cells and does not appear to be a high amount of crime. Figure 8.3 illustrates how the drawing of boundary lines can seriously impact the counts of crime and effectively make a real crime cluster disappear into an aggregate count of crime. While arbitrary coding units can be drawn in a manner that minimizes this problem, this is a problem that will always impact aggregate measures of crime.

Another related issue with the drawing of boundaries for aggregate crime units is the fact that they are often stable over time despite the growth and change of the city in which they are drawn. Specifically, boundary lines often don't change for 20 years or more, although the populations within the boundaries have changed dramatically. While the stability of boundaries can be beneficial for long-term trend analysis, changes within the population size and homogeneity can make statistical analysis difficult (Brantingham and Brantingham, 1984).

A more serious problem with the drawing of boundaries involves differences in the size of the different cells used for aggregation. In particular, the relative **size and shape** of the cells used for aggregation directly impact the results of statistical analysis involving aggregate data. In general as the size of a cell increases, correlations become stronger in strength, meaning it is more and more difficult to draw correct conclusions about the relationships between two areas as their size increases (Brantingham and Brantingham, 1984). This problem arises from the fact that crime data in aggregated units are averages of the individual points within each cell. Thus as you increase the number of incidents within each cell, the variability of the data becomes lost and data within differing cells becomes more similar leading to stronger correlations. It is important to underscore that these correlations are statistically true but practically invalid, in that the areas are more similar simply because there is more data and the data tends to create averages that are similar. Moreover, attempting to infer correct relationships between two different sized cells is particularly difficult, a problem that is particularly important when analyzing census tracts and police beats that are of varying sizes. As a general rule geographic units of vastly different sizes should not be used for comparison as the data within them is too different to accurately reflect real relationships (Brantingham and Brantingham, 1984). Importantly, collecting data in a standardized size, such as with arbitrary coding units, is a good way to prevent problems with incorrect correlations.

Another problem involving aggregate data involves attempting to **combine data with boundaries of differing shapes and sizes**. While census data and data collected at the police beat level are two of the more popular forms of data used in crime mapping, numerous other types of data are also available that may prove beneficial to understanding patterns of crime. Combining data is a process that is often used when overlaying data from different sources in order to create a new set of data that represents the two pieces of data that are of interest. The problem with combining data from different sources is that the boundaries may be different in shape and size and thus the data may not combine as accurately as necessary for proper inference and analysis. While most GIS packages have methods for combining different shaped data together, they do it in an arbitrary way that may not reflect the reality of the original distributions. Figure 9.4 provides an example of how combining school district data with crime data from police beats in order to determine crime per school district can result in incorrect relationships. Notice how the distribution of point data is skewed when aggregating it to the police beat and how in-turn this data is further skewed upon combining it with school district data. The resultant data provides a mistaken portrait of crime distributions in two different school districts. Although improvements in GIS software have helped to limit the problems with combining data of differing shapes, problems still exist that can lead to incorrect inferences about crime distributions. The problems are compounded when this data is then used to create policy, inform the public or is reported in research results.

The final problem associated with aggregated data involves how aggregate data is interpreted and is termed **ecological fallacy**. The concept underlying ecological fallacy is a relatively easy one, but one that is vitally important in terms of interpretation and understanding of aggregate crime data. Ecological fallacy is the idea that individual behavior cannot be inferred from aggregate data (Rossmo, 2000). In examining aggregate crime data, this is often a very attractive and common error, one that can lead to problems in both crime policy and public perception. An example of committing this type error in reasoning would be to state that individuals who are high school drop outs are more likely to commit crime than high school graduates based upon findings that there is a correlation between crime and high school graduation rates at the census tract level. This individual inference cannot be made simply because the relationship exits at the aggregate level. There is no way to infer individual behavior simply from relationships that exist at the aggregate level and to do so is to invite problems concerning the validity of the researchers work. The only way to prevent these types of errors in reasoning is to report findings on the aggregate level as aggregate level findings only and not to attempt to make leaps to individual-level behavior.

AGGREGATING POINT DATA

While many crime analysts and researchers would like to analyze crime data in its aggregate form, they are often provided crime data in point data format only and thus must transform the data. Before the advent of GIS, such as when Shaw and McKay were conducting their research on juvenile crime in Chicago (see Chapter 3), this aggregation would have to be done by hand. However, through the use of GIS, this task is now simply and easily completed.

1. Open ArcMAP and navigate to the Chapter 12 folder and add both the Houston.shp file and homicides file.

2. Right-click on the Houston and scroll down to "joins and Relates" and select "Join. . . ."
3. When the "Join Data" menu appears under the "What do you want to join to this layer" option, select "Join data from another layer based on spatial location." This will allow you to join the point data (Homicide locations) to the census tracts that each homicide occurred within.
4. Under the "Choose the layer to join to this layer" option, make sure that Homicides is selected. If it is not, use the drop-down menu to select it.
5. Leave all other default parameters selected.
6. Save the joined output in the Chapter 12 folder by clicking on the Open folder button in step 3 and scrolling to the Chapter 12 folder. Rename the file "crimecount."
7. When you return to the Join Data menu, click OK. You should now have a new layer named crimecount which contains all of the same data as the old Houston layer as well as a new category that contains the total homicides for each individual census tract.
8. Using what you learned in Chapter 2, create a new graduated color map using the aggregated crime data as the variable of interest.

Downloading Aggregate Data and Joining It with Existing Map Data

Over the last five years, there has been a dramatic increase in the availability of spatially enabled data via the Internet. Specifically, numerous government, non-profit, and private companies and individual citizens have been making available high-quality data in a format that is useful for spatial analysis. However, despite the increase in the amount of data available over the Internet, much of the data is difficult to find and or difficult to get in a useful format for spatial analysis. This last section of the chapter will provide students with a list of a few of the better Internet resources for spatial data as well as walk you through downloading and joining aggregate data to a map layer.

1. Open your browser and go to the following website: www.huduser.org. This website is part of the Housing and Urban Development (HUD) webpage and contains a wealth of data and information that can be useful for doing analysis of crime data.
2. When the page opens, click on the "Data Sets" link from the table of contents on the left hand side of the page. This will take you to a page that contains numerous different data sets that are available from HUD. Importantly, not all the datasets are in a format that can be downloaded and joined with a map file, and some of the data is available only via a CD or in a final report view.
3. When the "Data Sets" page opens, click on the "Geographic Information Systems" link from the right hand side table of contents. This will take you to the webpage that contains the different GIS data available for download from HUD.
4. When the GIS page opens, scroll down and click on the "Boundary Files Download Site." The boundary File Download page will walk you through how to download the boundary files for any county in the United States. In this case, we are going to download census tract files for Fayette County Kentucky.
5. Scroll to the bottom of the page to the "Select Summary Level" and choose the "080-Split Census Tract" option.
6. When the next page opens, scroll down and select "Kentucky" from the "Select a State Name" option.
7. Finally, when the last page opens, scroll down and select "Fayette County" from the list of counties in Kentucky. This will automatically start the downloading process in which a zipped file containing only the census tract data for Fayette County Kentucky is downloaded.

8. Unzip and extract the file named "21067_080," which is the census code for Fayette County Kentucky (Lexington, KY) census tract data.
9. Next on the HUD User webpage where you downloaded the Fayette County data, click on the "Data Sets" link on the left hand side. This will take you back to the dataset page where we will download our next data from.
10. When you get to the Data Sets webpage, click on the Consolidated Plan link on the right hand side. This will take you to the Consolidated Plan/CHAS 2000 data site.
11. Scroll down to the "Ways to Access the Data" area of the page and select "State Files." This will take you to the state data download page.
12. Scroll down to Kentucky and select it. This will automatically start the downloading process in which a zipped file contains data for the entire state of Kentucky.
13. Unzip the Kentucky Folder and extract all the contents to a location on your hard drive that is easy to access.

Joining Aggregate Data

The last stage of this process is the actual joining of the newly downloaded HUD data to the previously downloaded Boundary file for Lexington Kentucky. This process is crucial because it will allow the user to attach the HUD data to the basemap in such as manner that they will be able to use the data for analysis purposes. In particular, users will be able to make maps showing the areas where the income of owner occupied housing is lowest and overlay it with crime data.

1. Open ArcMap and add the 21067_080 file to the map. This is the basemap data for Fayette county KY that you downloaded and unzipped.
2. Click on "Add Data" and add the KY-F7080r table to the view. This is the table of HUD data that you downloaded and unzipped.
3. Right-click on the 21067_080 file and scroll down and select "Joins and Relates" and then select Join.
4. When the Join Data wizard appears, select "Join attributes from a table" in the drop-down menu of the "What do you want to join to the layer?" section. This will change the appearance of the wizard to questions that are relevant for joining the table with the basemap.
5. Choose "SUM080" as the field in the layer that the join will be based on in section 1.
6. If it is not already selected, make sure that the table "KY-F7080r" is selected in section 2 as the table to join to the layer.
7. Finally, if it is not already selected, choose SUM080 as the field in the table to base the join on. This is extremely important as for a join to work there must be a field in both the layer and the table that are the same. In this case the field is SUM080.
8. When the wizard has been completely filled out, click OK.

Analysis with Data: You should now be able to create amps using the added aggregate data from HUD. In particular you may want to look at two particular fields in the data.

F7C1: Owner-occupied income is less than 30 percent of HUD-adjusted median income for the city.

F7C5: Renter-occupied incomes in less than 30 percent of HUD-adjusted income for the city.

In both cases the results would indicate the locations of disproportionally low income home owners or renters. Included in the Chapter 12 folder is some crime data for Lexington KY that you may want to overlay in order to see if there is a correlation between the HUD data and crime locations.

Aggregate Data Sources

The last part of this chapter is just a simple discussion of some other places on the Internet to find freely available data that is relevant to analyzing and understanding crime patterns. Although some of the data will be easy to download and join with your existing layers, other sites are not as easy to use as the HUD site. When possible, a rating of the ease of data manipulation will be provided for each site.

1. HUD-User: Housing and Urban Development Website (www.huduser.gov): As already seen, this site has a wealth of data available that can be used in crime analysis. In particular, HUD-User provides census basemaps, data for analyzing housing and population demographics, and links to other housing data that can be ordered and used or analysis.

2. Geodata.gov (http://gos2.geodata.gov/wps/portal.gos): This site is billed as "Your one-stop for Federal, State & Local Geographic Data," and it contains the most complete set of links to freely available geospatial data. Of particular importance for crime analysis is the category "cultural, society, and demographic," which contains data on housing and structures, family and social services, education, and law enforcement and crime data. While the type of data available varies by the individual link, there is a great deal of excellent data available for crime analysis and visualization purposes.

3. National Historic Geographic Information System (www.nhgis.org): This excellent website provides historical boundary and statistical data for the United States all the way back to 1790. This data is especially useful to researchers and crime analysts who are trying to analyze both physical and demographic changes in urban areas over time. In particular, census tract level variables and their associated boundary files are available for as far back as 1930 in some locations all for free download. More importantly, the data has been created in such a way that it is easy to join the statistical data to the boundary files.

4. Census.gov (www.census.gov): This is the best and most complete location to find any and all census data for the United States. Importantly, while it may be a complete site in terms of the data available, the data is not generally provided in a very user friendly format. In particular, while downloads of data are available, getting them into a form where they can be attached to basic boundary files (census tracts or block group maps) is a long and not very easy process. In addition to downloads of traditional census data by location, the new American Community Survey data is also available. This data is a new nationwide survey designed to provide communities with an understanding of how they are changing.

EXERCISES

1. **Analyzing Point data and Aggregate Data:** Using the crime data in Chapter 12 for Lexington (crimes.shp), perform a hot spot analysis and do a visual analysis of crime in relation to median income levels. How would you characterize the association?

2. **Download Data:** Go to one of the links discussed in the chapter and try downloading and joining the data to the Fayette County basemap. In choosing data, make sure to find data that is relevant (see chapters to your analysis) and that can be joined. Importantly, only data that has a field similar to those within the 21067_080 layer can be joined.

Exploratory Spatial Data Analysis

GOALS: **1.** Understand the concept of exploratory spatial data analysis (ESDA).

   2. Understand the different ways to explore your aggregate data and how to interpret the results.

   3. Understand how to use GeoDa to explore your data and when and why to use it.

INTRODUCTION

While Workbook Chapter 12 provided an introduction to aggregate data issues, Workbook Chapter 13 will provide an introduction to the GeoDa software and how to use the software to explore your aggregate data. GeoDa is a free software program developed by Dr. Luc Anselin's Spatial Analysis Laboratory at the University of Illinois, Urbana-Champaign for the purpose of performing exploratory spatial data analysis (EDSA) on aggregate data. As opposed to Crimestat, which is used almost completely for analyzing point data, GeoDa is specifically designed to allow users to analyze data contained in aggregate form and provides no techniques for analyzing point data as such. The benefit of a program like GeoDa to crime analysts and researchers is its powerful ability to determine and visualize patterns, clusters, and outliers in aggregate level data. Specifically, GeoDa can be used to statistically determine if clusters of socially disorganized census block groups exist within a community and where they are in relation to high-crime areas. These analysis techniques are particularly important given that almost all social data (poverty level, housing vacancies, unemployment, etc.) associated with criminological theories such as social disorganization is collected and distributed only at the aggregate level. Thus using GeoDa allows crime analysts and researchers to determine clusters of crime and disorganization and the degree to which these clusters are related in space.

ESDA: EXPLORATORY SPATIAL DATA ANALYSIS

EDSA is the process of "summarizing spatial properties of the data, detecting spatial patterns in the data, formulating the hypotheses which refer to the geography of data, and identifying cases or subjects of cases that are unusual given their location on the map" (Haining, 2004:182). In essence, ESDA is the process of examining spatial data and determining the range of values for a distribution (median, inter quartile range) and if there are outliers in the data (values far outside the average) and where these values lie on a map. These distributions and their extreme values are then used to help better understand the data at hand and to drive the formulation of hypotheses and theory about the data. While determining median values, inter-quartile ranges, and outliers is all done with non-spatial techniques, ESDA allows users to view these distributions on the map. The value of this is that analysis of the data can take place not only in two dimensions using traditional techniques such as boxplots and scattergrams, but also in three dimensions using maps and geography. Thus, users can look at a distribution in a boxplot (to be explained below) and select all of the outliers in order to determine if these outliers contain some sort of spatial pattern. Conversely, users can select a geographic subset of the data (group of census block groups within a city) and determine if the data contain any outliers or if the distribution is normal in its distribution. The importance of ESDA is that it allows the user to better understand their data and to know whether their data contain extreme values and if so, where. As stated before, this information is then useful in creating hypotheses and formulating theories.

ESDA TECHNIQUES

While there are numerous different ESDA techniques, the focus of the discussion in this section will be on those techniques contained within GeoDa. Specifically, this section will discuss the different ESDA techniques contained within GeoDa and what information they provide. The following section will then walk the user through how to conduct these ESDA techniques and how to interpret the findings.

Boxplots

A boxplot is a useful tool for providing a simple five-number summary of a particular variable in your data (Fotheringham, Brunsdon, and Charlton, 2004). In particular, a boxplot provides a quick visual snapshot of the median value, quartiles, and outliers (high and low) for a variable in your data in order to assess whether it is skewed in one way or another. In order to better understand the value of the boxplot, it is best to break down the output of the boxplot into its individual parts, median value, quartiles, and outliers. The median value is simply the middle value or the mid point in a distribution (Fotheringham, Brundson, and Charlton, 2004). The importance of the median value is that it provides a good, stable indicator of an average value in your distribution. As opposed to the average, the median is less subject to outliers (extreme values within a distribution) and thus provides a more stable representation of a distribution. The quartiles in a boxplot consist of the lower and upper quartiles. The lower quartile is the location within a distribution in which 25 percent of the values are below it and 75 percent of the values are above it (Fotheringham, Brunsdon, and Charlton, 2004). Conversely, the upper quartile is the location within a distribution in which 25 percent of the values are above it and 75 percent of the values are below it. Importantly, the area between the upper and lower quartiles is called the interquartile range (IQR) and it contains the middle 50 percent of values in the distribution as well as the median value. The importance of the IQR is that it provides an indicator of the nature of your distribution. In particular, short compact IQRs in which the median value is in the true middle of the IQR indicate that the range of values within the distribution is smaller or less diverse than an IQR that is tall or elongated. Moreover, if the median value is closer to the lower or upper quartile, then it indicates that the distribution is not normally distributed, which may indicate the presence of extreme values or ouliers. The final aspect of the boxplot is the outlier. Outliers are values that are either below or above the IQR and indicate values that are generally extreme in nature. In analyzing crime data, it is common to find outliers as criminal behavior and crime locations are not normally distributed across society or a geographic landscape, but are instead focused in certain areas. Figure 13.1 (www.mappingcrime.org) provides an example of a boxplot of census level homicide totals for Houston created in GeoDa. In analyzing the boxplot, the IQR is fairly compact with the median (red line in the purple box) closer to the lower quartile, indicating a slightly skewed distribution but with a fair amount of high-value outliers. In analyzing the outliers (blue points coming out of the top of the IQR), a significant amount of them are well beyond the top quartile indicating many locations in which actual homicide counts are much higher than the median. Overall, this boxplot indicates that the majority of Houston does not have very high homicide totals at the census tract level, but that there are a fair amount of census tracts that experience very high amounts of homicide. In using the boxplot for crime analysis and pattern detection, it is often the extreme outliers that we are most interested in (highest and lowest homicides). As we will see when we explore GeoDa, the boxplot results are linked to the map so that users can select the outliers (or middle range points) and see where they lie geographically.

Histogram

A histogram is another simple method for representing a distribution of values within a variable (Fotheringham, Brunsdon, and Charlton, 2004). In a histogram, the range of values in a variable is divided into intervals (0–9, 10–19, 20–29, etc.) called bins and the number of values in each bin is counted and a bar graph is drawn indicating the height of each bin (Fotheringham, Brunsdon, and Charlton, 2004). This graph can then be analyzed to determine the general shape of the distribution, whether it is skewed and whether it has 1, 2, or several different peaks. As with using boxplots in analyzing crime, distributions are often skewed and it is those extreme values that are often most important in terms of determining high-crime areas and patterns of crime. Figure 13.2 (www.mappingcrime.org) provides a histogram of census level homicide totals for Houston created in GeoDa. In analyzing the histogram, it is apparent that it is highly skewed to the left (low homicide) as the majority of census tracts in Houston have no homicides or very little (left side of the graph). Specifically, 179 census tracts experience no homicide at all, with only a very few census tracts experiencing very high numbers of homicides (far right of the graph). When using GeoDa to analyze this histogram, the user can select the bin (bars on the graph) and they will be selected on the map, allowing a user to easily determine the geographic location and relative concentration of extreme values. Importantly, in creating a histogram the number and width of bins are important to both the creation and understanding of your distribution. Specifically, if you have very wide bins (0–60 homicides), you may miss important distinctions (outliers, 2 peaks, etc.), whereas if you have very narrow bins the possibility of detecting random variations becomes greater (Fotheringham, Brunsdon, and Charlton, 2004).

Scatter Plot

The last of the different ESDA methods in GeoDa that will be discussed is the scatter plot, a method used for determining the degree of association between two different variables (Fotheringham, Brunsdon, and Charlton, 2004). While many of the different techniques we have discussed in this workbook have been concerned with determining clusters of incidents (hot spots and kernel density interpolation), scatter plots are interested in determining the degree to which two variables are related—specifically, whether variable X (percent of families on public assistance) is associated with variable Y (total amount of homicides per census tract) and in what manner. A scatter plot can best be thought of as a collection of points that represent the relationship between two different variables, with each point having one coordinate on the X axis (homicides) and one on the Y axis (public assistance) (Fotheringham, Brunsdon, and Charlton, 2004). The main benefit of a scatter plot is that it allows for the determination of a relationship between the two variables as well as the direction of the relationship. Specifically, if the pattern of dots slopes upward from left to right, the association is positive (higher numbers of families on public assistance is associated with higher homicides), whereas is it slopes downward from left to right, the association is negative (higher numbers of families on public assistance is associated with lower homicides). While a scatter plot cannot determine causation (changes in homicide are related to changes in families on public assistance), it is a good method for determining causation and beginning to understand what variables may have causative impacts. Figure 13.3 (www.mappingcrime.org) provides a look at a scatter plot of the relationship between census level homicide totals for Houston and percent of families receiving public assistance that was created in GeoDa. In this case, the relationship slopes fairly strongly upward from left to right (as evidenced by the blue trend line), indicating that there is a fairly strong association between homicide incidents and the percent of families receiving public assistance. Again this does not indicate any level of causation in one direction or the other between the two variables, but rather only association.

ESDA IN GeoDa

As previously mentioned, GeoDa is a free software solution developed by Luc Anselin that is used for analyzing data at the aggregate level. While it is similar to Crimestat in that they are both developed and produced to be free tools for the analysis of spatially enabled data, there are some key differences between them. With the exception of the types of data analyzed by the software programs, the biggest difference between the two tools is the ability to view the data and analysis in GeoDa without needing a separate GIS program such as ArcGIS. This section of the lab will provide the user with a basic familiarity with GeoDa and how to use GeoDa for ESDA purposes.

Overview of GeoDa

1. After downloading and installing GeoDa from the textbook website (www.mappingcrime.org), start it from either the start menu or by double-clicking on the desktop icon. When GeoDa opens, you will see the main menu screen. Importantly, you cannot use any of the functions of GeoDa until you have added data to the project.
2. In order to add data, click on either the Open folder icon in the upper right corner or select "open project" from the file menu.
3. When the "GeoDa Project Setting" box appears, click on the open folder icon and navigate to Chapter 13 in the workbook and add Houston.shp. GeoDa will automatically select RECORD_ID as the key variable.
4. Click OK. You will now see a map of Houston on the screen and all of the menus and buttons will become available for use.

There are 12 different drop-down menus in GeoDa, eight of which are specific to the analysis and use of GeoDa and four of which are more general menus. In addition, many of the different analysis functions associated with the drop-down menus have associated dockable buttons that act as shortcuts to certain menu items. Importantly, all of these shortcut icon buttons are arranged by group and are dockable, implying they can be arranged in any fashion and moved around the map. In addition, if you hold the cursor over any of the button icons, GeoDa will tell you the function of the icon.

The first menu is the **Edit** menu, which contains several tools that allow the user to add new maps, duplicate maps, and add and remove layers to the maps. The second group of icon buttons is associated with these functions and they allow you to quickly open a new map, add or remove a layer, duplicate the main map, and copy data to a clipboard. The second menu is the **Tools** menu, which contains functions associated with creating weights for use in analysis, creating polygon maps from points, and exporting the data to different formats. The first group of icon buttons is associated with this drop-down menu and they allow the user to open and create weights, as well as analyze weights' characteristics. The third menu is the **Map** menu, which contains functions associated with different data visualization techniques. Specifically, users can create quantile, percentile, box, and standard deviation maps, as well as cartograms and map movies. These functions also have associated button icons located at the far left of the menu bar. The fourth menu is the **Explore** menu, which contains the techniques associated with EDSA. These techniques include histogram, scatter plot, box plot, parallel coordinate plot, 3D-scatter plot, and conditional plot, all with associated icon buttons in the fourth grouping from the left. The fifth menu is the **Space** menu, which contains techniques associated with determining spatial autocorrelation. In particular, these techniques include univariate and multivariate moran, Moran's I and LISA with EB rate, and univariate and multivariate LISA, all with associate button icons. The sixth menu is the **Regress** menu, which allows for a spatial regression analysis to be completed and has no associated button icon. The final menu of interest is the **Options** menu, which contains items associated with changing the color of the maps, saving map images, adding centroids to the data, and zooming in and out. As with the Regress menu, there are no associated button icons with these menu items.

DATA VISUALIZATION METHODS

While GeoDa contains several good techniques for use in ESDA, it also contains several good methods for data visualization, a key first stage in the ESDA process. In this section, we will discuss how to create and interpret quantile, percentile, and standard deviation maps.

Quantile Map

1. Under the Map menu, select Quantile.
2. When the "Variables Settings" menu appears, scroll down, select Homrate, and click OK. This is an already calculated homicide rate for each census tract within Houston. Importantly, if you have just raw counts of crimes, GeoDa can calculate rates using the smooth function under the map menu.
3. When the "Quantile Map" menu appears, it will ask you to determine the number of classes/groups you want to create. Unless you have a desire to create more classes, click OK to the default four classes.
4. The map now shows you the homicide rate in Houston, broken down into four different ranges (see Figure 13.4).

   Map Tip: In GeoDa, it is very easy to make duplicate maps in order to compare the results of multiple visualization techniques at one time. Simply select duplicate map from the Edit menu and an identical map (without the analysis) will be created.

Percentile Map

A percentile map takes all of the observations for a particular variable and groups the observations into different categories based on their percentile rank. Specifically, six different groups are created: less than 1 percent, 1–10 percent, 10–50 percent, 50–90 percent,

90–99 percent, and greater than 99 percent. The main advantage of this visualization technique is that it makes it easy to see where your extreme values are located within your study area as well as where the majority of your values are located. In a sense this is a non-statistical method for viewing extreme values with an eye toward clustering.

1. Under the Map menu select percentile.
2. When the "Variables Settings" menu appears, scroll down to select Homrate and click OK. The new map with the homicide rate broken down into six different percentiles should now appear (see Figure 13.5).

Interpretation: As discussed above, the benefit of the percentile map is that it allows the user to view their extreme values within their study area. In this case, there are six census tracts that have values above the 99th percentile located mostly near the center of Houston. While these are not necessarily statistical determinations in the classic sense, they are still useful as a precursor to ESDA.

Standard Deviation Map

The last data visualization technique to be discussed is the standard deviation map. In this visualization technique, data are assigned to groups based on where their relationship to the mean of the data. The major advantage of this technique is that by using the mean as a dividing point a contrast of values above and below the mean can be readily seen. Importantly, this technique works best for normally distributed data, which as discussed before, crime data rarely is.

1. Under the Map menu, select Std Dev.
2. When the "Variables Settings" menu appears, scroll down to select Homrate and then click OK. The new map with the homicide rate broken down by standard deviations should now appear (see Figure 13.6).

Interpretation. In this map, the vast majority of census tracts (390) are 1 standard deviation below the mean of 2.51 homicides, indicating that homicide rates are very low throughout the city. By contrast, the there are 18 census tracts that are 3 standard deviations above the mean, with the majority being concentrated near the center of the city. This indicates that there are census tracts that have much higher than average homicide rates and that they are clustered near the city center.

CONDUCTING ESDA WITH GeoDa

As earlier sections of this chapter have focused on explaining and understanding ESDA and the different techniques associated with ESDA, this part of the chapter will focus primarily on using GeoDa to perform ESDA as well as interpreting the results of the analysis.

1. With a map open, select Box Plot from the Explore drop-down menu.
2. When the "Variables Settings" menu appears, scroll down to select Homrate. The Box Plot results should appear as a floating window above the map (see Figure 13.7).

Interpretation: The IQR is the purple colored box with the red line running through it representing the media for the distribution. The blue dots running vertically through the middle of the IQR represent each different census tract, with the majority of values clustering between the 25th and 75th percentiles. The parallel red line just north of the

IQR is called a hinge and represents the 75th percentile of the distribution, with the parallel red line at the bottom of the IQR representing the 25th percentile of the values. Overall the distribution is fairly compact, with the majority of the values being near the media and a few outliers on the high side of the distribution. This indicates that homicide rates at the census tract level are consistently low across Houston, with a few census tracts having much higher than average homicide rates (outliers at the topmost portion of the box plot).

> **Map Tip:** All of the values in the box plot (blue dots) are dynamically linked with their constituent census tracts in the map. Thus, if you click and drag a box around the top outliers in the box plot (or any other values) those census tracts will be highlighted on the map (checkered yellow). This is called brushing and it is an excellent method for analyzing outliers in a distribution. In this case, the topmost outliers are concentrated in the general area of the city center.

Histogram

1. With a new open map, select open Histogram from the Explore drop-down menu.
2. When the "Variables Settings" menu appears, scroll down and select Homrate. The histogram results should appear as a floating window above the map (see Figure 13.8).

Interpretation: The vast majority of the census tracts (540) are contained within the first category (0–7.9371 homicides per 1,000). The rest of the values drop off dramatically, indicating that the distribution is very skewed toward lower homicide rates. In general, this would indicate that high homicide rates are concentrated in a relative few areas (42 census tracts). As with the other ESDA techniques, the results are dynamically linked, and thus selecting the six categories to the right of the one large category will allow the user to examine where the highest homicide census tracts are located.

Scatter Plot

1. With a new map open, select5 Scatter Plot from the Explore drop-down menu.
2. When the "Variables Settings" menu appears, scroll down and select Homrate for the first variable and DPubass for the second variable. Thus in this analysis we are looking to see the degree to which homicide rates are associated with public assistance. The Scatter Plot should appear as a floating window above the map (see Figure 13.9).

Interpretation: The red dots represent each individual value as it exists in both the homicide rate and public assistance. The vertical axis represents the homicide rate with higher values being higher up the axis, whereas the horizontal axis represents the values of public assistance, with higher values being farther to the right. The blue line in the middle of the values is called a trend line and is an approximation of the distribution. In this case, the line is slopping moderately upward from left to right indicating that there is a moderate positive association between homicide rates and public assistance. Practically, this indicates that both homicide rates and public assistance rates increase together. Importantly, this *does not* imply causation, but only association. Thus, this does not mean that higher public assistance rates lead to higher homicide rates.

EXERCISES

1. **Data Visualization:** Explore the distribution of juvenile homicide rates (juvyhom) in Houston using quantile, percentile, and standard deviation maps. How does it vary in its spatial distribution from the overall homicide rate?
2. **ESDA:** Using histograms, box plots, and scatter plots, explore the juvenile homicide rate in Houston. How does it vary in its spatial distribution and association in comparison with the overall homicide rate?

FURTHER READINGS

Stewart Fotheringham, A., C. Brunsdon, and M. Charlton (2004). *Quantitative Geography.* London, UK: Sage Publications.

Haining, R. (2004). *Spatial Data Analysis: Theory and Practice.* Cambridge, UK: Cambridge University Press.

Anselin, L. (2005). *Exploring Spatial Data with GeoDa: A Workbook.* http://www.geoda.uiuc.edu/

Spatial Autocorrelation

GOALS: 1. Understand the concept of spatial autocorrelation.

2. Understand the Moran's I method of spatial autocorrelation.

3. Understand local indicators of spatial association (LISA) statistics and how to use them.

INTRODUCTION

This last chapter in the workbook is designed to provide a discussion of how to use GeoDa to determine spatial autocorrelation of aggregate data and how to visualize these areas for use in determining clusters of aggregate data. In particular, through the use of Moran's I and local indicators of spatial association (LISA), clusters of aggregate data can be identified and visualized at both the global and local levels. This ability to determine clusters of aggregate data is particularly important for crime analysis given that some crime data (homicide rates) and variables associated with crime (poverty, residential mobility, etc.) are only collected at the aggregate level. Thus, as we will see, GeoDa is a particularly useful tool for exploring census data and attempting to determine underlying causes of crime on a community level. While spatial autocorrelation was discussed briefly in Workbook Chapter 7 as it relates to point level data, the discussion here will focus solely on its identification and visualization within aggregate level data.

SPATIAL AUTOCORRELATION ANALYSIS

As discussed in Workbook Chapter 7, spatial autocorrelation is the degree to which a variable is correlated with itself in space (Anselin, 2005). In particular, when high values of a variable correlate with high neighboring values, or low values correlate with nearby low values, it is termed **positive spatial autocorrelation** (Anselin, 2005). An example of positive spatial autocorrelation would be when census tracts with high homicide rates correlate with neighboring census tracts that also have high homicide rates. Generally, units of analysis (census tracts) that exhibit positive spatial autocorrelation are termed **clustered**. Thus census tracts with high homicide that are clustered together in a specific section of a city exhibit positive spatial autocorrelation. Conversely, when high values correlate with low neighboring values, it is termed **negative spatial autocorrelation** (Anselin, 2005). Crime incidents that exhibit negative spatial autocorrelation are termed **spatially independent** or **uniformly dispersed**. Thus, census tracts with high homicide rates that are uniformly distributed throughout a city would exhibit negative spatial autocorrelation. It is important to note that in cities most social phenomenon such as restaurants locations, population centers, and ethnic groups exhibit positive spatial autocorrelation (Levine, 2002b). This is important for crime research in that crime distributions may exhibit spatial autocorrelation simply because everything in the city exhibits positive spatial autocorrelation. While this measure is not used a great deal by practitioners conducting crime analysis, it is an important statistical tool for those conducting research into spatial patterns. Specifically, spatial autocorrelation measures can be used to determine the degree to which crime rates and variables associated with crime (poverty, residential mobility, etc.) that are only measured at the census block or census tract level are clustered within a city. In addition, these measures can also be used to determine the difference in spatial autocorrelation between two different crime types or the same crime at two different time periods.

As discussed earlier in Workbook Chapter 7, the two main tests for spatial autocorrelation are **Moran's I** and **Geary's C**, both of which are used to determine the degree of spatial autocorrelation in aggregate data. While, both of these tests are included within Crimestat, GeoDa includes only the Moran's I. However, in addition to the Moran's I test, GeoDa also includes a **local indicator of spatial association**, also known as **LISA**. These two tests are highly complementary and together provide an indication of both the extent of overall clustering in a dataset (Moran's I) and the location of local clusters within the data (LISA) (Anselin, 2005). From a crime analysis perspective, when used together these tests can determine if there is clustering of crime rates within a city as well as the location and significance of the clustering of these crime rates. In addition, these tests can also be used to assess the degree to which one variable changes in its clustering over time or the degree to which different variables have similar patterns of clustering within a city.

MORAN'S I

The Moran's I test applies only to zones that have associated continuous variables attached to them (census tracts with homicide rates) and it works by calculating the value of the variable at one location with the value of that variable at all other locations (Anselin, 1992). The output of a Moran's "I" test is similar to a correlation coefficient, in that it varies from −1.0 to +1.0, where positive values indicate positive spatial autocorrelation and thus clustering, and negative values indicate negative spatial autocorrelation and thus spatial randomness (Anselin, 1992). When nearby values have similar values (high homicide rate next to high homicide rate), the "I" value is higher, conversely when nearby values have dissimilar values (high homicide rate next to low homicide rate), the "I" value is low (Levine, 2002b). Thus, an analysis of homicide rates at the census tract level that produced an "I" value of 0.875 would indicate very high positive spatial autocorrelation and thus clustering of census tracts with high homicide rates. Conversely, an "I" value of −0.236 would indicate negative spatial autocorrelation and that census tracts with high homicide rates were randomly distributed near census tracts with low homicide rates.

LISA ANALYSIS

While Moran's I is a global indicator of spatial autocorrelation, meaning that it can provide a general indicator of clustering in an area, it cannot provide an indication of where the clustering occurs or if it is concentrated only within one part of the study area (Anselin, 2005). By contrast, LISA can provide an indicator of the presence of significant spatial clusters within the data (Anselin, 2005). Importantly, GeoDa provides an indicator of significant spatial clustering in a visual manner, outputting maps that indicate the location, type, and significance of the clustering.

On a practical manner, the Moran's I is used to determine local clustering, in which a window is passed over the data and dependence with other locations is examined only on the data within the window (Anselin, 1995). The specifications for the window of analysis are determined by spatial weights, of which there are two basic kinds, contiguity and distance weights (Anselin, 2005). Contiguity-based weights impose a neighborhood structure on the data based on shared borders of the data (Anselin, 2005). Within GeoDa, there are two kinds of contiguity weights, rook, in which areas are classified as neighbors if they share borders, and queen, in which areas are classified as neighbors if they share a border or point (Anselin, 2005). The main difference between these two weights is that queen will include all of the same neighbors as the rook method, while also including those areas that only touch at a corner rather than share a long border. Thus, queen weights include more areas as neighbors than does the rook method. In contrast to contiguity weights are distance-based weights, which are based on the distances between points rather than shared borders (Anselin, 2005). Distance-based weights work by drawing a radius around each point (usually a centroid of a census tract or similar type area) and then counting all of the points within this radius (Anselin, 2005). Thus, in using distance-based weights, the distance of the radius, which is user defined, is key to determining the number of neighbors used for determining clustering. In determining which type of weight to use, it is recommended that contiguity weights are used first and that analysis is done on the weights to determine the presence of islands or bimodal distributions (Anselin, 2005). If during the analysis the presence of islands or bimodal distributions is detected within the data, then distance-based weights should be used. Importantly, this does not mean that distance weights cannot be used instead of contiguity weights, merely it is a suggested method of analysis-based decision making for the creation of weights for use in Moran's I and LISA analyses.

CONDUCTING MORAN'S I ANALYSIS IN GeoDa

1. Open GeoDa.
2. When the main screen appears, click on the open a project icon and add Houston from the Chapter 14 folder.
3. Under the tools menu, select "Create" from within the Weights submenu. Alternatively, you can click on the middle of the three "W" icons from the menu screen.

This will open the Creating weights dialog box as the first thing that must be done before conducting a Moran's I or LISA analysis is to create a weights matrix. Importantly, we will create both a queen and rook weight and analyze them to determine which is best for use in the analysis.

4. When the "Creating Weights" box opens, select Houston from the Chapter 14 folder as the input file. Click on the Open folder icon to scroll to the Chapter 14 folder.
5. Save the output as "Queen" and save it in the Chapter 14 folder. In this first example, we will create a queen contiguity weight.
6. Select Record_ID from the drop-down menu as the ID variable for the weights file.
7. Click on the radio button next to "Queen Contiguity" and leave the order of contiguity at the default 1.
8. When all of the preparations are correct, click on Create. This will start the process of creating the queen weight file.

9. When the queen weight file is created, select "Create" again from the Tools menu. Now we are going to create a rook contiguity weight file so that we can analyze both files together to determine which is more appropriate for our use in this analysis.
10. Follow the same process described above used in creating the queen weight with the following exceptions:
    a. Save the output file as Rook in the Chapter 14 folder.
    b. Click on the radio button next to Rook Contiguity.
11. When the rook weight is created, select Properties from under the Tools menu and Weights submenu.
12. When the "Weight Characteristics" dialog box appears, click on the Open Folder icon and select Queen from the Chapter 14 folder.
13. Repeat the process again; however, this time select Rook from the Chapter 14 folder when the "Weight Characteristics" dialog box appears.
14. Place both weights histograms side by side in order to compare their distributions.

Interpretation

In order to determine which weight matrix to use, queen or rook, the histogram of both weights must be analyzed to determine the presence of strange features that could impact the spatial autocorrelation statistics (Anselin, 2005). In determining the presence of strange features, the two most important things to look for are the presence of islands or bimodal distributions. An island is a bar within the histogram that is discontinuous or separated from the other bars in the histogram. An island indicates the presence of locations that are isolated within the data and indicates that the method may not be a good way to group neighbors. In both of these distributions, there are no islands present. When no islands are found, the next step is to check for the presence of a bimodal distribution within the weights. A bimodal distribution is one that has two different peaks. In this case, neither distribution has a bimodal distribution. Thus, in this case both contiguity weights are free of strange features that may impact the spatial autocorrelation results. This leaves the question of which weight matrix to use. In this case, it would be acceptable to use either weight matrix, although the preference would be to use the queen weight as its distribution is closer to a normal distribution than the rook.

Conducting a Moran's I

1. Under the Space drop-down menu, select Univariate Moran. This is the option to select when performing a single variable Moran's I analysis.
2. When the "variables settings" dialog box appears, scroll down the variable list and select Homrate and click OK.
3. When the "Select Weight" dialog box appears, click on the open file icon and select queen.GAL from the Chapter 14 folder.
4. Click OK in order to run the analysis.

Interpretation of Moran's I Results

The Moran's I score for Homrate is 0.3267, which indicates that there is a moderate positive spatial autocorrelation. In a practical sense, this means that there is a moderate degree of spatial clustering of homicide rates at the census tract level within Houston. Importantly, the Moran's I does not indicate where the clustering occurs within Houston, only that there is some clustering. In order to determine the location and significance of the clustering, a LISA analysis must be conducted.

CONDUCTING A UNIVARIATE LISA ANALYSIS

1. Under the Space drop-down menu, select "Univariate LISA." This is the option to select when performing a LISA analysis.
2. When the "Variables Settings" dialog box appears, scroll down the variable list and select "Homrate" and click OK.
3. When the "Select Weight" dialog box appears, click on the open file icon and select queen. GAL from the Chapter 14 folder. Click OK to run the analysis.
4. When the "What windows to open?" dialog box appears, put check marks next to "The Significance Map" and "The Cluster Map" and then click OK. This will finish the analysis and open two new windows that will indicate where the clustering of "homrate" occurs within Houston as well as the degree of significance of this clustering.

Interpretation of LISA Analysis Results In the LISA analysis two maps are created, both of which need to be interpreted to understand the full degree of clustering of data within the study area. The first map is the clustering map, which indicates where the clustering occurs within the study area as well as the type of clustering that occurs. In the analysis at hand, red indicates areas where high homicide census tracts are next to high homicide census tracts, dark blue indicates where low homicide census tracts are next to low homicide census tracts, light blue indicates where low homicide census tracts are next to high homicides census tracts, and pink indicates where high homicides census tracts are next to low homicide census tracts. In Houston, clustering of high homicide rates is found in the center of the city and in the area slightly south of the city center. By contrast, the census tracts with the lowest homicide rates are clustered mostly on the outlying areas to the northwest and southeast of the city. Finally, there area a handful of census tracts where high homicide rates are adjacent to low homicide rate census tracts and these are mostly on the eastern side of Houston. Overall, the highest homicide rates are clustered in the center of the city with some pockets of high homicide rates radiating out on the eastern side of Houston and with the lowest homicide rates on the outlying areas of Houston. This pattern is fairly typical of large cities where the highest rates of crime are often found within the city center with crime decreasing the further from the center one travels. These results are similar to those hypothesized by Social Disorganization (see Chapter 3).

The other important output map is the significance map, which reports the level of statistical significance for the observations in the cluster map. The importance of this map is that it provides an indication of whether or not the clusters observed in the cluster map are statistically significant or are random in nature. In the analysis at hand, all of the clustering results are significant at the 0.05 or greater level (0.01 or 0.001), indicating that all of the clustered results are true clusters and not random fluctuations. It is important to note that these two results maps should be viewed together in order to determine if the areas of clustering are significant or not.

EXERCISES

1. **Juvenile Homicide:** Explore the distribution of juvenile homicide rates (juvyhom) in Houston by performing both a Moran's I and LISA analyses. How does it vary in terms of spatial autocorrelation from the overall homicide rate? Are there similar patterns of clustering?
2. **Structural Factors:** Explore the distribution of structural factors within Houston (such as family poverty or the poverty rate) by performing a Moran's I and LISA analyses. How does it vary in terms of spatial autocorrelation from the overall homicide rate? Are there similar patterns of clustering?

FURTHER READINGS

Stewart Fotheringham, A., C. Brunsdon, and M. Charlton (2004). *Quantitative Geography*. London, UK: Sage Publications.

Haining, R. (2004). *Spatial Data Analysis: Theory and Practice*. Cambridge, UK: Cambridge University Press.

Anselin, L. (2005). *Exploring Spatial Data with GeoDa: A Workbook*. Available on-line at: http://www.geoda. uiuc.edu/

Bibliography

Akers, R. (1977). *Deviant Behavior: A Social Learning Approach.* Belmont, CA: Wadsworth.

Akers, R. (1994). *Criminological Theory: Introduction and Evaluation.* Los Angeles, CA: Roxbury.

Alston, J. (1994). *The Serial Rapist's Spatial Pattern of Target Selection.* Unpublished master's thesis, Burnaby, British Columbia, Canada: Simon Fraser University, School of Criminology.

American Sickle Cell Anemia Foundation (2002). [On-line]. Available: www.ascaa.org.

Anderson, D. (1999, July). *Balancing Public and Private Rights in Mapping Crime: Two Axioms to Guide our Thinking.* Paper presented at the Crime Mapping and Data Confidentiality Roundtable at the Crime Mapping Research Center (CMRC). Retrieved from the National Institute of Justice website: www.ojp.usdoj.gov/nij/maps/Pubs/privacy/anderson.pdf.

Andresen, M. (2006). A spatial analysis of crime in Vancouver, British Columbia: A synthesis of social disorganization and routine activity theory. *Canadian Geographer* 50(4): 487–502.

Angel, S. (1968). *Discouraging Crime Through City Planning.* Berkeley, CA: Institute of Urban and Regional Development, University of California.

Annual Report on School Safety (1999). Retrieved January 14, 2001 from http://www.ed.gov/PDFDocs/InterimAR.pdf.

Annual Report on School Safety (2002). Washington, DC: U.S. Department of Education and U.S. Department of Justice.

Anselin, L. (1992). *Spacestat: A Program for the Statistical Analysis of Spatial Data.* Santa Barbara, CA: National Center for Geographic Information and Analysis, University of California.

Anselin, L. (1995). Local Indicators of Spatial Association-LISA. *Geographical Analysis* 27: 93–115.

Anselin, L., and Bera, A. (1998). Spatial Dependence in linear regression models with an introduction to spatial econometrics. In A. Ullah and D.A. Giles (Eds.) *Handbook of Applied Economic Statistics* (pp. 237–289). New York: Marcel Dekker.

Appleton, J. (1975). *The Experience of Place.* London: John Wiley & Sons.

Arata, C. (1999). Coping with rape. *Journal of Interpersonal Violence* 14(1): 62–78.

Avila, J. (Correspondent) (2002, October 7). Geographic profiling: A new technique being used by law enforcement. *NBC Nightly News.* New York: WNBC.

Bachman, R. (1991). An analysis of American Indian homicide: A test of social disorganization and economic deprivation at the reservation county level. *Journal of Research in Crime and Delinquency* 28(4): 456–471.

Bachman, R. (1994). Crime in nonmetropolitan America: A national accounting of trends, incidence rates, and idiosyncratic vulnerabilities. *Rural Sociology* 57: 546–560.

Bai, M. (1997). White storm warning: In Fargo and the prairie states, speed kills. *Newsweek,* 31 March: 66.

Baldwin, J., and A. Bottoms (1976). *The Urban Criminal: A Case Study in Sheffield.* London, England: Tavistok Press.

Balkwell, J. (1990). Ethnic inequality and the rate of homicide. *Social Forces* 69: 53–70.

Barclay, G., and C. Tavares (2002). International Comparisons of Criminal Justice Statistics 2000. London, England: Home Office.

Barker, M. (2000). The criminal range of small-town burglars. In D. Canter and L. Allison (Eds.), *Profiling Property Crimes* (pp. 59–73). Aldershot: Ashgate.

Bartol, C. (1996). Police psychology: Then, now, and beyond. *Criminal Justice and Behavior* 23: 70–89.

Baumer, E., Lauritsen, J., and R. Rosenfeld (1998). The influence of crack cocaine on robbery, burglary, and homicide rates: A cross-city, longitudinal analysis. *Journal of Research in Crime and Delinquency* 35(3): 316–340.

Beckett, K. (1997). *Making Crime Pay: Law and Order in Contemporary American Politics.* New York: Oxford University Press.

Bell, D., Carlson, J., and A. Richard (1998). The social ecology of drug use: A factor analysis of an urban environment. *Substance Use and Misuse* 33(11): 2201–2217.

Bellair, P. (1997[1996]). The consequences of crime for social disorganization theory: An examination of reciprocal effects between crime and social interaction. *Dissertation Abstracts International, A: The Humanities and Social Sciences* 56(10): 4154-A.

Bennell, C., and D. Canter (2002). Linking commercial burglaries by modus operandi: Tests using regression and ROC analysis. *Science and Justice* 42: 153–164.

Bennett, T., and R. Wright (1984). *Burglars on Burglary: Prevention and the Offender.* Brookfield, VT: Gower Publishing.

Bhati, A. (2005). Robust spatial analysis of rare crimes: An information-theoretic approach. *Sociological Methodology* 35 (1): 227–289.

Biderman, A., Johnson, L., McIntyre, J., and A. Weir (1967). *Report on a Pilot Study in the District of Columbia on Victimization and Attitudes Toward Law Enforcement.* Washington, DC: U.S. Government Printing Office.

Blau, J., and P. Blau (1982). The cost of inequality: Metropolitan structure and violent crime. *American Sociological Review* 47: 114–129.

Block, C. (1990). *Hot spots and Isocrime in Law Enforcement Decision Making*. Paper presented to the Conference on Police and Community Responses to Drugs. University of Illinois: Chicago.

Block, C. (1994). STAC hot spot areas: A statistical tool for law enforcement decisions. In *Proceedings of the Workshop on Crime Analysis Through Computer Mapping* (pp. 33–53). Chicago, IL: Criminal Justice Information Authority.

Block, C., and A. Christakos (1995). Major trends in Chicago homicide: 1965–1994. *Research in Brief*. Washington, DC: U. S. Department of Justice. National Institute of Justice.

Block, C., and R. Block (1995a). Street gang crime in Chicago. *Research in Brief*. Washington, DC: U.S. Department of Justice. National Institute of Justice.

Block, C., and R. Block (1998). Homicides in Chicago, 1965–1995 [Computer file]. 4th ICPSR version. Chicago, IL: Illinois Criminal Justice Information Authority [producer]. Ann Arbor, MI: Interuniversity Consortium for Political and Social Research [distributor].

Block, R., and C. Block (1995b). Space, place and crime: Hot spot areas and hot places of liquor-related crime. In J. E. Eck and D. Weisburd (Eds.), *Crime Prevention Studies: Vol 4. Crime and Place* (pp. 145–183). Monsey, NY: Criminal Justice Press.

Blumstein, A. (1995). Youth violence, guns, and the illicit drug industry. *Journal of Criminal Law and Criminology* 86: 10–36.

Blumstein, A. (1996). Linking gun availability to youth gun violence. *Law and Contemporary Problems* 59(1): 5–24.

Boba, R. (2005). *Crime Analysis and Crime Mapping*. Los Angeles, CA: Sage Publishing.

Bouley, E., and M. Vaughn (1995). Violent crime and modernization in Colombia. *Crime, Law, and Social Change* 23: 17–40.

Box, S., Hale, C., and G. Andrews (1988). Explaining fear of crime. *British Journal of Criminology* 28: 340–356.

Bowers, K., Johnson, S. D., and K. Pease (2004). Prospective hot-spotting: The future of crime mapping? *British Journal of Criminology* 44: 641–658.

Brantingham, P., and F. Faust (1976). A conceptual model of crime prevention. *Crime & Delinquency* 7: 284–295.

Brantingham, P., and P. Brantingham (1975). The spatial patterning of burglary. *Howard Journal of Penology and Crime Prevention* 14: 11–24.

Brantingham, P., and P. Brantingham (1978). Housing patterns and burglary in a medium size American city. In J. Scott and D. Dinitz (Eds.), *Criminal Justice Planning*. New York: Praeger.

Brantingham, P., and P. Brantingham (1981). *Environmental Criminology*. Beverly Hills, CA: Sage Publishing.

Brantingham, P., and P. Brantingham (1984). *Patterns in Crime*. New York: Macmillan.

Brantingham, P., and P. Brantingham (1991a). *Environmental Criminology*. Prospect Heights, IL: Waveland.

Brantingham, P., and P. Brantingham (1991b). Notes on the geometry of crime. In P. Brantingham and P. Brantingham (Eds.), *Environmental Criminology* (pp. 27–54). Prospect Heights, IL: Waveland.

Brantingham, P., and P. Brantingham (1993a). Environment, routine, and situation: Toward a pattern theory of crime. In R. Clarke and M. Felson (Eds.), *Routine Activity and Rational Choice. Advances in Criminological Theory*, Vol. 5. New Brunswick, NJ: Transaction Publishers.

Brantingham, P., and P. Brantingham (1993b). Nodes, paths and edges: Considerations on the complexity of crime and the physical environment. *Journal of Environmental Psychology* 13: 3–28.

Brantingham, P., and P. Brantingham (1995). Criminality of place: Crime generators and crime attractors. *European Journal on Criminal Policy and Research* 3: 5–26.

Brantingham, P., and P. Brantingham (1999). A theoretical model of crime hot spot generation. *Studies on Crime and Crime Prevention* 8(1): 7–26.

Brantingham, P., Brantingham, P., and D. Butcher (1986). Perceived and actual crime risks. In R. M. Figlio, S. Hakim, and G. F. Rengert (Eds.), *Metropolitan Crime Patterns* (pp. 139–159). Newark, NJ: Criminal Justice Press.

Brantingham, P., Brantingham, P., and P. Wong (1991). How public transit feeds private crime: Notes on the Vancouver "Sky Train" experience. *Security Journal* 1: 175–181.

Brener, N., Simon, T., Krug, E., and R. Lowry. (1999). Recent trends in violence-related behaviors among high school students in the United States. *JAMA* 282(5): 440.

Brezina, T. (1996). Adapting to strain: An examination of delinquent coping responses. *Criminology* 34(1): 39–60.

Bueermann, J. (1999, July). *Where is the Balance Between the Public's Right to Know and the Victim's Right to Privacy?* Paper presented at the Crime Mapping and Data Confidentiality Roundtable at the Crime Mapping Research Center (CMRC). Retrieved from the National Institute of Justice website: www. ojp.usdoj.gov/nij/maps/Pubs/privacy/ bueermann.pdf.

Buerger, M. E., Cohn, E. G., and A. J. Petronison (1995). Defining the "hot spots" of crime: Operationalizing theoretical concepts for field research. In J. E. Eck and D. Weisburd (Eds.), *Crime Prevention Studies: Vol. 4. Crime and Place* (pp. 237–257). Monsey, NY: Criminal Justice Press.

Bugl, P. (2001). [On-line]. Available: uhavax.hartford.edu/bugl/histepi.htm.

Bureau of Justice Statistics (1997). Retrieved from the Bureau of Justice Statistics website: www.ojp.usdoj.gov/bjs.

Bureau of Justice Statistics (2000). Retrieved from the University of Albany (State University of New York) website: www.albany.edu/sourcebook/1995/pdf/t420.pdf.

Bureau of Justice Statistics (2002). Criminal victimization. www.ojp.usdoj.gov/bjs.

Bureau of Justice Statistics (2006). Criminal victimization. Retrieved December 1, 2006 from http://ojp.usdoj.gov/bjs/cvictgen.htm.

Burgess, E. (1925). The growth of a city. In R. Park, E. Burgess, and D. McKenzie (Eds.), *The City*. Chicago, IL: University of Chicago Press.

Burquest, R., Farrell, G., and K. Pease (1992). Lessons from school. *Policing* 8: 148–155.

Bursik, R. (1988). Social disorganization and theories of crime and delinquency. *Criminology* 26: 519–551.

Bursik, R., and H. Grasmick (1993). *Neighborhoods and Crime: The Dimensions of Effective Social Control*. New York: Lexington.

Byers, B., and R. Zeller (2001). Official hate crime statistics: An examination of the "epidemic hypothesis." *Journal of Crime & Justice* 24(2): 73–85.

Camp, G. (1968). *Nothing to Lose: A Study of Bank Robbery in America*. Ph.D. dissertation. New Haven, CT: Yale University.

Canter, D., and S. Hodge (2000). Criminals' mental maps. In L. S. Turnbull, E. H. Hallisey, and B. D. Dent (Eds.), *Atlas of Crime: Mapping the Criminal Landscape* (pp. 186–191). Phoenix, AZ: Oryx.

Canter, D., and P. Larkin (1993). The environmental range of serial rapists. *Journal of Environmental Psychology* 13: 63–69.

Canter, D., Coffey, T., Huntley, M., and C. Missen (2000). Predicting serial killers' home base using a decision support system. *Journal of Quantitative Criminology* 16(4): 457–478.

Capone, D., and W. Nichols (1976). Urban structure and criminal mobility. *American Behavioral Scientist* 20: 199–213.

Carrington, P., and S. Moyer (1994). Gun availability and suicide in Canada: Testing the displacement hypothesis. *Studies on Crime & Prevention* 3: 168–178.

Carter, R., and K. Q. Hill (1978). Criminals' and non-criminals' perceptions of urban crime. *Criminology* 16: 353–371.

Carter, R., and K. Q. Hill (1979a). The criminal's image of the city and urban crime patterns. *Social Science Quarterly* 57: 597–607.

Carter, R., and K. Q. Hill (1979b). *The Criminal's Image of the City*. New York: Permagon.

Carter, R., and K. Q. Hill (1980). Area-images and behavior: An alternative perspective for understanding urban crime. In D. Georges-Abeyie and K. Harries (Eds.), *Crime: A Spatial Perspective* (pp. 193–204). New York: Columbia University.

Casady, T. (1999, July). *Privacy Issues in the Presentation of Geocoded Data*. Paper presented at the Crime Mapping and Data Confidentiality Roundtable at the Crime Mapping Research Center (CMRC). Retrieved from the National Institute of Justice website: www.ojp.usdoj.gov/nij/maps/Pubs/privacy/casady.pdf.

Castells, M. (1977). *The Urban Question: A Marxist Approach*. Cambridge, MA: MIT Press.

Cattarello, A. (2000). Community-level influences on individuals' social bonds, peer associations, and delinquency: A multilevel analysis. *Justice Quarterly* 17(1): 33–60.

Chaiken, J., Lawless, M., and K. Stevenson (1974). The impact of police activity on crime: Robberies on the New York City subway system. Report No. R-1424-NYC. Santa Monica, CA: Rand.

Chamlin, M., and J. Cochran (1995). Assessing Messner and Rosenfeld's institutional anomie theory: A partial test. *Criminology* 33(3): 411.

Chamlin, M., and J. Cochran (2006). Economic inequality, legitimacy, and cross-national homicide rates. *Homicide Studies* 10(4): 231–252.

Chapin, S. (1974). *Human Activity Patterns in the City: Things People Do in Time and Space*. New York: John Wiley & Sons.

Chun-Chung, C., Johnson, J., and M. Austin (2005). The status of low-income neighborhoods in the post-welfare reform environment: Mapping the relationship between poverty and place. *Journal of Health & Social Policy* 21(1): 1–32.

Cisneros, H. (1995). *Defensible Space: Deterring Crime and Building Community*. Washington, DC: U.S. Department of Housing and Urban Development.

Clark, P. J., and F. C. Evans (1954). Distance to nearest neighbor as a measure of spatial relationships in populations. *Ecology* 35: 445–453.

Clarke, R. (1983). Situational crime prevention: Its theoretical basis and practical scope. In M. Tonry, and N. Morris (Eds.), *Crime and Justice, An Annual Review of Research*, Vol. 4. Chicago, IL: University of Chicago Press.

Clarke, R. (1992). *Situational Crime Prevention: Successful Case Studies*. Albany, NY: Harrow and Heston.

Clarke, R. (1995a). *CPTED and Situational Crime Prevention in Public Housing*. Paper presented to the Technical Assistance Workshop on CPTED. Washington, DC: U.S. Department of Housing and Urban Development.

Clarke, R. (1995b). Situational crime prevention. In M. Tonry and D. Farrington (Eds.), *Building a Safer Society: Strategic Approaches to Crime Prevention. Crime and Justice*, Vol. 19. Chicago, IL: University of Chicago Press.

Clarke, R. (1997). *Situational Crime Prevention: Successful Case Studies*. Albany, NY: Harrow and Heston.

Clarke, R. (1998). The theory and practice of situational crime prevention. [On-line]. Available: www.e-doca.net/Resources/Articles/Clarke_the_theory_and_practice_of_situational_crime_prevention.pdf.

Clarke, R. (2001). Rational choice. In R. Paternoster and R. Bachman (Eds.), *Explaining Crime and Criminals*. Los Angeles, CA: Roxbury.

Clarke, R., and D. Cornish (1985). Modeling offenders' decisions: A framework for research and policy. *Crime and Justice: An Annual Review of Research* 6: 147–185.

Clarke, R., and D. Weisburd (1994). Diffusion of crime control benefits: Observations of the reverse of displacement. *Crime Prevention Studies* 2: 165–184.

Clarke, R., and M. Felson (1993). *Routine Activity and Rational Choice*. London: Transaction.

Clarke, R., and P. Mayhew (1989). Crime as opportunity: A note on domestic gas suicide in Britain and the Netherlands. *British Journal of Criminology* 29(1): 35–36.

Clarke, R. V., and D. B. Cornish (1985). Modeling offenders' decisions: a framework for research and policy. *Crime and Justice: An Annual Review of Research* 6: 147–85.

Classen, C., Field, N., Hoopman, C., Nevill-Manning, K., and D. Spiegel (2001). Interpersonal problems and their relationship to sexual revictimization among women sexually abused in childhood. *Journal of Interpersonal Violence* 16(6): 495–509.

Clayton, R. (1995). *Marijuana in the "Third World": Appalachia, U.S.A.* Boulder, CO: Lynne Reinner Publishers.

Cliff, A., and J. Ord (1973). *Spatial Autocorrelation.* London: Pion.

Cloward, R., and L. Ohlin (1960). *Delinquency and Opportunity: A Theory of Delinquent Gangs.* New York: The Free Press.

Cochran, J., Bromley, M., and K. Branch (2000). Victimization and fear of crime in an entertainment district crime "hot spot:" A test of structural-choice theory. *American Journal of Criminal Justice* 24(2): 189–201.

Cohen, J., and G. Tita (1999). Diffusion in homicide: Exploring a general method for detecting spatial diffusion processes. *Journal of Quantitative Criminology* 15(4): 451–493.

Cohen, J., Cork, D., Engberg, J., and G. Tita (1988). The role of drug markets and gangs in local homicide rates. *Homicide Studies* 2(3): 241–262.

Cohen, L., and M. Felson (1979). Social change in crime rate trends: A routine activity approach. *American Sociological Review* 44: 588–608.

Cohen, L., and D. Cantor (1980). The determinants of larceny: An empirical and theoretical study. *Journal of Research in Crime and Delinquency* 17(2): 140–159.

Cohen, L., Kluegel, J., and K. Land (1981). Social inequality and predatory criminal victimization: An exposition and a test of a formal theory. *American Sociological Review* 46: 505–524.

Cohn, D., and A. Lengel (2002, October 8). Bullets, locations hold clues to shootings: Investigators are using latest scientific tools in effort to solve series of crimes. *The Washington Post,* p. A11.

Coleman, A. (1985). *Utopia on Trial: Vision and Reality in Planned Housing.* London, England: Hilary Shipman.

Cook, P., and J. Laub (1998). The unprecedented epidemic in youth violence. In M. Tonry and M. Moore (Eds.), *Youth Violence. Crime and Justice: A Review of Research,* Vol. 24. Chicago, IL: University of Chicago Press.

Cork, D. (1999). Examining space-time interaction in city-level homicide data: Crack markets and the diffusion of guns among youth. *Journal of Quantitative Criminology* 15(4): 379–406.

Cornish, D. (1993). Theories of action in criminology: Learning theory and rational choice approaches. In R. Clarke and M. Felson (Eds.), *Routine Activity and Rational Choice, Advances in Criminological Theory,* Vol. 5. New Brunswick, NJ: Transaction.

Cornish, D., and R. Clarke (1986). *The Reasoning Criminal.* New York: Springer-Verlag.

Corzine, J., and L. Huff-Corzine (1992). Racial inequality and black homicide: An analysis of felony, non-felony, and total rates. *Journal of Contemporary Criminal Justice* 8: 150–165.

Costanzo, C., Halperin, W., and N. Gale (1986). Criminal mobility and the directional component in journeys to crime. In R. Figlio, S. Hakim, and G. Rengert (Eds.), *Metropolitan Crime Patterns.* Monsey, NY: Criminal Justice Press.

Coupe, T., and L. Blake (2006). Daylight and darkness targeting strategies and the risks of being seen at residential burglaries. *Criminology* 44(2): 431–464.

Covington, J. and R. Taylor (1991). Fear of crime in urban residential neighborhoods: Implications of between- and within-neighborhood sources for current models. *The Sociological Quarterly* 32(2): 231–249.

Cressie, N. (1991). *Statistics for Spatial Data.* New York: John Wiley & Sons.

Crimnotes (1995). Tallahassee, FL: The Florida State University Press.

Cromwell, P., Olson, J., and D. Avary (1991). *Breaking and Entering: An Ethnographic Analysis of Burglary.* Newbury Park, CA: Sage Publishing.

Crowe, T. (1991). *Crime Prevention Through Environmental Design: Applications of Architectural Design and Space Management Concepts.* Boston, MA: Butterworth-Heinemann.

Cusson, M. (1983). *Why Delinquency?* Toronto, Canada: University of Toronto Press.

D'Alessio, S., and L. Stolzenberg (1990). A crime of convenience: The environment and convenience store robbery. *Environment and Behavior* 22(2): 255–271.

del Carmen, A., and M. Robinson (2000). Crime prevention through environmental design and consumption control in the United States. *Howard Journal of Criminal Justice* 39(3): 267–289.

Dent, B. D. (1993). *Cartography: Thematic Map Design* (2nd ed.). Dubuque, IA: William C. Brown.

Donnermeyer, J. (1994). *Crime and violence in rural communities.* Paper presented to the 1994 annual meeting of the Academy of Criminal Justice Sciences. Chicago, IL.

Doran, B., and B. Lees (2005). Investigating the spatiotemporal links between disorder, crime, and the fear of crime. *The Professional Geographer* 57(1): 1–12.

Downs, R., and D. Stea (1977). *Maps in Minds: Reflections on Cognitive Mapping.* New York: Harper and Row.

Durkheim, E. (1893). *De la Division du Travail Social.* Paris: F. Alcan.

Durkheim, E. (1897). *Le Suicide.* Paris: F. Alcan.

Ebdon, D. (1988). *Statistics in Geography.* Oxford, England: Blackwell.

Eck, J. (1994). *Drug Markets and Drug Places: A Case-Control Study of the Spatial Structure of Illicit Drug Dealing.* Ph.D. Dissertation, University of Maryland.

Eck, J. (1997). Preventing crime at places. In crime prevention: What works, what doesn't, what's promising. www.ncjrs.org/works/

Eck, J. (1998). Preventing crime at places. In L. Sherman, D. Gottfredson, D. MacKenzie, J. Eck, P. Reuter, and S. Bushway (Eds.), *Preventing Crime: What Works, What Doesn't, What's Promising.* A report prepared for Congress.

Eck, J., and D. Weisburd (1995). *Crime and Place.* Monsey, NY: Criminal Justice Press.

Elliott, D., Wilson, W., Huizinga, D., Sampson, R., Elliott, A., and B. Rankin (1996). The effects of neighborhood disadvantage on adolescent development. *Journal of Research in Crime and Delinquency* 33: 389–426.

Environmental Systems Research Institute, Inc. (1998). *Introduction to Arcview GIS.* Redlands, CA: Environmental Systems Research Institute.

Erikson, K. (1966). *Wayward Puritans.* Boston, MA: Allyn & Bacon.

Evans, R. (2001). Examining the informal sanctioning of deviance in a chat room culture. *Deviant Behavior* 22(3): 195–210.

Farewell, D. (1999). *Specifying the Bandwidth Function for the Kernel Density Estimator.* Retrieved from the University of Cambridge Institute of Public Health website: www.iph.cam.ac.uk/bugs/documentation/coda/node44. html.

Farrell, G. (1994). *Why Does Repeat Victimization Occur?* Manchester, England: University of Manchester.

Farrell, G., and K. Pease (1993). Once bitten, twice bitten: Repeat victimization and its implications for prevention. Crime Prevention Unit Paper 46. London, England: Home Office.

Farrell, G., Phillips, C., and K. Pease (1995). Like taking candy: Why does repeat victimization occur? *British Journal of Criminology* 35(3): 384–399.

Farrington, D., Bowen, S., Buckle, A., Burns-Howell, T., Burrows, J., and M. Speed (1993). An experiment on the prevention of shoplifting. In R. Clarke (Ed.), *Crime Prevention Studies*, Vol. 1. Monsey, NY: Willow Tree Press.

Fattah, E. (1993[1991]). The rational choice/opportunity perspectives as a vehicle for integrating criminological and victiminological theories. In R. Clarke and M. Felson (Eds.), *Routine Activity and Rational Choice.* Advances in Criminological Theory, Vol. 5. New Brunswick, NJ: Transaction Publishers.

Feldkamp, R. (1996). Methamphetamine abuse and trafficking no longer regional: Epidemic is spreading. *Organized Crime Digest* 17(5): 1–4.

Felson, M. (1983). Ecology of crime. In S. Kadish (Ed.), *Encyclopedia of Crime and Justice.* New York: Free Press.

Felson, M. (1986). Linking the criminal choices, routine activities, informal control, and criminal outcomes. In D. Cornish and R. Clarke (Eds.), *The Reasoning Criminal: Rational Choice Perspectives on Offending.* New York: Springer-Verlag.

Felson, M. (1987). Routine activities and crime prevention in the developing metropolis. *Criminology* 25(4): 911–931.

Felson, M. (1994). *Crime and Everyday Life: Insights and Implications for Society.* Thousand Oaks, CA: Pine Forge Press.

Felson, M. (1995). Those who discourage crime. In J. Eck and D. Weisburd (Eds.), *Crime and Place.* Monsey, NY: Criminal Justice Press.

Felson, M. (2002). *Crime and Everyday Life: Insights and Implications for Society* (2nd ed.). Thousand Oaks, CA: Pine Forge Press.

Felson, M. (2008). *Crime and Everyday Life* (3rd ed.). Thousand Oaks, CA: Sage Publishing.

Felson, M., and R. Clarke (1998). Opportunity makes the thief: Practical theory for crime prevention. Police Research Paper 98. London, England: Crown Publishers.

Felson, M., Belanger, M., Bichler, G., Bruzinski, C., Campbell, G., Fried, C., Grofik, K., Mazur, I., O'Regan, A., Sweeney, P., Ullman, A., and L. Williams (1996). Redesigning hell: Preventing crime and disorder at the Port Authority bus terminal. In R. Clarke (Ed.), *Preventing Mass Transit Crime: Crime Prevention Studies*, Vol. 6. Monsey, NY: Criminal Justice Press.

Fernandez, K., and M. Kuenzi (2006). Crime and support for democracy: Revisiting modernization theory. Working Paper No. 64. Cape Town, South Africa: The Institute for Democracy in South Africa.

Figlio, R., Hakim, S., and G. Rengert (1986). *Metropolitan Crime Patterns.* Monsey, NY: Criminal Justice Press.

Fleissner, D., and F. Heinzelmann (1996, August). Crime prevention through environmental design and community policing. *National Institute of Justice Research in Action.*

Forrester, D., Chatterton, M., and K. Pease (1988). Why it's best to lock the door after the horse has bolted. *Police Review* 4: 2288–2289.

Fowles, R., and M. Merva (1996). Wage inequality and a regional culture of violence. *American Journal of Sociological Review* 36: 412–427.

Freud, S. (1962). *Civilization and Its Discontents.* New York: W. W. Norton.

Freudenburg, W., and R. Jones (1991). Criminal behavior and rapid community growth: Examining the evidence. *American Journal of Sociology* 92: 27–63.

Frischer, M., Anderson, S., Hickman, M., and H. Heatlie (2002). Diffusion of drug misuse in Scotland: Findings from the 1993 and 1996 Scottish Crime Surveys. *Addiction Research & Theory* 10(1): 83–95.

Fromm, E. (1976). *To Have or to Be?* Toronto, Canada: Bantam Books.

Frye, V., and S. Wilt (2001). Femicide and social disorganization. *Violence Against Women* 7(3): 335–351.

Gabor, T., and E. Gottheil (1987). Offender characteristics and spatial mobility: An empirical study and some policy implications. *Canadian Journal of Criminology* 26: 267–281.

Gabor, T., Baril, M., Cusson, M., Elie, D., LeBlanc, M., and A. Normandeau (1987). *Armed Robbery: Cops, Robbers and Victims.* Springfield, IL: Charles C. Thomas.

Gardiner, R. (1978). *Design for Safe Neighborhoods.* Washington, DC: U.S. Department of Justice.

Garling, T., and R. Golledge (1989). Environmental perception and cognition. In E. Zube and G. Moore (Eds.), *Advances in Environment, Behavior, and Design*, Vol. 2. New York: Plenum Press.

Garling, T., Lindberg, E., Carreiras, M., and A. Book (1986). Reference systems in cognitive maps. *Journal of Environmental Psychology* 6: 1–18.

Garofalo, J. (1987). Reassessing the lifestyle model of criminal victimization. In M. Gottfredson and T. Hirschi (Eds.), *Positive Criminology.* Newbury Park, CA: Sage Publishing.

Gates, L., and W. Rohe (1987). Fear and reactions to crime: A revised model. *Urban Affairs Quarterly* 22: 425–453.

Gebhardt, C. (1999, December). *Geocoding: Improving your Hit Rate.* Paper presented at the Crime Mapping Research Center's Annual Conference, Orlando, FL. Retrieved from the International Association of Crime Analysts website: iaca.net/resources/FAQs/hitrate.html

Genereux, R., Ward, L., and J. Russell (1983). The behavioral component in the meaning of places. *Journal of Environmental Psychology* 3: 43–55.

Gilbert, A., and J. Gugler (1982). *Cities, Poverty, and Development: Urbanization in the Third World.* New York: Oxford University Press.

Glyde, J. (1856). Localities of crime in Suffolk. *Journal of the Statistical Society of London* 19: 102–106.

Goffman, E. (1971). *Relations in Public: Micro Studies of the Public Order.* New York: Harper & Row.

Goldstein, A. (1994). *The Ecology of Aggression*. New York: Plenum Press.

Goldstein, H. (1979). Improving policing: A problem-oriented approach. *Crime & Delinquency* 4: 234–258.

Gorman, D., Zhu L., and S. Horel (2005). Drug 'hot spot,' alcohol availability and violence. *Drug and Alcohol Review* 24: 507–513.

Gottfredson, D., McNeil, R., and G. Gottfredson (1991). Social area influences on delinquency: A multi-level analysis. *Journal of Research in Crime and Delinquency* 28: 197–226.

Gottfredson, M., and T. Hirschi (1990). *A General Theory of Crime*. Stanford, CA: Stanford University Press.

Green, L. (1995). Cleaning up drug hot spots in Oakland, California: The displacement and diffusion effects. *Justice Quarterly* 12: 737–754.

Greenberg, S., and W. Rohe (1984). Informal social control. In R. Taylor (Ed.), *Urban Neighborhoods: Research and Policy*. New York: Praeger.

Greene, J., and R. Taylor (1988). Community-based policing and foot patrol: Issues of theory and evaluation. In J. Greene and S. Mastrofski (Eds.), *Community Policing: Rhetoric or Reality?* New York: Praeger.

Groff, E. (2007). Simulation for theory testing and experimentation: An example using routine activity theory and street robbery. *Journal of Quantitative Criminology* 23(2): 75–103.

Grubesic, T. H., and A. T. Murray (2002). *Detecting Hot Spots Using Cluster Analysis and GIS*. Paper presented at the Annual Conference of the Crime Mapping Research Center, Dallas, TX. Retrieved from the Crime Mapping Research Center website: www.ojp.usdoj.gov/cmrc/conferences/01conf/Grubesic.doc.

Guerry, A. M. (1833). *Essai sur la statistique morale de la France*. Paris: Cochard.

Hagan, J. (1994). *Crime and Disrepute*. Thousand Oaks, CA: Pine Forge Press.

Hagan, J., and R. Peterson (1994). Criminal inequality in America. In J. Hagan and R. Peterson (Eds.), *Inequality and Crime*. Stanford, CA: Stanford University Press.

Hamid, A. (1992). The development cycle of a drug epidemic: The cocaine smoking epidemic of 1981–1991. *Journal of Psychoactive Drugs* 24: 337–348.

Hammer, J., and E. Stanko (1985). Stripping away the rhetoric of protection: Violence to women, law and the state in Britain and the USA. *International Journal of the Sociology of Law* 13: 357–374.

Hanmer, J., and E. Stanko (1985). Stripping away the rhetoric of protection: Violence to women, law and the state in Britain and the U.S.A. *International Journal of the Sociology of Law* 13(4): 357–374.

Hansen, M. (2001, August). As a crime fighting tool geographic profiling hits criminal close to home. *ABA Journal* 35(3): 26–27.

Harer, M., and D. Steffesnmeier (1992). The different effects of economic inequality on black and white rates of violence. *Social Forces* 70: 1035–1054.

Harries, K. (1990). *Geographic Factors in Policing*. Washington, DC: Police Executive Research Forum.

Harries, K. (1999). *Mapping Crime: Principle and Practice*. Retrieved from the National Criminal Justice Reference Service website: www.ncjrs.org/html/nij/mapping/pdf.html.

Hazelwood, R., and J. Douglass (1980). The lust murderer. *FBI Law Enforcement Bulletin* 49(4): 18–22.

Heiland, H., and L. Shelley (1992). Civilization, modernization, and the development of crime and control. In H. Heitland, L. Sheley, and H. Katoh (Eds.), *Crime and Control in Comparative Perspectives*. Hawthorne, NY: Walter de Gruyter.

Henderson, K., and R. Lowell (2000). Reducing campus crime through high-definition mapping. In N. LaVigne and J. Wartell (Eds.), *Crime Mapping Case Studies: Successes in the Field*, Vol. 2 (pp. 3–11). Washington, DC: Police Executive Research Foundation.

Hesseling, R. (1994). Displacement: A review of the empirical literature. In R. Clarke (Ed.), *Crime Prevention Studies*, Vol. 1. Monsey, NY: Willow Tree Press.

Hickey, E. (1991). *Serial Murderers and Their Victims*. Pacific Grove, CA: Brooks/Cole.

Hickman, M. J. (1999). Computers and information systems in local police departments, 1990–1999. *Police Chief*, January: 50–56.

Hickman, M. J. (January 2001). "Computers and Information Systems in Local Police Departments, 1990–1999." *The Police Chief* 67(1): 50–56.

Hindelang, M., Gottfredson, M., and J. Garofalo (1978). *Victims of Personal Crime: An Empirical Foundation for a Theory of Personal Victimization*. Cambridge, MA: Ballinger.

Hipp, J., Bauer, D., Curran, P., and K. Bollen (2004). Crimes of opportunity or crimes of emotion? Testing two explanations of seasonal change in crime. *Social Forces* 82(4).

Hirschi, T. (1969). *Causes of Delinquency*. Berkeley: University of California Press.

Hope, T. (1982). Burglary in schools: The prospects for prevention. Home Office Research Paper 11. London, England: Home Office.

Howard, G., Newman, G., and W. Pridemore (2000). *Theory, Method, and Data in Comparative Criminology. Measurement and Analysis of Crime and Justice*. Washington, DC: U.S. Department of Justice.

Howlett, D. (1997, September 10). Easy-to-concoct drug often makes users turn violent. *USA Today*, p. A1.

Hoyt, H. (1943). The structure of American cities in the post-war era. *American Journal of Sociology* 48: 475–492.

Hsieh, C., and M. Pugh (1993). Poverty, income inequality, and violent crime: A meta-analysis of recent aggregate data studies. *Criminal Justice Review* 18(2): 182–202.

Huang, W. (1995). A cross-national analysis on the effect of moral individualism on murder rates. *International Journal of Offender Therapy and Comparative Criminology* 39: 63–75.

Hubbs, R. (1998). The Greenway rapist case: Matching repeat offenders with crime locations. In N. LaVigne and J. Wartell (Eds.), *Crime Mapping Case Studies: Successes in the Field* (Vol. 1, pp. 93–98). Washington, DC: Police Executive Research Forum.

Hunter, A. (1978). *Symbols of Incivility*. Paper presented to the annual meeting of the American Society of Criminology. Dallas, TX.

Indicators of School Crime and Safety, 2006. Retrieved December 20, 2006 from http://www.ojp.usdoj.gov/bjs/pub/ascii/iscs06.txt.

Jacobs, J. (1961). *The Death and Life of Great American Cities*. New York: Random House.

Jacobs, J., and J. Henry (1996). The social construction of a hate crime epidemic. *Law and Contemporary Problems* 86: 366–391.

Jefferis, E. (1999). *A Multi-Method Exploration of Crime Hot Spots*. Retrieved from the Crime Mapping Research Center website: www.ojp.usdoj.gov/cmrc/whatsnew/hotspot/intro.pdf.

Jeffery, C. (1977[1971]). *Crime Prevention Through Environmental Design*. Beverly Hills, CA: Sage Publishing.

Jeffery, C. (1990). *Criminology: An Interdisciplinary Approach*. Englewood Cliffs, NJ: Prentice-Hall.

Jeffery, C. (1996). *Mental Health and Crime Prevention: A Public Health Model*. Paper presented to the International Crime Prevention Practitioners Conference. Vancouver, Canada.

Jeffery, C., and D. Zahm (1993). Crime prevention through environmental design, opportunity theory, and rational choice models. In R. Clarke and M. Felson (Eds.), *Routine Activity and Rational Choice. Advances in Criminological Theory*, Vol. 5. New Brunswick, NJ: Transaction Publishers.

Jensen, E., and J. Gerber (1998). *The New War on Drugs: Symbolic Politics and Criminal Justice Policy*. Cincinnati, OH: Anderson.

Johnson, B., Golub, A., and J. Fagan (1995). Careers in crack, drug use, drug distribution, and nondrug criminality. *Crime and Delinquency* 41: 275–295.

Jones, M., and D. Jones (2000). The contagious nature of antisocial behavior. *Criminology* 38(1): 25–46.

Kawachi, I., Kennedy, B., and R. Wilkinson (1999). Crime: Social disorganization and relative deprivation. *Social Science and Medicine* 48(6): 719–731.

Kelsall, J. E., and P. J. Diggle (1995). Kernel estimation of relative risk. *Bernoulli* 1: 3–16.

Kennedy, L., and D. Forde (1990). Routine activities and crime: An analysis of victimization in Canada. *Criminology* 28(1): 137–152.

Kennedy, L., and D. Forde (1990a). Risky lifestyles and dangerous results: Routine activities and exposure to crime. *Sociology and Social Research: An International Journal* 74(4): 208–211.

Kirn, W. (1998). Crank. *Time*, 22 June: 24–27, 29–30, 32.

Kleck, G. (2005). *Point Blank: Guns and Violence in America* (2nd ed.). New York: Transaction.

Klein, M., Maxson, C., and L. Cunningham (1991). Crack, street gangs, and violence. *Criminology* 29: 623–650.

Knox, E. G. (1988). Detection of clusters. In P. Elliot (Ed.), *Methodology of Enquiries into Disease Clustering* (pp. 17–20). London: London School of Hygiene and Tropical Medicine.

Kobrin, S. (1959). The Chicago Area Project: A twenty–five year assessment. *Annals of the American Academy of Political and Social Science* 322: 19–29.

Kobrin, S. (1994). The Chicago Area Project—A 25 Year Assessment. *Annals of the American Society of Political and Social Science* 3: 19–29.

Larsson, D. (2006). Exposure to property crime as a consequence of poverty. *Journal of Scandinavian Studies in Criminology & Crime Prevention* 7(1): 45–60.

Land, K., McCall, P., and L. Cohen (1990). Structural covariates of homicide rates: Are there any invariances across time and space. *American Journal of Sociology* 95: 922–963.

Lasley, J. (1989). Drinking routines/lifestyles and predatory victimization: A causal analysis. *Justice Quarterly* 6: 529–542.

Lateef, B. (1974). Helicopter patrol in law enforcement: An evaluation. *Journal of Police Science and Administration* 2: 62–65.

LaVigne, N. (1994). Rational choice and inmate disputes over phone use on Rikers Island. In R. Clarke (Ed.), *Crime Prevention Studies*, Vol. 3. Monsey, NY: Criminal Justice Press.

Laycock, G., and N. Tilley (1995). Implementing crime prevention. In M. Tonry and D. Farrington (Eds.), *Building a Safer Society: Strategic Approaches to Crime Prevention. Crime and Justice: A Review of Research*, Vol. 19. Chicago, IL: University of Chicago Press.

LEAA Newsletter (1971). Summarized in Robinson, Matthew B. (1999). "The theoretical development of crime prevention through environmental design (CPTED)." *Advances in Criminological Theory* 8: 427–462.

LEAA Newsletter (1973). Summarized in Robinson, Matthew B. (1999). "The theoretical development of crime prevention through environmental design (CPTED)." *Advances in Criminological Theory* 8: 427–462.

LEAA Newsletter (1974). Summarized in Robinson, Matthew B. (1999). "The theoretical development of crime prevention through environmental design (CPTED)." *Advances in Criminological Theory* 8: 427–462. LeBeau, J. L. (1987). The methods and measures of centrography and the spatial dynamics of rape. *Journal of Quantitative Criminology* 3(2): 125–141.

LEAA Newsletter (1976). Summarized in Robinson, Matthew B. (1999). "The theoretical development of crime prevention through environmental design (CPTED)." *Advances in Criminological Theory* 8: 427–462.

LeBeau, J., and R. Coulson (1996). Routine activities and the spatial-temporal variation of calls for police service: The experience of opposites on the quality of life spectrum. *Police Studies* 19(4): 1–14.

LeBeau, J., and W. Corcoran (1990). Changes in calls for police service with changes in routine activities and the arrival and passage of weather fronts. *Journal of Quantitative Criminology* 6: 269–291.

Letkemann, P. (1973). *Crime as Work*. Englewood Cliffs, NJ: Prentice-Hall.

Levine, N. (2002a). Personal communication. July 2, 2002.

Levine, N. (2002b). *Crimestat: A Spatial Statistics Program for the Analysis of Crime Incident Locations* (*v2.0*). Ned Levine and Associates, Houston, TX, and the National Institute of Justice, Washington, DC. Retrieved from the National Archive of Criminal Justice Data website: www.icpsr.umich.edu/NACJD/crimestat.html.

Levine, N. (2006). Crime mapping and the Crime Stat program. *Geographical Analysis* 38(1): 41–56.

Levin, Y., and A. Lindesmith (1971). English ecology and criminology of the past century. *Journal of Criminology and Criminal Law* 27: 801–816.

Lewis, D., and G. Salem (1981). Community crime prevention: An analysis of a developing strategy. *Crime and Delinquency* 27: 405–421.

Lewis, D., and G. Salem (1986). *Fear of Crime: Incivility and the Production of a Social Problem.* New Brunswick, NJ: Transaction.

Lewis, D., and M. Maxfield (1980). Fear in the neighborhoods: An investigation of the impact of crime. *Journal of Research in Crime and Delinquency* 17: 60–89.

Ley, D. (1983). *A Social Geography of the City.* New York: Harper and Row.

Lockwood, D. (2007). Mapping crime in Savannah. *Social Science Computer Review* 25 (2): 194–209.

Loftin, C. (1986). Assaultive violence as a contagious process. *Bulletin of the New York Academy of Medicine* 62: 550–555.

Loukaitou-Sideris, A. (1999). Hot spots of bus stop crime: The importance of environmental attributes. *Journal of the American Planning Association* 65(4): 83–95.

Lowman, J. (1986). Conceptual issues in the geography of crime: Toward a geography of social control. *Annals of the Association of American Geographers* 76(1): 81–94.

Macdonald, J., and R. Gifford (1989). Territorial cues and defensible space theory: The burglars' point of view. *Journal of Environmental Psychology* 9: 193–205.

MacEachren, A. M. (1994). *Some Truth with Maps: A Primer on Symbolization and Design.* Washington, DC: Association of American Geographers.

Mack, J. (1964). Full-time miscreants: Delinquent neighborhoods and criminal networks. *British Journal of Sociology* 15: 38–53.

Maguire, M. (1982). *Burglary in a Dwelling.* London: Heinemann.

Maguire, M., and T. Bennett (1982). *Burglary in a Dwelling.* London: Heinemann.

Mahibir, C. (1988). Crime in the Caribbean: Robbers, hustlers, and warriors. *International Journal of the Sociology of Law* 16: 315–338.

Malleson, N. (2007). Agent-Based Modelling and Crime in Leeds. Paper presented at the Royal Geographic Society with IGB Conference, London, UK.

Mamalian, C. A., and N. G. La Vigne (1998). *The Use of Computerized Crime Mapping by Law Enforcement: Survey Results.* Washington, DC: U.S. Department of Justice, Office of Justice Programs, National Institute of Justice.

Manning, P. K. (2001). Technology ways: Information technology, crime analysis, and the rationalizing of policing. *Criminal Justice: The International Journal of Policy and Practice* 1(1): 83–104.

Marcus, J. (1996). *The Crime Vaccine: How to End the Crime Epidemic.* Baton Rouge, LA: Claitor.

Markovic, J. (2007). Not an article but a service available online at the IACP website. http://smart.gismapping.info/smart.

Markowitz, F., Bellair, P., Liska, A., and J. Liu (2001). Extending social disorganization theory: Modeling the relationships between cohesion, disorder, and fear. *Criminology* 39(2): 293–320.

Massey, J., Krohn, M., and L. Bonati (1989). Property crime and the routine activities of individuals. *Journal of Research in Crime and Delinquency* 26(4): 378–400.

Maume, D. (1989). Inequality and metropolitan rape rates: A routine activities approach. *Justice Quarterly* 6: 513–528.

Maxfield, M. (1984). The limits of vulnerability in explaining fear of crime: A comparative neighborhood analysis. *Journal of Research in Crime and Delinquency* 21: 233–250.

Maxfield, M. (1987). *Incivilities and Fear of Crime in England and Wales, and the United States: A Comparative Analysis.* Paper presented to the annual meeting of the American Society of Criminology. Montreal, Canada.

Mayall, A., and S. Gold (1995). Definitional issues and mediating variables in the sexual revictimization of women sexually abused as children. *Journal of Interpersonal Violence* 10(1): 26–44.

Mayhew, H. (1860). A visit to the Rookery of St. Giles and its neighborhood. Available online at http://learning.north.londonmet.ac.uk/history/Mayhew.pdf.

Mayhew, H. (1862). *London Labour and the London Poor: Those That Will Not Work, Comprising Prostitutes, Thieves, Swindlers, and Beggars,* Vol. 4. New York: Dover Publications. Reprinted in 1968.

Mayhew, P. (1981). Crime in public view: Surveillance and crime prevention. In P. Brantingham and P. Brantingham (Eds.), *Environmental Criminology.* Beverly Hills, CA: Sage Publishing.

Mayhew, P., Maung, N., and C. Mirrlees-Black (1993). The 1992 British Crime Survey. London, England: Home Office.

Mayhew, P., Clarke, R., Sturman, A., and J. Hough (1976). Crime as Opportunity. Home Office Research Study No. 34. London, England: Home Office.

Mazerolle, P., and J. Maahs (2000). General strain and delinquency: An alternative examination of conditioning. *Justice Quarterly* 17(4): 753–778.

Mazerolle, P., and L. Green (2000). Civil remedies and drug control: A randomized field trial in Oakland, California. *Evaluation Review* 24(2): 1–35.

McCormick, J., and P. O'Donnell (1993). Drug wizard of Wichita: Did the chemist concoct a killer narcotic? *Newsweek,* 21 June: 32.

McLafferty, S., Williamson, D., and P. G. McGuire (2000). Identifying crime hot spots using kernel smoothing. In V. Goldsmith, P. G. McGuire, J. H. Mollenkopf, and T. A. Ross (Eds.), *Analyzing Crime Patterns: Frontiers of Practice* (pp. 77–85). Thousand Oaks, CA: Sage Publishing.

McLoyd, V. (1990). The impact of economic hardship on black families and children: Psychological distress, parenting, and socio-emotional development. *Child Development* 61: 311–346.

McLoyd, V. (1998). Socioeconomic disadvantage and child development. *American Psychologist* 53(2): 185–204.

Mears, D., Scott, M., and A. Bhai (2007). Opportunity theory and agricultural crime victimization. *Rural Sociology* 72(2): 151–184.

Meeker, J. (1999, July). *Accountability for Inappropriate Use of Crime Maps and the Sharing of Inaccurate*

Data. Paper presented at the Crime Mapping and Data Confidentiality Roundtable at the Crime Mapping Resource Center (CMRC). Retrieved from the National Institute of Justice website: www. ojp.usdoj.gov/nij/maps/Pubs/privacy/ anderson.pdf.

Mencken, F., and C. Barnett (1999). Murder, nonnegligent manslaughter, and spatial autocorrelation in mid-South counties. *Journal of Quantitative Criminology* 15(4): 407–422.

Merriam-Webster's Collegiate Dictionary (2001). Definitions of culture and subculture. Retrieved January 11, 2001 from http://www.m-w.com.

Merriam-Webster's Collegiate Dictionary (2002). Definition for diffusion. Retrieved April 2, 2002 from http://www.m-w.com.

Merriam-Webster's Collegiate Dictionary (2007). Definition for displacement and epidemic. Retrieved February 28, 2007 from http://www.m-w.com.

Merton, R. (1938). *Social Theory and Social Structure.* New York: Free Press.

Messman-Moore, T., and P. Long (2000). Child sexual abuse and revictimization in the form of adult sexual abuse, adult physical abuse and adult psychological maltreatment. *Journal of Interpersonal Violence* 15(5): 489–502.

Messner, S. (1982). Poverty, inequality, and the urban homicide rate. *Criminology* 20: 103–114.

Messner, S., and K. Tardiff (1985). The social ecology of urban homicide: An application of the routine activity approach. *Criminology* 23: 241–267.

Messner, S., and R. Golden (1992). Racial inequality and racially disaggregated homicide rates: An assessment of alternative theoretical explanations. *Criminology* 30: 421–447.

Messner, S., Anselin, L., Baller, R., Hawkins, D., Deane, G., and S. Tolnay (1999). The spatial patterning of county homicide rates: An application of exploratory spatial data analysis. *Journal of Quantitative Criminology* 15(4): 423–450.

Miethe, T. (1991). Citizen-based crime control activity and victimization risks: An examination of displacement and free-rider effects. *Criminology* 29: 419–440.

Miethe, T., and R. Meier (1994). *Crime and Its Social Context: Toward an Integrated Theory of Offenders, Victims, and Situations.* Albany, NY: SUNY Press.

Miethe, T., Stafford, M., and J. Long (1987). Social differentiation in criminal victimization: A test of routine activities/lifestyle theories. *American Sociological Review* 52:184–194.

Miller, E. (1991). Crime's threat to land values and neighborhood vitality. In P. Brantingham and P. Brantingham (Eds.), *Environmental Criminology* (pp. 111–118). Prospect Heights, IL: Waveland.

Mone, G. (2003). Tracking bad guys. *Popular Science* 262(1): 68.

Monmonier, M. (1993). *Mapping It Out: Expository Cartography for the Humanities and Social Sciences.* Chicago: University of Chicago.

Monmonier, M. (1996). *How to Lie with Maps.* Chicago: University of Chicago Press.

Moore, D. (2002, October 23). TV movie to track investigations of Canadian criminal profiler. *Canadian Press Newswire.*

Morenoff, J., and R. Sampson (1997). Violent crime and the spatial dynamics of neighborhood transition: Chicago 1970–1990. *Social Forces* 76(1): 31–64.

Moriarty, L., and J. Williams (1996). Examining the relationship between routine activities theory and social disorganization: An analysis of property crime victimization. *American Journal of Criminal Justice* 21(1): 43–59.

Morris, T. (1957). *The Criminal Area.* New York: Routledge and Kegan Paul.

Mosher, C. (2001). Predicting drug arrest rates: Conflict and social disorganization perspectives. *Crime and Delinquency* 47(1): 84–104.

Murray, C. (1994). The physical environment. In J. Wilson and J. Petersilia (Eds.), *Crime.* San Francisco, CA: Institute for Contemporary Studies.

National Board for Crime Prevention (1994). *Wise After the Event: Tackling Repeat Victimization.* London, England: Home Office.

Nasar, J., and B. Fisher (1992). Design for vulnerability: Cues and reactions to fear of crime. *Sociological and Social Research* 76(2): 48–57.

National Crime Prevention Institute (1986). *Understanding Crime Prevention.* Louisville, KY: National Crime Prevention Institute.

Neapolitan, J. (1994). Cross-national variations in homicides: The case of Latin America. *International Criminal Justice Review* 4: 4–22.

Neapolitan, J. (1996). Cross-national crime data: Some unaddressed problems. *Journal of Criminal Justice* 19: 95–112.

Newman, G. (1999). *Global Report on Crime and Justice.* United Nations: Office for Drug Control and Crime Prevention, Centre for International Crime Prevention.

Newman, O. (1972a). *Defensible Space: Crime Prevention Through Urban Design.* New York: Macmillan.

Newman, O. (1972b). *Defensible Space: People and Design in the Violent City.* New York: Macmillan.

Newman, O. (1973). *A Design Guide for Improving Residential Security.* Washington, DC: Macmillan.

Newman, O. (1976). *Design Guidelines for Creating Defensible Space.* Washington, DC: National Institute of Law Enforcement and Criminal Justice.

Newman, O. (1996). *Creating Defensible Space.* Washington, DC: U.S. Department of Housing and Urban Development.

Nichols, W. (1980). Mental maps, social characteristics, and criminal mobility. In D. Georges-Abeyie and K. Harries (Eds.), *Crime: A Spatial Perspective* (pp. 156–166). New York: Columbia University.

Nisbett, R., and D. Cohen (1996). *Culture of Honor: The Psychology of Violence in the South.* Boulder, CO: Westview Press.

Nomiya, D., Miller, A., and J. Hoffman (2000). Urbanization and rural depletion in modern Japan: An analysis of crime and suicide patterns. *International Journal of Comparative and Applied Criminal Justice* 24(1–2): 1–18.

Office of the U.S. Surgeon General (2002). [On-line]. Available: www.osophs.dhhs.gov/ophs

Oh, J. (2005). Social disorganizations and crime rates in U.S. central cities: Toward an explanation of urban economic change. *Social Science Journal* 42(4): 569–582.

Olligschlaeger, A. (1997). Artificial neural networks and crime mapping. In D. Weisburd and J. T. McEwen (Eds.), *Crime Mapping and Crime Prevention* (pp. 313–347). Monsey, NY: Criminal Justice Press.

Olligschlaeger, A. (1999, July). *What is the Appropriate Model for Partnerships Between Law Enforcement Agencies and Researchers with Regard to Data Sharing?* Paper presented at the Crime Mapping and Data Confidentiality Roundtable at the Crime Mapping Research Center (CMRC). Retrieved from the National Institute of Justice website: www.ojp.usdoj.gov/nij/maps/Pubs/privacy/anderson.pdf.

Orleans, P. (1968). *Differential Cognition of Urban Residents: Effects on Social Scale of Mapping.* Paper presented at the American Sociological Association. Boston, MA.

Orleans, P. (1973). Differential cognition of urban residents: Effects of social scales on mapping. In R. M. Downs and D. Stea (Eds.), *Image and Environment* (pp. 115–130). Chicago, IL: Aldine.

Ortega, S., Corzine, J., Burnett, C., and T. Poyer (1992). Modernization, age structure, and regional context: A cross-national study of crime. *Sociological Spectrum* 12: 257–277.

Osgood, D., and A. Anderson (2004). Unstructured Socializing and rates of delinquency. *Criminology* 42(3): 519–549.

Osgood, D., and J. Chambers (2000). Social disorganization outside the metropolis: An analysis of rural youth violence. *Criminology* 38(1): 81–115.

Ousey, G. (1999). Homicide, structural factors, and the racial invariance assumption. *Criminology* 37: 405–426.

Ousey, G. (2000). Explaining Regional and Urban Variation in Crime: A Review of Research. In G. LaFree (Ed.), *The Nature of Crime: Continuity and Change.* Washington, DC: U.S. Department of Justice.

Packer, H. (1968). *The Limits of the Criminal Sanction.* Stanford, CA: Stanford University Press.

Park, R. (1915). The city: Suggestions for the investigation of human behavior in the urban environment. *American Journal of Sociology* 20: 577–612.

Park, R. (1952). *Human Communities.* Glencoe, IL: The Free Press.

Parker, K., and P. McCall (1997). Adding another piece to the inequality-homicide puzzle. *Homicide Studies* 1: 35–60.

Passas, N. (2000). Global anomie, dysnomie, and economic crime: Hidden consequences of neoliberalism and globalization in Russia and around the world. *Social Justice* 27(2): 16–44.

Pastore, A. L., and K. Maguire (Eds.). (2000). *Sourcebook of Criminal Justice Statistics.* Retrieved from the University of Albany (State University of New York) website: www.albany.edu/sourcebook.

Pate, A., Wycoff, M., Skogan, W., and L. Sherman (1986). *The Effects of Police Fear Reduction Strategies: A Summary of Findings from Houston and Newark.* Washington, DC: Police Foundation.

Paulsen, D., and R. Wilson (2008). Urban Growth simulation and Crime. Unpublished manuscript.

Paulsen, D. J. (2001a, December). *Mapping in Podunk: Issues and problems in the Implementation and Use of GIS in Small and Rural Law Enforcement.* Paper presented at the Crime Mapping Research Center's Annual Conference. Dallas, TX.

Paulsen, D. J. (2001b). *Mapping or not?: Results from the N.C. Police Chief Survey.* Unpublished manuscript.

Paulsen, D. J. (2002). Wrong side of the tracks: Assessing the role of newspaper coverage of homicide in socially constructing dangerous places. *Journal of Criminal Justice and Popular Culture* 9(3): 113–127.

Paulsen, D. J. (2003, March). To Map or not to map: Do crime maps have any measurable impact on patrol officers? Academy of Criminal Justice Sciences, Boston, MA.

Paulsen, D. J. (2005). "Testing Advanced Crime Series Prediction Methods." International Investigative Psychology Conference, December, London, UK. *Invited Presenter.*

Paulsen, D. J. (2006a). "Human vs. Machine: A comparison of the accuracy of Geographic Profiling Methods." *Journal of Investigative Psychology and Offender Profiling* 3(2): 77–89.

Paulsen, D. J. (2006b). "Connecting the Dots: Assessing the Relative Accuracy of Geographic Profiling Software." *Policing: An International Journal of Police Strategies and Management* 29(2): 306–334.

Paulsen, D. J. (2007). "Improving geographic profiling through commuter/marauder prediction." *Journal of Police Practice and Research* 8(4): 347–357.

Pease, K. (1992). The Kirkholt Project: Preventing burglary on a British public housing estate. In E. Clarke (Ed.), *Situational Crime Prevention: Successful Case Studies.* London, England: Heinemann.

Petee, T., and G. Kowalski (1993). Modeling rural violent crime rates: A test of social disorganization theory. *Sociological Focus* 26(1): 87–89.

Petee, T., Kowalski, G., and D. Duffield (1994). Crime, social disorganization, and social structure: A research note on the use of interurban ecological models. *American Journal of Criminal Justice* 19(1): 117–132.

Peters, V., Oetting, E., and R. Edwards (1992). Drug use in rural communities: An epidemiology. In R. Edwards (Ed.), *Drug Use in Rural American Communities.* New York: Haworth Press.

Petersilia, J., Greenwood, P., and M. Lavin (1977). *Criminal Careers of Habitual Criminals.* Santa Monica, CA: Rand Corporation.

Peterson, R., and L. Krivo (1993). Racial segregation and urban black homicide rates. *Social Forces* 59: 136–147.

Pettiway, L. (1995). Coping crack: The travel behavior of crack users. *Justice Quarterly* 12: 499–524.

Phillips, J. (1997). Variation in African-American homicide rates: An assessment of potential explanations. *Criminology* 35: 527–560.

Phillips, P. (1972). A prologue to the geography of crime. *Proceedings, Association of American Geographers* 4: 86–91.

Phillips, P. (1980). Characteristics and typology of the journey to crime. In D. Georges-Abeyie and K. Harries (Eds.), *Crime: A Spatial Perspective* (pp. 167–180). New York: Columbia University.

Polvi, N., Looman, T., Humphries, C., and K. Pease (1990). Repeat break-and-enter victimization: Time course and crime prevention opportunity. *Journal of Police Science and Administration* 17(1): 8–11.

Polvi, N., Looman, T., Humphries, C., and K. Pease (1991). The time course of repeat burglary victimisation. *British Journal of Criminology* 31: 411–414.

Potter, G., and V. Kappeler (1998). *Constructing Crime: Perspectives on Making News and Social Problems.* Prospect Heights, IL: Waveland Press.

Poyner, B. (1992). Situational crime prevention in two parking facilities. *Security Journal* 2: 96–101.

Poyner, B. (1997). Situational prevention in two parking facilities. In R. Clarke (Ed.), *Situational Crime Prevention: Successful Case Studies.* Albany, NY: Harrow and Heston.

Poythress, N., Otto, R., Darkes, J., and L. Starr (1993). APA's expert panel in the Congressional review of the USS Iowa incident. *American Psychologist* 48: 8–15.

Press, S. (1971). *On Effects of an Increase in Police Manpower in the 20th Precinct of New York City.* New York: RAND.

Pyle, G. (1974). *The Spatial Dynamics of Crime* (Research paper no. 159). Chicago, IL: University of Chicago Department of Geography.

Pyle, G. (1980). Systematic sociospatial variation in perspectives of crime location and severity. In D. Georges-Abeyie and K. Harries (Eds.), *Crime: A Spatial Perspective* (pp. 219–245). New York: Columbia University.

Quetelet, M. A. (1973). A treatise on man. In *Comparative Statistics in the Nineteenth Century* (pp. 25–75). Germany: Gregg International. (Reprinted from A treatise on man, by M. A. Quetelet, 1842, Edinburgh: William and Robert Chambers.)

Ratcliffe, J. (2006). A temporal constraint theory to explain opportunity-based spatial offending patterns. *Journal of Research in Crime & Delinquency* 43(3): 261–291.

Ratcliffe, J., and M. McCullagh (2001a). Chasing ghosts: Police perception of high-crime areas. *British Journal of Criminology* 41: 330–341.

Ratcliffe, J. H. and M. J. McCullagh (2001b). Crime, repeat victimisation and GIS. In: K. Bowers and A. Hirschfield (Eds.), *Mapping and Analysing Crime Data*, Chapter 3 (pp. 61–92). London: Taylor & Francis.

Redfield, H. (1880). *Homicide, North and South.* Philadelphia, PA: Lippincott.

Reinarman, C. (1995). Crack attack: America's latest drug scare, 1986–1992. In J. Best (Ed.), *Images of Issues: Typifying Contemporary Social Problems.* New York: Aldine de Gruyter.

Reinarman, C., and H. Levine (1989). Crack in context: Politics and media in the making of a drug scene. *Contemporary Drug Problems* 16: 116–129.

Reiss, Jr., A. (1985). *Policing a City's Central District: The Oakland Story.* Washington, DC: U.S. Department of Justice, National Institute of Justice.

Reiss, A., and J. Roth (1993). *Understanding and Preventing Violence.* Washington, DC: National Academy Press.

Rengert, G. (1989). Behavioural geography and criminal behavior. In D. Evans and D. Herbert (Eds.), *The Geography of Crime* (pp. 161–175). New York: Routledge.

Rengert, G. (1991). Burglary in Philadelphia: A critique of an opportunity structure model. In P. Brantingham and P. Brantingham (Eds.), *Environmental Criminology* (pp. 189–202). Prospect Heights, IL: Waveland.

Rengert, G., and J. Monk (1982). Women in crime. In G. Rengert and A. Monk (Eds.), *Women and Social Change* (pp. 7–10). New York: Kendall Hunt.

Rengert, G., and J. Wasilchick (1985). *Suburban Burglary: A Time and Place for Everything.* Springfield, IL: Charles C. Thomas.

Rengert, G., and W. V. Pelfrey (1997). Cognitive mapping of the city center: Comparative perceptions of dangerous places. In D. Weisburd and T. McKewan (Eds.), *Crime Mapping and Crime Prevention: Crime Prevention Studies*, Vol. 8 (pp. 193–217). Monsey, NY: Criminal Justice Press.

Rengert, G., Piquero, A., and P. Jones (1999). Distance decay reexamined. *Criminology* 37(2): 427–445.

Reppetto, T. (1974). *Residential Crime.* Cambridge, MA: Ballinger.

Rhodes, W., and C. Conly (1991). Crime and mobility: An empirical study. In P. Brantingham and P. Brantingham (Eds.), *Environmental Criminology* (pp. 167–188). Prospect Heights, IL: Waveland.

Rice, K., and W. Smith (2002). Socioecological models of automotive theft: Integrating routine activity and social disorganization approaches. *The Journal of Research in Crime and Delinquency* 39(3): 304–336.

Richardson, F. (2002, October 9). Locator software may aid in search. *Boston Herald*, p. 6.

Riley, D. (1987). Time and crime: The link between teenager lifestyle and delinquency. *Journal of Quantitative Criminology* 3(4): 339.

Robinson, M. (1997). *Ecology and Crime: Lifestyles, Routine Activities, and Residential Burglary Victimization.* Ph.D. dissertation. Tallahassee: Florida State University.

Robinson, M. (1998a). Accessible targets, but not advisable ones: The role of "accessibility" in student apartment burglary. *Journal of Security Administration* 21(1): 29–43.

Robinson, M. (1998b). High aesthetics/low incivilities: Criminal victimizations and perceptions of risk in a downtown environment. *Journal of Security Administration* 21(2): 19–32.

Robinson, M. (1999). Lifestyles, routine activities, and residential burglary victimization. *Journal of Crime & Justice* 22(1): 27–56.

Robinson, M. (2000). Preventing burglary through a systems approach. *American Journal of Criminal Justice* 24(2): 169–179.

Robinson, M. (2002). *Justice Blind? Ideals and Realities of American Criminal Justice.* Upper Saddle River, NJ: Prentice-Hall.

Robinson, M. (2004). *Why Crime? An Integrated Systems Theory of Antisocial Behavior.* Upper Saddle River, NJ: Prentice-Hall.

Robinson, M. (2005). *Justice Blind? Ideals and Realities of American Criminal Justice* (2nd ed.). Upper Saddle River, NJ: Prentice Hall.

Robinson, M. (2008). *Death Nation: The Experts Explain American Capital Punishment.* Upper Saddle River, NJ: Prentice Hall.

Robinson, M., and K. Mullen (2001). Crime on campus: A survey of space users. *Crime Prevention and Community Safety: An International Journal* 3(4): 33–46.

Robinson, M., and R Scherlen (2007). *Lies, Damned Lies, and Drug War Statistics*. Albany, NY: State University of New York Press.

Robinson, M., and S. Roh (2007). Crime on campus: Spatial aspects of calls for police service at a regional comprehensive university. In J. Sloan and B. Fisher (Eds.), *Campus Crime: Legal, Social, and Police Perspectives* (2nd ed.). Springfield, IL: Charles Thomas Publishing.

Robinson, J., Lawton, B., Taylor, R., and D. Perkins (2003). Multilevel longitudinal impacts of incivilities: Fear of crime, expected safety, and block satisfaction. *Journal of Quantitative Criminology* 19(3): 237–274.

Roh, S., and W. Oliver (2005). Effects of community policing upon fear of crime: Understanding the causal linkage. *Policing: An International Journal of Police Strategies & Management* 28(4): 670–683.

Rohe, W., and R. Burby (1988). Fear of Crime in Public Housing. *Environment and Behavior* 20: 700–720.

Rollin, J. (1997). The social ecology of crime in Saginaw, Michigan. *Dissertation Abstracts International, A: The Humanities and Social Sciences* 58(2): 0591-A.

Roncek, D., and P. Maier (1991). Bars, blocks, and crimes revisited: Linking the theory of routine activities to the empiricism of "hot spots." *Criminology* 29(4): 725–753.

Rose, D., and T. Clear (1998). Incarceration, social capital, and crime: Implications for social disorganization theory. *Criminology* 36(3): 441–479.

Rosenfeld, R., Bray, T., and A. Egley (1999). Facilitating violence: A comparison of gang-motivated, gang affiliated, and nongang youth homicides. *Journal of Quantitative Criminology* 15(4): 495–516.

Ross, N. (1994). *Repeat Victimization*. Paper presented to the National Board for Crime Prevention. London, England, UK.

Rossmo, D. K. (1994). Targeting victims: Serial killers and the urban environment. In T. O'Reilly-Fleming and S. Egger (Eds.), *Serial and Mass Murder: Theory, Research and Policy* (pp. 133–153). Toronto, Canada: University of Toronto.

Rossmo, D. K. (1995a). Place, space, and police investigations: Hunting serial violent criminals. In J. Eck and D. Weisburd (Eds.), *Crime and Place* (pp. 217–235). Monsey, NY: Criminal Justice Press.

Rossmo, D. K. (1995b). Multivariate spatial profiles as a tool in crime investigation. In C. R. Block, M. Dabdoub, and S. Fregly (Eds.), *Crime Analysis Through Computer Mapping* (pp. 65–97). Washington, DC: Police Executive Research Forum.

Rossmo, D. K. (1997). Geographic profiling. In J. Jackson and D. Bekerian (Eds.), *Offender Profiling: Theory, Research and Practice* (pp. 159–175). West Sussex, NY: John Wiley & Sons.

Rossmo, D. K. (2000). *Geographic Profiling*. Boca Raton, FL: CRC Press.

Rossmo, K. D. (1993). Target patterns of Serial Murderers: A Methodological Model. *American Journal of Criminal Justice* 17(2): 1–21.

Rountree, P., and B. Warner (1999). Social ties and crime: Is the relationship gendered? *Criminology* 37(4): 789–813.

Russell, D., and R. Bolen (2000). *The Epidemic of Rape and Child Sexual Abuse in the United States*. Beverly Hills, CA: Sage Publishing.

Sacco, V., and L. Kennedy (2002). *The Criminal Event: Perspectives in Space and Time*. Belmont, CA: Wadsworth.

Sacks, H. (1972). Notes on police assessment of moral character. In D. Sundow (Ed.), *Studies in Social Interaction* (pp. 280–293). New York: Free Press.

Sampson, A., and C. Phillips (1992). *Multiple Victimization: Racial Attacks on an East London Estate*. Home Office Crime Prevention Unit Paper 36. London, England: Home Office.

Sampson, R. (1985). Race and criminal violence: A demographically disaggregated analysis of urban homicide. *Crime & Delinquency* 31: 47–82.

Sampson, R. (1995). The community. In J. Wilson and J. Petersilia (Eds.), *Crime*. San Francisco: ICS Press.

Sampson, R. (2000). A neighborhood-level perspective on social change and the social control of adolescent delinquency. In L. Crockett and R. Silbereisen (Eds.), *Negotiating Adolescence in Times of Social Change*. New York: Cambridge University Press.

Sampson, R., and B. Groves (1989). Community structure and crime: Testing social disorganization theory. *American Journal of Sociology* 94: 774–802.

Sampson, R., and J. Wooldredge (1987). Linking the micro- and macro-level dimensions of lifestyle-routine activity and opportunity models of predatory victimization. *Journal of Quantitative Criminology* 3(4): 371–393.

Sampson, R., and S. Raudenbush (1999). Systematic observation of public places: A new look at disorder in urban neighborhoods. *American Journal of Sociology* 105(3): 603–651.

Sampson, R., and S. Raudenbush (2001, February). Disorder in urban neighborhoods: Does it lead to crime? *National Institute of Justice Research in Brief*. Washington, DC: U.S. Department of Justice.

Sampson, R., and W. Wilson (1994). Toward a theory of race, crime, and urban inequality. In J. Hagan and R. Peterson (Eds.), *Inequality and Crime*. Stanford, CA: Stanford University Press.

Sampson, R., and W. Wilson (1995). Toward a theory of race, crime, and urban inequality. In Hagan, J. and Peterson, R. (Eds.), *Crime and Inequality*. Stanford, CA: Stanford University Press.

Sampson, R., and W. Wilson (2000). Toward a theory of race, crime, and urban inequality. In S. Cooper (Ed.), *Criminology*. Madison, WI: Coursewise.

Sampson, R., Raudenbush, S., and F. Earls (1997). Neighborhoods and violent crime: A multi-level study of collective efficacy. *Science* 277: 398–462.

Scherdin, M. (1986). The halo effect: Psychological deterrence of electronic security systems. *Information Technology and Libraries* 5: 232–235.

Scherdin, M. (1992). The halo effect: Psychological deterrence of electronic security systems. In R. Clarke (Ed.), *Situational Crime Prevention: Successful Case Studies*. Albany, NY: Harrow and Heston.

Schmitz, P., Cooper, A., Davidson, A., and K. Rossouw (2000). Breaking alibis through cell phone mapping. In N. LaVigne and J. Wartell (Eds.), *Crime Mapping Case Studies: Successes in the Field*, Vol. 2 (pp. 65–71). Washington, DC: Police Executive Research Foundation.

Sellin, T. (1938). *Culture Conflict and Crime*. New York: Social Science Research Council.

Shannon, L. (1988). *Criminal Career Continuity: Its Social Context.* New York: Human Sciences Press.

Shapiro, J. (1998). Psychotherapeutic utilization of prevention education in treatment for sexually abused children. *Journal of Child Sexual Abuse* 7(2): 105–121.

Shaw, C. (1930). *The Jackroller.* Chicago, IL: University of Chicago Press.

Shaw, C. R., and E. D. Myers (1929). The juvenile delinquent. In *The Illinois Crime Survey* (pp. 645–732). Chicago, IL: Illinois Association for Criminal Justice and Chicago Crime Commission. (Reprinted 1968, Montclair: NJ: Patterson-Smith).

Shaw, C. R., and H. D. McKay (1929a). *Delinquency Areas.* Chicago, IL: University of Chicago Press.

Shaw, C. R., and H. D. McKay (1929b). *Juvenile Delinquency and Urban Areas.* Chicago, IL: University of Chicago Press.

Shaw, C. R., and H. D. McKay (1942). *Juvenile Delinquency and Urban Areas* (5th ed.). Chicago, IL: University of Chicago Press.

Shaw, C. R., and M. Moore (1931). *The Natural History of a Delinquent Career.* New York: Greenwood Press.

Shaw, C. R., McKay, H., McDonald, J., Hanson, H., and E. Burgess (1938). *Brothers in Crime.* Chicago, IL: University of Chicago Press.

Sherman, L. W. (1990). Police crackdowns: Initial and residual deterrence. In M. Tonry and N. Morris (Eds.), *Crime and Justice: A Review of Research,* Vol. 12. Chicago, IL: University of Chicago Press.

Sherman, L. W. (1998). Evidence-Based Policing. Washington, DC: Police Foundation.

Sherman, L. W., and D. Weisburd (1995). General deterrent effects of police patrol in crime hot spots: A randomized controlled trial. *Justice Quarterly* 12(4): 625–648.

Sherman, L. W., and D. P. Rogan (1995). Deterrent effects of police raids on crack houses: A randomized, controlled experiment. *Justice Quarterly* 12(4): 755–781.

Sherman, L. W., Gartin, P. R., and M. E. Buerger (1989). Hot spots of predatory crime: Routine activities and the criminology of place. *Criminology* 27(1): 27–55.

Sherman, L. W., Gottfredson, D., MacKenzie, D., Eck, J., Reuter, P., and S. Bushway (1998, July). Preventing crime: What works, what doesn't, what's promising. *NIJ Research in Brief.* [On-line]. Available: www.ncjrs.org/pdffiles/171676.pdf.

Shihadeh, E., and G. Ousey (1996). Metropolitan expansion and black social dislocation: The link between suburbanization and center-city crime. *Social Forces* 75: 649–666.

Shihadeh, E., and G. Ousey (1998). Industrial restructuring and violence: The link between entry-level jobs, economic deprivation, and black and white homicide. *Social Forces* 77: 185–206.

Siegel, L. (1995). *Criminology* (5th ed.). Minneapolis/St. Paul, MN: West.

Silver, E. (1999). Violence and mental illness from a social disorganization perspective: An analysis of individual and community risk factors. *Dissertation Abstracts International, A: The Humanities and Social Sciences* 60(6): 2236-A.

Simcha-Fagan, O., and J. Schwartz (1986). Neighbourhood and delinquency: An assessment of contextual effects. *Criminology* 24: 667–703.

Simon, M., and J. Shepherd (2007). The elements and prevalence of fear. *British Journal of Criminology* 47:154–162.

Simons, R., Chao, W., Conger, R., and G. Elder (2001). Quality of parenting as mediator of the effect of childhood defiance on adolescent friendship choices and delinquency: A growth curve analysis. *Journal of Marriage & the Family* 63(1): 63–79.

Simons, R., Johnson, C., Conger, R., and G. Elder Jr. (1998). A test of latent trait versus life-course perspectives on the stability of adolescent antisocial behavior. *Criminology* 36(2): 217–243.

Skogan, W. (1981). On attitudes and behaviors. In D. Lewis (Ed.), *Reactions to Crime.* Beverly Hills, CA: Sage Publishing.

Skogan, W. (1986). Fear of crime and neighborhood change. In A. Reiss and M. Tonry (Eds.), *Communities and Crime.* Chicago, IL: University of Chicago Press.

Skogan, W. (1990). *Disorder and Decline.* Berkeley: University of California Press.

Skogan, W. (1991). *Disorder and Decline.* New York: Free Press.

Skogan, W., and M. Maxfield (1981). *Coping with Crime: Individual and Neighborhood Reactions.* Beverly Hills, CA: Sage Publishing.

Skolnick, J. (1966). *Justice Without Trial: Law Enforcement in a Democratic Society.* New York: John Wiley & Sons.

Smith, D., and G. Jarjoura (1988). Social structure and criminal victimization. *Journal of Research in Crime and Delinquency* 25(1): 27–52.

Smith, M. (1992). Variations in correlates of race-specific urban homicide rates. *Journal of Contemporary Criminal Justice* 8: 137–149.

Smith, W., Frazee, S., and E. Davison (2000). Furthering the integration of routine activity and social disorganization theories: Small units of analysis and the study of street robbery as a diffusion process. *Criminology* 38(2): 489–523.

Snook, B., Canter, D., and C. Bennell (2002). Predicting the Home Location of Serial Offenders: A Preliminary Comparison of the Accuracy of Human Judges with a Geographic Profiling System. *Behavioral Science and the Law* 20: 109–118.

Snook, B., Taylor, P., and C. Bennell (2004). Geographic Profiling: The Fast, Frugal, and Accurate Way. *Applied Cognitive Psychology* 18: 105–121.

Snook, B., Zito, M., Bennell, C., and P. Taylor (2005). On the Complexity and Accuracy of Geographic Profiling Strategies. *Journal of Quantitative Criminology* 21: 1–26.

Spano, R., and S. Nagy (2005). Social guardianship and social isolation: An application and extension of lifestyle/routine activities theory to rural adolescents. *Rural Sociology* 70(3): 414–437.

Sparks, R. (1981). Multiple victimization: Evidence, theory, and future research. *Journal of Criminal Law and Criminology* 72: 762–778.

Stahura, J., and J. Sloan (1988). Urban stratification of places, routine activities and suburban crime rates. *Social Forces* 66(4): 1102–1118.

Stark, R. (1987). Deviant places: A theory of the ecology of crime. *Criminology* 25(4): 893–909.

Stark, R. (1996). Deviant places: A theory of the ecology of crime. *Criminology* 25(4): 893–909.

Stephenson, L. K. (1980). Centrographic analysis of crime. In D. E. Georges-Abeyie and K. Harries (Eds.), *Crime: A Spatial Perspective* (pp. 146–155). New York: Columbia University.

Stevenson, J. (2001). *Principles of Infectious Disease and Epidemiology.* [On-line]. Available: www.cas. muohio.edu/~stevenjr/mbi111/disprinepid111.html

Stewart, P., and G. Sitaramiah (1997). America's heartland grapples with rise of dangerous drugs. *Christian Science Monitor,* 13 November.

Stinchcombe, A., Adams, R., Heimer, C., Schepple, K., Smith, T., and D. Taylor (1980). *Crime and Punishment: Changing Attitudes in America.* San Francisco, CA: Jossey-Bass.

Stoks, F. (1983). Assessing urban public space environments for danger of violent crime—Especially rape. In D. Joiner, G. Brimikombe, J. Daish, and D. Kernohan (Eds.), *Proceedings on the Conference on People and Physical Environment Research.* Ministry of Works and Development, Wellington, New Zealand.

Stretesky, P., Schuck, A., and M. Hogan (2004). Space matters: An analysis of poverty, poverty clustering, and violent crime. *Justice Quarterly* 21(4): 817–841.

Sutherland, E. (1947). *Principles of Criminology* (4th ed.). Philadelphia: Lippincott.

Taylor, M., and C. Nee (1988). The role of cues in simulated residential burglary. *British Journal of Criminology* 28: 396–401.

Taylor, R. (1996). Neighborhood responses to disorder and local attachments: The systemic model of attachment, social disorganization, and neighborhood use value. *Sociological Forum* 11(1): 41–74.

Taylor, R. (1997). Social order and disorder of street blocks and neighborhoods: Ecology, microecology, and the systemic model of social disorganization. *The Journal of Research in Crime and Delinquency* 34(1): 113–155.

Taylor, R. (2001). The ecology of crime, fear, and delinquency: Social disorganization versus social efficacy. In R. Paternoster and R. Bachman (Eds.), *Explaining Crime and Criminals.* Los Angeles, CA: Roxbury.

Taylor, R., and A. Harrell (1996). *Physical Environment and Crime.* National Institute of Justice Research Report. Washington, DC: U.S. Department of Justice.

Taylor, R., Shumaker, S., and S. Gottfredson (1985). Neighborhood level links between physical features and local sentiments, deterioration, fear of crime and confidence. *Journal of Architectural Planning and Research* 21: 261–275.

Thacher, D. (2004). The rich get richer and the poor get robbed: Inequality in U.S. criminal victimization, 1974–2000. *Journal of Quantitative Criminology* 20(2): 89–116.

Thomas, E, and L. Wolfer (2003). The crime triangle: Alcohol, drug use, and vandalism. *Police Practice & Research* 4(1): 47–61.

Thomas, T., and F. Znaniecki (1958[1920]) . *The Polish Peasant in Europe and America.* New York: Dover Publications.

Thrasher, F. M. (1927). *The Gang.* Chicago, IL: University of Chicago Press.

Tiffany, W., and J. Ketchel (1979). Psychological deterrence in robberies of banks and its application to other institutions. In J. Kramer (Ed.), *The Role of Behavioral Sciences in Physical Security.* National Bureau of Standards.

Tilley, N. (1993). *The Prevention of Crime Against Small Businesses: The Safer Cities Experience.* Home Office Crime Prevention Unit Paper 45. London, England: Home Office.

Tita, G., and E. Griffiths (2005). Traveling to violence: The case for a mobility-based spatial typology of homicide. *Journal of Research on Crime and Delinquency* 42(2): 275–308.

Torrens, P. (2003). "SprawlSim: Modelling sprawling urban growth using automata-based tools." In D. Parker, T. Berger, and S. Manson (Eds.), *Agent Based Models of Land-Use and Land-Cover Change* (pp. 72–79). Belgium: LUCC International Project Office.

Toy, C. (1992). Coming out to play: Reasons to join and participate in Asian gangs. *Journal of Gang Research* 1(1): 13–29.

Trickett, A., Osborn, D., Seymour, J., and K. Pease (1992). What is different about high crime areas? *British Journal of Criminology* 32: 250–265.

Trojanowicz, R., Kappeler, V. E., and L. K. Gaines (2002). *Community Policing: A Contemporary Perspective.* Cincinnati, OH: Anderson.

Trypak, S. (1975). Newark high-impact anti-crime program: Street lighting project interim evaluation report. Newark, NJ: Office of Criminal Justice Planning.

Tunnell, K. (1994). *Choosing Crime: The Criminal Calculus of Property Offenders.* Chicago, IL: Nelson-Hall Publishers.

Tyson, A. (1996). Drug abuse is quiet scandal in America's countrysides. *Christian Science Monitor,* 16 September.

van Kesteren, J., Mayhew, P., and P. Nieuwbeerta (2001). Criminal Victimisation in Seventeen Industrialized Countries: Key Findings from the 2000 International Crime Victims Survey. Website: www.minjust.nl.

Veysey, B., and S. Messner (1999). Further testing of social disorganization theory: An elaboration of Sampson and Groves's "community structure and crime." *The Journal of Research in Crime and Delinquency* 36(2): 156–174.

Vieraitis, L. (2000). Income inequality, poverty, and violent crime: A review of the empirical evidence. *Social Pathology* 6(1): 24–45.

Vold, G. (1958). *Theoretical Criminology.* New York: Oxford University Press.

Vold, G., Bernard, T., and J. Snipes (1998). *Theoretical Criminology* (4th ed.). New York: Oxford University Press.

Vold, G., Bernard, T., and Snipes, J. (2001). *Theoretical Criminology* (5th ed.). New York: Oxford University Press.

Von Kappen, P., and J. De Keijser (1997). Desisting distance decay: On the aggregation of individual crime trips. *Criminology* 35(3): 505–515.

Voss, H., and D. Petersen (1971). *Ecology, Crime and Delinquency.* New York: Meridith Corporation.

Walker, S. (1998). *Sense and Nonsense About Crime and Drugs.* Belmont, CA: Wadsworth.

Wallis, A. (1980). *Crime Prevention Through Environmental Design: An Operational Handbook.* Washington, DC: U.S. Department of Justice.

Walsh, A. (2002). *Biosocial Criminology: Introduction and Integration*. Cincinnati, OH: Anderson Publishing.

Walsh, D. (1980). *Break-Ins: Burglary from Private Houses*. London: Constable.

Warden, J., and J. Shaw (2000). Predicting a residential break-in pattern. In N. LaVigne and J. Wartell (Eds.), *Crime Mapping Case Studies: Successes in the Field* (Vol. 2, pp. 73–79). Washington, DC: Police Executive Research Foundation.

Warner, B., and G. Pierce (1993). Reexamining social disorganization theory using calls to the police as a measure of crime. *Criminology* 31(4): 493–517.

Warner, B., and P. Rountree (1997). Local social ties in a community and crime model: Questioning the systemic nature of informal social control. *Social Problems* 44(4): 520–536.

Warr, M. (1990). Dangerous situations: Social context and fear of victimization. *Social Forces* 68: 891–907.

Wartell, J., and J. T. Thomas (2001). *Privacy in the Information Age: A Guide for Sharing Crime Maps and Spatial Data*. Washington, DC: National Institute of Justice. Retrieved from website: www.ncjrs.org/pdffiles1/nij/188739.pdf.

Wartell, J., and J. T. McEwen (2001). *Privacy in the Information Age: A Guide for Sharing Crime Maps and Spatial Data*. Washington, DC: Institute for Law and Justice.

Websdale, N. (1998). *Rural Women Battering and the Justice System*. Thousand Oaks, CA: Sage Publishing.

Weisburd, D. (1997). *Reorienting Crime Prevention Research and Policy: From the Causes of Criminality to the Context of Crime*. NIJ Research Report. Washington, DC: U.S. Department of Justice.

Weisburd, D., and T. McEwen (1997). Introduction: Crime mapping and crime prevention. In D. Weisburd and J. T. McEwen (Eds.), *Crime Mapping and Crime Prevention* (pp. 1–23). Monsey, NY: Criminal Justice Press.

Weisburd, D., Bushway, S., Lum, C., and S. Yang (2004) Trajectories of crime at places: A longitudinal study of street segments in the city of Seattle. *Criminology* 42(2): 283–321.

Weisheit, R., and J. Donnermeyer (2000). *Change and Continuity in Rural America. The Nature of Crime: Continuity and Change*. Washington, DC: U.S. Department of Justice.

Weisheit, R., Falcone, D., and E. Wells (1994, September). Rural crime and rural policing. *National Institute of Justice Research in Action*. Washington, DC: U.S. Department of Justice.

Wekerle, G., and C. Whitzman (1995). *Safe Cities: Guidelines for Planning Design and Management*. New York: Van Nostrand Reinhold.

Wells, E., and R. Weisheit (1998). *Rural Gangs: Are They a Problem?* Paper presented to the annual meeting of the American Society of Criminology. Chicago, IL.

Welsh, W., Stokes, R., and J. Greene (2000). A macro-level model of school disorder. *Journal of Research in Crime and Delinquency* 37(3): 243–283.

Wikstrøm, P. (Ed.). (1995). Self-control, temptations, frictions and punishment. An integrated approach to crime prevention. *Integrating Crime Prevention Strategies: Propensity and Opportunity*. Stockholm.

Wikstroem, P. (1998). Communities and crime. In M. Tonry (Ed.), *The Handbook of Crime and Punishment*. New York: Oxford University Press.

Williams, K., and R. Flewelling (1988). The social production of criminal homicide: A comparative study of disaggregated rates in American cities. *American Sociological Review* 53: 421–431.

Willmer, M. (1970). *Crime and Information Technology*. Edinburgh, Scotland: Edinburgh University Press.

Wilson, J. (1968). The urban unease: Community vs. city. *The Public Interest* 12: 25–39.

Wilson, J. and G. Kelling (1982). Broken windows: The police and neighborhood safety. *The Atlantic Monthly*, March: 29–38.

Wilson, W. (1987). *The Truly Disadvantaged: The Inner City, the Underclass, and Public Policy*. Chicago, IL: University of Chicago Press.

Witt, R. (1999). Crime and economic activity: A panel data approach. *The British Journal of Criminology* 39(3): 391–400.

Witt, R., Clarke, A., and N. Fielding (1999). Crime and economic activity: A panel data approach. *British Journal of Criminology* 39(3): 391–400.

Wood, E. (1961). *Housing Design: A Social Theory*. New York: Citizens' Housing and Planning Counsel of New York.

World Health Organization (2002). [On-line]. Available: www.who.int/gtb.

Wright, R., and S. Decker (1994). *Burglars on the Job: Streetlife and Residential Break-Ins*. Boston, MA: Northeastern University Press.

Wright, J., and P. Rossi (1983). *Armed and Considered Dangerous: A Survey of Felons and Their Firearms*. Hawthorne, NY: Aldine de Guyer.

Wrobleski, H., and K. Hess (1993). *Introduction to Law Enforcement and Criminal Justice*. St. Paul, MN: West.

Zhu, L., Gorman D., and S. Horel (2004). Alcohol outlet density and violence: A geospatial analysis. *Alcohol and Alcoholism* 39(4): 369–375.

Zimring, F. (1996). Kids, guns, and homicide: Policy notes on an age-specific epidemic. *Law and Contemporary Problems* 59: 25–37.

Index